Up against the Sprawl

Up against the Sprawl
Public Policy and the Making of Southern California

Jennifer Wolch, Manuel Pastor Jr., and
Peter Dreier, Editors || Foreword by Michael Dear

*Published in Association with the
Southern California Studies Center
of the University of Southern California*

University of Minnesota Press
Minneapolis || London

The University of Minnesota Press gratefully acknowledges the contribution of
The John Randolph Haynes and Dora Haynes Foundation in support of this project.

An earlier version of chapter 1 was originally published as "Unraveling Southern California's
Water/Growth Nexus: Metropolitan Water District Policies and Subsidies for Suburban
Development, 1928–1996," by Steven P. Erie and Pascale Joassart-Marcelli, in *California
Western Law Review* 36, no. 2 (spring 2000): 267–90. Reprinted by permission of California
Western Law Review.

An earlier version of chapter 2 was originally published as "Rethinking Environmental
Racism: White Privilege and Urban Development in Southern California," by Laura Pulido,
in *Annals of the Association of American Geographers* 90, no. 1 (2000): 12–40. Reprinted by
permission of Blackwell Publishers.

Published by the University of Minnesota Press
111 Third Avenue South, Suite 290
Minneapolis, MN 55401-2520
http://www.upress.umn.edu

Library of Congress Cataloging-in-Publication Data
Up against the sprawl : public policy and the making of Southern
California / Jennifer Wolch, Manuel Pastor Jr., and Peter Dreier,
editors ; foreword by Michael Dear.
      p. cm.
  "Published in Association with the Southern California Studies
Center of the University of Southern California."
  Includes bibliographical references and index.
  ISBN 0-8166-4297-4 (hc : alk. paper) — ISBN 0-8166-4298-2 (pb : alk. paper)
  1. Cities and towns—California, Southern—Growth. 2. Urban policy—California,
Southern. 3. Land use, Urban—California, Southern. I. Wolch, Jennifer R. II. Pastor,
Manuel, Jr., 1956- III. Dreier, Peter.
  HT384.U52C2586 2004
  307.76′09794′9—dc22
                                    2004006607

Printed in the United States of America on acid-free paper

The University of Minnesota is an equal-opportunity educator and employer.

12 11 10 09 08 07 06 05 04   10 9 8 7 6 5 4 3 2 1

Contents

Part III. Which Way L.A.?

Foreword

Michael Dear

The challenges of "urban sprawl" sit atop the agenda of many researchers and policy makers throughout the world. Although there is no consensus about what sprawl actually is, most agree that protecting the environment, boosting civic engagement, and sharing prosperity are keys to managing sprawl.

But there is a deeper common question underlying these concerns that must be answered before any effective response to sprawl can be articulated: *What is the appropriate role of government in managing urban growth and change?* Under this rubric falls a kaleidoscope of urban issues, including the actions of land and property markets, transportation, pollution, migration, and environmental protection/conservation. Questions on the role of government are especially pertinent now, because after many decades of deregulation and privatization, the apparatus of urban and regional planning in the United States has been reduced to a minor regulatory function of local governments. Moreover, just as the gloved hand of government is being withdrawn (at least in the urban sphere), the invisible hand of the market is learning new tricks. The rules governing urban growth and change have altered drastically under the impetus of globalization and the information revolution. Cities are now manufactured as much by global forces as they are by local or national dynamics. Indeed, many scholars and commentators now believe that a global network of "world cities" will be the dominant force in twenty-first-century geopolitics.

If the new rules governing urban growth have altered as much as I believe they have, then it is imperative that we figure out new policies to manage the altered forms of urban growth and change. This book tackles these difficult issues head-on, by asking, What has been, and what should be, the role of public policy in shaping growth and change in our cities? All too often, this fundamental issue is ignored by those who (mistakenly) claim that public policy makes little practical difference, or who are ideologically predisposed to reject any form of public intervention. Even advocates of "public-private partnerships" (who have coined the term *governance* to describe such a hybrid) still cannot evade the question of what we *should* expect our elected governments to do about cities. The contributors to this book use the case of Southern California to reveal just how significant public policy has been in the making of Los Angeles, and how vital it is to the region's future.

In truth, the hand of government has been present in most of our major cities since their inception. For instance, the earliest Spanish colonial settlements in Southern California were laid out in accordance with Spain's Laws of the Indies, which prescribed in precise detail such things as street width, location of a central square, and so on. In these same borderlands, after the 1848 Treaty of Guadalupe Hidalgo had ceded vast acreages of Mexican territory (including Alta California) to the United States, a different set of land development rationalities, or intentionalities, was introduced. Land was surveyed, private ownerships established (often ignoring the titles of Mexican and indigenous landholders), and formal land markets instituted. Much later, closer to our present times, Los Angeles was placed on a firm economic foundation by early-twentieth-century public investments in water and transportation infrastructure (especially rail and port facilities). So Los Angeles, like most other cities, can trace its pivotal historical moments to periods when enlightened public investments made possible a new city.

Yet, curiously, at the beginning of the twenty-first century, there are few (if any) examples of enlightened public policies directed toward cities, despite the litany of challenges facing our urban areas. Indeed, the well-being of our nation's cities managed to find its way onto current national agendas solely as a consequence of the terrorist attacks of September 11, 2001. Such neglect does not mean that America lacks the tools to address urban issues—it's just that most of the direct policy armamentarium is locked away at municipal level, where it is overwhelmingly focused on the regulation of local land use, through "zoning" laws. Such laws can tell you how many houses can be built on a city lot or how many parking spaces are required for a new shopping center. But zoning cannot tell you how to make your city competitive in a global marketplace, how to deal with racism and inequality, how to stop pollution or save critical habitat. Zoning laws represent a codification and classification of permissible land uses within a municipal boundary; they constrain possible urban futures, but rarely give us the means of creating a boldly reimagined urban future.

At the federal and state levels, there are few precedents for urban public policy, in the sense of direct interventions targeted at local or regional land-use planning and development. However, both levels of government have extensive options regarding policies that may indirectly influence cities. For example, one of the most important federal policies influencing the growth of cities has been the tax relief granted mortgage interest payments, which is generally regarded as the principal impetus toward post-1945 suburbanization in this country. Other important policies, such as those relating to health, welfare, and education, became de facto urban programs because the cities are where large numbers of people in need live; in effect, the agglomeration of people in cities concentrates certain amounts of government expenditure in specific neighborhoods.

Governments also make direct investment in cities, to build dams, freeways, schools, and universities; they sign international treaties that promote regional growth; and in myriad ways—for better or worse—government expenditures influence where jobs are going, whether or not transportation will be available, and what kind of housing opportunities will be on offer. Although private markets—comprising individuals and corporations, bankers and homemakers, commuters and artists—are engaged in creating great cities, they do so under circumstances that are everywhere enabled and constrained by public policy.

Cities have always been centers of entrepreneurial innovation, social and cultural melting pots, and hotbeds of political experimentation. For some, they represent the "cradle of civilization." If, in a twenty-first-century world of city-regions such as Los Angeles, local and geopolitical futures are intimately tied to the fate of a small number of world cities, are we prepared to manage the metropolis in ways that can sustain our economic, social, and environmental well-being? Has Southern California—long a poster child for urban sprawl—now exhausted its supply of available land at the metropolitan fringe? Home to sixteen million residents already, will the region be able to accommodate the six million new residents expected during the next two decades without new urban policies and development practices designed to keep the city healthy and livable?

Some municipalities in Southern California, and nationwide, have begun to experiment with "smart growth" tools, new regionalist frameworks, and urban sustainability programs. More and more states are interested in statewide as well as regional land-use plans. And the federal government's regulations on habitat conservation and endangered species are increasingly shaping patterns of suburban expansion. But we need a much clearer knowledge base before we can translate our goals for a preferred urban future into a practical vision that will take hold in our collective imaginations and help us remap the twenty-first-century metropolis as a place of shared prosperity, social justice, and environmental health.

This book provides such a knowledge base. Its contributors include some of our foremost urban scholars, and their findings will have theoretical and applied relevance not only for Southern California but for the rest of urban America as well.

Acknowledgments

We thank the Southern California Studies Center at the University of Southern California, the Irvine Foundation, the National Science Foundation's Program in Geography and Regional Science, and the Haynes Foundation for financial support. We are also especially grateful to Michael Dear of the Southern California Studies Center and to Bruce Katz and Amy Liu of the Brookings Institution Center on Urban and Metropolitan Policy for their guidance, support, and encouragement at critical moments in the development of this project. Thanks are due to many others who contributed to producing the volume: Pascale Joassart-Marcelli, who helped manage the project and assisted in so many vital ways; Alejandro Alonso, Dallas Dishman, Javier Huizar, and Jim Sadd for their assistance with graphics and geospatial analysis; David Deis for his superb cartography; and USC's Richard Parks and Billie Shotlow for their ongoing administrative assistance. Finally, we are indebted to Carrie Mullen and the staff at the University of Minnesota Press for their skillful work on, and commitment to, *Up against the Sprawl*.

Introduction. Making Southern California: Public Policy, Markets, and the Dynamics of Growth

Jennifer Wolch, Manuel Pastor Jr., and Peter Dreier

Every weekday, millions of commuters in the Los Angeles area creep along in traffic from home to work (Willon 2001). Exemplars of the region's economic success, two-income couples leave their suburban homes in separate cars, usually heading in different directions, sometimes to jobs in the central city but increasingly to jobs in other suburbs or edge cities. On the way to work, they detour to drop their kids off at school or child care, complicated maneuvers given that few such services are centralized or coordinated to tie with work patterns. Occasionally, traffic reaches gridlock levels and tempers flare, as dramatically parodied in the 1993 film *Falling Down*. Meanwhile, the less wealthy steam in their own anger, squeezed into the nation's most overcrowded bus system and taking long hours to travel short distances.

Even as frustration spills over into road (and sometimes bus rider!) rage, some portray Los Angeles as the exemplar of free and open consumer choice. The suburban sprawl perfected to a developer's art form in Southern California is said to reflect the spirit of American individualism and the workings of the unfettered market. Hollywood's studios are perfectly located in this mecca for entrepreneurs and dreamers. As portrayed in Hollywood films, television shows, novels, and books, Southern California is the place where people come to remake themselves. Once they arrive, they often prefer to live alone and apart, in neatly separated housing with tidy but small lawns, amid vast shopping malls, linked by roads and highways. It is a world of individuals, with little concern for old-fashioned ideas like neighborhood, community, and social fabric.

Is the pattern of how people live, work, and commute really just a matter of individual choice? Are the booms at the edges and the shortfalls in inner cities—from which banks, jobs, and shopping opportunities have exited to suburbs—simply matters of consumer preference, with businesses simply following consumers to the next residential frontier? If the companies building factories and offices prefer outlying suburbs to city neighborhoods, isn't that just because land prices and production costs are cheaper in the suburbs, enabling them to compete in the regional, national, or even global marketplace? If farmers and other landowners choose to sell their property on the urban outskirts to developers to build housing, or shopping malls, or office parks, aren't they operating within the rules of the free market, seeking the highest price and thus the "best use" for their holdings? Who can rightly blame them— or indeed anyone—for the resulting metropolitan sprawl, so characteristic of Los Angeles and other metro areas?

The view that American metro areas developed primarily because of market forces and consumer preferences underpins "public choice" theories of metropolitan governance and population dynamics. Public choice theorists view the multiplicity of local governments within metropolitan areas as creating an intergovernmental marketplace parallel to the private market. Just as shoppers can choose from among brands of towels, toothpastes, and television sets, households can choose where to live from an array of cities and suburbs, with each jurisdiction representing a distinct bundle of amenities and services at a distinct price in housing and taxation. In this view, fragmented metropolitan areas do not reflect a problem to be addressed; rather, they signal a cornucopia of choices that maximize household satisfaction.

These basic ideas of public choice theory have been used to justify sprawl and metropolitan spatial inequality as the normal workings of human nature and market forces. Indeed, the resulting urbanization patterns have been celebrated as manifestations of American individualism, allowing the creation of "the first mass upper-middle class" (Siegel 1999) unplanned by public officials or government bureaucrats.

Such views, however, ignore the fact that although people do make individual choices among alternatives in housing, business location, and transportation, these private choices are profoundly shaped by public policies that are often invisible to those whose lives are affected by them on a daily basis. Indeed, government policies affect every aspect of how people make those choices and what they have to choose from. Joel Garreau's (1991) famous celebration of the virtues of "edge cities" ignores the fact that these areas have grown around and depend entirely on public-funded highways and, in some cases, airports and government facilities, including universities and research centers. They have been influenced by federal and state policies, including mortgage subsidy programs, highway-building programs, and tax systems, as in California, that encourage the development of large-scale malls on vast tracts of open space. From the "free market" perspective, this system seems to work: central-city and suburban governments all compete for residents and private investment, and both home buyers and business owners make their own choices. In reality, however, these choices are not the products of free markets. In fact, the rules of the game—shaped by government policies—do not give all people and places equal chances to succeed. Urban poverty, suburban sprawl, and metropolitan segregation are the consequences of government policies as much as they are the result of consumer preferences or business efficiency (Dreier, Mollenkopf, and Swanstrom 2001).

Although the notion that public policy influences the geography of opportunity is accepted in many metropolitan areas on the East Coast, Los Angeles is sometimes portrayed as the grand exception in American urbanism—the city that "breaks the rules." Diverse, fragmented, polarized, and ungovernable, a metropolis without geographic center or unifying civic culture, Southern California is said to have grown without benefit of planning or policy. But in fact, federal, state, and local public policies have profoundly shaped the region and continue to do so today. Government policies have promoted the L.A. region's intertwined dilemmas of urban sprawl and the deterioration of older communities, undermining its sustainability by creating deep-seated and overlapping social, economic, and environmental problems.

In this way, L.A.'s story is similar to the tales that might be told of other major metropolitan regions in the United States. In fact, like much else in Southern California, it may be an exaggerated version of the broader American story. Not only has the region felt the impacts of the usual suspects—federal defense spending and transportation and housing policies—it has also been shaped by immigration policies, water and environmental policies, and even local and state tax policies (Hise 1997; Scott and Soja 1996). Not only has the region experienced the changing racial and ethnic diversity now characteristic of most U.S. metropolitan areas, it has become so diverse that no single group has a majority of the region's population. Not only has it experienced the tensions of urban disinvestment and sprawl, it has been home to two of the country's severest social explosions: the Watts rebellion of 1965 and the vast multiracial uprising of 1992.

This book explores how government policy has shaped the development of greater Los Angeles, tackling the myth of market choice and pointing to the key roles of government policies, often driven (or at least significantly influenced) by business priorities. But the contributors to this volume do not simply recount the horrors visited on the region and its people—although there is plenty of that to go around. Instead, they and we contend that the escalating challenges facing Los Angeles, including widening divides along the lines of income, race, and geography, have led some residents to develop innovative approaches to taming these economic and political forces, often through grassroots organizing and creative public policy making. L.A., long viewed as the poster child for unsustainable growth and inequality, may in fact offer lessons for other urban areas in forging progressive policy reforms.

This book brings together the research and ideas of twenty individuals, but it differs from many other edited volumes in at least one important way: it is the result of a process and not a moment. The various authors were not simply brought together for a conference and a single exchange; instead, the three editors convened a group that met consistently for a period of two years, sharing ideas, visions, and preliminary chapter drafts. This intensive process was matched by a series of conversations with those conducting similar research efforts and discussions in several other metropolitan areas under the auspices of the Brookings Institution's Center on Urban and Metropolitan Policy. The end result, we hope, offers an unusual unity of purpose, coherence of story, and commitment of effort.

We are, after all, lovers of Los Angeles. For us, the area's many problems have long presented the opportunity for change and challenge. The region's very fragmentation compels researchers, policy makers, and activists to explore ways to bring people together. The travails of excessive sprawl, the alienation of suburban life, and the basic outrage of severe economic misery amid so much prosperity force us to contemplate the possibility of new ways to organize our metropolis. Its extraordinary income gaps create the need for—if not the inevitability of—new social movements to improve the conditions of daily life. And the fact that government policy helped produce so many of these ill effects suggests that government policy—and not market mechanisms—will also be needed to bring about change.

Whether these challenges are met with creative thinking is yet to be seen. In the rest of this introduction we place these problems and possibilities in broader context by introducing the history of the region and offering a framework for analysis of that history. We then outline the organization of this volume, detailing the contributions of the authors and pointing to some common threads in their analyses.

Building Southern California

Southern California is the second-largest metropolitan area in the United States in terms of population size. More than sixteen million people live in the 177 cities, five counties (Los Angeles, Orange, Riverside, San Bernardino, and Ventura), and 35,000 square miles that comprise the region. (About 14,000 of those square miles are "urbanized"—inhabited by human beings; see Figure I.1.)

One hundred years ago, few knowledgeable people could have predicted that this region would become a magnet for human migration and settlement. The varied and extreme topography, climate, and river systems make it an improbable site for a major urban region (Schoenherr 1992). The area's mediterranean climate produces hot, dry summers and winters with low average precipitation but intense storms that can cause flooding. Beneath the region lie faults that generate devastating earthquakes (Sherman et al. 1998). Steep, landslide-prone mountains surround the coastal plain, creating a barrier to offshore air currents and causing inversion layers that trap air contaminants, giving Los Angeles the reputation (as well as the reality) of being one of the world's smoggiest cities. And periodic hot, dry winds, topographic features, and fire-adapted vegetation promote wildfires that chronically threaten the region, increasing risks of floods, landslides, and debris flows (Sherman et al. 1998).

By 1870, only 15,000 residents lived in Los Angeles County, but between 1870 and 1880 the population doubled and then tripled to 90,000 between 1880 and 1890 (Table I.1). This boom was mostly due to the completion of government-subsidized transcontinental rail lines. Migrants came from the Midwest in search of wealth and the region's pristine environment. Native-born *Californios* were displaced and Chinese laborers and other people of color were harshly marginalized from the emerging social and economic life dominated by white settlers and an emergent urban growth regime dominated by railroad men, newspaper publishers, merchants, and bankers.

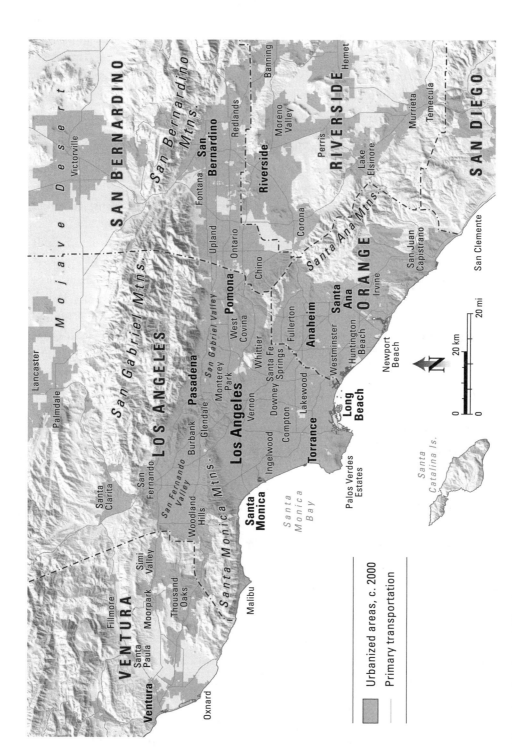

Figure I.1. Southern California region, Los Angeles and vicinity.

By 1900, 170,000 people lived in L.A. and another 80,000 people lived in small centers—such as Riverside, San Bernardino, Ventura, and Anaheim—that emerged in outlying counties. Between 1900 and 1920 the population soared as a result of agricultural expansion, business boosterism, town building, land speculation, and business-attracting antiunion policies. None of this would have been possible without a variety of government-sponsored, large-scale infrastructure projects, which local business leaders actively advanced (Erie 1992). The Los Angeles Aqueduct promoted the development of Los Angeles as an "infinite suburb." The Metropolitan Water District removed constraints to growth by building the Colorado River Aqueduct (Davis 1996). Flood control projects "regulated" the area's rivers and permitted floodplain development.[1] Civic leaders promoted construction of the nation's largest storm-drain system, made possible by massive federal subsidies, to handle urban surface runoff into the Pacific Ocean.[2]

Key to the region's growth was an extensive transportation infrastructure built primarily by government agencies, with public tax dollars, at the behest of a powerful urban growth coalition led by the *Los Angeles Times*, the Los Angeles Chamber of Commerce, Merchants and Manufacturers Bank, and large-scale industrialists. Determined to wrest control of vital infrastructure away from private water, electricity, and traction companies, this coalition municipalized infrastructure and sought to use it to build the region's economic base. The coalition also attracted public funds to complete a complex system of publicly owned ports, airports, and surface transportation. The federally subsidized Ports of Los Angeles and Long Beach helped shift the regional economy from one based primarily on land speculation toward one based mostly on industry. A decentralized airport system—which initially included a number of airports linked to aircraft manufacturers and military installations that later became general airports—is now anchored by Los Angeles International Airport (LAX), one of the largest airports in the world (Southern California Association of Governments [SCAG] 2000, 76–78).

Table I.1. Population growth in Southern California by county (in thousands), 1870–2025

Year	Los Angeles	Orange	San Bernardino	Riverside	Ventura	Total
1870	15	—	4	—	—	19
1880	33	—	8	—	5	46
1890	101	14	25	—	10	151
1900	170	20	28	18	14	250
1910	504	34	57	35	18	648
1920	936	61	73	50	28	1,150
1930	2,209	119	134	81	55	2,597
1940	2,786	131	161	106	70	3,253
1950	4,152	216	282	170	115	4,934
1960	6,011	709	501	303	199	7,724
1970	7,042	1,421	682	457	378	9,981
1980	7,478	1,932	893	664	530	11,496
1990	8,863	2,411	1,418	1,170	669	14,531
2000	9,519	2,846	1,709	1,545	753	16,374
2025 (forecast)	12,339	3,403	2,778	2,832	951	22,303

Sources: Soja and Scott (1996, 3). Figures from 2000 are from U.S. Census, Summary File 1. Forecast from 2025 is from SCAG (2001, 9).

Private investors used their political influence to promote these government projects and then used their entrepreneurial skills to profit from them. For example, by the early twentieth century, the nation's largest metropolitan transit system, with more than 1,100 miles of tracks—the Pacific Electric Red and Yellow Car companies—linked Los Angeles's relatively small downtown to lower-density suburbs. Land speculators created streetcar systems to inflate agricultural land values by improving accessibility to downtown employment. Thus transit infrastructure investments made by private parties, rather than government, led initial waves of exurbanization.

However, the public transit system that initially promoted development soon outlived its usefulness—if not to passengers (actually, ridership steadily increased), at least to business leaders. Powerful organizations and individuals—the automobile, bus, and tire industries; public officials; and consumers, who (influenced by both the declining maintenance of the public transit system and the lure of the "freedom" promised by the automobile) perceived cars as more efficient or profitable—all demanded auto infrastructure rather than continued investment in rail transit. They persuaded the region's public officials that the car was the way of the future, and the trolley system was gradually dismantled, making it less convenient and attractive to riders. Between 1919 and 1929, auto registrations in Los Angeles skyrocketed to one car for every three residents. By the 1960s, the streetcar system had completely disappeared, and cars reinforced public and private decisions to disperse residence and employment.

Meanwhile, the region continued to grow. Between the two world wars, the region's population roughly doubled, with L.A. County reaching 2.7 million. The region recovered faster from the Great Depression than did the rest of the nation. Southern California also became the biggest branch-plant auto-manufacturing zone in the country as well as the largest consumer market for cars. Aircraft and movie production also expanded and new industries emerged, such as chemicals, apparel, and furniture. A continuous belt of factories soon extended from downtown L.A. to the ports at Long Beach and San Pedro. By 1940, manufacturing employment growth rates in Los Angeles were among the highest in the nation. But residential and labor markets became increasingly divided by race, with workers of color enjoying limited access to the region's better-paying jobs and more desirable neighborhoods.

World War II (and the later conflicts in Korea and Vietnam) prompted the U.S. Department of Defense to exploit the region's existing aircraft manufacture and Pacific location, producing a regional concentration of defense-related industries. The region became a center of the "military-industrial complex." Population grew to almost 10 million by 1970 as workers migrated in for good defense jobs. Large-scale home builders, along with banks and insurance companies, as well as industrialists seeking to secure worker housing, used their political influence to promote suburbanization, building homes for the growing workforce, and benefiting handsomely from the transformation of the region's agricultural land into housing tracts. The resulting boom in home building literally changed the region's landscape. Once-rural areas such as the San Fernando Valley and the outlying counties, especially Orange County (where population grew tenfold from 1940 to 1970), became prime examples of America's suburban auto-centered shopping mall culture.

As people moved into these new areas, they sought greater control over such things as property taxes, the schools, and who their future neighbors might be. Unlike other democratic societies, where the national government sets some standards over land use and taxes, federal and state governments in the United States encourage the proliferation of semiautonomous local governments. Between 1940 and 1960, nearly sixty cities incorporated in Southern California, a process made easier by public policy in the form of the "Lakewood system," in which municipalities could contract with counties for essential services (Fulton 2001). Many of these new suburbs sought to limit property tax growth and to utilize local zoning power to limit apartment construction. In combination with redlining by banks and the federal housing administration, along with racial steering by real estate agents and builders, this worked to erect invisible barriers to African Americans and Latinos—and, in turn, led to eruptions of civil unrest during the 1960s and 1990s.[3]

Sprawl and rapid population growth fueled demand for new schools and services. Fortunately for the fiscal health of municipalities, housing prices rose as well, allowing local governments to pay for infrastructure with increased property taxes. Some home owners, however, rebelled, and the political backlash led to the passage of Proposition 13 in 1978, a California state law that capped increases in individual tax bills and thereby limited the ability of local governments to raise revenues. The law had enormous unanticipated consequences, including a rapid decline in the quality of public education in many areas. It also fueled cities' and suburbs' growing dependence on local sales taxes to pay for basic services.

To generate these sales taxes, cities and suburbs began competing for retail stores that could generate much-needed revenue. These "bidding wars" forced localities to engage in self-defeating efforts to attract shopping malls and retailers by giving away the fiscal stores. One consequence of this was further sprawl, leading to traffic jams and pollution. During 1970–90, the two eastern counties in the region, Riverside and San Bernardino, were transformed from rural areas to highly urbanized areas, characterized by land-extensive retail development and massive logistics and warehousing firms. Increasingly, these inland subregions served as affordable-housing reservoirs for Orange County workers priced out of that county's rapidly inflating housing market, making for desperately congested east-west roadways.

Still, growth continued in both the central city and the outlying areas of the region. While individual choices and market dynamics played a role, demand was also driven by government-sponsored infrastructure projects primed, in turn, by the efforts of an urban growth coalition determined to keep Los Angeles at the center of the rapidly spreading metropolis. Massively expanded port facilities acted as a linchpin for the region's global trade, in turn fueling development of a large, decentralized transportation sector linked to rail facilities, trucking, and warehousing. Beginning in the 1960s, the Los Angeles World Airports, the airport enterprise district of the city of Los Angeles, acquired Ontario and Palmdale Airports. Major plans are currently under way to increase LAX's capacity to serve global travelers (Erie, Kim, and Freeman 1999). By the 1980s, rail transit also returned to the public agenda. Mayor Tom Bradley and L.A.'s downtown business community successfully pushed for a controversial system of fixed and light rail lines around downtown and to suburbs. According to Giuliano (chapter 5, this volume), by 1997 $7 billion had been spent on or was committed to this system, which is often described as both inefficient and inequitable.

The historic infrastructure and development-oriented local growth regimes, however, came increasingly under challenge during the 1990s. As globalization and the neoliberal trade policies in much of Latin America and Asia swelled the ranks of immigrant workers in Southern California, the numbers of the working poor grew. Low-wage workers reinvigorated a flagging labor movement that, joining with other progressive forces, engineered "living wage" laws and other challenges to the region's governing regime. At the same time, using federal environmental laws, environmentalists erected barriers to developers' ability to engage in business-as-usual suburban expansion. Meanwhile, the growing suburban areas of the region became increasingly alienated from downtown-oriented political elites as well as from the increasingly minority neighborhoods at the region's core. This alienation became so severe that by the turn of the twentieth century well-organized business leaders and home owner groups in the suburban San Fernando Valley section of Los Angeles—an area with more than one million residents—had mobilized a movement to "secede" from L.A., reversing the successful annexation efforts of the first half of the twentieth century. This movement ultimately failed at the ballot box, but it proved a powerful illustration that old-fashioned downtown growth-regime politics and policies—especially as played out in the form of land-use planning—had reached the limits of their effectiveness and faced serious contestation from a variety of social movements and stakeholder groups.

In sum, public policy played a dramatic role in the creation and fragmentation of Southern California. An area that nature seemed to mark as less inhabitable was transformed by railroads and aqueducts into a real estate developer's paradise. The subsequent destruction of the rail infrastructure in favor of the automobile favored outward sprawl even as defense spending helped transform the region into a manufacturing center. The fragmentation of local governmental units within the region, as well as local zoning laws, allowed for the suburbanization of the landscape even as tax policy pushed the process by fueling new outward growth and new infrastructure spending facilitated the increasingly far-flung location of economic activities.

Public choice theory and its story of consumer preferences is therefore inadequate to explain our current dilemma: much as Hollywood has made dreams into films, public policy has shaped millions of individual choices into the collective narrative that is Southern California. And much as earlier social movements have challenged persistent policy patterns around civil rights, environmental standards, and labor regulations, a new set of actors has arisen in both the Los Angeles metro area and the nation to challenge the sprawl that federal, regional, and local policies have produced. Unfortunately, like Southern California itself, the movement is fragmented, ranging from suburbanites worried about further development to inner-city residents seeking a just share of regional prosperity—and the jury is still out on whether these strands will come together to be more than the sum of their disparate parts.

The Region and Its People

Although the region's most explosive growth occurred during the settling period of the early and mid-twentieth century, Southern California's population has continued to expand in recent decades. Between 1980 and 2000, the region's population zoomed from 11.5 million to 16.4 million, a gain of more than 40 percent. Los Angeles County, the largest California county, with more than 9.5 million people, grew by more than 2 million residents (27 percent). Orange County grew by 47 percent. Riverside and San Bernardino Counties—the so-called Inland Empire—more than doubled in population, adding almost 1.7 million. As a result, Los Angeles County has become far less dominant than it was a century ago. By 2040, population in the outlying counties is expected to equal that of L.A. County.

The city of Los Angeles remains by far the largest municipality in the region, with almost 4 million residents. The region also includes eleven other cities with populations over 150,000, the largest being Long Beach (461,522) in L.A. County and Santa Ana (337,977) and Anaheim (328,014) in Orange County (SCAG 2001, 9). However, most of the fastest-growing cities—some with population growth rates over 100 percent—are located on the region's fringe.

Meanwhile, the region has become the most diverse "multicultural" metropolis in the nation, perhaps in the world; indeed, demographer William Frey (2001) has termed it a "melting pot metro." A large wave of immigrants from Asia, Europe, and especially Mexico and other parts of Latin America led the change. By 1990, the region was home to almost a quarter of the nation's immigrants (Myers 1996). More than one in four residents were foreign-born, and among these, half arrived after 1985. Some 80 percent emigrated from Asia or Latin America as globalization and free trade policies were played out and intensified long-standing migration patterns.[4] By the year 2000, 30 percent of the region's residents, and nearly 36 percent of L.A. County residents, were foreign-born.[5] The more rapid pace of population growth in the outlying counties reflects a trend occurring within L.A. County as well: through the 1990s, new immigrants increasingly settled directly in suburbs characterized by concentrations of immigrants and ethnic businesses (see Table I.2).

Despite this, in 2000 the most affluent communities remained predominantly white. Almost half of the region's cities still had majority white populations, with percentages higher in outlying counties (Myers and Park 2001). At the same time, cities that already had Latino majorities in 1980 had become even more Latino over the ensuing two decades, underscoring trends toward increasing racial separation at the municipal level (Fulton et al. 2000). Segregation did begin to break down in many of L.A.'s older neighborhoods, with blacks and Latinos, and in some cases Asians and whites, living in close proximity. This situation created the potential for both conflict and cooperation—and L.A. saw much of both during the 1990s, ranging from disputes between African American residents and Korean shopkeepers to joint efforts among low-wage workers of all races to improve labor conditions through unionization.

What does the future hold? The Los Angeles region is expected to add more than 6 million residents over the next twenty years, to top 22 million persons in 2020. If current racial trends continue, diversity will increase, not as much from immigration as from the natural increase due to the sons and daughters of immigrants. Meanwhile, the diversity at the aggregate scale will be matched by increasing separation at the local level—except in poor neighborhoods. Public policy, especially the national change in immigration policies over the last three decades, has played a dramatic role in making this picture, and new public policies will have to be part of the solution.

Economy and Inequality

Southern California's economy, as measured by employment, more than tripled in size during the second half of the twentieth century. Like the United States overall, postwar Southern California was characterized by rapid growth in durable manufacturing industries, such as automobiles, tires, aerospace, and defense. The 1970s brought drastic changes, with an increase in service industries (especially business services) and a decline in the share of manufacturing. However, the trend toward "deindustrialization" was less dramatic in Southern California than in other parts of the country because of a new wave of "reindustrialization" of mostly nondurable manufactures, including a garment industry deeply tied to the region's fashion design facilities. However, both deindustrialization and reindustrialization brought problems: middle-class, typically unionized, blue-collar manufacturing jobs disappeared, replaced by low-wage, nonunionized labor. Both phenomena contributed to regional poverty and inequality.

As this restructuring proceeded, economic activity shifted from central cities and old industrial zones to outer suburbs. In the earlier boom period for manufacturing,

Table I.2. Ethnic composition (in 2000) and changing proportion of foreign-born residents in Southern California counties (1980–2000)

Race/Ethnicity	Percentage of population by race/ethnicity in 2000					
	Los Angeles	Orange	Riverside	San Bernardino	Ventura	Region
Anglo/white	30.9	51.1	50.9	43.8	56.6	38.9
African American	9.4	1.4	6.0	8.6	1.7	7.2
Latino	44.6	30.8	36.2	39.2	33.5	40.3
Asian Pacific	12.1	13.8	3.6	4.8	5.3	10.5
Year	Percentage of foreign-born residents					
	Los Angeles	Orange	Riverside	San Bernardino	Ventura	Region
1980	22.3	13.3	10.0	7.7	12.7	18.5
1990	32.7	23.9	14.8	13.2	17.0	27.1
2000	36.2	29.9	19.0	18.6	20.7	30.9

Sources: U.S. Census Summary Tape File 1, 1980, and Summary File 3, 2000; California Department of Finance, January 1998.
Note: Race/ethnicity does not add to 100 percent because of "other" category, including Native Americans and mixed race.

between 1950 and 1970, plants spread southeast, eventually reaching northern Orange County and stimulating the first wave of suburbanization. Later, in the 1980s and 1990s, new technology and business/financial service clusters developed in Orange and Ventura Counties and in the northwest of San Fernando Valley. However, the traditional blue-collar areas of southeastern Los Angeles County were left behind and declined rapidly as production moved overseas and south to Mexico. Meanwhile, Riverside and San Bernardino Counties benefited from an increased rate of industrialization and rapid retail growth. Not surprisingly, given the accelerated population growth and housing development in those areas, construction also increased in the four outlying counties, especially Riverside.

The early 1990s recession hobbled Southern California's economy. Almost half a million jobs were lost between 1990 and 1994, and the region did not recover its pre-recession job level until mid-1997.[6] However, the effects were uneven geographically. Los Angeles County and, to a lesser extent, Orange County suffered the biggest losses. This helped to accelerate a trend of decentralization of employment: although the majority of the region's jobs are still found in Los Angeles County, an increasing share is located in outlying areas.

Indeed, by the late 1990s, the Los Angeles-Long Beach Primary Metropolitan Statistical Area had one of the nation's most decentralized employment patterns, with only about 7 percent of all jobs located within a three-mile radius of downtown, compared with about 45 percent in New York, 26 percent in Boston, and 19 percent in Chicago (Glaeser, Kahn, and Chu 2001). Even though Los Angeles County hosts the nation's seventh-largest high-tech industrial base, measured in terms of per capita high-tech jobs, Orange and Ventura Counties surpass Los Angeles in terms of average per capita high-tech output: $9,180 and $5,081, respectively, compared with L.A.'s $4,520 (U.S. Conference of Mayors and National Association of Counties 2000). This suggests a concentration of high-tech activity in suburban areas, and, indeed, in the early 1990s many areas of Los Angeles County continued to lose high-tech employment to outlying counties, triggered in part by bidding wars between municipalities within the region to attract high-tech investment.

Like many urban areas, Los Angeles suffers from a mismatch between where people live and where jobs are located, although the picture in L.A. is more complex than that in older East Coast cities. For example, job density (jobs per 100 persons) remains high in the L.A. region's older areas, especially in inner Los Angeles County and northern Orange County, and in some areas the number of jobs available exceeds the total population. However, these areas' neighborhoods often suffer from high unemployment and poverty because the jobs available do not necessarily correspond to local residents' skills and so are held by commuting suburbanites. Moreover, job growth in these areas is slow, leading to fewer opportunities for youth just entering the labor market (Pastor and Marcelli 2000).

In downtown and East Los Angeles, for example, there were more than 200 jobs per 100 working-age residents, but total jobs decreased by almost a fifth between 1990 and 1994. This contrasts with areas in outlying counties, where job density was often below 50 jobs per 100 working-age persons while job growth was over 30 percent. Surprisingly, the former central areas continued to experience more rapid population growth (although at a lower percentage rate) than outlying counties, leading to a growing absolute spatial mismatch between labor supply and demand in those zones. Partly as a result, median household incomes have been substantially lower in Los Angeles County than in Orange and Ventura Counties, with the Inland Empire also suffering because it is one step outside the ring of affluence (Figure I.2).

Another aspect of the spatial disparity is illustrated in Figure I.3, in which we plot the poverty rates for 1989 and 1999 for the city of Los Angeles, the rest of the county of Los Angeles, and the rest of the Southern California area outside of Los Angeles County. As might be expected, poverty rates are dramatically higher in the city and decline as one moves outward from the center. However, one striking fact is that the increase in poverty over the past decade has been quite substantial everywhere. For example, the 2.9 percentage point increase in the poverty rate for those under age eighteen in the city of Los Angeles is nearly matched by a 2.7 percentage point increase in the same poverty rate for those in the areas of Southern California outside of Los Angeles County—and given that the 1989 base was so much lower, the fact is that the poverty rate rose twice as fast in the rest of the region. This expansion of the poverty problem has been illustrated in other areas by Myron Orfield (1997) and has been used to argue for a natural coming together of city and suburban interests.[7]

However, even as poverty has spread through the counties, it remains highly concentrated in certain neighborhoods, a phenomenon that exacerbates the problems of spatial mismatch and weak social networks and also weakens the political bases for coalitions. One standard concentration measure—calculating the proportion of poor living in high-poverty tracts—shows that 48 percent of people below 150 percent of the official poverty threshold lived in high-poverty census tracts in Southern California in 2000, compared with 41 percent in 1990 and 33 percent in 1980.[8] This ghettoization was higher in Los Angeles County, where the proportion grew from 41 percent in 1980 to 48 percent in 1990, rising to 56 percent by 2000. Poverty is less concentrated in other parts of the region, but it nevertheless increased rapidly between 1980 and 2000.

More generally, Los Angeles has one of the widest income gaps of any metro area, and the 1990s brought little relief. For example, median income for households in the top 20 percent of the income distribution in 1995–98 was more than seven times that for the bottom 40 percent (see Figure I.4). While the top 20 percent of the income distribution added more than $5,500 in income (in 2001 dollars) between 1991–94 and 1995–98, the lowest 40 percent of the distribution actually saw a decline in real incomes. The latter part of the region's economic recovery brought relief to those at the bottom, due to both tightness in labor markets and a mobilized set of unions and community actors that pushed for living wage laws and other measures; unfortunately, the downturn that took hold in California in early 2001 eroded these advances.[9]

Income inequality between racial groups also grew during the 1990s, especially between white households on the one hand and African American and Latino households on the other. Asian households are not far behind white households in median

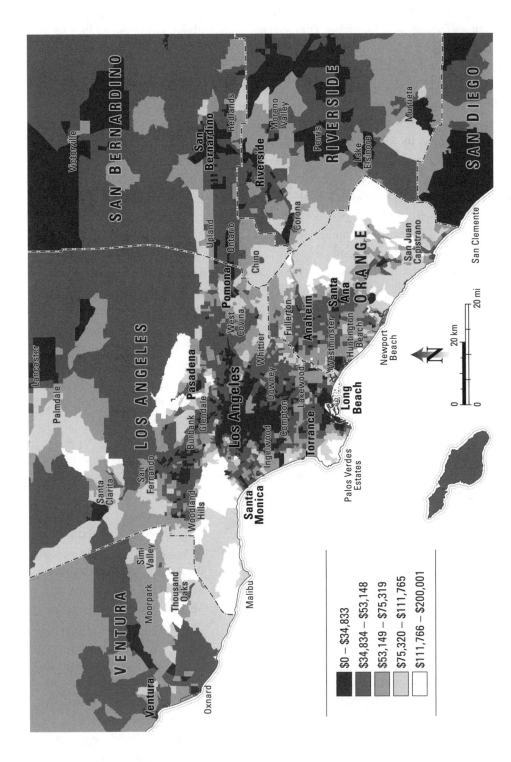

Figure I.2. Median household income, 1999 (in U.S. dollars).

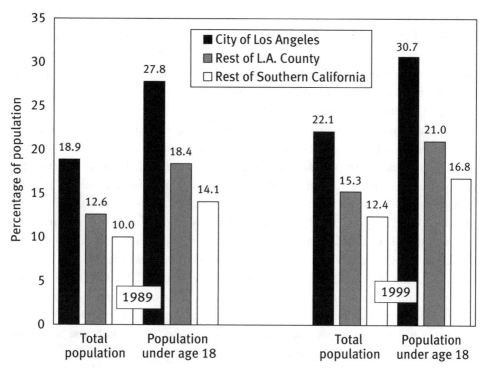

Figure I.3. Poverty rates in Southern California, 1989 and 1999.

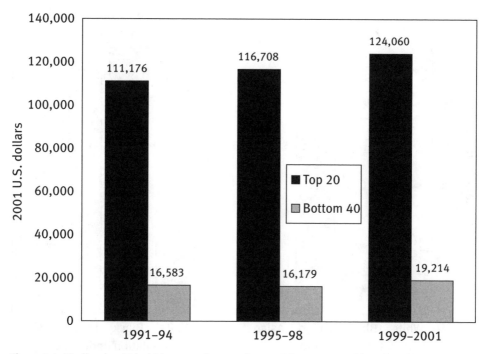

Figure I.4. Median household income changes for top 20 percent and bottom 40 percent of the income distribution in Southern California during the 1990s.

income but this is partly because Asian households tend to be larger, with greater numbers of income earners but lower per capita income. Figure I.5 illustrates the poverty rates for ethnic groups, showing the pattern for all of Southern California for both all ages and those under the age of 18; although the pattern is even more dramatic for the central city of Los Angeles, this graph shows startling racial disparities, with especially troubling gaps for children.

Economic inequality by race is deeply rooted in the bifurcation of employment opportunities in the region due to geography, skill, and connections. Latinos and African Americans disproportionately live in areas (mostly L.A. County) where the early 1990s recession caused the highest job losses, while whites dominate in areas with sustained job growth (mostly Orange, Riverside, and Ventura Counties). The higher-end service jobs that have emerged often have educational requirements beyond the skill levels of many workers of color.[10] And even when geography and skill come together, many residents lack the social connections that help link people to good-paying employment. Recent research shows that social networks pay off for Southern California's white workers but not as much for other groups. In particular, although Latinos often have contacts to secure employment, these contacts typically lead them to low-wage work that does not always reflect their skills and allows for limited upward mobility (Goldman 1997).

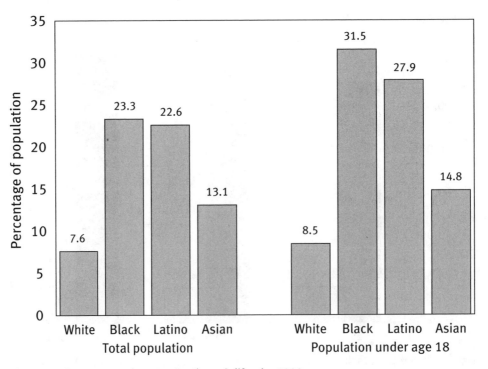

Figure I.5. Poverty rates by race, Southern California, 1999.

With all these factors driving the economy, many of Southern California's low-income residents get their poverty the old-fashioned way: they earn it. They work at jobs that pay low wages and provide few benefits. In 1990, more than 52 percent of poor persons in the region lived in households with at least one full-time worker; by 1998, the proportion had risen to 57 percent. Their situation has been exacerbated by the federal welfare reform law of 1996, which pushed many former welfare recipients into the workforce, leaving them in many cases poorer than they were before. Meanwhile, the percentage of households in which at least one member has health insurance declined from 66.3 percent in 1990–94 to 63.9 percent in 1995–98, with L.A. County's rate nearly 9 percent lower than the rest of the region. For the working poor, the federal earned income tax credit (EITC) provides additional revenues, although many eligible workers, especially new immigrants, do not take advantage of it. In L.A. County, 775,000 residents earned $1.2 billion in EITC refunds in 1997 (Berube and Forman 2001).

As noted, the twenty-first century began with a major downturn in the national and California economies, with the recessionary malaise subsequently exacerbated by the aftereffects of the September 11, 2001, terrorist attacks. These played special havoc with L.A.'s tourism industry—airlines, hotels, restaurants, and related sectors laid off many workers. In the wake of welfare reform, the recession will likely have a devastating impact on new entrants into the labor force, leading to greater unemployment without a safety net. As a result of both welfare reform and a severe shortage of affordable housing, homelessness remains a serious problem in Southern California.

Housing and Public Finance

At the same time much of the population in metropolitan L.A. is poor, housing remains expensive. The region suffers from a severe shortage of affordable housing and, in some areas, serious overcrowding and slum conditions. In 1998, the average Southern California household spent 37 percent of pretax wages ($15,500) on housing (one of the highest figures in the nation). About 14 percent of households were burdened with severe housing costs (twice the national average), and 15 percent suffered from overcrowding (twice as high as any other major metropolitan area). The home ownership rate (49 percent) is lower than any U.S. metro area except New York and well below California and U.S. averages. According to the National Low-Income Housing Coalition, a worker must earn two to three times the minimum wage to afford an average one-bedroom apartment in metropolitan Los Angeles. Almost half of poor renters must pay either more than half their income for rent or live in extremely inadequate housing units.[11] Again, this is one of the highest figures in the country (Southern California Studies Center [SC2] 2001).

The affordability index—the share of households that can afford a median-priced home—had fallen to 34 percent in Orange County and 39 percent in L.A. County by the end of the 1990s (SCAG 2000, 49–51). Although rental affordability—measured by the percentage of income spent on rent—was worse in central Los Angeles and Orange Counties, affordability problems were still widespread. According to the American

Housing Survey, for example, in L.A. County 45 percent of all renters paid more than they could afford in 1985, and this share rose to 49 percent by 1995—prior to the postrecession rent escalations.

The capacity of government to respond to the housing crisis is limited, partly because, like many other metropolitan areas, Southern California has a highly fragmented governmental structure. In 1997, the region was made up of five counties, 177 cities, and more than 1,100 special districts. Coordinating land use and housing production—particularly since Proposition 13 made housing a losing fiscal proposition[12]—is a challenge.

Moreover, the fiscal capacities of the region's cities vary widely, with those most in need often among those least able to respond. In 1982, per capita fiscal capacity was $502 for the region, with a low of $384 in San Bernardino County and a high of $516 in both Los Angeles and Orange Counties.[13] By 1997, the average fiscal capacity for the region had risen to $641 (in 1997 constant dollars), with the largest increases having occurred in Orange, Los Angeles, and Ventura Counties. Conversely, fast-growing San Bernardino and Riverside dropped considerably ($449 and $477, respectively), defying the conventional wisdom that "trickle-down" exurbanization results in newly developing suburban communities that are wealthier and have higher capacity to provide basic services.

In other words, some cities can barely afford to collect the garbage and maintain the streets. Paradoxically, the cities with the poorest residents and least vibrant commercial sectors have to ask their residents and businesses to dig deeper into their pockets to pay for basic services. This exacerbates the flight of families and firms with choices to flee the troubled cities for more affluent areas. In search of sales tax revenues, cities compete for auto malls and consumer outlets. But fiscal zoning is often impossible for the poorest cities—exemplified by the failure of an auto mall, hotel facilities, and other regional attractions in the city of Compton. Local municipalities are forced to rely on fees that are often regressive and, as such, may exacerbate income disparities.[14]

Beyond the fiscal impediments to coordinated planning lies another problem: the region's political life has also become increasingly fragmented. Until the 1960s, L.A. was governed, for better and sometimes for worse, by a small group of cohesive, conservative elites. Since then, the region's business and corporate leaders have become disconnected from one another and less politically effective. There are no longer any *Fortune* 500 companies headquartered in Los Angeles, nor is there a major bank headquartered in the nation's second-largest city. The transformation of greater Los Angeles as a "branch office" region is symbolized most dramatically by the fact that the region's dominant daily newspaper—the *Los Angeles Times*—was recently purchased by the Chicago-based Tribune Company.

The small and medium-sized businesses that now dominate the region's economy have found it difficult to step up to the civic leadership plate. And while it is still the region's cultural and media center, the city of Los Angeles no longer dominates Southern California as it once did. L.A.'s Mayor and city council members, as well as the city's business leaders, are merely part of the cacophony of political voices within the larger metropolitan area.

Especially since the enactment of Proposition 13, each municipality has adopted a "go it alone" strategy for economic development, and the region has resisted attempts to strengthen regional government. Indeed, the outlying counties and even the cities within Los Angeles County itself seem to share only one political perspective: an aversion to being seen as part of the city of Los Angeles. Even within the city itself, small but very vocal groups have established movements in several areas—including the San Fernando Valley and the harbor-area community of San Pedro—to break off from Los Angeles and form their own municipal governments.

The general fragmentation within and across cities has brought one positive trend: with other sectors weakened, community-based organizations as well as labor unions have grown in numbers and influence. These sectors create the potential for a political force that could challenge the widening economic disparities within the region. But without a common agenda—and a broad constituency—even these progressive forces are unlikely to promote regional approaches to metropolis-wide problems in areas such as infrastructure, planning, and housing. A new Los Angeles will likely require that these grassroots voices rise up and articulate a crosscutting regional approach. Fortunately, this has begun to happen in arenas as diverse as economic policy, transportation development, and environmental inequities.

Transportation and Environment

One place where popular voices have aggressively challenged the status quo is in the world of transportation. Daily life in greater L.A. is characterized by traffic congestion for drivers and frustrating delays and overcrowding for bus riders. Compared with other metro areas, few people use the region's limited subway and light rail systems.

Between 1980 and 2000, the region made major transportation investments in a subway system, light rail lines, and an interurban commuter rail system. In addition, there was a 54 percent growth in freeway miles between 1982 and 1997 (Texas Transportation Institute 1999). Most of the largest projects were located in Orange County, along its north-south axis, and in northern L.A. County and the Inland Empire.[15]

Additions to transportation system capacity and population growth, in part, fueled an increase in total auto vehicle miles traveled (VMT) as well as per capita VMT. After small reductions following the early 1990s recession and an expansion in transportation capacity, regionwide daily VMT grew by 19 percent between 1994 and 1997. This increase dramatically outstripped population growth as auto users drove more miles (SCAG 2000, 73–76). Between 1982 and 1999, VMT increased by 65 percent in Los Angeles and 123 percent in the Inland Empire, compared with population increases of 27 percent and 56 percent, respectively. In Los Angeles County, hours of delay per capita per year rose from thirty-one in 1982 to fifty-six in 1999, resulting in increased air pollution and more than 1.1 million gallons of wasted fuel, for a total delay-related cost of almost $12.5 billion, the highest in the nation. In the Inland Empire, annual

hours of delay per person rose from six in 1982 to thirty-eight in 1999 (Texas Transportation Institute 2001).

At the same time, total public transit trips declined from their 1985 high, despite
a 12 percent increase during the 1990s. And the *share* of the population utilizing
public transit fell from thirty-four transit trips per thousand population in 1990 to
thirty-two in 1997, despite heavy investment in transit in L.A. County (SCAG 1999,
71). By century's end, 93 percent of all regional commuters were still using cars (SCAG
2000, 73–76).

The region's public transit system mirrors the economic and racial inequality of
the larger society. The Metropolitan Transportation Authority (MTA), L.A. County's
transportation commission, runs a bus fleet and three rail operations, channels funds
to sixteen suburban municipal bus operators, and also created Metrolink, a regional
commuter rail system with five lines converging in downtown. In an effort to reduce
auto congestion and associated pollution, the MTA's expenditures during the 1990s
favored rail line riders (including commuters from outlying areas) over severely neglected central L.A. County bus riders. Although in 1992 buses carried 94 percent of
all MTA riders (mostly low-income people of color), only about 30 percent of the
MTA's $2.6 billion capital and operating budget went to buses, leading to severe over-
crowding on key routes—up to 140 percent of capacity.[16] In contrast, the three rail
lines carried less than 6 percent of riders, mostly white and affluent, but received 71
percent of the budget. Each rider on a Metrolink train received a $41 subsidy in 1994,
compared with a bus rider's $1.17, and security expenditures per rider were 43 times
higher in 1994 on rail lines than on MTA buses. The MTA has been further criticized
for the fact that lines with a higher share of passengers of color got lower subsidies
and that suburban bus operators, with mostly white ridership, received higher MTA
subsidies than its own bus riders, leading to disparities in fares and service quality.

These disparities led the Bus Riders Union, a grassroots organization expressly
formed to represent poor (often immigrant) bus riders, to a successful federal civil
rights suit that claimed the MTA discriminated against transit riders of color. The suit
resulted in a consent decree forcing the MTA to alter its fare policies, purchase additional buses, and extend service. Although controversy continues over implementation
of these changes and MTA compliance, the capacity of the working poor to organize
on this key issue of transportation reflects the burgeoning of new community movements for justice throughout the region (Pastor 2001).

The environmental movement has also been revitalized in—and has helped to
revitalize—the area. For much of the past fifty years, L.A. has been viewed as the
nation's smog capital. By the mid-1970s, the region exceeded federal lead standards
during the entire year and federal ozone standards during almost half the year. But
smog is not the only problem. Widespread fears about groundwater contamination
arose in the 1970s and 1980s when contaminated wells in the San Fernando and San
Gabriel valleys were declared federal Superfund sites. By the late 1990s, 40 percent
of Southern California's wells were contaminated (SC2 2001).

Air pollution and well contamination are both closely related to the sheer volume of solid waste the region produces—50,000 tons of garbage per day in Los Angeles County alone. Although landfilled solid waste declined during the early 1990s recession, volumes subsequently increased as the region recovered. Many cities have not complied with the state's 1989 Integrated Waste Management Act, which mandated a 25 percent reduction in the 1990 levels of solid waste by 1995 and a 50 percent reduction by 2000 (SCAG 2000, 58). As in many metropolitan areas, illegal dumping and seepage of toxic wastes from industrial facilities or storage tanks contaminate groundwater and soils, leaving vacant "brownfields" too costly to clean up.

Yet the news is not all bad. During the past 25 years, the region has also dramatically reduced pollution, prodded along by federal Environment Protection Agency enforcement and community pressure. According to the South Coast Air Quality Management District (SCAQMD 2002), the number of Stage 1 smog alerts averaged 113 days a year in the 1976–78 period, but fell to only 4 days a year in the 1997–99 period. Of course, the region still fails to meet federal standards for ozone and fine particulates, and the consequences are high—one estimate suggests that the cost to the region is $9.4 billion in annual health-related expenses. Air toxics, diesel emissions linked to expansion of heavy-duty trucking, the popularity of sport utility vehicles, and high traffic densities all continue to threaten the region's environment (Hricko et al. 1999). But it is getting better, and public policy has played a key role in that shift.

Community pressure is also important, particularly around the notion of "environmental justice." As it turns out, pollution is not an equal opportunity problem. Although the entire region faces unhealthful exposure, the probability of dying from air pollution–related causes varies across counties, from an estimated 55 deaths for every 100,000 residents in Orange County to 79 in L.A. County, to 122 in the Inland Empire (SCAG 2000). The region also has pollution "hot spots," especially near large-scale refineries and chemical plants. Partly because these are often in older, minority neighborhoods, people of color have higher lifetime cancer risks due to air pollution from all sources than do whites (64 versus 49 deaths for every 100,000).[17] Differences persist even when one controls for the level of income of residents (see Figure I.6).

This has led to a vibrant environmental justice movement, which has pressed the SCAQMD to abandon an emissions credit program that was contributing to hot spots and forced the district's board to adopt both environmental justice principles and new, stricter standards for facility emissions. Environmental justice groups have also joined together with local social justice organizations and new social movement groups concerned with the quality of neighborhood life to fight not only against disproportionate exposure to pollution, but for a fairer distribution of environmental amenities such as access to urban parks and open space. Again, the severity of the problems has created an opportunity: communities have realized that public policy matters and have begun organizing new movements to shift policy in their favor.

Sprawl Hits the Wall

In contrast, the new "smart growth" movement has gathered less momentum in Southern California. This reflects, in part, the fact that organizations representing the have-nots—such as unions and community groups—have not yet forged a clear agenda on the issue of growth. At the same time, the obvious need to address unfettered sprawl and its consequences has pushed some municipalities to adopt a variety of limited smart growth measures, encouraged by middle-class constituents and environmental groups concerned about traffic congestion, increases in population without the capacity to provide schools and basic infrastructure, and other problems.

As it turns out, the image of the Los Angeles region as the nation's sprawl capital is somewhat misleading. The L.A. region is, in fact, characterized by clusters of dense development spread out over a large land area—what one observer has called "dense sprawl."[18] A useful benchmark is the land actually devoted to urban uses, as measured by the National Resources Inventory. Using this measure, between 1982 and 1992, regional population grew by almost 25 percent, while urbanized land increased only about 20 percent. Southern California was one of only two large metro areas where population grew faster than urbanized land. By 1997, the Los Angeles region had attained a density of 8.31 persons per urbanized acre—higher than the New York region (Fulton et al. 2001, 6).

True, in parts of the region, some people live in huge homes on large lots. But many more people live in the region's older urban areas, mainly because of larger households among immigrant families and "doubling up" by the poor in overcrowded housing. Between 1990 and 2000, household size in the region increased approximately

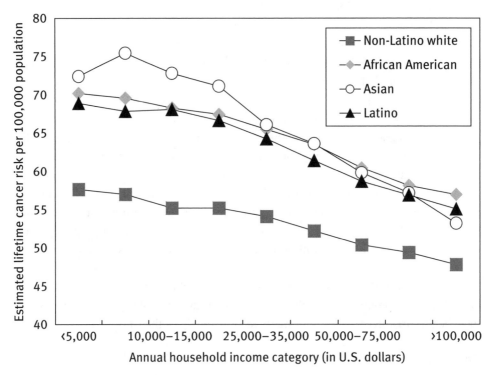

Figure I.6. Estimated lifetime cancer risk from ambient hazardous air pollutant exposures, by income and race, Southern California, 1990.

7 percent, from roughly 2.9 to about 3.1 persons per household (SC2 2001). Density in the hub cities of central Los Angeles County increased dramatically, from about 7,500 persons per square mile in 1975 to about 12,000 persons per square mile in 1995 (Fulton et al. 2000). In general, densities have risen in older, more central parts of the region as well as on the fringes (Figure I.7).

This trend is likely to continue. Indeed, most new housing developments are relatively dense—and certainly far denser than in other metropolitan areas (especially outside of the West). This is not to say that outward growth has been stopped. Despite relatively high densities, the sheer size of the region and its rapid population growth meant that more than 400,000 acres of land were urbanized between 1982 and 1997 (Fulton et al. 2001, 5). But this has actually led to a shortage of developable land in the region. Significant portions of undeveloped land are either too steep or ecologically sensitive, or are farmlands, state and national forests, or lands protected by conservation efforts through the federal Endangered Species Act (ESA) and the state-level Natural Community Conservation Planning (NCCP) program (Figure I.8). Sprawl, it seems, has hit the wall. The future of Southern California will depend on new strategies to allow residents to live together more effectively.

Smart growth—the idea of investing in central-city infrastructure and steering growth inward and toward greater density—would therefore seem to be an obvious way to address some of the region's most serious dilemmas. It would also seem to have appeal to members of the burgeoning social justice movements, at least to the extent that such a strategy could reverse the privileges enjoyed by those who have sprawled away from the central city. But for such a framework to gain traction, leaders from all over the region will first have to challenge the traditional view that Southern California's future must inevitably follow the same trajectory as its past—outward, toward the region's edges.

Civic leaders will need new skills and new coalitions. They will need to recognize the connections between inner-city distress and suburban challenges, stressing the connections between land-use policies and the possibilities for social justice. They will need to understand that denser urban living has worked well where it has been well planned and can be a way to accommodate unstoppable increases in population due to immigration and birth. Most important, the region's business, civic, and political leaders will need to recognize the extent to which public policy—and not just the market—has played a major role in the region's evolution and to understand that a different set of public policies is now necessary to address the region's problems. This book is an attempt to contribute to that task.

The Plan of This Book

We have argued that Southern California's rapid demographic, economic, social, political, and environmental transformations since World War II have produced a complex metropolis characterized by (1) a rapidly growing and diversifying population that is becoming denser but continues to consume urban fringe land; (2) insufficient infrastructure leading to overcrowded schools and housing and major traffic congestion;

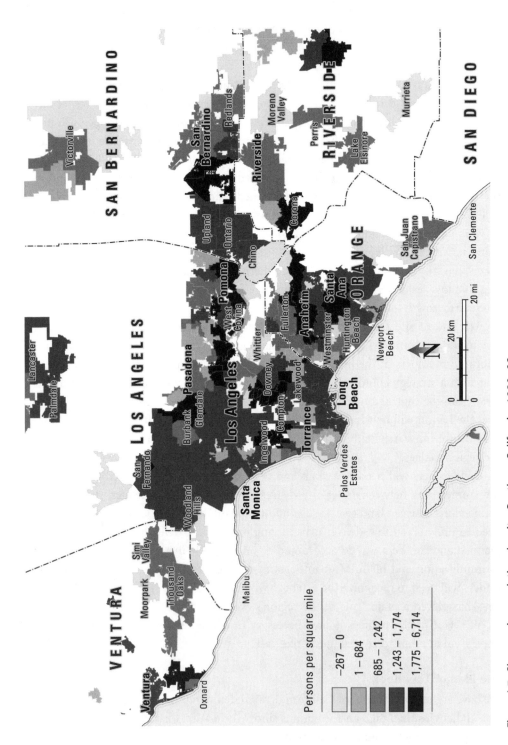

Figure I.7. Changes in population density, Southern California, 1980–98.

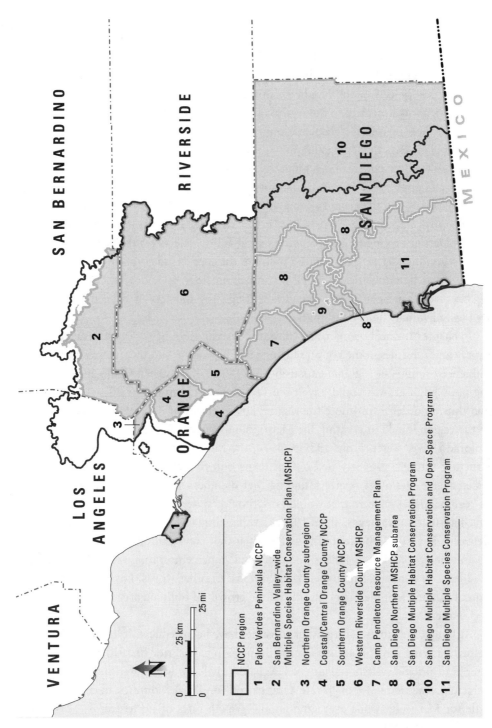

Figure I.8. Natural Community Conservation Planning (NCCP) program subregional planning areas, Southern California.

(3) rising ethnic, racial, and income group polarization linked to economic restructuring, welfare reforms, and local fiscal relations; and (4) severe environmental stresses that are unevenly distributed by race and location and also endanger native plants and animals. These characteristics are not simply the result of individual actions; they are closely linked, directly or indirectly, to public policies.

The chapters in Part I of this volume, "Policy Pathways," pick up this story by exploring key aspects of the region's history: infrastructure for growth, in particular water, which was so central to the region's development trajectory, and how, over time, industrial, housing, and transportation policies shaped the region's geography of race and class. Part II, "Up against the Sprawl," then turns to contemporary patterns and the role of key policies in shaping the contours of sprawl. These include housing markets and population distribution, transportation infrastructure and opportunities, fiscal dynamics and the region's geography of poverty, and environmental outcomes. The chapters in Part III, "Which Way L.A.?" consider how some communities and stakeholders are trying to grapple with sprawl and its effects on the economy, equity, and environment. Here, we provide a précis of the chapters to come, highlighting their findings and how together they tell a compelling story of Southern California as a region made—and constantly remade—through the impacts of collective action as well as individual choices and market dynamics.

In chapter 1, Erie, Freeman, and Joassart-Marcelli examine the broad issue of water supply and subsidies in the region's history, and how water supply practices in the past influenced rounds of regional expansion. Very little of Southern California's staggering population growth could have occurred without cheap imported water supplies, and thus, in order to promote the region, Los Angeles and several other major cities in the region joined in creating the Metropolitan Water District (the Met) to acquire Colorado River water. From 1929 to 1970, the Met financed its water supply infrastructure through property taxes. As it turns out, the city of Los Angeles and, to a lesser degree, the other twelve founding Met members supported most capital costs of regional infrastructure that would later provide water to newer suburbs. But being first had its disadvantages: since 1929, L.A. has drawn 8 percent of total Met water deliveries but paid 17 percent of total Met financial "contributions" from member districts, whereas San Diego, for instance, received 26 percent of total water delivered but paid only 18 percent of financial contributions. In other words, Los Angeles and the other founding Met members subsidized the growth of outlying areas, contributing to regional expansion.

Although the cross-county water subsidies have been reduced in recent years, they helped pave the way for suburban growth in the region. Prior to 1970, when the Met altered its pricing system, the city of L.A. paid heavily for Met water but grew at a 2.2 percent average annual growth rate. Orange and San Diego Counties, in contrast, paid little for Met water while averaging annual growth rates of up to almost 12 and 14 percent, respectively. The same relationship holds for all twenty-seven Met agencies: member areas with deeper water subsidies grew faster than areas with lower rates of subsidy. After 1970, outright subsidies paid by L.A. were eliminated, but the Met's basic goal remained: to ensure that water supply would not constrain growth (Fulton 2001). The obvious political question is why the central city continued to support the fiscal hemorrhage. Erie, Freeman, and Joassart-Marcelli grapple with this question, convincingly pointing out that a combination of shortsightedness by public officials and the political influence of developers and their allies likely played a role. But the main point is simple: sprawl resulted from subsidy and public policy, not just consumer choice.

In her exploration in chapter 2 of the driving forces behind the region's historical urbanization patterns, especially its racial formation, Pulido begins by pointing to the disparities in exposure to environmental dangers in the region. After first describing the basic patterns, Pulido argues that conventional approaches to understanding environmental inequality, which focus, for example, on whether there is intentional siting of polluting facilities in communities of color, often paint an incomplete picture. She suggests that the disparities in exposure are rooted in broader historical patterns of urban growth and sprawl—and that the "white privilege" inherent in that urbanization pattern is itself rooted in the society's basic set of institutions and power relations.

Pulido then traces the evolution of Southern California, showing how public policies reinforced existing patterns of racial privilege—for example, policies that made it easy for whites, but not people of color, to move out into suburban communities to avoid the environmental and other problems associated with older areas. In particular, the city of L.A.'s early zoning ordinance created an initial and long-lasting divide between the Westside, reserved for white, middle-class housing and population-serving retail and commerce, and the Eastside, destined for industrial development and worker housing, much of it multifamily. With rapid industrialization came increasing environmental pollution, as well as increasing numbers of African Americans from the South and international immigrants, especially from Mexico. Whites, unwilling to live near racial minorities if they could avoid it, sought—and were able—to escape both degraded environments and communities of color by moving out.

Critical to empowering this set of decisions were successive federal housing policies that provided mortgage subsidies to white households moving into "safe" suburban communities. This left older, more affordable neighborhoods to lower-income minority populations who were politically disempowered and unable to fight further industrialization by polluting factories. Although many discriminatory housing policies have now been abandoned, mortgage markets continue to treat people of color differently, reinforcing historical patterns of white advantage inscribed in the region's geography and social relations, and exacerbating intraregional disparities that in part drive sprawl.

Picking up directly from Pulido's contention that mortgage markets are still not color-blind, Aldana and Dymski review the legacy of housing policy in chapter 3: federal tax breaks for home owners; the Federal Housing Administration's mortgage insurance program, which "redlined" older urban areas; and the concentration of federally subsidized housing in already low-income areas, particularly those with large minority populations, that exacerbated the ghettoization of the poor. The important twist in these authors' contribution is the documentation that proves this is not merely a historical phenomenon. They show how the current regional patterns of residential segregation continue to be exacerbated by a variety of government policies today. For example, despite reform efforts, mortgage lending is still characterized by racial disparities, even when other variables that may explain why banks deny loan applications—especially household income—are factored in. African Americans, for instance, are at a significant disadvantage in obtaining conventional loan approval, with approval rates ranging from 57 to 71 percent below those of white applicants with the same income, debt, and other characteristics considered by lenders. Latino applicants in every Southern California county (except Ventura) are also at a disadvantage, having lower approval rates, all other things being equal.

Aldana and Dymski also note that federal policy has long promoted suburbanization by allowing home owners to deduct their mortgage interest and property taxes from their taxable income—a tax break not available to renters—thus not only encouraging home ownership but also encouraging consumers to buy bigger homes than they could otherwise afford, typically in suburban areas. Using careful and conservative calculations, they suggest that home owner mortgage deductions on homes purchased in 1997 alone range from 6.6 times (Los Angeles County) to 20 times (Orange County) the total value of subsidies for low-income housing in that year. At a more micro or neighborhood level, mortgage interest deductions for homes disproportionately flow toward the lowest-poverty areas, suggesting that the largest housing subsidies in the region go to already affluent neighborhoods. These disparities in federal housing subsidies have had enormous consequences in terms of both exacerbating economic inequalities and promoting sprawl (Gyourko and Sinai 2001).

The book next turns, in Part II, "Up against the Sprawl," to consider the contemporary patterns of public policy influence in four different areas: immigration, transportation infrastructure, fiscal policies, and the environment. Considering policies that influence the size and distribution of population, in chapter 4 Marcelli takes up the recent argument that it is population growth from immigration that fuels suburbanization and sprawl. Some environmental and restrictionist groups argue that population pressures from new arrivals lead to the outward push of white residents. This contributes to increasing differences in ethnic composition between city and suburb, making alliances on regional policy difficult. Meanwhile, conservatives add, immigrants settle into welfare dependence—indeed, many are attracted by high benefits in the first place.

Marcelli offers a more complex picture. New immigrants have historically settled first in central cities, partly because they typically find jobs and housing through social networks and so often elect to settle where family, friends, and conationals reside; once they assimilate and achieve economic success, however, they move out to the suburbs. Marcelli shows that although most new arrivals do settle in older central communities of Southern California, an increasing *share* of all immigrants now plan to move immediately into suburbs. Los Angeles County has continued to receive slightly more than two-thirds of all legal permanent residents intending to reside in Southern California, but this tendency weakened between 1990 and 1996.[19] The share of immigrants planning to reside in Los Angeles County fell from 76 to 68 percent, while Orange, San Bernardino, and Ventura Counties experienced slightly increased shares and Riverside County's roughly doubled, from 2.6 to 5.1 percent.

Breaking the geography into even smaller areas, Marcelli finds that those areas attracting the largest numbers of immigrants do have higher proportions of foreign-born persons than other areas, reflecting needs for public transportation, affordable housing, job and language training programs, and other antipoverty services. However, and paradoxically, most new immigrants go to areas where relatively few funds are allocated to reduce poverty or cushion the hardships associated with poverty. Moreover, employment-based immigration policies that favor workers whose skills help to address domestic labor shortages may be promoting suburbanization, because new immigrants disproportionately select communities with employment opportunities and rapid job growth. Thus policies attracting immigrants who are better prepared for economic success—the sort of policies most often pushed by those who question the value of immigration—may have promoted decentralization.

Giuliano's contribution to the contemporary infrastructure policy story in chapter 5 focuses on transportation, and in particular transportation planning. Reviewing the recent history of transportation policy, especially federal policy since the Reagan years, she argues that after the large-scale federal highway–oriented investments of the postwar era, transportation planning and funding increasingly devolved to state and local governments. During the 1980s, the federal government reduced transit subsidies. This shifted the burden to lower tiers of government, prompting the passage of county-level sales taxes to fund transit that became de facto transportation plans for the region.

The passage of the Intermodal Surface Transportation Efficiency Act of 1991 increased the flexibility as well as the funding for regional metropolitan planning agencies responsible for transportation and established a framework for regional transportation planning (especially through act's requirements for conformity between air quality and transportation plans). But, as Giuliano demonstrates, in Southern California the opportunity to develop a genuinely regional transportation plan was squandered in favor of further devolution to counties. Why? Giuliano suggests that the balance of power favored cities and counties over regional levels of government. This is due, in part, to the long-standing reluctance of cities and counties to subject themselves to regional mandates unless required to do so by the federal government. It is also due to the incredible complexity of funding mechanisms that politicized the planning process and the increased importance of local funding to the overall transportation funding mix.

The consequences of these trends included a regressive shift of costs to local residents; a shift toward requiring developers to finance improvements, which exacerbated housing affordability problems; and a pattern of transportation infrastructure investment that varies dramatically from county to county, leaving the region without a coherent transportation vision or strategy.

Giuliano concludes with three compelling case studies of how the lack of transportation planning in the region has played out. One example focuses on the struggle between L.A. County's MTA and the Bus Riders Union, mentioned above, that is rooted in the MTA's strategy of promoting subways and commuter rail projects at the expense of the vast majority of its customers—bus riders. This strategy did not succeed in altering the type of transportation utilized by the region's residents, but did lead to a dramatic deterioration of bus service in central Los Angeles County— particularly when the agency attempted to shift mounting subway project costs onto the backs of bus riders through increased fares and reduced service. Giuliano's second example relates to the conflict between Riverside and Orange Counties over toll roads and debates over how to relieve congestion created by the lack of affordable housing in job-rich Orange County and the lack of an adequate job base in the more affordable Riverside County. Finally, Giuliano considers the case of airport planning, another example fraught with political struggle involving airport neighbors, environmentalists, local governments, and the region's metropolitan planning organization, in which little regional planning for burgeoning passenger and freight traffic has occurred. In all three cases, the lack of regional planning has reinforced the region's decentralized, deeply fragmented, and dysfunctional approach to transport.

This section of the book next considers the region's fiscal policy and its ramifications. In chapter 6, Musso leads with a study of how the region's fiscal picture has changed dramatically since the passage of Proposition 13 in 1978 shifted fiscal power from localities to the state. Since that time, local governments have continually faced the specter of fiscal austerity and stress. Once primarily reliant on property taxes to finance services and infrastructure, localities have had to search for alternative sources of revenue. They now rely on diversified portfolios of revenue streams, the most significant elements of which are nonproperty fees and taxes, especially utility user taxes, and sales taxes.

These shifts have had a number of repercussions. One is that thirty new cities have incorporated since 1978, largely in order to gain control over land-use and fiscal decisions. Another is that local finance has probably become more efficient, as service costs are transferred to direct users, but it has also become increasingly regressive, as new and more regressive tax instruments have become more important. Third, an increasing number of local governments have experimented with outsourcing (or privatization) of service delivery, a shift that has implications for the living standards of lower-paid workers. Lastly, although the share of sales taxes as a share of total revenues has actually declined regionwide, the search for sales tax revenue, often largely exportable, has led to the "fiscalization of land use" in the region as jurisdictions compete frantically to attract sales tax dollars. This amounts to a beggar-thy-neighbor, zero-sum game that undermines the fiscal health of all those jurisdictions engaged in this competition.

Musso also considers the intrametropolitan geography of fiscal capacity and fiscal stress, finding extreme variability in fiscal capacity across the region. At the high end, cities such as Rolling Hills, Hidden Hills, and Beverly Hills topped the list with between $3,500 and $4,000 in per capita fiscal capacity. In contrast, in the cities with lowest fiscal capacity, such as Gardena, Coachella, and Blyth, per capita rates are less than $400. Moreover, Musso shows that patterns of fiscal capacity and stress run counter to received wisdom in two regards: first, older cities are no more likely than newer cities to experience low fiscal capacity; and second, cities located in the central portions of the region do not necessarily have lower fiscal capacity than those in the outlying areas, especially the Inland Empire, where newer, working-class communities face high levels of fiscal stress as they attempt to provide new infrastructure to support their growing populations. Indeed, 40 percent of the ten cities in the region with the lowest fiscal capacity are located in the Inland Empire, and 60 percent of the ten cities with the highest fiscal capacity are located in L.A. County—not the distant suburbs. Nevertheless, because the coastal and hillside areas of the region gained fiscal capacity over the 1980s and 1990s, they can attract better-off residents in low-fiscal-capacity/high-fiscal-stress jurisdictions seeking more favorable tax-service packages—and hence the region's fiscal picture is also an integral part of the sprawl story.

In chapter 7, Joassart-Marcelli, Musso, and Wolch explore the geographic distribution of federal spending in Southern California, and what it means for regional structure. Despite devolution, which in some policy arenas has involved reductions in federal funding to lower-level governments, the federal government continues to spend billions of dollars that find their way to local areas. Between 1994 and 1996, the federal government spent an average of $77.4 billion per year in Southern California—almost 25 percent of the gross regional product. Of this amount, $12.3 billion were allocated to antipoverty programs, including individual welfare payments and housing subsidies, as well as place-based housing, education, and health projects. The allocation of these funds to cities is critical at a time when many local governments must cope with escalating demands for infrastructure and urban services linked to rising poverty, despite severe limitations in their ability to raise local revenues.

Joassart-Marcelli, Musso, and Wolch examine both the level and the distribution of this federal spending. They find that real per capita federal spending in Southern California decreased almost 4 percent between 1983–85 and 1994–96, but note that this was largely driven by sharp defense spending cuts. Not surprisingly, Los Angeles County received the largest absolute share of federal dollars channeled to the region. Its mix included a disproportionately large share of what the authors term "redistributive" funds—spending on poverty and welfare programs. But on a per capita basis, Orange County residents received much higher levels of expenditures than did residents of other counties (partly because of infrastructure spending), and Riverside and San Bernardino saw their low averages actually decline over the period.

Although these county patterns are illustrative, city-level differences are even sharper. Low-income inner suburbs in the old industrial belt running from south-central Los Angeles County through the Inland Empire and selected working-class suburbs in the outlying counties attract below-average per capita amounts of both antipoverty and other federal funding, whereas the city of L.A., coastal cities, and scattered cities in outlying suburbs receive more-than-average federal expenditures per person, with L.A. ranking high only because its high poverty attracts antipoverty dollars. Still, on a per capita basis, federal funds tend to go disproportionately to cities with lower poverty rates, which only deepens metropolitan inequality.

Indeed, people in the richest 20 percent of the region's cities (those with the lowest poverty rates) receive on average almost twice as much as people in the poorest 20 percent of cities. This is largely because of the allocation of nonredistributive expenditures that constitute most (more than 80 percent) of all federal spending and seem to favor wealthier cities. Moreover, Joassart-Marcelli et al. note that both discretionary local fiscal capacity and fiscal effort have had positive influences on the allocation of redistributive federal funds to Southern California cities. Thus redistributive federal expenditures fail to alleviate fiscal disparities. To the contrary, they often help cities that can more easily afford to help themselves (e.g., can provide matching funds for federal and state programs). Moreover, population growth actually has a negative impact on the amount of nonredistributive expenditures. This finding indicates that the allocation of federal funds may not necessarily go to cities with the highest need for infrastructure development and new services.

In short, federal spending patterns serve to deepen rather than equalize fiscal disparities between cities while failing to address the problems of poorer cities, typically located in the urban core, and older industrial suburbs. In common parlance, the rich cities got richer thanks to federal subsidies, in part because of their greater ability to apply for and attract federal funds, and to match federal funds where such matches are called for. These dynamics fuel population and business out-migration and metropolitan fringe development.

In chapter 8, Pincetl rounds out the discussion of recent policy legacies by examining strategies the region has used for habitat conservation. Sprawl has, as noted above, consumed land on the urban fringes and threatened both open space and particular native animals and plants. Seeking to find political and policy levers to influence the broader questions of growth, environmentalists in the past frequently wielded the ESA as a tool to stop developers. This strategy was cumbersome, expensive, and piecemeal, and it eventually spurred the development of the NCCP program, directed by the California Department of Fish and Game. NCCP was initially designed to protect the California gnatcatcher's coastal sage scrub habitat in advance of potential development and listing, but it has become a model for other species and places.

In NCCP's initial form, participation was voluntary and collaboration was limited. As a result, although some landowners and governments voluntarily complied, six months after creation of the NCCP program more than 2,000 acres of the gnatcatcher habitat were nevertheless destroyed. Federal intervention, particularly the formal declaration of the gnatcatcher as a threatened species, helped put teeth in the process, and since 1991, NCCP collaborative groups have developed eleven subregional conservation plans (amounting to subregional land-use planning) that involve 6,000 square miles in Southern California. Thus far, some 150,000 acres have been preserved, and NCCP programs are now incorporated into city and county general plans. Although they have their limitations and could use even more federal support and strength, NCCP programs represent a rare example of the translation of regional consensus building around an environmental agenda into local land-use policy.

This discussion of mixed successes in directing land use in the region, even where strong federal legislation provides an impetus to do so, sets the stage for the book's final section, "Which Way L.A.?" The contributions in this section ponder how communities have attempted to manage and direct growth through local measures, and also how a variety of stakeholders are now trying to grapple with sprawl and its effects on economic well-being, social justice, and the environment. In chapter 9, Joassart-Marcelli, Fulton, and Musso review the general history of growth management policies in the region. Despite the federal constraints related to endangered species protection described by Pincetl, policies to manage growth are adopted primarily at the local level. Joassart-Marcelli et al. report that between 1989 and 1992, more than half of Southern California cities adopted new measures designed to manage growth, such as land-use tools, incentive programs, and development restrictions. However, between 1995 and 1998, this proportion fell to less than a quarter, with no clear connection between growth management activity in the two periods. In the 1989–92 period, only 16 percent of all growth management activity involved some form of zoning restrictions, rising to one-third by 1995–98. Not surprisingly, then, the sharpest declines were in local efforts to limit commercial development. In other words, by the mid-1990s, local governments in Southern California began rethinking their prior efforts to restrict such development as shopping malls, industrial and office parks, and other types of commercial investment.

Clearly, environmental protection and efforts to preserve community character triggered the initial spurt in growth management efforts. But why would municipalities halt such efforts only a few years later, particularly when the problems that led to the initial wave of growth control measures were still serious? The authors argue that these trends reflect a shift in fiscal imperatives brought by the early 1990s recession for cities facing the twin pressures of Proposition 13's fiscal constraints and the growing local burden of service provision. Between 1989–92 and 1995–98, cities that became involved in growth management were typically neither the fastest growing nor the densest. They usually enjoyed greater fiscal capacity, lower poverty and unemployment, higher proportions of white residents, and lower proportions of immigrants and Latinos. However, between 1989 and 1992, housing characteristics seem to have been the most important influences on growth management activity. Cities with lower vacancy rates but good housing conditions (i.e., higher property values and less overcrowding) tended to adopt growth restrictions, and other sorts of city characteristics were not critical. In the second period, however, socioeconomic, institutional, and fiscal characteristics became very important. Cities with high poverty and unemployment rates were much less likely to adopt growth management measures. Whereas fiscally healthier cities were more likely to approve such measures, those cities that were more dependent on revenue from sales taxes—generated by retail businesses— were less likely to do so.

Thus wealthier cities often used growth management to maintain fiscal strength and to avoid inflows of poorer residents, whereas poorer communities that suffered most from the recession saw development as a way to promote job creation and housing improvement and thus avoided growth management efforts. Given the playing field on which they are forced to operate, it may appear rational for all cities to engage in these efforts. When they do so, however, their activities contribute to further sprawl and even greater concentrations of poverty and unemployment. Rather than encouraging the sharing of prosperity in good times and sacrifice in lean years, these practices widen the already serious disparities between the haves and the have-nots within the region.

One reaction to the challenges of effective local growth management has been the rise of smart growth. In chapter 10, Gearin explores the smart growth movement, the rationales and lingo of which have come to dominate policy discussions about the future of the region. She shows how the movement has appropriated arguments, concepts, and tools from other schools of planning thought, particularly ideas about "new regionalism" and "urban sustainability." She also dissects the origins of the smart growth movement and investigates its diverse policies and implementation approaches. About half of the smart growth policies she identifies seek to direct growth or preserve land. In contrast, relatively few tools are aimed at reducing reliance on automobiles, redesigning communities, increasing livability, or shifting the housing market (to make it either more locationally or energy efficient). Most smart growth policies are implemented through incentive-based or regulatory tools, with only a few examples of market-based approaches. And most are pursued by local governments, closely followed by states and regions.

Gearin shows that in Southern California—as one might expect, given its far-flung, diverse, and fragmented character—smart growth has been pursued piecemeal by localities rather than being guided by any regional vision or organizational entity such as a regional government. The movement has significant potential, in part because smart growth is a large tent under which many stakeholders can comfortably shelter. But the term's very generality leaves it open to widely divergent interpretations. In reality, the region's smart growth movement remains largely about directing growth and land use rather than making the region more equitable or protecting its environment. Nevertheless, according to Gearin, smart growth could become a potent force for regional coordination and could pave the way for a more inclusive and sustainable Southern California.

Turning to a specific set of local efforts to pursue smart growth in chapter 11, Ryan, Wilson, and Fulton investigate Ventura County's recent ballot-box initiatives—Save Open Space and Agricultural Resources (SOAR), which in 1999 created urban growth boundaries around the county's major cities. SOAR—actually several autonomous measures passed by cities and county voters that require voter approval of any development proposed outside of the limit lines—is the region's first and thus far only experiment with urban growth boundaries. The authors utilize the GIS-based California Urban and Biodiversity Analysis model to predict future urban growth patterns and their impact on habitat extent and quality in Ventura County. Using the most current population projections and the model's parameters, they then estimate the future configuration of development in the county, comparing six alternative policy scenarios, ranging from a scenario lacking development constraints to others with varied levels of environmental and sensitive habitat protections, including one representing SOAR.

The results reveal that the growth policies represented by the six scenarios produce radically different geographic patterns of growth in Ventura County. The county should be able to accommodate projected growth under five of the six scenarios, but, significantly, the adoption and enforcement of SOAR will consume nearly two-thirds of the county's potentially developable land, involve the loss of five thousand additional acres of prime agricultural land, and limit growth unless residential densities are increased in the future. This raises the question of whether the political coalitions that led to the passage of SOAR will be able to hold together as growth pressures mount. Early challenges to the urban limit lines suggest otherwise: the first three of four challenges to SOAR boundaries in the cities of Ojai and Ventura (to build outside limit lines) won voter approval. But this may be related to the nature of the development proposals themselves—each was linked to church expansion and/or development of community playing fields. How other sorts of developments—such as residential subdivisions or office parks—would fare remains to be seen. However, the increased density necessary to accommodate future growth is probably not so high as to be politically unacceptable. The county's existing densities are relatively low, and its cities offer many opportunities for infill development.

SOAR explicitly addresses the challenge of sprawl through land-use controls, but many other attempts to improve the region's economic, social, and environmental picture have used other approaches. The final chapter in this volume, by Marks, Gearin, and Armstrong, focuses on seven experiments aimed at promoting smart growth, sustainability, and regional cooperation: the Gateway Cities Partnership, a twenty-seven-city collaboration for economic development, remarkable in its ability to organize and create opportunities for residents in some of the most distressed cities in the metro area; Orange County's NCCP and Riverside's Integrated Planning efforts, large-scale examples of habitat conservation and smart growth planning on a subregional basis; the Cool Schools Program, a partnership between L.A. Unified School District, the city's Department of Water and Power, and grassroots nonprofit organizations that removes concrete and plants trees at local schools to make them healthier places for children and to help the city become more sustainable; Village Green, a transit-oriented, smart growth residential development that shows that properly designed high-density communities are attractive and viable in the marketplace; the Bus Riders Union, organized by the nonprofit Labor/Community Strategy Center to pressure the behemoth MTA to provide more and better-quality bus service for the region's poorest transit riders; and the city of Santa Monica's Sustainable City Program, one the most wide-reaching local sustainability programs in the nation. All of these efforts are innovative—some because of their unusual objectives, others because of the strange bedfellows involved, still others due to their ability to organize some of the most disenfranchised groups in the region. But as Marks, Gearin, and Armstrong make clear, all of these efforts also face enormous challenges, including clashing interests among local residents and stakeholders, free-rider problems that reduce support and participation in large-scale efforts, and structural obstacles to progressive change in California, such as state-local fiscal relations. To a greater or lesser extent, leaders involved in these efforts have addressed such challenges by drawing on formal authority to instigate action, offering side payments to induce partners to participate, and using salesmanship to create a broad base of support for their initiatives. In so doing—and by producing tangible results that promote smart growth, sustainability, and regionalism—they show that, despite obstacles, there are workable approaches to addressing sprawl and its discontents.

Toward a New Regional Agenda in Southern California

What are the common threads among all the contributions to this book? The first is simple: the Southern California region has been shaped by public policies. That is, rather than supporting the image of an unplanned region molded by the market and individual choices, the evidence suggests that the current configuration is the result of actions at every level of government. Growth, exurbanization, economic inequality, racial segregation, environmental destruction, and sprawl were not simply accidents; they were intentionally produced, often through collective decisions, typically spurred by the most politically influential sectors within the region.

The second common thread is that these public policies have generally been both negative and incoherent. Tax policy, for example, has given cites an incentive to work at cross-purposes, and even major federal policies that explicitly mandate regional planning have largely failed to engender powerful regionalism. Part of the reason is that leadership is fragmented, as old elites have collapsed and new movements struggle to gain ground. Unfortunately, the usual solutions advocated by "new regionalists" for coalition building, such as alliances between central cities and suburbs to promote regional tax-base sharing, are most improbable here, where the very terms of reference (central city, inner-ring suburb) do not apply. Market-based solutions—such as congestion pricing, conservation easements, and location-efficient mortgages—have often made economic sense, but even these have enjoyed limited purchase with policy makers. Instead, "stealth regionalism"—for example, under the guise of the ESA—has become a force for regional planning, but only in some parts of the metropolis and only for land-use management; policies to alleviate inequality have been the losing partner in the usual trinity of economy, environment, and equity that many new regionalists offer. This general mix has left virtually untouched major problems that can be addressed only (or most effectively) on a regional scale.

The third common strand is that solutions are, in fact, possible. Many of the policies examined here originated at the federal level, are deeply entrenched, and have powerful constituencies. Because so many federal policies fundamentally structure the rules of the game for metropolitan regions, it is crucial that such regions revise or remove those that have deleterious urban consequences. Funding formulas could be changed to promote fiscal equalization, and regulatory powers could be expanded or modified to promote regional cooperation and integrated planning. At the state and local levels there is also latitude, for example, to require additional provision of affordable housing in affluent communities and to eliminate the perverse incentives for fiscal zoning and beggar-thy-neighbor municipal competition for sales tax revenues.

The trick is to build new political coalitions around three interacting strategies: equity-based regionalism, a focus on greater sustainability, and a coordinated smart growth agenda. Equity-based regional planning seeks to raise wages, ensure health care coverage for all workers, provide affordable housing close to job opportunities, and expand the use of tax credits to aid low-wage workers and their households. This approach, pursued by community-based organizations and labor groups, starts from the recognition that making connections to larger regional dynamics and opportunities is the best avenue out of economic deprivation and inequality—and it critically relies on securing middle-class and suburban allies by noting that evidence suggests that metropolitan regions paying more attention to reducing central-city poverty, city/suburban differentials, and inequality actually grow faster (Pastor et al. 2000).

Sustainability involves tracking regional land consumption, establishing resource and pollution benchmarks, and setting goals for the future. An important step would be to add sustainability criteria to standard environmental impact reports, making determinations based at least partly on a proposed project's impact on overall sustainability goals. Cities and counties could create local sustainability programs that set targets for environmental remediation, pollution reduction, and conservation. They could also develop "green" building and landscaping codes and support emergent green industries that enhance energy efficiency, restore local ecosystems, reduce waste, and encourage ecological restoration of local rivers.

Smart growth fits into all of this. This part of the agenda would require the integration of land-use, economic, and transportation planning. Given that the regional council of governments currently lacks real power, new collaborative and crosscutting organizational structures may need to be created to carry out this crucial task. Southern California might also follow Maryland's example regarding the direction of infrastructure and other state spending to built-up areas by earmarking state funds to encourage smart growth planning and development and to provide incentives for urban land recycling and infill development as well as development of high-density, transportation-oriented neighborhoods.

As difficult as all this might seem, there is increasing evidence that Southern California residents are "getting it." Local innovations may be modest, but they are also rays of hope. Low-income bus riders have joined together to defend the transportation necessities of the working poor. Business organizations have banded together to promote new industry "clusters" in some of their region's poorest neighborhoods and cities. Environmentalists have come to work with corporations and others on new strategies to protect both the land and the wealth of species that it hosts. Many housing developers now recognize the growing necessity for higher densities and mixed-income developments. The challenge for the future will be connecting such new approaches to business and development to the vibrant energies of social and environmental movements, and in turn to the public policy arena, where community voices need to be heard and allowed to shape policy decisions.

We ourselves are quite hopeful. Throughout the L.A. region and other metropolitan areas, there is a growing sense that the urban wasteland and alienated suburbs of the past must be replaced by regional landscapes where opportunities—for employment, income, environmental access, and political power—are more widely shared. Southern California, we have argued, is the place where people come to remake themselves. But the place itself was formed by public policy decisions—and it is high time for us together to remake the region.

Notes

1. The Los Angeles Drainage Area Project, for instance, with seventeen debris basins, three major flood control dams, forty-eight miles of channelization, and more than a hundred bridges, kept floodwaters at bay and allowed development of the foothills (Keil and Desfor 1996).

2. Efforts to control or eradicate nature to facilitate development also permeated public policies toward dealing with the region's natural hazards. Once declared disaster areas, parts of the region affected by floods, fires, and other "acts of nature" routinely attract public funds to subsidize rebuilding in the very same high-risk zones and to underwrite additional hazard control projects (see Davis 1996, 1998).

3. Miller (1981) argues clearly that the incorporation efforts under the Lakewood system were intended to benefit wealthier Anglo residents: by drawing boundaries around themselves and contracting for essential services, such residents were able to lower their tax rates while leaving the poor and their needs concentrated in unincorporated areas of the county and therefore paid for from general county coffers. As such, incorporation under this system was "a 'revolt of the rich against the poor,' carried out by exit rather than voice" (9).

4. Studies of the distribution of adult undocumented Latino immigrants in Los Angeles County reveal their high concentration in the older core communities, but also in the San Fernando Valley and Pomona (in the eastern San Gabriel Valley). In these places, they constitute between 15 and 30 percent of the total population (Marcelli 1998, 17–20).

5. These figures come from the 2000 U.S. Census supplemental survey (see http://www.census.gov).

6. For employment figures from the various counties that constitute Southern California, see the Labor Market Information Division page on the California State Employment Development Department's Web site, http://www.edd.calmis.ca.gov.

7. The poverty rate figures in this chapter are taken from the U.S. Census Summary File 3 for both 1990 and 2000.

8. High-poverty areas are defined as those tracts with proportions of population in poverty greater than one standard deviation above the mean regional poverty rate, or above 38 percent (see Jargowsky and Bane 1991).

9. The figures on median household income are taken from the U.S. Census Current Population Survey, March Supplements, 1992 through 2002.

10. Although the higher educational attainment of whites helps to explain some of the racial disparity in income, it does not fully explain the growing disparities, as the educational levels of the workforce have actually been rising over time.

11. The city of Los Angeles has especially severe problems with inadequate housing units. The Blue Ribbon Citizens' Committee on Slum Housing, in a report released July 28, 1997, noted that there were more than 150,000 substandard apartments in the city of Los Angeles—about one out of every seven rental units within the city (City of Los Angles 1997).

12. As a result of Proposition 13 and subsequent measures, the property tax is effectively limited to 1 percent of market value, assessed value growth is capped, and voter approval is required for any tax increases. Revenues from the fixed 1 percent property tax rate are allocated by the counties to cities and other local governments primarily based on state formulas created in 1978.

13. These figures are derived from chapter 6 in this volume, in which Musso assesses total fiscal capacity by calculating a "representative" income burden measure for discretionary revenues to which intergovernmental grants, sales tax revenues, and property tax revenues are added. Conceptually, this index measures the revenue a city would raise if it were to collect discretionary taxes, fees, and other revenues at a percentage of personal income equal to the regional average rate, adjusted upward for the intergovernmental grants, sales tax, and property tax allocated to the municipality under state law.

14. To the extent that cities have homogeneous populations, such user fees would not have a regressive impact *within* a city. Nonetheless, income variation *across* cities would imply that fees have a regressive impact from a regional perspective.

15. As part of these investments, five hundred miles of high-occupancy vehicle lanes were constructed by 1999, mostly in southern L.A. and Orange counties (SCAG 2000, 73–76).

16. Statistics in this section are derived from the summary of evidence, *Labor Community Strategy Center v. MTA*, from the federal consent decree requiring the MTA to address the court's finding of discriminatory disparate impact on citizens of color (accessed May 26, 2000, Institute for Global Communications Web site, http://www.igc.org/lctr/smmry2.html).

17. Race is consistently related to the distribution of risks, even when one also controls for not just income but residential location near industrial, commercial, and transportation land uses. This suggests that people of color are more apt to live near more polluting land uses, such as freeways with high volumes of diesel traffic and heavy emitters of industrial toxic waste (Morello-Frosch, Pastor, and Sadd 2001).

18. This term was coined by William Fulton.

19. Data from the Immigration and Naturalization Service on the intended place of residence of new legal permanent residents for 1990 to 1996 were aggregated from zip codes to Public Use Microdata Areas to be matched with the 1990 Census Public Use Microdata Samples.

Works Cited

Berube, Alan, and Benjamin Forman. 2001. *Rewarding Work: The Impact of the Earned Income Tax Credit in Greater Los Angeles.* Washington, DC: Brookings Institution Center on Urban and Metropolitan Policy.

City of Los Angeles. 1997. "The Blue Ribbon Citizens' Committee on Slum Housing." http://www.cityofla.org/LAHD/slumhsg.pdf.

Davis, Mike. 1996. "Water Pirates and the Infinite Suburb." *Capitalism, Nature, Socialism* 7:81–84.

———. 1998. *Ecology of Fear: Los Angeles and the Imagination of Disaster.* New York: Metropolitan.

Dreier, Peter, John Mollenkopf, and Todd Swanstrom. 2001. *Place Matters: Metropolitics for the Twenty-First Century.* Lawrence: University Press of Kansas.

Erie, Steven P. 1992. "How the Urban West Was Won: The Local State and Economic Growth in Los Angeles, 1880–1932." *Urban Affairs Review* 27(4): 519–54.

Erie, Steven P., Thomas P. Kim, and Gregory Freeman. 1999. *The LAX Master Plan: Facing the Challenge of Community, Environmental and Regional Airport Planning.* Los Angeles: University of Southern California, Southern California Studies Center.

Frey, William. 2001. "Melting Pot Suburbs: A Census 2000 Study of Suburban Diversity." Washington, DC: Brookings Institution Center on Urban and Metropolitan Policy.

Fulton, William. 2001. *The Reluctant Metropolis: The Politics of Urban Growth in Los Angeles.* Baltimore: Johns Hopkins University Press.

Fulton, William, Madelyn Glickfeld, Grant McMurran, and June Gin. 2000. *A Landscape Portrait of Southern California's Structure of Government and Growth.* Claremont, CA: Claremont Graduate University Research Institute.

Fulton, William, Rolf Pendall, Mai Nguyen, and Alicia Harrison. 2001. *Who Sprawls Most? How Growth Patterns Differ across the U.S.* Washington, DC: Brookings Institution Center on Urban and Metropolitan Policy.

Garreau, Joel. 1991. *Edge City: Life on the New Frontier.* New York: Doubleday.

Glaeser, Edward L., Matthew Kahn, and Chenguan Chu. 2001. *Job Sprawl: Employment Location in U.S. Metropolitan Areas.* Washington, DC: Brookings Institution Center on Urban and Metropolitan Policy.

Goldman, Abigail. 1997. "A Hidden Advantage for Some Job Seekers." *Los Angeles Times,* November 28.

Gyourko, Joseph, and Todd Sinai. 2001. *The Spatial Distribution of Housing-Related Tax Benefits in the United States.* Washington, DC: Brookings Institution Center on Urban and Metropolitan Policy.

Hise, Greg. 1997. *Magnetic Los Angeles: Planning the Twentieth-Century Metropolis.* Baltimore: Johns Hopkins University Press.

Hricko, Andrea, Kim Preston, Hays Witt, and John Peters. 1999. "Air Pollution and Children's Health." In *Atlas of Southern California,* vol. 3. Los Angeles: University of Southern California, Southern California Studies Center.

Jargowsky, Paul A., and Mary Jo Bane. 1991. "Ghetto Poverty in the United States, 1970–80." In *The Urban Underclass,* ed. Christopher Jencks and Paul E. Peterson. Washington, DC: Brookings Institution.

Keil, Roger, and Gene Desfor. 1996. "Making Local Environmental Policy in Los Angeles." *Cities* 13:303–14.

Marcelli, Enrico. 1998. "Undocumented Latino Immigrants." In *Atlas of Southern California,* vol. 2. Los Angeles: University of Southern California, Southern California Studies Center.

Miller, Gary J. 1981. *Cities by Contract: The Politics of Municipal Incorporation.* Cambridge: MIT Press.

Morello-Frosch, Rachel, Manuel Pastor Jr., and James Sadd. 2001. "Environmental Justice and Southern California's Riskscape: The Distribution of Air Toxics Exposures and Health Risks among Diverse Communities." *Urban Affairs Review* 36:551–78.

Myers, Dowell. 1996. "Immigration: Past and Future." University of Southern California, School of Urban Planning and Development, Lusk Center Research Institute.

Myers, Dowell, and Julie Park. 2001. "Racially Balanced Cities in Southern California, 1980–2000." Public research report 2001–05. University of Southern California, School of Policy, Planning and Development.

Orfield, Myron. 1997. *Metropolitics: A Regional Agenda for Community and Stability.* Washington, DC: Brookings Institution.

Pastor, Manuel, Jr. 2001. "Looking for Regionalism in All the Wrong Places: Demography, Geography and Community in Los Angeles County." *Urban Affairs Review* 36:747–82.

Pastor, Manuel, Jr., Peter Dreier, J. Eugene Grigsby III, and Marta López-Garza. 2000. *Regions That Work: How Cities and Suburbs Can Grow Together.* Minneapolis: University of Minnesota Press.

Pastor, Manuel, Jr., and Enrico A. Marcelli. 2000. "Men 'n the Hood: Skill, Spatial, and Social Mismatches among Male Workers in Los Angeles County." *Urban Geography* 12(6):474–96.

Schoenherr, Allan A. 1992. *A Natural History of California.* Berkeley: University of California Press.

Scott, Allen J., and Edward W. Soja, eds. 1996. *The City: Los Angeles and Urban Theory at the End of the Twentieth Century.* Berkeley: University of California Press.

Sherman, Douglas, et al. 1998. "Natural Hazards." In *Atlas of Southern California,* vol. 2. Los Angeles: University of Southern California, Southern California Studies Center.

Siegel, Fred. 1999. "The Sunny Side of Sprawl." *New Democrat,* March, http://www.ppionline.org.

Soja, Edward W., and Allen J. Scott. 1996. "Introduction to Los Angeles: City and Region." In *The City: Los Angeles and Urban Theory at the End of the Twentieth Century,* ed. Allen J. Scott and Edward W. Soja. Berkeley: University of California Press.

South Coast Air Quality Management District. 2002. "Historic Ozone Air Quality Trends." http://www.aqmd.gov/smog/03trend.html.

Southern California Association of Governments. 1999. *The State of the Region 1999.* Los Angeles: SCAG.

———. 2000. *The State of the Region 2000.* Los Angeles: SCAG.

———. 2001. *The State of the Region 2001.* Los Angeles: SCAG.

Southern California Studies Center. 2001. *Sprawl Hits the Wall: Confronting the Realities of Metropolitan Los Angeles.* Los Angeles: University of Southern California, Southern California Studies Center/Brookings Institution Center on Urban and Metropolitan Policy.

Texas Transportation Institute. 1999. "Annual Urban Mobility Study." Texas A&M University System, http://www.mobility.tamu.edu.

———. 2001. "Annual Urban Mobility Study." Texas A&M University System, http://www.mobility.tamu.edu.

U.S. Conference of Mayors and National Association of Counties. 2000. "US Metro Economies: Leading America's New Economy." http://www.mayors.org/citiesdrivetheeconomy/index2.html.

Willon, Phil. 2001. "As Inland Empire Grows, Freeway Commute Slows." *Los Angeles Times,* October 30.

PART I
Policy Pathways

1 | W(h)ither Sprawl? Have Regional Water Policies Subsidized Suburban Development?

Steven P. Erie, Gregory Freeman, and Pascale Joassart-Marcelli

Regional Water Policies, Subsidies, and Growth

Have regional water policies in Southern California favored the suburbanizing periphery at the expense of the central city? We seek to answer that question in this chapter. We examine here the history of the water policies of the Metropolitan Water District of Southern California (MWD or Metropolitan), the mammoth twenty-six-member-agency water wholesaler serving more than 16 million customers in 250 communities.[1] Of particular interest are the equity and growth effects of MWD's policies. A guiding question is the extent to which the city of Los Angeles, owing to its large early investments in the Colorado River Aqueduct and limited use of MWD water, subsidized water provision to fast-growing outlying areas such as San Diego and Orange Counties, thus wittingly or unwittingly underwriting suburban sprawl in Southern California. The lengthy period examined here, 1928–96, covers nearly the entire life of MWD, from its creation through two very different financing regimes (pre-1970, based on property taxes, versus post-1970, based on water charges) to the advent of agricultural-to-urban water transfers, which today are being hailed as promoting smart growth and environmental sustainability.

The pattern of growth in Southern California during the period examined here has been one of massive and unrelenting suburban development. Since 1928, the population of metropolitan Southern California (which includes both the Los Angeles and San Diego regions) has increased tenfold, from fewer than 2 million to more than 18 million residents. The city of Los Angeles, the original urban core, has grown from 1 million to 3.8 million residents—a 280 percent increase. The rest of Southern California has experienced far more prodigious growth—1,300 percent, from 1 million to 14.3 million in population. Although the city of Los Angeles was the region's pre-Depression-era growth leader, in the immediate post–World War II era the rest of

Los Angeles County witnessed fast-paced suburbanization. By the 1960s, the fastest-growing areas were San Diego and Orange Counties. More recently, the Inland Empire (San Bernardino and Riverside Counties) has emerged as the region's growth leader.

Population growth estimates for the region suggest little slackening in the fervid pace of growth. Southern California is forecast to grow by 6.2 million residents in the period from 2000 to 2020, the equivalent of adding more than the entire metropolitan Boston, Dallas, or Atlanta populations, and almost as much as the entire San Francisco Bay Area population.[2] The fastest-growing areas are predicted to be the exurban periphery: western Riverside County, San Bernardino County, northern Los Angeles County, southern Orange County, and northern and southern San Diego County. The prospect of continued suburban sprawl and the potential costs for the region's environment, quality of life, public services, and infrastructure have pushed "smart growth" or sustainable development to the forefront of policy discussions in the region and in California as a whole (Center for Continuing Study of the California Economy 1998).

Devising policies to encourage sustainable development requires an understanding of the dynamics of suburbanization, which are complex and multifaceted. Transportation technology (e.g., the streetcar and automobile), cultural values, and federal highway and housing policies have been major contributory factors (Jackson 1985; Fishman 1987; Garreau 1991). Local and state policies have furthered processes of suburbanization. These include zoning and land-use controls, municipal incorporation and taxation policies, and, in the case of Southern California, the provision of county services to newly incorporated suburbs (Teaford 1976; Danielson 1976; Gottdiener 1977; Miller 1981; Logan and Molotch 1987).

In the semiarid West, there is widespread recognition that water has played a crucial role in development (Wiley and Gottlieb 1982; Worster 1985; Reisner 1986; Hundley 1992). Without the massive infrastructure that was put in place over the last century to supply water to both urban and agricultural areas, most western states would have been unable to sustain the rapid population growth they have experienced. Yet few studies have examined how water policy may be an important contributory factor to suburban development *within* regions such as Southern California. In one of the few intraregional analyses, Robert Gottlieb (1988) argues that the founders of MWD "immediately established policies that were favorable to newly developing areas rather than the city [of Los Angeles] itself. . . . These policies were designed to draw on the tax base of the developed areas while creating pricing incentives for water use and development of the new areas" (126).

Was this indeed the case? Did MWD's founders deliberately establish and implement long-term policies favoring suburban development? We argue here that although there have been significant MWD water subsidies, particularly before 1970, favoring the periphery, this has primarily been due to reasonable miscalculations on the part of MWD's founders. Our alternative hypothesis is that a relentless drive for secure water supplies led the city of Los Angeles to miscalculate the benefits and costs of membership in MWD, inadvertently resulting in a large subsidy for water provision to the rest of Southern California. Los Angeles paid most of the cost of MWD's initial infrastructure, financed through property taxes that relied heavily on the urban core, but it also expected to take a proportional share of water deliveries. When lawsuits over Colorado River water rights threatened MWD's supplies, L.A. instead secured additional independent water. L.A. did not fully claim its anticipated share of MWD water, even while still paying for the infrastructure that supplied it. By its actions, Los Angeles subsidized MWD's infrastructure and freed up additional affordable Metropolitan water deliveries for fast-growing outlying areas in Southern California.

We develop our argument in five parts, based on MWD data (MWD 2000). First, we present a brief history of MWD, focusing on its capital financing and water policies under two different financing regimes, one based on property taxes (pre-1970) and the other on water charges (post-1970). Second, we develop a subsidy measure applied to the two regimes based on MWD member agency financial contributions relative to water deliveries. Using this measure, we test whether the urban core (e.g., Los Angeles) subsidized water provision to the suburbanizing periphery (e.g., Orange and San Diego Counties). Third, we try to explain evident urban-to-suburban water subsidies, considered either as the intentional product of development-oriented MWD policy makers or as a miscalculation on the part of Los Angeles water officials who, for fiduciary reasons, allowed it to persist for years. Fourth, we test the relationship between urban subsidy and suburban growth under the two different MWD financing systems. Finally, looking toward the future, we consider water transfers, the region's most recent water initiative, and assess their implications for subsidies and suburban sprawl.

MWD: A Policy History

Very little of Southern California's staggering population growth to date could have occurred without an adequate supply of affordable imported water. The region's climate is semiarid, and local water supplies can support a population of only one million. In the early twentieth century, the city of Los Angeles pioneered the development of imported water supplies, completing its aqueduct from the Owens Valley in 1913 (Ostrom 1953; Hoffman 1981; Kahrl 1982). This allowed L.A. to grow from one-half million to two million residents.

In 1928, Los Angeles and its suburbs joined in creating the Metropolitan Water District in order to finance, construct, and operate the Colorado River Aqueduct to bring fresh supplies of imported water from the Colorado River. In effect, MWD created a "water wall" around Los Angeles, breaking up the city's water monopoly, which had been used as a potent force for territorial expansion.[3] Los Angeles's boundaries today are roughly the same as they were in 1928. In this fashion, MWD helped underwrite the postwar suburbanization of Los Angeles County, as more than fifty new cities were incorporated. They formed municipal water districts that were annexed to MWD (Erie and Joassart-Marcelli 2000).

From the 1940s onward, as Colorado River water became available, outlying areas such as San Diego annexed themselves to MWD. As a result, Metropolitan's service area has grown to encompass most of urban Southern California. In the early 1950s, MWD established a new policy, known as the Laguna Declaration, that pledged the agency to find a permanent water supply for the region and to provide water to anyone who requested it in MWD's service territory.[4] In 1960, California voters approved the MWD-supported State Water Project (SWP), bringing a fresh supply of imported water (albeit representing only one-half of the California Aqueduct's full capacity) from Northern California for distribution by Metropolitan and its member agencies (Schwarz 1991).

To finance these various infrastructure projects, MWD initially relied on property taxes and annexation fees rather than water charges. In the early years of its existence, property taxes provided the bulk of MWD's revenues. Although Colorado River water did not make its way to Southern California until 1941, when the aqueduct finally was completed, MWD began collecting property taxes in 1929 to finance the $220 million project. Property taxes remained the principal means of MWD financing through the 1960s because capital projects could not generate revenue until they were completed, and early water sales were inadequate for project financing. By the mid-1940s, MWD was awash in water but not customers, forcing the agency to sell water below cost in order to encourage greater purchases by member agencies as well as possible annexations to Metropolitan. In 1947, MWD charged only $15 per acre-foot for treated domestic water, a price that slowly rose to $49 by 1970; by 1996, however, this rate had increased to $426 (MWD 1972, 1997).

Los Angeles, whose taxpayers paid 75 percent of the costs of the Colorado River Aqueduct, drew little MWD water—only 8 percent of total deliveries—because the city continued to develop its own water supplies. In the 1930s, Los Angeles extended its system to the Mono Lake Basin. Later, in 1970, the city completed a second aqueduct to the Owens Valley. Owens Valley water was far cheaper because it featured a gravity-flow system, whereas MWD needed costly pumping plants to move its Colorado River water over desert mountains.

Starting in the 1960s, MWD began shifting its capital financing from taxes to water sales. By then, nearly all of the urban coastal plain had been annexed to Metropolitan. Now it was easier for MWD to raise water prices to recover costs. The SWP, begun in 1960 and completed in 1972–73, served as a major catalyst for capital finance restructuring. Los Angeles demanded that the SWP, with its more expensive water, be financed by water sales rather than taxes. San Diego, however, resisted. The San Diego County Water Authority (SDCWA), MWD's largest customer, drew 25 percent of its water but had paid only 10–13 percent in annexation charges (representing back taxes plus interest) and property taxes since joining MWD in 1946.

The conflict between Los Angeles and San Diego resulted in MWD's slowly shifting much of its capital financing from property taxes to water rates. In 1960, the MWD board of directors adopted a new policy requiring that at least one-half of all capital expenses plus all operating and maintenance costs be borne by water sales revenues.[5] This partially allayed Los Angeles's concern that MWD would continue to rely heavily on tax revenues. A subsequent Los Angeles lawsuit and, in 1978, the passage by California's voters of Proposition 13, sharply reducing property tax rates and revenues, furthered the shift in MWD capital financing to water sales.[6]

As a result, there are two distinct MWD fiscal regimes: pre- and post-1970. Figure 1.1 shows the sharp shift in Metropolitan capital financing circa 1970. The figure displays annual capital contributions from taxes (and annexation fees paid by new member agencies) and water sales, 1929–96, in constant 1996 dollars. Before 1970, virtually all MWD capital projects were paid for by property taxes. After the early 1970s, as SWP water flowed into Southern California, water sales became a major source of capital financing. Metropolitan's uniform or postage-stamp water rates (in which all member agencies paid the same amount for similar kinds of water) now were raised to include most capital, operating, and maintenance charges.

By 1995, however, new capital financing policies were being created. In response to reduced water deliveries, sales, and revenues produced by a lengthy drought coupled with the financing needs of an ambitious capital improvement program, MWD adopted a new rate structure designed to shift capital costs away from variable water sales toward new, more stable charges. These included a readiness-to-serve (RTS) charge to meet debt service needs by guaranteeing water reliability and quality under normal demand, a standby charge for unimproved land benefiting from legal access to MWD water, and a new-demand charge (since suspended) to recover capital costs associated with meeting new demands on Metropolitan's system.[7]

The shift in capital financing circa 1970, coupled with an increase in water rates to reflect the actual cost of service, dramatically altered MWD's revenue sources.

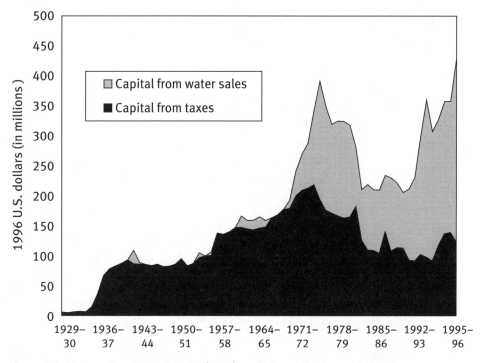

Figure 1.1. Metropolitan Water District (MWD) capital contributions, 1929–96.

Figure 1.2 contrasts the components of total MWD revenue (in current dollars) between the 1929–70 period and the 1970–96. In the pre-1970 period, property taxes and annexation fees accounted for 75 percent of agency revenue, whereas water sales amounted to only one-quarter of MWD revenue. Property taxes not only were the principal source of early capital financing, they also were used to pay a significant share of operating costs. By 1960, one-third of MWD's ad valorem tax rate was devoted to general purposes rather than bond service (MWD 1972, 146). Metropolitan had been forced to keep water prices artificially low to make its water financially attractive to member agencies relative to groundwater usage, and to encourage annexations to MWD. This strategy of giving water away, forcing continued reliance on property taxes as the agency's principal revenue source, appeared to work. The original thirteen member agencies, which had joined MWD between 1928 and 1931, later were joined by thirteen additional agencies annexed to Metropolitan between 1942 and 1963. San Fernando joined in 1971.[8]

For the post-1970 period, the relative magnitude of the two revenue streams was reversed. Water sales now accounted for 75 percent of total agency revenue. In contrast, taxes, fees, and other charges generated only one-quarter of MWD revenue. Increased water sales revenues reflected both the shift in capital financing and MWD's willingness to raise water rates as annexation was completed.

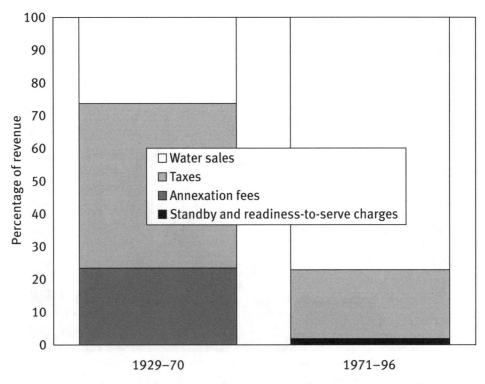

Figure 1.2. Components of total revenue collected by MWD (in current U.S. dollars), 1929–70 and 1971–96.

Member Agency Subsidies

Measuring Subsidies: A Unit Cost Approach

We define subsidies in terms of MWD member agencies' total real (inflation-adjusted) financial contributions (water charges, property taxes, annexation fees, and so on) relative to the amount of water they received.[9] This average unit cost approach is quite sensible in a cooperative structure such as MWD, as it provides a direct link between financial contributions and tangible benefits to member agencies. In general, water deliveries to the original members have not matched their contributions.

From the time of MWD's creation in 1928 to 1996, the city of Los Angeles paid more than twice its share of MWD's financial contributions (17 percent) relative to the share of MWD water received (8 percent). In contrast, San Diego, for example, received a 35 percent greater share of MWD water (26 percent) than its proportion of financial contributions (19 percent). The disparity can be traced to the fact that the city of Los Angeles, and to a lesser extent the other founding member agencies of Metropolitan, underwrote most of MWD's early capital costs, particularly for the Colorado River Aqueduct.

Figure 1.3 shows the relationships between financial contribution and water delivery for the city of Los Angeles, the rest of Los Angeles County, and the other counties served by Metropolitan for the period 1929–96. Data on water sales, taxes, assessed

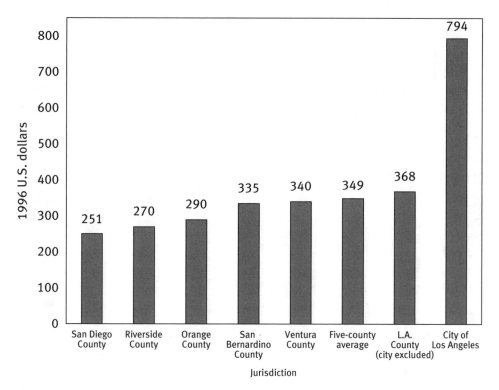

Figure 1.3. Unit cost per acre-foot of MWD water delivered, by county and the city of Los Angeles, 1929–96.

valuations, total capital costs, annexation charges, fees, and revenues were gathered from MWD annual reports between 1929 and 1996 (MWD 1996). We have chosen counties as our primary unit of analysis because counties and their political subdivisions, not water agencies, make land-use decisions and thus shape patterns of growth. Given the major historical financing role played by the city of Los Angeles, the figure shows data for the city separately. The ratios represent the total real contribution to MWD (in 1996 dollars) per acre-foot of water delivered to each jurisdiction. Note the substantial differences in unit water costs for the city of Los Angeles relative to the rest of Southern California. Los Angeles paid $794 per acre-foot of water, more than double the $349 average. In contrast, San Diego, Riverside, and Orange Counties paid only $251, $270, and $290 per acre-foot, respectively.

What explains these substantial unit cost disparities? Figure 1.4 disaggregates MWD financial contributions (in 1996 dollars) for these jurisdictions into four components: water sales, property taxes, annexation fees, and other charges. Thus 74 percent of Los Angeles's financial contribution to Metropolitan has come from taxes, compared with less than 24 percent from water sales. In sharp contrast, only 28 percent of the San Diego County Water Authority's total contribution has come from taxes and annexation fees, and 70 percent has come from water sales. Similarly, two-thirds of Orange and Riverside Counties' member agency contributions to Metropolitan have come from water sales and only one-third from taxes and annexation charges.

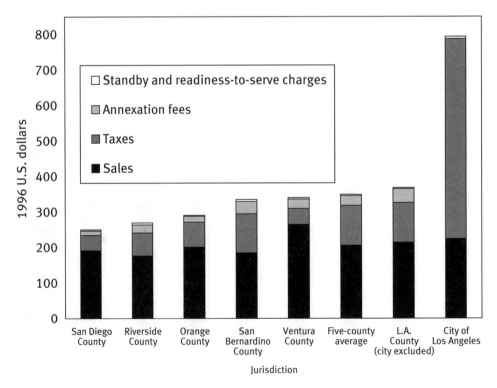

Figure 1.4. Types of MWD financial contributions per acre-foot of MWD water delivered, by county and the city of Los Angeles, 1929–96.

As both Figures 1.3 and 1.4 reveal, the greatest disparities between MWD water deliveries and financial contributions are between the city of Los Angeles and the counties of San Diego, Riverside, and Orange. Between 1929 and 1996, Los Angeles drew only 8 percent of total MWD water deliveries but paid (in 1996 dollars) 25 percent of total property taxes, 23 percent of capital charges, and 17 percent of total MWD financial contributions. In contrast, the SDCWA received 26 percent of MWD's total water delivered, but, in real terms, paid only 13 percent of MWD's taxes, 15 percent of the capital budget, and 18 percent of overall MWD's financial contributions. Similarly, Orange County's five member agencies drew 21 percent of MWD water deliveries and paid only 16 percent of MWD taxes, 17 percent of capital costs, and 18 percent of revenue.

As Figure 1.5 illustrates, there are important disparities between particular member agencies. For instance, most of Orange County's disparity is produced by one agency, the Municipal Water District of Orange County (MWDOC). The county's three smallest agencies, Anaheim, Santa Ana, and Fullerton, were MWD founders, joining between 1928 and 1931. A fourth agency, Coastal MWD, annexed in 1942. However, MWDOC, the county's largest agency, which draws 70 percent of its Metropolitan water deliveries, did not join MWD until 1951. Riverside County's member agencies with low unit costs are Eastern and Western MWD, having joined Metropolitan in 1951 and 1954, respectively.

Changing Subsidy Patterns: Pre- and Post-1970

The pronounced shift in MWD capital financing and revenue sources circa 1970 suggests that there may be different subsidy patterns in the pre- and post-1970 eras. Figure 1.6 shows this to be the case. Here we measure the magnitude of the financial overpayment or underpayment to Metropolitan (in 1996 dollars) relative to actual water deliveries for the city of Los Angeles, the rest of L.A. County, and the other counties served by MWD, for the periods 1929–70 and 1971–96. The figure shows that most of the interagency subsidies occurred in the pre-1970 period. In the 1929–70 period, the city of Los Angeles overpaid $1.42 billion and the rest of L.A. County overpaid $59 million in MWD contributions relative to water deliveries. In contrast, the San Diego County Water Authority underpaid $701 million relative to MWD deliveries, and Orange County member agencies underpaid $631 million. MWDOC, with a $531 million underpayment, generated most of Orange County's subsidy. Riverside County's pre-1970 subsidy was much smaller ($173 million), reflecting its limited MWD purchases given ample groundwater supplies. In essence, Riverside's member agencies joined MWD to provide for future growth. However, there is little early subsidy pattern evident for MWD member agencies in San Bernardino and Ventura Counties.

Figure 1.6 demonstrates that after 1970, with the postage-stamp water rate rising to reflect most MWD expenses, suburban subsidies were significantly reduced, but not eliminated. Los Angeles continued to overpay—the city by $487 million and the county by $250 million—and San Diego to underpay (by $621 million) while Orange and Riverside Counties' subsidies largely were eliminated.

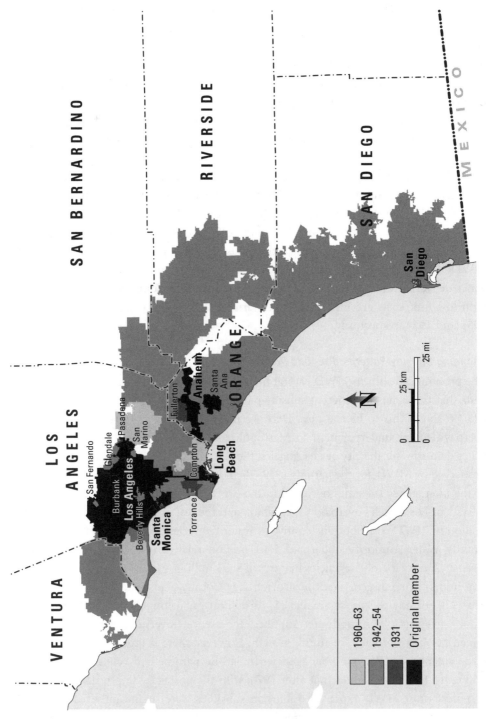

Figure 1.5. Dates of entry of member agencies into Metropolitan Water District of Southern California. Areas in white depict no data.

To control for differences in member agency size, water deliveries, and financial contributions, Figure 1.7 shows the real cost per acre-foot of water delivered for both periods. As in Figure 1.3, unit cost is obtained by dividing the total financial contribution of each member agency by the quantity of water delivered. Figure 1.7 shows that there were significant early cost disparities. For 1929–70, the city of Los Angeles paid $1,670 per acre-foot of MWD water, while member agencies in Ventura (Calleguas MWD) and San Bernardino (Chino Basin MWD) Counties paid $439 and $655, respectively. Given that Ventura and San Bernardino unit costs for 1929–96 closely approximate the overall regional average, these pre-1970 figures are anomalous. Calleguas only joined MWD in 1960 to receive State Water Project deliveries and, through 1970, had paid annexation charges but had received little MWD water. Chino Basin, which joined in 1951, chose to draw little MWD water in the pre-1970 period relative to its payment of annexation fees.

The high pre-1970 unit costs make the city of Los Angeles appear a fiscal profligate. Yet, as noted, L.A. early on relied heavily on its own water supplies, taking few MWD deliveries before the advent of the SWP. Hence the retail cost of water to Los Angeles customers remained relatively low and did not represent an inhibitor to development. Also of note is the high early unit cost for the remainder of Los Angeles County—$453. From 1928 to 1931, ten of L.A.'s suburbs had joined MWD, fully contributing to the financing of the Colorado River Aqueduct while generally drawing on Metropolitan water as a supplemental source.

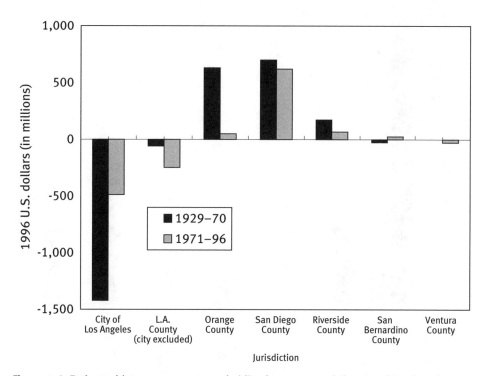

Figure 1.6. Estimated interagency water subsidies by county and the city of Los Angeles, 1929–70 and 1971–96.

In dramatic contrast, in the pre-1970 era, San Diego, Riverside, and Orange County water agencies paid only $211, $229, and $199 per acre-foot, respectively. As noted, their low unit costs were driven by small assessed valuations (and thus low annexation fees and early property taxes) coupled with large water deliveries, particularly for agricultural use. For example, SDCWA and MWDOC paid $34 million and $32 million in annexation charges, respectively, which represent 10 percent shares of total MWD annexation charges. After 1970, however, as MWD's water rates were raised substantially, unit cost disparities among member agencies were reduced.

Los Angeles's Capital Subsidies: Developers' Calculus, or Demand/Supply Miscalculations?

The large unit cost disparities between Los Angeles and San Diego, Riverside, and Orange Counties raises the inevitable question of why the city of Los Angeles so heavily contributed to early MWD capital financing, in effect subsidizing water provision to suburbanizing outlying areas. Why would the MWD's board of directors—initially dominated by the city of Los Angeles—allow such subsidies to be created, and later to persist? Assuming the board members were rational actors, there are two broad possible explanations: either development-oriented board members used their position to promote subsidies encouraging growth because doing so enhanced their profit

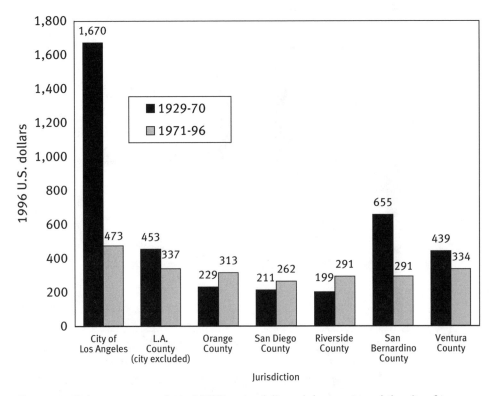

Figure 1.7. Unit cost per acre-foot of MWD water delivered, by county and the city of Los Angeles, 1929–70 and 1971–96.

opportunities or water policy makers made good-faith decisions that seemed reasonable at the time but nonetheless proved to be mistakes. Here, we suggest that the latter is the more compelling account.

One explanation, popularized by the movie *Chinatown*, suggests that L.A.'s MWD directors were acting in their capacity as regional developers and investors. According to Gottlieb (1988):

> Though the city of Los Angeles's representatives dominated the new MET [MWD] board and management, they immediately established policies that were favorable to newly developing areas rather than the city itself. They did so in part as developers in their own right, and as participants and leaders in the urban-development complex that transcended the boundaries of particular municipalities. These policies were designed to draw on the tax base of the developed areas while creating pricing incentives for water use and development of the new areas. (126)

Thus by supplying plentiful, affordable water to undeveloped areas, MWD supposedly oiled the region's growth machine that would turn desert land into profitable real estate investments. Although MWD ultimately did play an important part in making Southern California's growth possible, Gottlieb's explanation conflates the eventual outcome with the alleged motives of the original policy makers.

Undoubtedly, some of the early MWD board members had strong personal economic incentives to promote development in Southern California. However, the 1928 Metropolitan Water District Act was written several years before there was even a board to be filled with development-oriented members. In actuality, the bill's drafters were two public attorneys: William Burgess Mathews, former L.A. city attorney, Department of Water and Power (DWP) attorney, and first MWD general counsel; and James Howard, the Pasadena city attorney and Mathews's successor as MWD's general counsel.

These attorneys and MWD supporters such as William Mulholland were motivated primarily by the need to finance a secure water supply for Los Angeles. In the 1920s, L.A. experienced both explosive population growth and a lengthy drought. Projecting into the future, the L.A. Chamber of Commerce estimated that, at current growth rates, the city's population would reach 4.2 million by 1960 and 5.1 million by 1970. Given the apparently stratospheric demand the city would eventually face, Los Angeles water officials searched frantically for new supplies. The city of Los Angeles could not build the Colorado River Aqueduct on its own, as Mulholland initially had wanted, because the project's $220 million price tag (in 1928 dollars) would far exceed, in conjunction with existing municipal debt, the city's bonding capacity of 15 percent of assessed valuation.

In effect, MWD was created as a debt-pyramiding scheme for Los Angeles and its suburbs. It provided an additional 15 percent bonding capacity and, importantly, reduced the voter approval threshold from two-thirds (for DWP municipal bonds) to a simple majority (for MWD special district bonds) (see Erie 1992). In 1931, even with a poor economy, L.A.-area voters overwhelmingly approved (83 percent in favor) the aqueduct bond, adding new property taxes representing 13 percent of overall assessed valuation. City of Los Angeles taxpayers paid 75 percent of MWD's substantial start-up infrastructure costs.

Yet, for both the MWD bill's drafters and L.A. water officials, these costs seemed reasonable in the late 1920s. Given presumed rampant future demand, these policy makers assumed that Los Angeles would draw a substantial portion of MWD water deliveries, greatly reducing if not eliminating the city's delivery/contribution disparity. Although they acted reasonably, however, they made two miscalculations. First, they overestimated local demand, particularly with the coming of the Great Depression. Second, they overestimated the security of their new water supplies. In the 1930s, Arizona sought congressional redress and began filing federal lawsuits against California to reallocate Colorado River allotments. As a result, L.A. policy makers realized their Colorado River priority rights were less secure than originally thought and began developing their own more secure municipal water sources (see Erie and Joassart-Marcelli 2000).

The new supplies from the Owens Valley and Mono Basin allowed the city of Los Angeles to draw far less water from MWD than it had originally planned, despite its heavy initial infrastructure investment. Thus it was a single-minded drive for *secure* water supplies to meet supposed burgeoning demand that led the city of Los Angeles inadvertently to subsidize water—and, ultimately, growth—in the rest of Southern California.

The question remains, however, as to why these tax-based capital subsidies persisted until the 1970s. Although some MWD directors may have pursued self-interested development agendas, as Gottlieb suggests, there were other forces at work. One credible explanation is that as MWD board directors were installed, they acted primarily as guardians of Metropolitan's fiduciary interests. As Gottlieb (1988) admits, "After Colorado River water arrived in the Basin in 1941, so much surplus water was available at first that MET practically offered to give it away for free in order to establish a more substantial revenue base" (126). Below-cost water charges and low annexation fees encouraged the rest of Southern California to join MWD. This enhanced the agency's long-term revenue stream and allowed for later readjustments in the relative financial burdens of older and newer member agencies. Given that MWD's appointed-board governance system was shielded from voters and close public scrutiny, the agency could pursue these long-term financial goals with little fear of protest from L.A. taxpayers and ratepayers, who disproportionately paid for MWD's steep start-up capital costs.

Another explanation for capital subsidy persistence is that Los Angeles acquiesced because it continued to derive substantial benefit from MWD. In exchange for financing most of the Colorado River Aqueduct and bestowing its substantial Colorado River water entitlement on MWD, the city was offered substantial inducements.[10] The Metropolitan Water District Act conferred preferential rights to water, such as during times of scarcity, on the basis of property taxes and other financial contributions for MWD capital and operating costs, exclusive of water sales.[11] In 1996, Los Angeles had a preferential claim to 24 percent of MWD water relative to SDCWA's 13 percent claim and MWDOC's 11 percent share (MWD 1996).

In effect, Los Angeles ended up treating MWD as an expensive drought insurance policy should its Owens Valley supplies prove insufficient. Los Angeles also was assured a major role in MWD policy making when assessed valuation, the basis for property taxes levied, became the basis of board representation and voting. To protect smaller member agencies, however, the MWD enabling legislation gave Los Angeles only 50 percent of the initial weighted vote—in effect guaranteeing it a veto—even though, on the basis of assessed valuation, the city was entitled to 75 percent. By 1960, however, with the State Water Project offering additional secure MWD supplies, Los Angeles's MWD directors pressed for a shift in capital financing from property taxes to water charges. As noted, heavy water users such as San Diego fought, but could only delay, this shift.

Thus the city of Los Angeles's original intention was to secure MWD water for fast-growing Los Angeles, not to subsidize the rest of Southern California. Its heavy capital investment became a subsidy only after urban demand lessened and the security of Colorado River water supplies had been undermined. The city could have chosen to rely on less secure MWD supplies, but instead sought independent Owens Valley municipal supplies and accepted its massive MWD investment as a supplemental water source and drought insurance policy.

Testing the Subsidy-Growth Relationship

Untangling the empirical relationship between MWD capital financing and water rate policies, and resulting interagency subsidies, on the one hand and the region's suburban sprawl on the other is complicated by both conceptual and data issues. Regional growth is a complex, multifaceted phenomenon; it is not driven solely by any single variable. In addition to secure, affordable water supplies, key growth determinants include land availability and price, zoning and land-use controls, local taxes, infrastructure (such as transportation), education, and amenities. Yet our ability to undertake a multivariate analysis here is hindered by the fact that data for many demographic, economic, and policy variables are available only at the county and city levels, not for MWD member agencies that are not coterminous with county or city boundaries. Some member agencies span both incorporated and unincorporated areas, making data comparability and analysis difficult. Further, a multivariate analysis would ideally employ a lag variable where population growth in a given period is regressed over water subsidy in a previous period, a difficult task given the long aggregate periods used here.

Even using simple, bivariate correlations, we need to approach the subsidy-growth relationship with care. Subsidies arose from the early tax-based capital financing structure of MWD, not through differential incremental water prices for member water agencies. Given that developers in the city of Los Angeles and in the subsidized, later-joining areas faced similar prices for water (the so-called postage-stamp rate), the relationship between subsidies and urban growth is obviously not as simple as a bivariate analysis suggests. Nonetheless, using only one independent variable (i.e., subsidies) to determine how that factor correlates with a dependent variable (urban growth) is valid for a first cut. Thus we want to emphasize the exploratory and suggestive nature of our results and the need for additional research.

We have performed a correlation analysis between the subsidy scores for twenty-seven MWD member agencies, expressed as their real cost per acre-foot of MWD water delivered and their average annual population growth rates since joining Metropolitan.[12] As Figure 1.8 shows, there are wide variations in average annual growth rates for the city of Los Angeles, the remainder of Los Angeles County, and the other counties served by Metropolitan in the periods 1929–70 and 1971–96. Because of the smaller population base in the pre-1970 period, early growth rates are much higher than later rates and show greater variation. Both the city of Los Angeles and L.A. County, because they already were settled, experienced lower annual growth rates than sparsely settled Orange, San Diego, and Ventura Counties. Subregional differences persisted after 1970, with annual population increases in Riverside and San Bernardino Counties four times as great as those in the city and county of Los Angeles.

Figure 1.9 compares unit water costs per acre-foot and average annual population growth rates for the three leading cases of fiscal transfers from central cities to suburbs: the city of Los Angeles, San Diego County, and Orange County, 1929–70 and

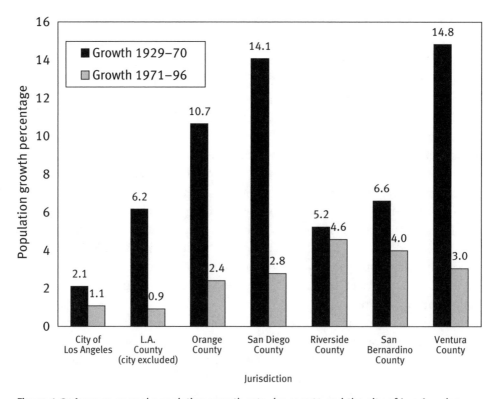

Figure 1.8. Average annual population growth rate, by county and the city of Los Angeles, 1929–70 and 1971–96.

1971–96. The figure illustrates the early relationship between subsidy and growth for these three key jurisdictions. Prior to 1970, Los Angeles paid dearly for its MWD hookup but grew only at a moderate 2.2 percent annual rate. In contrast, San Diego and Orange Counties paid little for MWD infrastructure and water provision in the earlier period but experienced double-digit annual growth rates. For all three jurisdictions, however, the relationship between water and growth weakened substantially after 1970.

The early subsidy-growth relationship also appears to hold for all twenty-seven MWD member agencies (reduced by consolidation to twenty-six in 2001). Figure 1.10 displays the correlation between member agency real (inflation-adjusted) cost per acre-foot of water delivered and average annual population growth rate for 1929–70. The relationship appears robust, with $R^2 = .3838$. Moreover, as the figure illustrates, the San Diego County Water Authority and the Municipal Water District of Orange County represent the two key agencies with the highest subsidy index and some of the highest average annual population growth rates. This contrasts sharply with the city of Los Angeles, which experienced a combination of slower growth rates and a low subsidy score.

Finally, Figure 1.11 displays the correlation for the member agency subsidy-growth relationship for 1971–96. As expected, for the later period the correlation is sharply

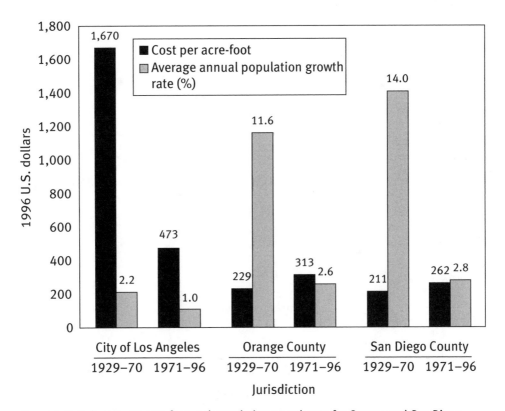

Figure 1.9. Unit cost per acre-foot and population growth rate for Orange and San Diego Counties and the city of Los Angeles, 1929–70 and 1971–96.

reduced but not eliminated, with R^2 = .1361. Thus MWD capital financing and water pricing after 1970 appear much less growth inducing.

Our results suggest that the subsidy-growth relationship for MWD member agencies was surprisingly strong for the pre-1970 period—when MWD relied primarily on property taxes for revenue. This topic needs further research, but in the interim, our tentative findings fit both the historical record and common sense. Had Los Angeles not gone ahead and invested $4.5 billion to develop the Owens Valley and Mono Basin supplies, and instead shifted its demand to MWD to deliver 200,000 acre-feet per year, it would have left substantially less water for everyone else in Southern California. Shortages could have affected other MWD customers, with predictably dire consequences for regional growth. Thus, by developing its own water sources, L.A. significantly reduced demand on MWD, relieved MWD of having to develop additional supplies, and provided a form of free drought insurance for other member agencies.

By limiting its claims on MWD water deliveries, Los Angeles in effect allowed its heavy early MWD capital investment to serve as a subsidy and inducement for later-joining agencies. Another L.A. contribution to suburban growth involved the MWD water that the city did not use when it chose to develop its more secure municipal supplies. By making more Colorado River water available for others, Los Angeles in effect made the water supply of all other MWD agencies that much more secure. This also relieved upward pressure on the price of water.

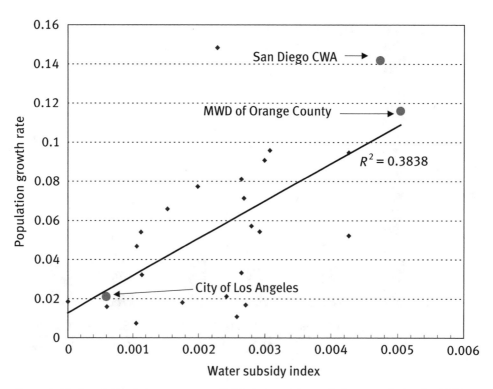

Figure 1.10. Correlation between water subsidy index and population growth rate by MWD member agency, 1929–70.

Plentiful, inexpensive MWD water sent strong signals to developers, businesses, agriculture, and potential home buyers that the suburban periphery could support massive development. This was the sine qua non for regional development and concomitant suburban sprawl. Consider which of these two possibilities was more likely: (1) the existence of MWD without a growing periphery to buy its water or (2) a growing periphery without MWD to supply water. Only the first is plausible. In San Diego, for example, that region's small Colorado River water appropriation (the city of San Diego filing in 1926 for only 112,000 acre-feet), inability to build its own aqueduct, and limited local groundwater supplies would have left it insufficient water to grow without MWD.

Water Transfers: Do They Promote Smart Growth?

Situations such as San Diego's have encouraged the development of new water policies, particularly agriculture-to-urban water transfers, which involve the purchase or lease of water supplies. Approved in 1998, the landmark transfer agreement of up to 200,000 acre-feet per year from the Imperial Irrigation District (IID) to the SDCWA has been hailed as a promising "smart growth" solution to the looming water shortage in urban Southern California. In 1999, MWD outlined its own plans to buy water on the open market. Such transfers are supported by many environmentalists who believe that, as a result, fewer dams and aqueducts will be constructed (LaRue 1998; Perry 1999).

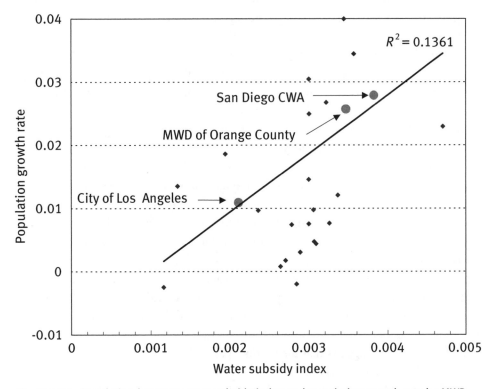

Figure 1.11. Correlation between water subsidy index and population growth rate by MWD member agency, 1971–96.

Yet very little is known about the actual effects of water transfers on growth. Nor is much known about their impact on capital facility needs and financing or on cost-of-service equity among the region's water agencies. Our analysis of the equity and growth effects of past and current MWD policies provides a valuable baseline for the contemporary debate about transfers (Erie 1997; Brackman and Erie 1999).

Past MWD Policies: The Track Record on Equity and Growth

This analysis suggests that MWD's pre-1970 policy of relying on ad valorem property taxes for capital financing and many operating expenses produced substantial cost-of-service disparities between member agencies and favored new suburban development at the expense of the central city and older suburbs. MWD's founding member agencies, such as the city of Los Angeles, paid their full complement of property taxes but, in general, used the system as a limited supplemental water source. In contrast, agencies such as the SDCWA joined MWD in the postwar era, paid relatively small annexation fees, and relied on MWD as a primary water source. The result was a substantial early water provision subsidy of more than $1.3 billion from Los Angeles, both city and county, to suburbanizing San Diego and Orange Counties.

How fair was this early tax-based financing system? Should new suburban areas have been subsidized by established urban centers like Los Angeles in the same way that a nation might protect infant industries or parents might indulge a child until maturity? According to Gottlieb (1988), an argument can be made that MWD's founders and early directors were pursuing a policy of enlightened self-interest, creating a suburban hinterland and thus greater economic opportunities for the core urban center. As noted, a strong case also can be made that when faced with a possible stranded asset such as the Colorado River Aqueduct, MWD officials pursued a rational long-term strategy of encouraging low-cost annexations and subsidized water sales so that rates could be raised at a later date. One wonders what the thirteen original member agencies' MWD costs would have been if outlying areas had not been encouraged with financial incentives to join the Metropolitan family.

Yet there is growing evidence that such subsidies have unwanted consequences. Because beneficiaries fight ferociously to maintain their privileged status, subsidies have a tendency to become self-perpetuating. The protracted battle over shifting MWD capital financing from property taxes to water rates offers vivid testimony in this regard. In recent years, with central-city decline and rampant suburban sprawl, it has become clear that urban centers can no longer be called upon to subsidize the suburban periphery. Indeed, there is growing realization that the fate of metropolitan areas depends fundamentally on the prosperity of the central city (Rusk 1995; Pastor et al. 2000). Smart growth advocates now call for the elimination of subsidies encouraging sprawl. Because newly developed areas require greater capital investments, a cost-of-service logic suggests that they should pay additional, not reduced, charges for services such as water provision.

MWD's post-1970 shift from tax-based financing to a water charge structure featuring substantial cost recovery has resulted in a much more equitable and less growth-inducing water policy. The new rate system reduced many cost-of-service disparities among member agencies and resulting subsidies. Yet, Los Angeles's subsidy of water provision to other member agencies, particularly San Diego, continued—although at one-half the level as previously. As noted, since 1970 the city of Los Angeles and L.A. County have overpaid $737 million and San Diego has underpaid $621 million relative to their respective water deliveries. Although a portion of San Diego's lower water costs are due to agricultural discounts (which come with lessened water reliability), MWD's continued reliance on property taxes for up to one-third of its capital financing (designed to generate a stable dedicated revenue stream and thus lower borrowing costs) saddles Los Angeles, with its large tax base, with a disproportionate share of MWD costs.

Overall, between 1929 and 1996 the taxpayers and ratepayers of the city of Los Angeles have overpaid $1.9 billion and L.A. County residents have overpaid $309 million relative to their MWD water usage. In contrast, San Diego County residents have underpaid $1.3 billion, Orange County residents have underpaid nearly $700 million, and those living in Riverside County have underpaid $225 million relative to their MWD water usage. As a result, the metropolitan core has subsidized water provision to the suburbanizing periphery by more than $2.2 billion.

But MWD's strategy of piggybacking much of its costs onto water charges has not been without risks. It made the majority of its capital financing dependent on water sales and revenues. In the early 1990s, as MWD embarked on an ambitious capital program while suffering drought-induced declines in water sales and revenues, the limitations of this rate structure became evident. Hence MWD adopted new charges—readiness-to-serve, standby, and new-demand rates—to firm up capital financing and create greater equity between established and rapidly growing areas for financing the capital projects needed to accommodate new growth. Yet the postage-stamp rate and new growth charges created incentives for major customers such as the San Diego County Water Authority to reduce their large and growing MWD capital financing burdens by purchasing non-MWD water through transfers.

The IID/SDCWA Water Transfer: Are There Subsidy and Growth Effects?

A question needs to be raised, whether water transfers such as the landmark IID/SDCWA agreement are more about guaranteeing water reliability or reducing the recipient's capital financing burdens. Another nagging question is whether such large-scale transfers, hailed by many environmentalists, entail further subsidies, urban growth, and environmental degradation.

Although SDCWA claims it is buying reliability given its limited preferential rights to MWD water, the state Water Code governing water shortage emergencies appears to make preferential rights unenforceable. Instead, critics have argued that San Diego is seeking to insulate itself from a fair share of MWD capital project financing, such as for the $2.2 billion Eastside Reservoir, by positioning itself to purchase less water from (and furnish less revenue to) Metropolitan in the future.

The IID transfer also could help insulate San Diego from proposed growth-based fees, such as Metropolitan's now-suspended new-demand charge, designed to recover system development costs to meet the needs of fast-growing areas. Also of concern is whether transfers, by reducing supply pressures, might lessen the incentive for sustainable-development policies such as conservation and reclamation. In back-to-the-future fashion, transfers may herald a return to regional water policies that are growth inducing and result in significant cost-of-service inequities.

To be made workable, the IID/SDCWA deal requires substantial subsidies, although this time directly from the state (and possibly federal) government rather than indirectly (and inadvertently) from Los Angeles. As we have noted, MWD receives 75 percent of its revenues from variable water sales, and 80 percent of its costs are fixed. Thus any reduction in water revenues by a member agency seeking to substitute transfers for MWD purchases could result in significant cost shifting to other member agencies. In 1998, the California State Legislature approved $235 million in general fund moneys to compensate non-San Diegans for the adverse financial impacts of the IID/SDCWA transfer on other MWD member agencies. This is a subsidy paid for by the California taxpayers. The deal's escalating environmental mitigation costs may require an additional $60 million federal subsidy.

Do water transfers like the IID/SDWCA deal encourage smart growth and protect the environment? A strong contrary case can be made that such transfers actually further urban growth and may hurt the environment. The San Diego Association of Governments estimates that the county will add nearly one million new residents in the next twenty years. The Imperial Valley transfer helps ensure that such massive growth can indeed occur.

In addition to possible environmental degradation in rapidly growing San Diego, this transfer also has potentially adverse environmental and economic consequences in the Imperial Valley and across the Mexican border, in Mexicali. Conservation measures such as lining the All-American Canal threaten to reduce agricultural seepage into the Salton Sea significantly. This will necessitate costly mitigation efforts—and possible federal subsidies—to maintain water and salinity levels in the Salton Sea, a fragile ecosystem that is one of the major stops for migrating birds on the Pacific flyway. Lessened seepage from the Imperial Valley also threatens to reduce the water supply available to Mexicali-area farmers. Thus the IID/SDCWA water transfer, widely hailed as a smart growth model for the region and nation, is in actuality a cautionary tale of new subsidies for urban growth, threatened environmental degradation, and the need for costly (and subsidized) mitigation.

In conclusion, our findings suggest a complex relationship between regional water policy and suburban development, and between the city of Los Angeles and its older suburbs and the rest of suburban Southern California. The Metropolitan Water District, ostensibly the creature of "imperial Los Angeles," for forty years heavily subsidized suburban sprawl and the regional periphery, particularly San Diego and Orange Counties, at the expense of the taxpayers and ratepayers of the metropolitan center. A post-1970 policy shift reduced L.A.'s suburban subsidization to one-half of its previous level, but did not end the intraregional conflicts over who benefits and pays for water.

San Diego, Metropolitan's most heavily subsidized customer, likes to portray itself as a David fighting for water independence against the dictatorial MWD Goliath headquartered in Los Angeles. San Diego's preferential status, which in the past was paid for by Los Angeles city and county residents, now could come disproportionately at the expense of the region's fastest-growing areas—Riverside and San Bernardino Counties. Thus the future friction point in regional water politics may not be between Los Angeles and San Diego but between the "old" (San Diego and Orange) and "new" (Riverside and San Bernardino) growth peripheries.

Ultimately, the question of the region's water policies and its subsidized beneficiaries recalls a Thomas Nast cartoon about the Tweed Ring, the political machine that ran New York City in the Civil War era. Nast portrays the most notorious grafters standing in a circle, each pointing his finger at the culprit next to him. So, too, with the politics of water subsidies in Southern California. The region's "usual suspects" are eager to point fingers at each other rather than pay their fair share for water provision, environmental mitigation, and sustainable development.

Notes

This research was supported by a grant from the Southern California Studies Center, University of Southern California, and the James Irvine Foundation. We wish to thank Jennifer Wolch, Manuel Pastor Jr., Robert V. Phillips, Michael Schudson, Gary Arant, Howard Williams, and Harold Brackman for their thoughtful comments on earlier drafts of the manuscript. We are also grateful to Larry LaCom, Metropolitan Water District Graphic Services Department, for providing the MWD's member-agency base map.

1. MWD member agencies (and dates of entry) are as follows: Anaheim (1928), Beverly Hills (1928), Burbank (1928), Glendale (1928), Los Angeles (1928), Pasadena (1928), San Marino (1928), Santa Ana (1928), Santa Monica (1928), Fullerton (1931), Long Beach (1931), Torrance (1931), Compton (1931), San Diego County Water Authority (1946), West Basin MWD (1948), Pomona Valley MWD (1950), Eastern MWD (1951), Chino Basin MWD (1951), MWD of Orange County (1951), Foothill MWD (1953), Central Basin MWD (1954), Western MWD of Riverside County (1954), Las Virgines MWD (1960), Calleguas MWD (1960), Upper San Gabriel Valley MWD (1963), and San Fernando (1971).

2. Population figures as of April 2000 for the Boston-Worcester-Lawrence, MA-NH-ME-CT, consolidated metropolitan statistical area (CMSA) (5,819,100); Dallas–Forth Worth, TX, CMSA (5,221,801); Atlanta, GA, metropolitan statistical area (4,112,198); and the San Francisco-Oakland-San Jose, CA, CMSA (7,039,362) are from the U.S. Bureau of the Census (2001). California projections for Imperial, Los Angeles, Orange, Riverside, San Diego, San Bernardino, and Ventura Counties are from the State of California, Department of Finance (2001).

3. Interview with Robert V. Phillips, former general manager, Los Angeles Department of Water and Power, June 1, 1995.

4. The Laguna Declaration states: "The Metropolitan Water District of Southern California is prepared, with its existing governmental powers and its present and projected distribution facilities, to provide its service area with adequate supplies of water to meet expanding and increasing needs in the years ahead. The District now is providing its service area with a supplemental water supply from the Colorado River. When and as additional water resources are

required to meet increasing needs for domestic, industrial and municipal water, the Metropolitan Water District of Southern California will be prepared to deliver such supplies." See also "Statement of Policy Approved by the Board of Directors of the Metropolitan Water District of Southern California, December 16, 1952" (MWD 1996).

5. See Board of Directors of the Metropolitan Water District of Southern California, Resolution 5821 (1960), MWD Executive Office, Los Angeles.

6. In 1960, SDCWA's MWD directors resisted raising MWD water rates to include payments of principal and interest on bonded debt. Later, Metropolitan's board of directors considered setting a higher price for SWP supplies (to include capital costs) relative to Colorado River water. According to an unofficial history of Metropolitan Water District Act provisions: "SDCWA and other heavy water users resisted the concept of any such difference [in water price based on] source amendment to the Act [to section 133, derived from the original act's section 5(10) and section 6(8) (Stats. 1961, ch. 862)]. A majority of the board, though, approved . . . a legislative draft containing this concept. However, the [Los Angeles] City's Department of Water and Power then entered into a Memorandum of Understanding with SDCWA (in order to dissuade the Authority from lobbying for defeat of the bill). The Memorandum contained these points: . . . [t]he legislation is permissive only" (Flewelling n.d., 93). Finally, starting in 1979 with the settlement of a lawsuit brought by the city of Los Angeles regarding MWD water and tax rate-setting policies, MWD began to implement fully a water charge-based system of capital financing (Flewelling n.d., 92–107). See also MWD Resolution 5821 (1960); Board of Directors of the Metropolitan Water District of Southern California, Resolution 7446 (1972), MWD Executive Office, Los Angeles; Board of Directors of the Metropolitan Water District of Southern California, Minutes, November 13, 1979, p. 9, MWD Executive Office, Los Angeles.

7. See Board of Directors of the Metropolitan Water District of Southern California, Resolutions 8464–65 (1995), MWD Executive Office, Los Angeles.

8. The merger of MWD member agencies Coastal MWD and MWD of Orange County in January 2001 reduced the number of MWD members to its current total of twenty-six.

9. Alternative definitions of subsidy—based on stand-alone costs and incremental costs— lead to the same conclusion: a subsidy relationship existed between original MWD members, particularly the city of Los Angeles, and later joiners such as San Diego County (Erie 2000, 149).

10. On June 28, 1924, the city of Los Angeles filed with the state authorities for a flow of 1,500 cubic feet per second—equivalent to 1.1 million acre-feet annually—from the Colorado River. Los Angeles's original filing, which was transferred to Metropolitan, represents 90 percent of MWD's Colorado River priority rights. MWD's other Colorado River entitlement consists of the city of San Diego's 112,000 annual acre-feet. San Diego granted its filing to MWD upon annexation in 1946 (see MWD 1939, 36; Schwarz 1991, 84–86).

11. See Metropolitan Water District Act, sec. 5½, ch. 323, California Statutes 1931. Preferential rights now appear in sec. 135 of the Metropolitan Water District Act, ch. 209, California Statutes 1969, as amended (see MWD 1996).

12. As we have noted, there are now twenty-six member agencies. However, in the period 1928–96, there were twenty-seven. The analysis is based on twenty-seven agencies.

Works Cited

Brackman, Harold, and Steven P. Erie. 1999. "Managing California's New Water Wars." In *California Policy Options*, ed. Daniel J. B. Mitchell and Patricia Nomura, 45–50. Los Angeles: University of California, School of Public Policy and Social Research.

Center for Continuing Study of the California Economy. 1998. "Land Use and the California Economy: Principles for Prosperity and Quality of Life." http://www.calfutures.org.

Danielson, Michael N. 1976. *The Politics of Exclusion.* New York: Columbia University Press.

Erie, Steven P. 1992. "How the Urban West Was Won: The Local State and Economic Growth in Los Angeles, 1880–1932." *Urban Affairs Quarterly* 27:519–51.

———. 1997. "A San Diego/Imperial Valley Water Deal: Who Stands to Gain? Who to Lose?" *Metro Investment Report,* June, 19–20.

———. 2000. "'Mulholland's Gifts: Further Reflections upon Southern California Water Subsidies and Growth." *California Western Law Review* 37:147–60.

Erie, Steven P., and Pascale Joassart-Marcelli. 2000. "Unraveling Southern California's Water/Growth Nexus: Metropolitan Water District Policies and Subsidies for Suburban Development, 1928–1996." *California Western Law Review* 36:267–90.

Fishman, Robert. 1987. *Bourgeois Utopias: The Rise and Fall of Suburbia.* New York: Basic Books.

Flewelling, George. n.d. "Derivation and History of Various Metropolitan Water District Act Provisions." Unpublished manuscript.

Garreau, Joel. 1991. *Edge City: Life on the New Frontier.* New York: Doubleday.

Gottdiener, Mark. 1977. *Planned Sprawl: Private and Public Interests in Suburbia.* Beverly Hills, CA: Sage.

Gottlieb, Robert. 1988. *A Life of Its Own: The Politics and Power of Water.* New York: Harcourt Brace Jovanovich.

Hoffman, Abraham. 1981. *Vision or Villainy: Origins of the Owens Valley–Los Angeles Water Controversy.* College Station: Texas A&M University Press.

Hundley, Norris, Jr. 1992. *The Great Thirst: Californians and Water, 1770s–1990s.* Berkeley: University of California Press.

Jackson, Kenneth T. 1985. *Crabgrass Frontier: The Suburbanization of the United States.* New York: Oxford University Press.

Kahrl, William. 1982. *Water and Power: The Conflict over Los Angeles' Water Supply in the Owens Valley.* Berkeley: University of California Press.

LaRue, Steve. 1998. "Historic Imperial Water Deal Approved." *San Diego Union Tribune,* April 30, A1.

Logan, John R., and Harvey L. Molotch. 1987. *Urban Fortunes: The Political Economy of Place.* Berkeley: University of California Press.

Metropolitan Water District of Southern California. 1939. *History and First Annual Report.* Los Angeles: MWD.

———. 1972. *Thirty-fourth Annual Report.* Los Angeles: MWD.

———. 1996. *Source Materials on Metropolitan Water District Act § 135 Preferential Rights.* Los Angeles: MWD.

———. 1997. *Fifty-ninth Annual Report.* Los Angeles: MWD.

——— 2000. "Water Delivery in Acre Feet by Member Agency through March 31, 1996"; "Taxes by Member Agencies through March 31, 1996"; "Total Capital Costs [by Member Agencies], Nominal Value and Present Value [through Fiscal Year 1995-96]"; "Total Revenue Collected by MWDSC from the Member Agencies through March 31, 1996." Los Angeles: MWD.

Miller, Gary J. 1981. *Cities by Contract: The Politics of Municipal Incorporation.* Cambridge: MIT Press.

Ostrom, Vincent. 1953. *Water and Politics: A Study of Water Policies and Administration in the Development of Los Angeles.* Los Angeles: Haynes Foundation.

Pastor, Manuel, Jr., Peter Dreier, J. Eugene Grigsby III, and Marta López-Garza. 2000. *Regions That Work: How Cities and Suburbs Can Grow Together.* Minneapolis: University of Minnesota Press.

Perry, Tony. 1999. "MWD to Buy Water on the Open Market." *Los Angeles Times,* August 10, A3.

Reisner, Marc. 1986. *Cadillac Desert: The American West and Its Disappearing Water.* New York: Viking.

Rusk, David. 1995. *Cities without Suburbs,* 2d ed. Washington, DC: Woodrow Wilson Center Press.

Schwarz, Joel. 1991. *A Water Odyssey: The Story of the Metropolitan Water District of Southern California.* Los Angeles: MWD.

State of California, Department of Finance. 2001. *Interim County Population Projections.* Sacramento: State of California.

Teaford, Jon C. 1976. *City and Suburb: The Political Fragmentation of Metropolitan America, 1850–1970.* Baltimore: Johns Hopkins University Press.

U.S. Bureau of the Census. 2001. "Ranking Tables for Metropolitan Areas: Population in 2000 and Population Change from 1990 to 2000" (PHC-T-3). http://www.census.gov.

Wiley, Peter, and Robert Gottlieb. 1982. *Empires in the Sun: The Rise of the New American West.* New York: Putnam.

Worster, Donald. 1985. *Rivers of Empire: Water, Aridity, and the Growth of the American West.* New York: Pantheon.

2 | Environmental Racism and Urban Development

Laura Pulido

The concept of environmental racism—the idea that nonwhites in the United States are disproportionately exposed to pollution—emerged more than ten years ago with the United Church of Christ (UCC) study *Toxic Wastes and Race in the United States* (1987).[1] Given the social, ecological, and health implications of environmental hazards, researchers have sought to determine *whether* inequalities exist, to understand the reasons for any such disparities, and to make recommendations (Cutter 1995). Although these are obviously important research contributions, the study of environmental racism is important for an additional reason: it helps us understand racism.

Unfortunately, scholars of environmental racism have not seriously problematized racism, opting instead for a de facto conception based on individual malicious acts. By reducing racism to hostile discriminatory acts, many researchers (with the notable exception of Bullard 1990) miss the role of structural and hegemonic forms of racism in contributing to inequalities. Indeed, structural racism has been the dominant mode of analysis in other substantive areas of social research, such as residential segregation (Massey and Denton 1993) and employment patterns (Kirschenman and Neckerman 1991), since at least Myrdal's *An American Dilemma* (1944). Not only has the environmental racism literature become estranged from social science discussions of race, but, in the case of urban studies, it is divorced from urban geography. Because racism is understood as discrete acts that *may* be spatially expressed, it is not seen as a sociospatial relation both constitutive of the city and produced by it. Yet pollution concentrations are inevitably the product of relationships among distinct places, including industrial zones, affluent suburbs, working-class suburbs, and downtown areas, all of which are racialized.

In this chapter, I use Los Angeles as a case study to explain that the emphasis on siting of pollution sources, although obviously important, must be located in larger urban processes, and that this requires us to "jump scales" in our analysis and also explicitly consider the value of various sorts of public policy (Smith 1993). This is especially true given recent findings that pollution concentrations are closely associated with industrial land use (Baden and Coursey 1997; Boer et al. 1997; Pulido, Sidawi, and Vos 1996; Anderton, Anderson, Oakes, et al. 1994; Colten 1986). This research recasts issues of intentionality and scale, as it requires us to examine the production of industrial zones, their relation to other parts of the metropolis, and the processes and policies by which these patterns evolve.

After all, few can dispute that U.S. cities are highly segregated. Can we attribute this simply to discriminatory lenders and landlords? No. Residential segregation results from a diversity of racisms. Moreover, there is growing evidence that racial responses are often unconscious, the result of lifelong inculcation (Devine 1989; Lawrence 1987). Thus an exclusive focus on discriminatory acts, such as sitings, ignores the facts that all places are racialized and that race informs all places. By contrast, a focus on "white privilege" enables us to develop a more structural, less conscious, and more historicized understanding of racism. It differs from hostile individual discriminatory acts in that it refers to the privileges and benefits that accrue to white people by virtue of their whiteness. White privilege, together with overt and institutionalized racism, reveals how racism shapes places. Hence, instead of asking if an incinerator was placed in a Latino community because the owner was prejudiced, I ask, Why is it that whites are not comparably burdened with pollution (see Szasz and Meuser 1997)? In the case of Los Angeles, industrialization, decentralization, and residential segregation are keys to this puzzle. Because industrial land use is highly correlated with pollution concentrations and people of color, the crucial question becomes, How did whites distance themselves from both industrial pollution and nonwhites? And what sorts of policy tools did they use to further this process?

Racism and White Privilege

Because there are multiple motives and forms of racism (Goldberg 1993; Cohen 1992; Omi 1992), there are various ways of analyzing racisms. In this chapter I consider racism from only two perspectives: scale and intention. Scale is an important analytic tool in any attempt to understand racism in that it is both defined by and transcends it. Consider the various scales at which racism exists: the individual, the group, the institution, the society, the world. Although all are distinct scales, there are dialectical relations among them. So, for instance, an individual racist act is just that, an act carried out at the level of the individual. Nonetheless, that individual is informed by regional and/or national racial discourses, and his or her act informs and reproduces racial discourses and structures at higher scales. Thus we can focus on a particular scale of racism, but we must always be cognizant of its relationship to other scales.

A second crucial issue is the question of intent. Although most social science scholars acknowledge the existence of institutional and structural racism, popular understandings focus heavily on individual malicious intent. Many people believe that a hostile motive is necessary for an action or inequality to qualify as racist. Yet "white privilege" is a concept not dependent on or defined in terms of intentionality. It refers to the hegemonic structures, practices, and ideologies that reproduce whites' privileged status. In this scenario, whites do not necessarily *intend* to hurt people of color, but because they are unaware of their white-skin privilege, and because they accrue social and economic benefits by maintaining the status quo, they inevitably do. White privilege thrives in highly racialized societies that espouse racial equality, but in which whites will not tolerate either being inconvenienced in order to achieve racial equality (Lipsitz 1998; Delgado 1995; Quadagno 1994; Edsall and Edsall 1991) or being denied the full benefits of their whiteness (Harris 1993). White privilege is powerful and pervasive precisely *because* few whites are aware of the benefits they receive simply from being white and that their actions, without malicious intent, may undermine the well-being of people of color.

The concept of white privilege allows us to see how the racial order works to the benefit of whites, whether in the form of economic and political benefits (Ignatiev 1995; Oliver and Shapiro 1995; Almaguer 1994; Harris 1993) or psychological ones (Roediger 1991; Fanon 1967). White privilege is distinct both from white supremacy, a more blatant and acknowledged form of white dominance (Fredrickson 1981), and from individual discriminatory acts, but it flourishes *in relation* to these other forms. Because most white people do not see themselves as having malicious intentions, and because they associate racism with malicious intent, whites exonerate themselves of racist tendencies, all the while ignoring their investment in white privilege. It is this ability to sever intent from outcome that allows whites to acknowledge that racism exists yet seldom identify themselves as racists.

A brief example will demonstrate how the concept of white privilege allows us to historicize environmental racism: a polluter locates near a black neighborhood because the land is relatively inexpensive and adjacent to an industrial zone. This is not a malicious, racially motivated discriminatory act. Instead, many would argue that it is economically rational. Yet it is racist in that it (1) is made possible by the existence of a racial hierarchy, (2) reproduces racial inequality, and (3) undermines the well-being of that community. Moreover, the value of black land cannot be understood outside of the relative value of white land, which is a historical product. White land is more valuable by virtue of its whiteness (Oliver and Shapiro 1995), and thus it is not as economically feasible for the polluter to purchase such land. Nor is it likely that the black community's proximity to the industrial zone is a chance occurrence. Given the federal government's role in creating suburbia, whites' opposition to integration, and the fact that black communities have been restricted to areas that whites deem undesirable, can current patterns of environmental racism be understood outside of a racist urban history?

The final issue of white privilege is, At whose expense? It is impossible to privilege one group without disadvantaging another. White privilege comes at the expense of nonwhites. Historically speaking, suburbanization can be seen as a form of white privilege, as it has allowed whites to live in inexpensive and clean residential environments

(Jackson 1980). It has been a privilege denied to most people of color, but one for which they have also borne the cost, both in terms of the erosion of central-city quality of life and in their direct subsidization of white suburbia through their tax dollars (Guhathakurta and Wichert 1998). The concept of white privilege is useful in the discussion of suburbanization and environmental racism because it shifts our understanding of racism beyond discrete siting acts while also emphasizing the spatiality of racism.

Racism and Space in Environmental Racism Research

Siting and Intentionality in Discrete Acts of Racism

Although an earlier generation of scholars explored the relationship between demographics and pollution (Berry 1977), it was not until the 1980s that these issues were framed as environmental justice (McGurty 1995; see Szasz and Meuser 1997 for a complete review). The initial literature on environmental racism documented discriminatory outcomes (Bullard 1990; UCC 1987; U.S. General Accounting Office 1984) but did not delve into the processes producing them. Drawing on traditional social science understandings of racism, Bullard (1996) has argued that discriminatory outcomes are evidence of racism, regardless of the mechanism (siting, housing discrimination, job blackmail), precisely because of the racist nature of the economy and the larger social formation. Subsequent scholarship, however, has not only challenged the existence of environmental racism but has produced an overly restrictive conception of racism.[2] As a result, the *siting* of pollution sources, as a discrete and conscious act, is often analyzed solely with respect to the locations of racially subordinated groups (Bullard 1996), without sufficient attention to the larger sociospatial processes that produce such patterns. Likewise, interpretations of environmental racism are considered suspect without "proof" of intentionality. Some scholars assert that if an industry moves to an already polluted locale, and the motive is unknown, claims of racism cannot be substantiated. This is predicated on an understanding of racism as discrete hostile acts. In effect, the *siting* of environmental hazards becomes the expression of a potentially racist act.

SITING

The emphasis on siting is significant for two reasons. First, it reproduces an erroneous understanding of urban dynamics as it separates larger sociospatial processes from explanations of environmental inequity. Second, it is the only mechanism considered in terms of discrimination. This can be seen, for instance, in the way that discriminatory siting is carefully distinguished from market forces, which supposedly are nonracist. Neither the narrow conception of racism nor the fetishizing of siting helps us understand the nature of environmental racism in an urban context. In particular, it does not recognize that space is essential to the (re)production of a particular racial formation, nor does it acknowledge the fundamental relationship between racism and the production of industrial zones, pollution, and residential areas (Arnold 1998).

In effect, intentionality has become the litmus test as to whether or not a racist act has been committed. Intentionality not only underlies discussions of racism but also serves several purposes in defining it, as critical legal race scholars have pointed out (Armour 1997; Crenshaw et al. 1995; Delgado 1995). First, the requirement of intentionality reduces the likelihood of viewing collective actions as racist, as it is more difficult to prove group intent than individual intent. Second, the emphasis on intentionality allows for a continual contraction in the definition of racism, as seen in recent court rulings (e.g., *Washington v. Davis*). Finally, the requirement of malicious intent exonerates entire dimensions of the social arena, including the unconscious, from contributing to racial inequality (Devine 1989; Lawrence 1987). The normal functioning of the state and capitalism are thus naturalized, as racism is reduced to an aberration.[3]

A good example of limiting the domain of racism can be seen in conceptions of the market. Instead of viewing the market as both constituted by racism and an active force in (re)producing racism, scholars have treated it as somehow operating outside the bounds of race (for fuller discussions, see Pulido 1996; Mohai and Bryant 1992). This is troubling, given the extent to which discrimination and racism have been proven in the "free market," including in employment, banking, and housing. Do not these various forces shape a city and influence where pollution will be concentrated? Such a limited conception of racism prevents us both from grasping the power and spatiality of racism and from identifying its underlying effectiveness in perpetuating environmental injustice.

Scale and Racism

In addition to siting and intent, spatial scale is also implicated in producing a narrow conception of racism, as it too reflects normative understandings of race and space. Scale is a major methodological issue in the environmental racism literature (Bowen et al. 1995; Cutter 1995; Perlin et al. 1995; Zimmerman 1993). Not only have researchers examined environmental inequity at different scales, they have also debated the question of the most appropriate scale. Evidence suggests that different units of analysis, such as counties, zip codes, or census tracts, may produce different findings. For instance, county-level data may reveal a pattern of environmental racism that is not clear in a census tract analysis of the same area (Bowen et al. 1995; Anderton, Anderson, Rossi, et al. 1994). Moreover, as Neil Smith (1993) has argued, we need to recognize scale as socially constructed, rather than treat it as a "methodological preference for the researcher" (96). Aside from appreciating the fuzzy edges of spatial units, we must recognize that places are the products of specific sets of social relations (Massey 1994; Soja 1989). Moreover, the relevant social relations do not reside solely within the spatial unit under consideration. Rather, places are produced by other places, through what Massey (1994) calls "stretched out" social relations. Thus our analysis must not only operate at several scales simultaneously, it must also consider the functional roles of those places and their interconnections. This has implications for how we use scale in studies of racism. We must bear in mind that the selected scale of analysis may not necessarily coincide with the scale of racist activity. If racism is constitutive of the urban landscape and various types of racisms operate simultaneously, then racism and its consequences do not necessarily cease at the edges of census tracts or city boundaries.

Accordingly, instead of treating spatial units as if they exist in a vacuum, the study of industrial pollution requires that we not limit our focus to the individual facility, but rather address the larger industrial zone in which it is located (Arnold 1998). In turn, we must understand the industrial zone in relation to working-class suburbs, affluent suburbs, "inner cities," and downtown areas.[4] All of these places represent specific class relations that are functionally linked. At the same time, all of these places are racialized, and racism works in particular ways in their formation and evolution.

Collectively, the three practices described above—the emphasis on siting, intentionality, and a static conception of scale—have a limited ability to explain the geography of urban environmental hazards, particularly their concentration in industrial zones (Baden and Coursey 1997; Sadd et al. 1999; Pulido et al. 1996; Anderton, Anderson, Oakes, et al. 1994; Cutter and Tiefenbacher 1991). In a national study of transfer, storage, and disposal facilities (TSDFs), Anderton, Anderson, Oakes, et al. (1994) found that "the clearest and most consistent finding across the country is the apparent association between the location of TSDFs and other industrial enterprises" (239).[5] This finding suggests the need to clarify the relationships among industrial zones, suburbanization, inner cities, and race. As Been (1993) has suggested:

> Many factories and other sources of hazardous waste were traditionally located in the center city because of greater access to transportation and markets. In some cities, developers provided cheap housing for workers in the surrounding areas. As *workers moved away*, either because factories closed or because more desirable housing became affordable elsewhere, the cheap housing in the center cities became disproportionately populated by the poor and by people of color. (1017; emphasis added)

The process of how "workers moved away" is one key to understanding contemporary patterns of environmental racism.

Environmental Racism, Urban Space, and White Privilege in Southern California

Environmental Racism in Los Angeles County

Six systematic studies of environmental racism have been conducted in Los Angeles (five at the county level and one at the city level), examining three environmental hazards: uncontrolled toxic waste sites (UCC 1987), TSDFs (Boer et al. 1997), and air toxins based on the Toxic Release Inventory (TRI) (Sadd et al. 1999; Pulido et al. 1996; Burke 1993; Szasz et al. 1993). Table 2.1 summarizes the methods and findings of these studies.[6] All found that nonwhites were disproportionately exposed. Most vulnerable were working-class Latinos.

The fact that three different hazards have been examined sheds light on distinct aspects of urban environments. For instance, uncontrolled waste sites are often abandoned, thereby illuminating past industrial activities (Newton 1998; Krieg 1995; Colten 1986). Data from the TRI, which lists facilities emitting at least two hundred pounds of air toxins annually, reflect largely contemporary industrial activities. TSDFs, despite their relatively small number, receive an inordinate amount of attention because they are high-profile projects requiring extensive permitting. In cities, they are often located in industrial zones because of their hazardous nature as well as their proximity to waste generators.

The first study to suggest that environmental racism exists in Los Angeles was that conducted by the United Church of Christ. This study, which was national in scope, examined the distribution of uncontrolled hazardous waste sites in major cities, including Los Angeles. The researchers found that Latinos in Los Angeles were disproportionately exposed owing to a concentration of waste sites in the eastern part of the city. Out of fifty-seven waste sites, thirty-five (61.4 percent) were located in zip codes that were at least 50 percent Latino (UCC 1987).[7] This area is not only one of

Table 2.1. Summary of six studies examining environmental hazards in Los Angeles

Study	Hazard	Unit of analysis	Analytic methods	Findings
United Church of Christ (1987)[a]	Abandoned toxic waste sites	City of L.A. (except harbor connector) zip codes	Descriptive analysis	Latinos disproportionately affected
Burke (1993)	Facilities emitting air toxins (TRI)	Urbanized L.A. County census tracts	Bivariate mapping, generalized linear modeling, logit analysis	Latinos disproportionately affected
Szasz et al. (1993)	Facilities emitting air toxins (TRI)	L.A. County census tracts	Difference of means, regression analysis, comparison of means, two-way regression analysis	Black and Latino households earning $20–$40,000 disproportionately affected
Pulido et al. (1996)	Air toxin emission clusters (TRI)	Urbanized L.A. County census tracts	Descriptive and historical analysis	Latinos disproportionately affected
Boer et al. (1997)	Transfer, storage, and disposal facilities	L.A. County census tracts	Visual analysis, univariate and multivariate analyses	Working-class blacks and Latinos disproportionately affected
Sadd et al. (1999)	Air toxins (TRI) (facilities, size of emissions, relative toxicity)	Six Southern California county (Los Angeles, Orange, Ventura, Riverside, San Bernardino, and Imperial) census tracts	Univariate comparisons, binomial logit, ordered logit, tobit regression analysis	Blacks and Latinos in urbanized, central L.A. disproportionately affected

Note: TRI = Toxic Release Inventory.
[a] The primary UCC study examined the relationship between commercial hazardous waste facilities and community demographics. The study of abandoned hazardous wastes was a smaller component of the larger project and was less methodologically rigorous.

the older industrial zones, it is also a long-standing Chicano barrio (Pulido et al. 1996; Sanchez 1993; Romo 1983). The area is legendary for its foul-smelling air and has been dubbed the most polluted zip code in the state (Kay 1994).

The next group of studies examined facilities releasing air toxins. Figure 2.1 is a map displaying the data analyzed in the Sadd et al. (1999) study.[8] This data set contains by far the largest number of pollution events. Burke (1993) identified three key variables associated with census tracts containing TRI facilities: the high presence of minority populations (primarily Latinos), lower incomes, and high population densities. Sadd et al. (1999) found that sites were concentrated in the "heavily urbanized metropolitan Los Angeles area . . . in which the percentage of African American or Latino residents exceeds the mean for the study area" (111). They, along with Szasz et al. (1993), also found that facilities were concentrated in working-class areas, rather than poor or wealthy ones (see also Cutter and Solecki 1996). The Pulido et al. (1996) study focused on emission clusters and found that the largest concentration of sites was located in the greater East Los Angeles and South Los Angeles areas.[9]

The final types of hazards that have been studied are TSDFs. Figure 2.2 represents data on TSDFs analyzed by Boer et al. (1997). These researchers found a pattern similar to that noted by Sadd et al. (1999) and Szasz et al. (1993): the disproportionate exposure of working-class communities of color. Using a multivariate model, Boer et al. found that "race remains a factor along with industrial land use and employment in manufacturing; rising income, on the other hand, has a positive, then a negative effect on the probability of TSDF location" (795). They found that 5.2 percent of blacks and Latinos lived in census tracts containing TSDFs, whereas only 2.9 percent of whites did.

The results of these six studies suggest important racial and spatial patterns associated with these three forms of pollution. First, it appears that most industrial hazards in Southern California are concentrated in the greater central and southern part of Los Angeles County. This older core is inhabited predominantly by people of color, and whites live on the periphery. Within this large zone, one group of hazards follows a major transportation corridor, the I-5 freeway and the railroad, stretching from East Los Angeles through downtown and into the eastern San Fernando Valley. A second major grouping forms a wide swath from downtown to the harbor. This distribution reflects both contemporary and historic industrial patterns. Second, as previously stated, all of these studies found evidence of environmental racism, even when income was taken into account. This substantiates Perlin et al.'s (1995) finding that pollution is concentrated in a few large urban areas with substantial minority populations. Third, working-class Latinos, and to a lesser extent African Americans, are disproportionately affected. This reflects patterns of residential segregation as well as Latinos' historic and continuing role as the region's low-wage working class (Scott 1996b; Morales and Ong 1993; Ong and Blumenberg 1993). What is significant is the degree to which almost no whites live in these areas and therefore are not exposed to the hazards under consideration. There is simply far less pollution in the outlying areas. I maintain that we can understand these contemporary patterns only

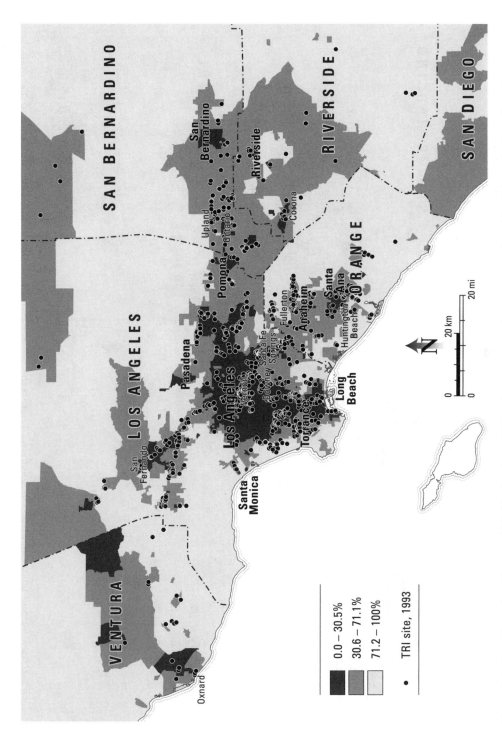

Figure 2.1. Non-Hispanic white population in Southern California (percentage by census tract) and facilities releasing air toxins according to the Toxic Release Inventory (TRI).

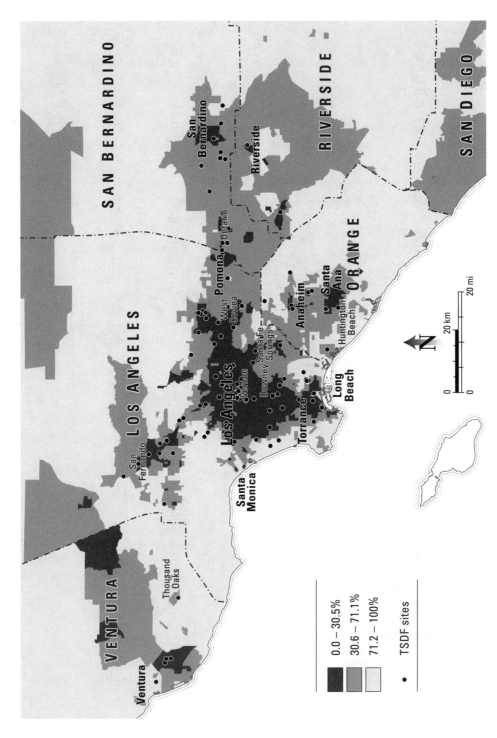

Figure 2.2. Non-Hispanic white population in Southern California (percentage by census tract) and transfer, storage, and disposal facilities (TSDFs).

by examining the historical development of urban space at the regional scale and that these processes are inherently racialized. Although some forms of environmental racism are directly attributable to overt acts of discrimination, white privilege has contributed to this larger pattern.

The Historical Geography of White Privilege and Environmental Racism in Los Angeles

The data suggest that people of color's disproportionate exposure to pollution in Los Angeles is not the result of chance. Although the geography of environmental racism is the result of millions of individual choices, those choices reflect a particular racial formation and are responses to conditions deliberately created by the state and capital (Hise 1997; Harvey 1985; Walker 1981). My goal here is to show the historical evolution of these patterns and how racism contributed to the spatial patterns associated with environmental racism.

Before I present this historical geography, however, it is useful to consider how Los Angeles is both similar to and different from other urban areas. Although the nature and definition of suburbia is contested (Kling, Olin, and Poster 1995; Sharpe and Wallock 1994; Garreau 1991; Fishman 1987), there is no denying that urban regions have undergone a fundamental restructuring over the past five decades, as whites and middle-class persons of all colors have moved outward, with significant consequences for inner cities. This process of deconcentration has been described as a "massive regional dispersal of population, industry, and commerce" entailing "the restructuring of both the central city and the outlying areas" (Gottdiener and Kephart 1995, 33–34).

Los Angeles has not escaped these profound shifts, but its experience is also unique (Dear and Flusty 1998; Soja 1989, 1996; Davis 1992). Unfortunately, the reality of Los Angeles is often obscured by the many misconceptions about the region (Soja 1996). For example, because of L.A.'s legendary sprawl, many overlook the historical and contemporary significance of the region's inner cities. Inner cities are often considered to be sites of poverty and pathos, but this is too simple a reading. Although both the Eastside barrio and South-Central L.A. are home to poor people of color, they are also the sites of vibrant communities and an assortment of industry and warehousing. In addition, because of the influence of Hollywood and Disneyland, many do not realize that Los Angeles County is the leading manufacturing county in the nation. Accordingly, the historical geography of industry has been a powerful force in shaping the region (Soja 1989).

Suburbanization is also unique in Los Angeles. Although the region did not pioneer the suburb, suburbia peaked in Los Angeles, as real estate speculation and "living the good life" became economic and social cornerstones of the region (Fishman 1987). Finally, many U.S. cities have historically been characterized by bipolar racial structures (usually black/white), only recently becoming multiracial. In contrast, Los Angeles has always been racially diverse. This is important in that the longtime presence of various racial/ethnic groups illustrates how nonwhites have differentially experienced racism, underscoring the profundity of white privilege.

EARLY RESIDENTIAL AND INDUSTRIAL PATTERNS, 1848–1920S

Early suburbanization emanated partly from the refusal of middle-class whites to live near people of color and new immigrants. Whites pursued suburbanization for many reasons, but regardless of their motives, their choice was predicated on white privilege. Historian Robert Fogelson (1993) has pointed out that soon after the Anglo takeover of Los Angeles (1848), the city was transformed from a spatially clustered community to a rapidly expanding city. This transformation was driven by several forces, including a growing population, land speculation, and the fact that many newly arrived white Angelenos were native-born and refused to live near socially subordinated groups. Fogelson argues that because the whites who came to Los Angeles were relatively secure financially, they were more concerned with lifestyle issues than with economic survival, and their affluence led them to embrace suburbia. Hence whites' residential desires and real estate interests were two of the more powerful forces that shaped early Los Angeles:

> The unique dispersal of Los Angeles reflected not so much its chronology, geography, or technology as the exceptional character of its population. It was not like Chicago . . . inhabited largely by impoverished and insecure European immigrants, who . . . were confined to the city's teeming tenements and crowded ghettos. . . . Los Angeles was populated principally by native Americans with adequate resources and marketable skills, who faced the problems of adjustment confidently because of a common language and similar background. . . . Moreover, the native Americans came to Los Angeles with a conception of the good community which was embodied in single-family houses, located on large lots, surrounded by landscape lawns, and "isolated" from business activities. Not for them multi-family dwellings . . . separated by cluttered streets and . . . industry. Their vision was epitomized by the residential suburb. (144)

In addition to the exclusionary desires of white Angelenos, suburbanization was also promoted by industrialists who sought to provide housing for working-class whites as a means of avoiding labor unrest. According to one promotional brochure:

> The real secret of the efficiency of the workers of Southern California may be found in their home life. . . . A tenement is unknown here and the workers live in their own little bungalows surrounded by plenty of land for fruits, vegetables and flowers, and where children romp and play throughout the entire year. . . . This spells contentment and contentment spells efficiency. (Los Angeles Chamber of Commerce 1926, n.p.)

As whites moved outward, Chicanos, African Americans, Japanese Americans, Chinese Americans, and the remnant Indian population were relegated to San Pedro, Watts, and the central city (including downtown and the Eastside) (Anderson 1996; Horne 1995; Sanchez 1993; Romo 1983; Warren 1986–87). Beginning in the 1920s, residential segregation was violently enforced (Massey and Denton 1993; deGraff 1970). As a result, for the thousands of "Mexicans, Japanese, and Negroes who lived amidst commerce and industry in the small ghettos of central Los Angeles and San Pedro there were a million white Americans who resided in the suburbs sprawling north to Hollywood, east to Pasadena, south to Long Beach, and west to Santa Monica" (Fogelson 1993, 147). These early differences in environmental quality were codified by zoning laws in the 1920s that resulted in the concentration of industrial activity in nonwhite and immigrant areas (Zoning Map Company 1930). For example, the zoning of Boyle Heights, what is today part of the Chicano Eastside, did not provide for any buffers between the multiunit residential and industrial zones.

This early process of white out-migration was characterized by various forms of racism. For one, the fact that nonwhites were considered undesirable reflects a racial hierarchy. More conscious was the exclusion of people of color from white housing developments. Although most developers practiced overt discrimination, denying housing to people of color, they may have had distinct motives. Some may have opposed nonwhites living with whites, for example, whereas others may simply have realized that the presence of nonwhites would reduce property values. Regardless of the motives, however, *all* these actions were predicated on white privilege and served to undermine the well-being of people of color.

Until the 1920s, the Los Angeles industrial sector was weak and clustered downtown due to limited infrastructure. During the 1920s, however, civic leaders sought to build the region's manufacturing base in order to diversify the economy. Between 1919 and 1933, Los Angeles County rose from twenty-seventh to sixth in the nation in terms of the value of manufactured goods (Los Angeles Chamber of Commerce 1934). Several factors guided this growth, including the success of the "branch plant" strategy, capital's desire to escape organized labor and zoning regulations (Los Angeles Chamber of Commerce 1929), and the coordinated efforts of industrialists, developers, and planners to transform Los Angeles's landscape from one based on tourism and land speculation to one based on manufacturing (Hise 2001; Fogelson 1993).

The resulting manufacturing and residential geographies have had an enduring influence. *Mexicanos* and industry were continually pushed eastward from the central Plaza, toward the Los Angeles River (Romo 1983; Sanchez 1993), further cementing the barrio's role as an industrial district. Industrialists and planners chose to develop this site, given its proximity to the railroad, in hopes of generating cargo tonnage (Los Angeles Central Manufacturing District 1923). Partly because of the existing industrial infrastructure (railroads, industrially zoned land, already contaminated land) and the availability of a large pool of low-wage labor, the Eastside remains an important industrial area.

The production of urban space in Los Angeles in the 1920s shows how race and class influenced the location of both residential and industrial districts. Affluent whites moved to residential suburbs such as Pasadena, Rancho Palos Verdes, and Beverly Hills, areas that were never seriously threatened by industrial activity. Instead, industry developed in conjunction with nonwhite spaces (the Eastside and south of downtown) and the white working class. As previously mentioned, industrialists' desire to avoid labor unions (concentrated downtown) and to placate white labor through home ownership led to the development of industrial suburbs. The creation of communities such as Torrance, Huntington Park, and Bell, located in the southern and southeast portions of Los Angeles County, offered a suburban experience to all whites, regardless of class (Parson 1984). The strength of the color line can be seen in the way Bell, for instance, boasted of providing "homes for industrial workers [with] no Negroes and very few Mexicans and Chinese." Likewise, Compton described itself as having "inexpensive homes of individuality, where flowers and gardens may be grown the year-round. White help prevails" (Los Angeles Chamber of Commerce 1925, n.p.). As suburbanization continued, what were once the near suburbs became the inner city as white workers moved away and people of color subsequently took their place, a process known as *ethnic succession*.[10] Consequently, wealthy whites were never systematically burdened by pollution, and working-class whites were able to escape by taking advantage of new housing opportunities. Thus, regardless of class differences, all whites enjoyed white privilege, albeit to varying degrees.

Residential and Industrial Expansion in the World War II Era

The Depression and World War II greatly intensified the process of white suburbanization, but instead of this being a private project, the state actively subsidized suburbanization, to the detriment of people of color living in the central city (Guhathakurta and Wichert 1998; Ebner 1987). Not only did whites continue their outward migration, but millions of newly arrived white Angelenos settled in the suburbs. In contrast, newly arriving African Americans and *Mexicanos* were relegated, respectively, to the ghetto and the barrio. And Japanese Americans, on their postwar release from concentration camps, clustered in black and brown spaces, such as the Crenshaw area west of downtown and Boyle Heights, as well as rural communities such as Gardena (Warren 1986–87).

The economic growth triggered by defense dollars provided jobs, and housing these workers created a construction boom. Hise (1993) has argued that this period is pivotal to explaining the contemporary fragmentation of Southern California: "The emergence of Los Angeles as a fully urbanized region occurred around a set of decentralized industrial growth poles . . . [and the] industrial and housing policy associated with the defense emergency accelerated this emergent pattern of decentralization" (97–98).

Federal policies such as Titles I and VI of the Federal Housing Act (FHA) sought to increase the housing supply (Doti and Schweikart 1989), and did so in an overtly racist way. Perhaps of greatest significance was the institutionalization of redlining practices by the Home Owners Loan Corporation (HOLC) and FHA. Although intended to protect small home owners from foreclosure, the HOLC practice of ranking neighborhoods in descending order from "A" to "D" had profound consequences for future urban development. "A" ratings were reserved for "newer, affluent suburbs that were strung out along curvilinear streets well away from the problems of the city"

(Jackson 1980, 424). At the other extreme were nonwhite neighborhoods. Indeed, HOLC's survey of the Los Angeles area shows the suburban communities of Pasadena, Beverly Hills, Santa Monica, and Palos Verdes as all "A" areas. Working-class white communities were ranked "B," and black, Latino, and Asian neighborhoods (primarily on the Eastside, in central Los Angeles, and south of downtown) were ranked "C" and "D" (Federal Home Loan Bank Board 1939). A confidential report by the survey team illustrates the degree to which black and brown people were considered a problem and potential threat to white residential development:

> Negroes do not constitute a racial problem in the area as a whole, for although they too have been increasing rapidly in number, their ratio to the total county population has remained constant since 1890. The Negro race is fairly well confined to a few sections within the county. They occupy one large area southwest of the business district. . . . Although Beverly Hills shows a larger than average number of Negroes, these are made up entirely of servants *and they do not own property in the community*. . . . The major racial problem existing in Los Angeles, and one which is not revealed by the census data, is that created by the large numbers of Mexicans, who are classed as Whites by the Census Bureau. . . . While many of the Mexican race are of high caliber and descended from the Spanish grandees who formerly owned all the territory in southern California, *the large majority of Mexican people are a definite problem locally* and their importation in the years gone by to work the agricultural crops has now been recognized as a mistake. (Bowden and Mayborn 1939, n.p.; emphases added)

The results of such overt and institutionalized forms of racism were evident in dramatic urban inequalities. For instance, despite the outlawing of restrictive covenants in 1948 (legislation that Californians subsequently repealed), less than 2 percent of the housing financed with federal mortgage insurance was made available to blacks (Anderson 1996). Moreover, in 1955 the ratio between single-family and multifamily housing starts was more than nine to one in Los Angeles (Cohan 1956). Because Mexican Americans and blacks were largely excluded from the new suburbs, the limited production of multifamily units meant greater crowding in the barrio and ghetto. Minority communities were also disadvantaged insofar as massive funds were channeled into suburbia. Not only did this mean that less money was available for inner-city development, but such projects were often built literally at the expense of nonwhites. For example, Los Angeles's freeways, on which the suburban structure was predicated, were largely built *through* communities of color, particularly Chicano neighborhoods, resulting in severe disruption to these communities and their housing stock (Avila 1998). The result of these practices was evident in growing racial and economic polarization. In 1960, the average annual income in central and eastern Los Angeles was $5,916, whereas it was $8,575 in the outlying, newly urbanizing areas (Los Angeles Times 1965).[11]

A related segregation tool was suburban city incorporation. The exclusionary nature of suburbanization is underscored by the fact that once people arrived, they sought to insulate their investment through incorporation. Not only did this protect their tax dollars, it offered them more control over local land use, including industry, schools, and the ability to exclude outsiders through, for example, restrictive covenants, advertising practices, and minimum lot-size standards (Miller 1981; Babcock and Bosselman 1973). Because incorporation offered communities greater autonomy, overt racism flourished. In Torrance, for instance, whites fiercely resisted an integration campaign led by the Congress of Racial Equality, a civil rights group. White opposition ranged from parades held by Nazis and Klansmen to white home owners' planting American flags and signs on their lawns saying, "Without property rights there are no human rights" (Weeks 1963). Between 1955 and 1960, twenty-five communities incorporated in Los Angeles County (Miller 1981), resulting in a total of more than seventy-six incorporated cities (Los Angeles Times 1965).[12] The issue of incorporation versus suburbanization demonstrates the multiple forms of racism shaping the region. For some, moving to suburbia might simply have been a way of taking advantage of an opportunity afforded by their white skin. Although this opportunity is *predicated* on institutionalized racism, incorporation is potentially a more conscious and deliberate act aimed at maintaining privilege (often in the form of property values). Indeed, what is significant is not that some whites refused to live among non-whites, but the extent to which social status and a desired quality of life are predicated on homogeneous whiteness.

> That suburbanites effectively wall out those unlike themselves after arriving [in suburbia], however, suggests that a major force driving their migration is the wish to escape racial and class intermingling. In the United States, *upward mobility and social status are predicated on living apart from racial and economic groups considered inferior*. . . . Thus, it is not simply the racism of individuals but also the collectively perceived threat that race and class differences pose to homeownership and social standing that drives suburbanites to keep their territory segregated. (Sharpe and Wallock 1994, 9; emphasis added)

This quote emphasizes the connection between individual actions and social structures. Although some suburban whites undoubtedly had malicious intentions, others did not. Yet, in order to preserve and fully exploit the privilege associated with whiteness, presumably well-intentioned individuals respond to market forces and social structures in ways that reinforce racist hierarchies.

This process highlights not only the spatiality of racism but also the fact that space is a resource in the production of white privilege. Indeed, neighborhoods are not merely groupings of individuals, homes, and commerce, they are *constellations of opportunities* with powerful consequences for both the recipient and nonrecipient populations. Although whites must go to ever-greater lengths to achieve them, relatively homogeneous white spaces are necessary for the full exploitation of whiteness (Frankenberg 1993).

Beginning in the 1950s, L.A.'s urban exodus was driven by the relocation of key industries and government services. Led by Northrop, Hughes, and Lockheed, aerospace firms left central Los Angeles in a leapfrog pattern, creating industrial agglomerations (Scott 1996a; Lockheed Aircraft Corporation 1953). As a result, good-paying defense jobs shifted to Los Angeles's periphery (Law, Wolch, and Takahashi 1993), and racial and economic polarization became more entrenched. There was a strong relationship between the defense industry and white workers. White workers followed the industry, and the industry moved to areas amenable to whites. For instance, labor market surveys described Fullerton as undergoing a "significant expansion in industries related to the missile program" (California Department of Employment 1960) and as having a labor force that was primarily "native-born white" (California Department of Employment 1952).

Many factors contributed to this industrial and urban decentralization. In addition to population growth, new production methods required larger lots, which were increasingly hard to find in Los Angeles. Indeed, 76 percent of capital investment in L.A. in 1955 was spent on existing businesses as they sought to expand (Banks 1956). In addition, many residents had a desire to escape congestion and various quality-of-life concerns, which greatly intensified after the Watts riots in 1965. Consequently, new communities were built along Los Angeles's periphery, including the San Fernando Valley, the South Bay, and Orange County (Kling et al. 1995; Scott 1990). Between 1960 and 1965, Los Angeles County experienced a population growth rate of 21.4 percent, whereas Orange County averaged 137.5 percent (Los Angeles Times 1965). Despite Orange County's exceptional growth, however, relatively few people of color moved there. In 1964, Los Angeles's population was 19.2 percent nonwhite, but Orange County's was only 8.8 percent nonwhite (Los Angeles Chamber of Commerce 1964).

Aside from affordable housing and good-paying jobs, white Angelenos were lured to the suburbs by new, attractive, segregated communities such as Irvine, the quintessential planned community. The developer, the Irvine Company, believed that both affordable housing and racial integration would reduce property values and deter desirable buyers. One official explained that a multiracial advertisement "would scare off every white person I had even the slightest hopes of getting" (quoted in Schiesl 1995, 68).

Nonetheless, with a decrease in overt racism and a strong economy, people of color began to enjoy more housing options. The San Gabriel Valley became the path of upward mobility for Chicanos. Asian Americans became increasingly dispersed throughout the region, and, in the 1970s, a decrease in racism allowed blacks to move beyond central and southern Los Angeles.

CONTEMPORARY PATTERNS

In recent years, immigration has dramatically affected both the economy and residential patterns of the L.A. region. Between 1970 and 1990, the Asian population of Los Angeles increased by 451 percent (Cheng and Yang 1996), and from 1980 to 1990, the Latino population rose from two million to well over three million (Morrison and Lowry 1994). Although these new arrivals settled throughout the region, many clustered in eastern, central, and southern Los Angeles. At the same time, African

Americans, while still heavily concentrated in southern Los Angeles, have been moving east to the "Inland Empire"; some have even left California to return to the South (Johnson and Roseman 1990).

New immigrants have moved into the spaces left by black and brown out-migration because they are affordable and accessible. Immigrants do not settle randomly; rather, their decisions about where to live are informed by the geography of past racial regimes. As a result, central Los Angeles continues to be a nonwhite space (Allen and Turner 1997). This growth is juxtaposed to the loss of 352,000 whites between 1980 and 1990 (Sabagh and Bozorgmehr 1996). White "holdout" communities feel their days are numbered. According to a resident in one such centrally located white community, Lakewood, "I've got three blacks [families] on my block, right now . . . and well, you know the problem with blacks, they have friends, and they have visitors. That is the problem. We can't encourage our people to stay if this keeps up. Our housing stock has stayed pretty solid, but some people can't be encouraged much more to stay" (quoted in Brill 1996, 110).

The complexion of Orange County, particularly the inland areas, has changed considerably in recent years as the numbers of Latinos and Asian/Pacific Islanders have grown. Nonetheless, blacks still constitute only 1.8 percent of the county's population (Roseman and Lee 1998). The net result of all these shifts is that although people of color can now be found throughout the region, they are concentrated in the mature suburbs: the eastern San Fernando Valley and the San Gabriel Valley.[13] Central Los Angeles remains almost completely nonwhite, and whites continue to congregate along the region's periphery.

Many of the industries and land uses associated with environmental hazards are concentrated in central Los Angeles and, to a lesser extent, along industrial arteries. Both blacks and Latinos are disproportionately exposed, but for somewhat different reasons. As the most segregated population, black Angelenos were confined to southern Los Angeles beginning in the 1920s (deGraff 1970). Although many blacks have left, southern Los Angeles is still heavily black (Allen and Turner 1997) and contains portions of an old industrial corridor. Despite the fact that blacks were only intermittently hired in them, southern Los Angeles housed many Fordist industries, the majority of which left in the 1970s and 1980s (Oliver, Johnson, and Farrell 1993). This "rust belt" not only harbors various environmental hazards, but as a politically weak and industrially oriented area, it attracts projects such as incinerators and the proposed Pacific Pipeline (Aspen Environmental Group 1993). Thus blacks' exposure to environmental hazards is largely a function of severe spatial containment and the historic practice of locating hazardous land uses in black areas.

In contrast, Latinos' exposure is more a function of their role as low-wage labor within the racialized division of labor and the historic relationship between the barrio and industry. Latinos have *always* lived close to industry, but, unlike blacks, they have at times been hired by industry in large numbers (Morales and Ong 1993; Ong and Blumenberg 1993). Latinos' contemporary exposure cannot be understood outside of industrial and immigration shifts. Over the past twenty years, the region has undergone a simultaneous industrial decline and expansion (Soja 1989). The finance and service sectors have grown dramatically, but manufacturing declined in Los Angeles in the 1980s. In the 1990s, however, a selective reindustrialization was realized (Scott 1996b) by high-technology industries and low-wage Latino labor. As a result, Latinos live near industry, because both are concentrated in central Los Angeles and industrial corridors, and they are exposed on the job (Ong and Blumenberg 1993). Thus their exposure is a function of their class and immigrant status as well as their racial position. As Latinos, they live where brown and black people have historically lived, or in spaces vacated by the white working class.

Environmental hazards are concentrated in central Los Angeles (including the inner suburbs) in several distinct ways. First, because a significant portion of these communities are industrially zoned, industry continues to locate there (Cordoba Corporation 1987). However, because of the poverty of central Los Angeles, land fragmentation, and poor services, few of the large, well-financed firms in growth sectors locate there. Instead, small polluting activities and large-scale hazards, such as incinerators, are drawn to these areas, and "cleaner industries are dissuaded from locating in the area because of the toxic contamination" (Los Angeles Design Action Planning Team 1990, 12). According to one official from Paramount, an inner suburb in southeast L.A. County, "We provide a place for industry that nobody wants" (quoted in Flanigan 1999, C1). Scott (1996b) has pointed out that low-technology, labor-intensive industries are now clustered near downtown; metallurgical and machinery industries are found in old industrial zones throughout the region, including the eastern San Fernando Valley, South-Central L.A., and northern Orange County; and high-technology industries are located on the fringe (see also Kaplan 1998).

Consider the Eastside and Southeast Planning Districts in the city of Los Angeles. In both cases, 20 percent of the land is zoned as industrial (City of Los Angeles 1988; Garrow, Lau, and Loong 1987). Not surprisingly, both of these communities were targets for incinerator projects in the 1980s. The city of Los Angeles proposed a waste-to-energy incinerator for South-Central, but Concerned Citizens of South Central Los Angeles, a group of largely African American women, successfully resisted the project. In the second case, the city of Vernon, southeast of downtown L.A. and adjacent to Boyle Heights, proposed a hazardous waste incinerator. This time, the city of Los Angeles assisted the Mothers of East L.A. in defeating the project (Blumberg and Gottlieb 1989).

Conflicting land uses are also a serious problem that intensifies potential environmental hazards. One planning document described the Eastside as consisting of

> small, older, single family homes situated between or adjacent to large commercial and industrial buildings. . . . The noise, dirt, heavy truck and trailer traffic along industrial/residential edges also severely detracts from the quality of life of nearby residents. Views from homes to loading docks, auto wrecking and repair yards, and heavy machinery do not provide the amenities traditionally associated with residential life. (Garrow et al. 1987, 54)

Beyond the general unsightliness, such land uses pose a severe threat to residents. Because of the lack of buffers and the hazardous nature of industry, there have been mass evacuations, school contaminations (Frammolino 1999), explosions (Sahagun 1989) and workers killed (Malnic and Ramos 1997), and potential cancer clusters have been identified (Gold 1999). Newer suburban communities do not appear to have the same concentration of hazardous industrial activities and enjoy more effective zoning and land-use regulations. Overall, there are simply fewer pollution clusters along the coast (see Figures 2.1 and 2.2). With the exception of the port, coastal communities are cleaner (and whiter) than the central city. Aside from the fact that the suburbs house better-capitalized firms more likely to have the best available technology, the coastal breeze blows pollution inland, thus further cleansing the coastal suburbs. Clearly, such unequal geographies have resulted not from any single decision or act, but from a complex process of highly racialized urban development over the course of 150 years.

Conclusion

I have argued that the emphasis on siting, intentionality, and scale have contributed to the conceptualization of both racism and space as discrete objects rather than as social relations. I have sought to challenge this approach by employing the concept of white privilege, which offers a more structural and spatial understanding of racism. The history of suburbanization reveals that although many forces contributed to decentralization, it was largely an exclusionary undertaking. Moreover, the state has played a central role in crafting Southern Californians' choices and landscapes. The concept of white privilege allows us to see how environmental racism has been produced—not only through the conscious targeting of people of color (as in the incinerator cases) but through the larger processes of urban development, including white flight, in which whites have sought to exploit fully the benefits of their whiteness.

From a policy perspective, my argument highlights the need to direct more attention to industrial zones and pollution clusters, rather than just the siting process and individual facilities. Although the latter are clearly important, particularly in terms of future pollution, most industrial pollution does not involve new sitings; rather, it is the product of already existing facilities, land uses, and zoning. In Los Angeles, explanations of, and remedies for, environmental inequality must include careful consideration of residential patterns, land use, and industrial development. But of course, as important as these measures are, the problem of environmental racism will be resolved only when racial inequality ceases to exist.

Notes

1. A word on terminology is in order. In early studies, the term *environmental racism* was used to denote disparate patterns in certain groups' exposure to pollution. Over time, the term *environmental equity* became popular as it was more inclusive, encompassing both racial and economic disparities. However, many activists also saw the use of the latter term as an effort to depoliticize the antiracist consciousness underlying the movement. Moreover, as Heiman

(1990) has pointed out, the term *environmental (in)equity* implies that the problem is with the allocation of pollution and environmental hazards, rather than with a particular economic system. Activists eventually adopted the term *environmental justice*, as it is inclusive and also indicates a politicized conception of the problem. While supportive of the environmental justice movement, I use the term *environmental racism* in this chapter, as I am highlighting racial disparities. At times I also use *environmental inequities* to refer to allocation issues.

2. In most cases, scholars simply want to establish whether such inequalities exist. However, there has also been a move on the part of both corporations and politically conservative institutions to refute such claims (Anderton, Anderson, Rossi, et al. 1994; Anderton, Anderson, Oakes, et al. 1994; Boerner and Lambert 1994; see also Goldman 1996).

3. The notion of racism as an aberration, or as an irrationality, is an entrenched part of the liberal discourse on racism. For a critique, see Crenshaw et al. (1995).

4. I place the term *inner city* in quotes to denote the fact that it is both socially constructed and problematic as a policy and social science concept.

5. Anderton et al.'s work has been widely criticized on several grounds. Their finding of no environmental racism has been challenged on methodological grounds (Been 1995), as has their participation in industry-supported research (Goldman 1996, 132–34). Nonetheless, their observations concerning industrial land uses have been increasingly corroborated.

6. For purposes of this chapter, Southern California is limited to Los Angeles and Orange Counties.

7. Although the UCC study was based on 1980 U.S. Census data and is therefore somewhat dated, this part of the city has only become more Latino since the study was conducted. Latinos now constitute upward of 90 percent of the population in eastern Los Angeles (see Allen and Turner 1997).

8. Many thanks to Jim Sadd and Environmental Data Resources, Inc., for allowing me to use this data set. In Figures 2.1 and 2.2, I have overlaid environmental hazards data from the Sadd et al. (1999) and Boer et al. (1997) studies, respectively, on 1990 census data.

9. The single largest emitter was an oil refinery in Torrance, an ethnically mixed, middle-income city (see also Burke 1993); however, at a more refined scale, we found that the neighborhoods immediately adjacent to the refinery were primarily nonwhite (Pulido et al. 1996).

10. This is an important issue that few have seriously addressed: the historic exposure to environmental hazards of the white working class. The fact that working-class whites may have been disproportionately exposed in the past does not detract from the argument that environmental racism exists today. Rather, it suggests the changing nature of race and the need to historicize its spatiality.

11. I reached these figures by averaging the reported incomes for the following communities as identified in the *Los Angeles Times* media market. For the inner city, I included the areas designated Northeast, East, Central, and Southeast. For the periphery, I included the San Fernando Valley, Glendale, South Coast, and Orange County (Los Angeles Times 1965, 15, M-12).

12. An important impetus for this incorporation boom was the planned community of Lakewood, which pioneered a contract-based form of municipal government (Brill 1996, 98). Many communities emulated this plan during what has been called the "Lakewoodization" of Southern California (Davis 1992, 166).

13. This is in keeping with research findings suggesting that despite people of color's growing presence in suburbia, they remain segregrated and live in more marginal suburbs (Phelan and Schneider 1996).

Works Cited

Allen, J., and E. Turner. 1997. *The Ethnic Quilt: Population Diversity in Southern California.* Northridge: California State University Northridge, Center for Geographical Studies.

Almaguer, T. 1994. *Racial Fault Lines: The Historical Origins of White Supremacy in California.* Berkeley: University of California Press.

Anderson, S. 1996. "A City Called Heaven: Black Enchantment and Despair in Los Angeles." In *The City: Los Angeles and Urban Theory at the End of the Twentieth Century,* ed. A. J. Scott and E. W. Soja, 336–64. Berkeley: University of California Press.

Anderton, D., A. Anderson, J. Oakes, and M. Fraser. 1994. "Environmental Equity: The Demographics of Dumping." *Demography* 31(2):229–48.

Anderton, D., A. Anderson, P. Rossi, J. Oakes, M. Fraser, E. Weber, and E. Calabrese. 1994. "Hazardous Waste Facilities: 'Environmental Equity' Issues in Metropolitan Areas." *Evaluation Review* 18(2):123–40.

Armour, J. D. 1997. *Negrophobia and Reasonable Racism: The Hidden Costs of Being Black in America.* New York: New York University Press.

Arnold, C. 1998. "Planning Milagros: Environmental Justice and Land Use Regulation." *Denver University Law Review* 76(1):1–153.

Aspen Environmental Group. 1993. *Pacific Pipeline Project: Draft Environmental Impact Report, Executive Summary.* Sacramento: California Public Utilities Commission.

Avila, E. 1998. "The Folklore of the Freeway: Space, Culture, and Identity in Postwar Los Angeles." *Aztlan* 23(1):15–32.

Babcock, R., and F. Bosselman. 1973. *Exclusionary Zoning.* New York: Praeger.

Baden, B., and D. Coursey. 1997. "The Locality of Waste Sites within the City of Chicago: A Demographic, Social and Economic Analysis." Working paper 97-2. University of Chicago, Irving B. Harris Graduate School of Public Policy Studies.

Banks, F. 1956. "An Industry Puts Up $190,000,000." *Midwinter: Los Angeles Times 75th Anniversary,* January 3, pt. I, 63–64.

Been, V. 1993. "What's Fairness Got to Do with It? Environmental Justice and the Siting of Locally Undesirable Land Uses." *Cornell Law Review* 78:1001–85.

———. 1995. "Analyzing Evidence of Environmental Justice." *Journal of Land Use and Environmental Law* 11(1):1–36.

Berry, B. J. L., ed. 1977. *The Social Burdens of Environmental Pollution: A Comparative Metropolitan Data Source.* Cambridge, MA: Ballinger.

Blumberg, L., and B. Gottlieb. 1989. "Saying No to Mass Burn." *Environmental Action,* January/February, 28–30.

Boer, J., J. Sadd, M. Pastor Jr., and L. Snyder. 1997. "Is There Environmental Racism? The Demographics of Hazardous Waste in Los Angeles County." *Social Science Quarterly* 78(4):793–810.

Boerner, C., and T. Lambert. 1994. "Environmental Justice?" Policy Study 21. Center for the Study of American Business, St. Louis, MO.

Bowden, T., and D. Mayborn. 1939. "Confidentiality Report of a Survey in Metropolitan Los Angeles, California. For the Division of Research and Statistics. Home Owners Loan Corporation. Records Relating to the City Survey Files, 1935–40." Record group 95, box 101. National Archives and Records Administration, College Park, MD.

Bowen, W., M. Salling, K. Haynes, and E. Cyran. 1995. "Toward Environmental Justice: Spatial Equity in Ohio and Cleveland." *Annals of the Association of American Geographers* 85(4):641–63.

Brill, A. 1996. "Lakewood, California: 'Tomorrowland' at 40." In *Rethinking Los Angeles*, ed. M. J. Dear, H. E. Schockman, and G. Hise, 97–112. Thousand Oaks, CA: Sage.

Bullard, R. D. 1990. *Dumping in Dixie*. Boulder, CO: Westview.

———. 1996. "Environmental Justice: It's More Than Waste Facility Siting." *Social Science Quarterly* 77(3):493–99.

Burke, L. 1993. "Environmental Equity in Los Angeles." Master's thesis, University of California, Santa Barbara, Department of Geography.

California Department of Employment, Research and Statistics Division. 1952. *Community Labor Market Surveys*. California Historical Society, L.A. Area Chamber of Commerce Collection, Special Collections, box 71, University of Southern California, Los Angeles.

———. 1960. *Community Labor Market Surveys*. California Historical Society, L.A. Area Chamber of Commerce Collection, Special Collections, box 71, University of Southern California, Los Angeles.

Cheng, L., and P. Yang. 1996. "Asians: The 'Model Minority' Deconstructed." In *Ethnic Los Angeles*, ed. R. Waldinger and M. Bozorgmehr, 305–44. New York: Russell Sage Foundation.

City of Los Angeles, Department of City Planning. 1988. "Southeast Los Angeles District Plan."

Cohan, C. 1956. "Southland Building at New Peak." *Midwinter: Los Angeles Times 75th Anniversary*, January 3, pt. I, 44–45.

Cohen, P. 1992. "'It's Racism What Dunnit': Hidden Narratives in Theories of Racism." In *"Race," Culture and Difference*, ed. J. Donald and A. Rattansi, 62–103. London: Sage.

Colten, C. 1986. "Industrial Wastes in Southeast Chicago: Production and Disposal, 1870–1970." *Environmental Review* 10:93–106.

Cordoba Corporation. 1987. "Final Application, Eastside Employment Incentive Area." City of Los Angeles, Community Development Department.

Crenshaw, K., N. Gotanda, G. Peller, and K. Thomas, eds. 1995. *Critical Race Theory: The Key Writings That Formed the Movement*. New York: New Press.

Cutter, S. 1995. "Race, Class and Environmental Justice." *Progress in Human Geography* 19:107–18.

Cutter, S., and W. Solecki. 1996. "Setting Environmental Justice in Space and Place: Acute and Chronic Airborne Toxic Releases in the Southeastern U.S." *Urban Geography* 17(5):380–99.

Cutter, S., and M. Tiefenbacher. 1991. "Chemical Hazards in Urban America." *Urban Geography* 12(5):417–30.

Davis, M. 1992. *City of Quartz: Excavating the Future in Los Angeles*. New York: Vintage.

Dear, M. J., and S. Flusty. 1998. "Postmodern Urbanism." *Annals of the Association of American Geographers* 88(1):50–72.

deGraff, L. B. 1970. "The City of Black Angels: Emergence of the Los Angeles Ghetto, 1890–1930." *Pacific Historical Review* 39(3):323–52.

Delgado, R. 1995. *The Rodrigo Chronicles: Conversations about America and Race*. New York: New York University Press.

Devine, P. 1989. "Stereotypes and Prejudice: Their Automatic and Controlled Components." *Personality and Social Psychology* 56(1):5–18.

Doti, L., and L. Schweikart. 1989. "Financing the Postwar Housing Boom in Phoenix and Los Angeles, 1945–1960." *Pacific Historical Review* 58(2):173–91.

Ebner, M. 1987. "Re-reading Suburban America: Urban Population Deconcentration, 1810–1980." In *American Urbanism: A Historiographical Review*, ed. H. Gillette Jr. and Z. L. Miller, 227–42. Westport, CT: Greenwood.

Edsall, T., and M. Edsall. 1991. *Chain Reaction*. New York: W. W. Norton.

Fanon, F. 1967. *Black Skins, White Masks*. New York: Grove.

Federal Home Loan Bank Board, Division of Research and Statistics. 1939. Residential Security Maps, secs. 1–4. Record group 95, box 101. National Archives and Records Administration, College Park, MD.

Fishman, R. 1987. *Bourgeois Utopias: The Rise and Fall of Suburbia*. New York: Basic Books.

Flanigan, J. 1999. "Downey Takes Lead to Revive Gateway Cities." *Los Angeles Times*, June 16, C1, C4.

Fogelson, R. 1993. *The Fragmented Metropolis: Los Angeles, 1850–1930*. Berkeley: University of California Press.

Frammolino, R. 1999. "Report Lists L.A. Schools That Pose Toxic Risks." *Los Angeles Times*, June 26, B1, B5.

Frankenberg, R. 1993. *White Women, Race Matters: The Social Construction of Whiteness*. Minneapolis: University of Minnesota.

Fredrickson, G. 1981. *White Supremacy: A Comparative Study of Race in American and South African History*. New York: Oxford University Press.

Garreau, J. 1991. *Edge City: Life on the New Frontier*. New York: Doubleday.

Garrow, P., J. Lau, and S. Loong. 1987. *Urban Ecology and Design for the Eastside Incentive Area*. Los Angeles: Department of City Planning.

Gold, M. 1999. "A School, Factories and Plenty of Fear." *Los Angeles Times*, February 27, A1, A20–21.

Goldberg, D. T. 1993. *Racist Culture: Philosophy and the Politics of Meaning*. Cambridge, MA: Blackwell.

Goldman, B. 1996. "What Is the Future of Environmental Justice?" *Antipode* 28(2):122–41.

Gottdiener, M., and M. Kephart. 1995. "The Multinucleated Metropolitan Region: A Comparative Analysis." In *Postsuburban California: The Transformation of Orange County since World War II*, ed. R. Kling, S. Olin, and M. Poster, 31–54. Berkeley: University of California Press.

Guhathakurta, S., and M. Wichert. 1998. "Who Pays for Growth in the City of Phoenix: An Equity-Based Perspective on Suburbanization." *Urban Affairs Review* 33(6):813–38.

Harris, C. 1993. "Whiteness as Property." *Harvard Law Review* 106(8):1709–91.

Harvey, D. 1985. *The Urbanization of Capital*. Baltimore: Johns Hopkins University Press.

Heiman, M. 1990. "From 'Not in My Backyard!' to 'Not in Anybody's Backyard!': Grassroots Challenges to Hazardous Waste Facility Siting." *American Planning Association Journal* 56:359–62.

Hise, G. 1993. "Home Building and Industrial Decentralization in Los Angeles: The Roots of the Postwar Urban Region." *Journal of Urban History* 19(2):95–125.

———. 1997. *Magnetic Los Angeles: Planning the Twentieth-Century Metropolis*. Baltimore: Johns Hopkins University Press.

———. 2001. "Constructing 'Nature's Workshop': Industrial Districts and Urban Expansion in Southern California, 1910–1950." *Journal of Historical Geography* 27(1):74–92.

Horne, G. 1995. *Fire This Time: The Watts Uprising and the 1960s*. Charlottesville: University of Virginia Press.

Ignatiev, N. 1995. *How the Irish Became White*. New York: Routledge.

Jackson, K. 1980. "Race, Ethnicity, and Real Estate Appraisal: The Home Owners Loan Corporation and the Federal Housing Administration." *Journal of Urban History* 6(4):419–52.

Johnson, J., and C. Roseman. 1990. "Increasing Black Outmigration from Los Angeles: The Role of Household Dynamics and Kinship Systems." *Annals of the Association of American Geographers* 80(2):205–22.

Kaplan, K. 1998. "Tech Coast: Entrepreneurs and Officials Seek to Ride an Innovation Wave to Rival That of Silicon Valley." *Los Angeles Times*, March 9, D1, D12.

Kay, J. 1994. "California's Endangered Communities of Color." In *Unequal Protection: Environmental Justice and Communities of Color*, ed. R. D. Bullard, 155–88. San Francisco: Sierra Club Books.

Kirschenman, J., and K. Neckerman. 1991. "We'd Love to Hire Them, But . . . The Meaning of Race for Employers." In *The Urban Underclass*, ed. C. Jencks and P. E. Peterson, 203–32. Washington, DC: Brookings Institution.

Kling, R., S. Olin, and M. Poster. 1995. "The Emergence of Postsuburbia: An Introduction." In *Postsuburban California: The Transformation of Orange County since World War II*, ed. R. Kling, S. Olin, and M. Poster, 1–30. Berkeley: University of California Press.

Krieg, E. 1995. "A Socio-historical Interpretation of Toxic Waste Sites: The Case of Greater Boston." *American Journal of Economics and Sociology* 54(1):1–14.

Law, R., J. Wolch, and L. Takahashi. 1993. "Defense-less Territory: Workers, Communities, and the Decline of Military Production in Los Angeles." *Environment and Planning: Government and Policy* 11:291–315.

Lawrence, C. 1987. "The Id, the Ego and Equal Protection: Reckoning with Unconscious Racism." *Stanford Law Review* 39:317–88.

Lipsitz, G. 1998. *The Possessive Investment in Whiteness*. Philadelphia: Temple University Press.

Lockheed Aircraft Corporation. 1953. "168 Communities Contribute to Lockheed Leadership." *Los Angeles Times Annual Midwinter*, January 2. California Historical Society, L.A. Area Chamber of Commerce Collection, University of Southern California, Los Angeles.

Los Angeles Central Manufacturing District. 1923. *Central Manufacturing District of Los Angeles*. California Historical Society, L.A. Area Chamber of Commerce Collection, University of Southern California, Los Angeles.

Los Angeles Chamber of Commerce. 1964. *The Researcher: 1964 Statistical Summary*. California Historical Society, L.A. Area Chamber of Commerce Collection, box 64, University of Southern California, Los Angeles.

Los Angeles Chamber of Commerce, Industrial Department. 1925. *Industrial Communities of Los Angeles Metropolitan Area*. California Historical Society, L.A. Area Chamber of Commerce Collection, Special Collections, University of Southern California, Los Angeles.

———. 1926. *Facts about Industrial Los Angeles: Nature's Workshop*. California Historical Society, L.A. Area Chamber of Commerce Collection, Special Collections, University of Southern California, Los Angeles.

———. 1929. *General Industrial Report of Los Angeles County, CA and Surrounding Communities*. California Historical Society, L.A. Area Chamber of Commerce Collection, Special Collections, University of Southern California, Los Angeles.

———. 1934. *General Industrial Report of Los Angeles County, California*. California Historical Society, L.A. Area Chamber of Commerce Collection, Special Collections, University of Southern California, Los Angeles.

Los Angeles Design Action Planning Team. 1990. "Boyle Heights, Los Angeles." Los Angeles City Archive, Planning Department.

Los Angeles Times. 1965. *Los Angeles 1965: Market and Media.* California Historical Society, L.A. Area Chamber of Commerce Collection, box 118, University of Southern California, Los Angeles.

Malnic, E., and G. Ramos. 1997. "Explosion Kills 4, Injures 25 at L.A. Toy Factory." *Los Angeles Times,* November 6, A1, A30–31.

Massey, D. B. 1994. *Space, Place, and Gender.* Minneapolis: University of Minnesota Press.

Massey, D. S., and N. A. Denton. 1993. *American Apartheid: Segregation and the Making of the Underclass.* Cambridge, MA: Harvard University Press.

McGurty, E. 1995. "The Construction of Environmental Justice: Warren County North Carolina." Ph.D. diss. University of Illinois, Urbana-Champaign.

Miller, G. J. 1981. *Cities by Contract: The Politics of Municipal Incorporation.* Cambridge: MIT Press.

Mohai, P., and B. Bryant. 1992. "Environmental Racism: Reviewing the Evidence." In *Race and the Incidence of Environmental Hazards: A Time for Discourse,* ed. B. Bryant and P. Mohai, 163–246. Boulder, CO: Westview.

Morales, R., and P. Ong. 1993. "The Illusion of Progress: Latinos in Los Angeles." In *Latinos in a Changing U.S. Economy: Comparative Perspectives on Growing Inequality,* ed. R. Morales and F. Bonilla, 55–84. Newbury Park, CA: Sage.

Morrison, P., and R. Lowry. 1994. "A Riot of Color: The Demographic Setting." In *The Los Angeles Riots,* ed. M. Baldassare, 19–46. Boulder, CO: Westview.

Myrdal, G. 1944. *An American Dilemma: The Negro Problem and Modern Democracy.* New York: Harper & Row.

Newton, M. 1998. "L.A. to Get $3.3 Million for Pollution Cleanup." *Los Angeles Times,* March 18, B1, B8.

Oliver, M., J. Johnson, and W. Farrell. 1993. "Anatomy of a Rebellion: A Political-Economic Analysis." In *Reading Rodney King, Reading Urban Uprising,* ed. R. Gooding-Williams, 117–41. New York: Routledge.

Oliver, M. L., and T. M. Shapiro. 1995. *Black Wealth, White Wealth: A New Perspective on Racial Inequality.* New York: Routledge.

Omi, M. 1992. "Shifting the Blame: Racial Ideology and Politics in the Post–Civil Rights Era." *Critical Sociology* 18:77–98.

Ong, P., and E. Blumenberg. 1993. "An Unnatural Trade-Off: Latinos and Environmental Justice." In *Latinos in a Changing U.S. Economy: Comparative Perspectives on Growing Inequality,* ed. R. Morales and F. Bonilla, 207–25. Newbury Park, CA: Sage.

Parson, D. 1984. "Organized Labor and the Housing Question: Public Housing, Suburbanization and Urban Renewal." *Society and Space* 1:75–86.

Perlin, S., R. Setzer, J. Creason, and K. Sexton. 1995. "Distribution of Industrial Air Emissions by Income and Race in the United States: An Approach Using the Toxic Release Inventory." *Environmental Science Technology* 29(1): 69–80.

Phelan, T., and M. Schneider. 1996. "Race, Ethnicity, and Class in American Suburbs." *Urban Affairs Review* 31(5):659–80.

Pulido, L. 1996. "A Critical Review of the Methodology of Environmental Racism Research." *Antipode* 28(2):142–59.

Pulido, L., S. Sidawi, and R. Vos. 1996. "An Archaeology of Environmental Racism in Los Angeles." *Urban Geography* 17(5):419–39.

Quadagno, J. 1994. *The Color of Welfare.* New York: Oxford University Press.

Roediger, D. R. 1991. *The Wages of Whiteness: Race and the Making of the American Working Class*. New York: Verso.

Romo, R. 1983. *East Los Angeles: History of a Barrio*. Austin: University of Texas Press.

Roseman, C., and S. Lee. 1998. "Linked and Independent African American Migration from Los Angeles." *Professional Geographer* 50(2):204–14.

Sabagh, G., and M. Bozorgmehr. 1996. "Population Change: Immigration and Ethnic Transformation." In *Ethnic Los Angeles*, ed. R. Waldinger and M. Bozorgmehr, 79–107. New York: Russell Sage Foundation.

Sadd, J., M. Pastor, J. Boer, and L. Snyder. 1999. "Every Breath You Take . . . The Demographics of Point Source Air Pollution in Southern California." *Economic Development Quarterly* 13(2):107–23.

Sahagun, L. 1989. "Toxic Neighbors: Measure Would Force Metal Platers out of Residential Areas." *Los Angeles Times*, August 28, Metro sec., 1, 6.

Sanchez, G. 1993. *Becoming Mexican American: Ethnicity, Culture and Identity in Chicano Los Angeles, 1900–1945*. New York: Oxford.

Schiesl, M. J. 1995. "Designing the Model Community: The Irvine Company and Suburban Development, 1950–88." In *Postsuburban California: The Transformation of Orange County since World War II*, ed. R. Kling, S. Olin, and M. Poster, 55–91. Berkeley: University of California Press.

Scott, A. J. 1990. *Metropolis: From Division of Labor to Urban Form*. Berkeley: University of California Press.

———. 1996a. "High-Technology Industrial Development in the San Fernando Valley and Ventura County: Observations on Economic Growth and the Evolution of Urban Form." In *The City: Los Angeles and Urban Theory at the End of the Twentieth Century*, ed. A. J. Scott and E. W. Soja, 276–310. Berkeley: University of California Press.

———. 1996b. "The Manufacturing Economy: Ethnic and Gender Divisions of Labor." In *Ethnic Los Angeles*, ed. R. Waldinger and M. Bozorgmehr, 215–44. New York: Russell Sage Foundation.

Sharpe, W., and L. Wallock. 1994. "Bold New City or Built Up Burb? Redefining Contemporary Suburbia." *American Quarterly* 46(1):1–30.

Smith, N. 1993. "Homeless/Global: Scaling Places." In *Mapping the Futures: Local Cultures, Global Change*, ed. J. Bird, B. Curtis, T. Putnam, G. Robertson, and L. Tickner, 87–119. London: Routledge.

Soja, E. W. 1989. *Postmodern Geographies: The Reassertion of Space in Critical Social Theory*. New York: Verso.

———. 1996. "Los Angeles, 1965–1992: From Crisis-Generated Restructuring to Restructuring-Generated Crisis." In *The City: Los Angeles and Urban Theory at the End of the Twentieth Century*, ed. A. J. Scott and E. W. Soja, 426–62. Berkeley: University of California Press.

Szasz, A., and M. Meuser. 1997. "Environmental Inequalities: Literature Review and Proposals for New Directions in Research and Theory." *Current Sociology* 45(3):99–120.

Szasz, A., M. Meuser, H. Aronson, and H. Fukarai. 1993. "The Demographics of Proximity to Toxic Releases: The Case of Los Angeles County." Paper presented at the meetings of the American Sociological Association, Miami, FL.

United Church of Christ, Commission for Racial Justice. 1987. *Toxic Wastes and Race in the United States*. New York: United Church of Christ.

U.S. General Accounting Office. 1984. *Siting of Hazardous Waste Landfills and Their Correlation with Racial and Economic Status of Surrounding Communities.* Washington, DC: U.S.GAO.

Walker, R. 1981. "A Theory of Suburbanization: Capitalism and the Construction of Urban Space in the United States." In *Urbanization and Urban Planning in Capitalist Society,* ed. M. J. Dear and A. J. Scott, 383–429. New York: Methuen.

Warren, W. 1986–87. "Maps: A Spatial Approach to Japanese American Communities in Los Angeles." *Amerasia* 13(2):137–51.

Weeks, P. 1963. "700 March for Integration in Torrance Tract." *Los Angeles Times,* June 30, 1, 12.

Zimmerman, R. 1993. "Social Equity and Environmental Risk." *Risk Analysis* 13(6):649–66.

Zoning Map Company. 1930. *The Los Angeles Zoning Atlas.* California Historical Society, L.A. Area Chamber of Commerce Collection, Special Collections, box 66, University of Southern California, Los Angeles.

3 | Urban Sprawl, Racial Separation, and Federal Housing Policy

Carolyn B. Aldana and Gary A. Dymski

Increasingly, scholars are viewing federal policies as playing a critical role in the creation of urban sprawl and racial segregation in U.S. metropolitan areas (see, e.g., Nivola 1999). This causative role of the federal government is seen most clearly in past policies, such as federal support for interstate construction and Federal Housing Administration (FHA) housing loans in the 1950s. These two policies interacted to facilitate the movement of whites to new suburban enclaves while denying home-ownership opportunities to minorities. But while this historical role is now readily acknowledged, the continuing role of federal policy in the ongoing processes of urban sprawl and in evolving patterns of racial separation and integration has received little attention and is not well understood.

In this chapter, we take up this challenge by analyzing patterns in Southern California, a place that is considered both a capital of sprawl and a bastion of racial tension. We argue that both historically and now, federal policies have interacted with housing market forces to exacerbate the racial separation, income segmentation, and urban sprawl that have come to define this region's growth. If these results of federal policy were intentional in the past, they are perhaps unintended today; nonetheless, federal housing-related policies remain nonneutral with respect to both urban sprawl and the degree of racial residential separation.

Our view that federal housing-related policies remain an active element in shaping the urban landscape is not universally shared. Many analysts regard federal policies and market forces as distinct, even as substitutes or competitors. For example, some scholars assert that a government-led system for financing mainstream housing and for providing low-income housing was replaced after 1980 by a market-driven system (see, e.g., Wachter 1990; Diamond and Lea 1992; Downs 1985). The inference is that the elimination of wasteful subsidies permitted the emergence of a more efficient housing allocation mechanism. This perspective embodies the idea that once government gets out of the way, spatial development can more clearly reflect consumer and business preferences.

The idea that preferences underlie observed outcomes is a powerful theme in much writing on urban spatial patterns. A vast literature, spawned by Becker (1971), explains how racial discrimination in housing and other markets arises from some people's "taste" for being with their own kind. There can be little doubt that personal discrimination of this sort remains a key source of racial inequality in the contemporary United States (see Ondrich, Stricker, and Yinger 1998). More recently, Gordon and Richardson (2000) have argued that suburban sprawl is an optimal urban form because consumers like it.

Economists' widespread use of preference-based models, together with the reduced role of government allocation and regulation, can suggest that any continued patterns of urban sprawl and racial separation observed today are preference based and in some sense "optimal." One central point of the contributions to this volume is that this view is untenable. The apparently microeconomic context of housing choice is embedded in the societal dynamics surrounding the construction and maintenance of the urban built environment, and these dynamics reflect political decisions and influences at many levels. This means that urban sprawl cannot be interpreted as simply reflecting consumer "choices." It also means that racial preferences per se cannot explain residential patterns of racial segregation (Clark 1993). Other factors are also involved, and federal housing policy is one of those contributing factors.

Indeed, federal housing-related policies have provided the context in which racial separation and urban sprawl have arisen and persisted. Market forces and federal policies together have generated the urban landscape—both in the earlier era of heavier regulation and in the deregulated era of today.

In the next section, we show how federal home-ownership and lower-income housing policies contributed directly to urban sprawl and racial separation before 1990. We then discuss federal policies and market processes in the 1990s. FHA housing finance receives special attention due to its unique role, past and present, in Southern California's residential process.

Federal Home-Ownership Policies and Racial Spatial Inequality through 1990

Housing affordability has been a chronic problem in Southern California. Carey McWilliams (1973) observed a half century ago that the region's residents were caught between continually rising land and housing prices and chronically depressed wage levels. This housing affordability problem has not lessened with time. One measure of housing affordability is the ratio of median rent to median income: a ratio of 30 percent or more is a benchmark indicator of unaffordable housing. In 1990, about half the census tracts in Southern California had (median-to-median) ratios higher than 30 percent; Figure 3.1 shows the situation by 1999. Further, the unaffordable-housing threshold is more likely to be crossed as income levels fall.

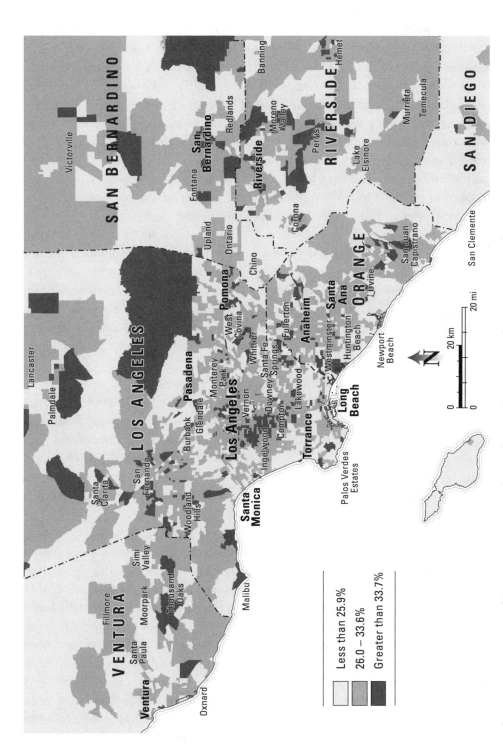

Figure 3.1. Percentage of income spent on rent in Southern California, 1999 (from census tracts).

Racial exclusion has also been a fixture in the region since eastern settlers first came to California (Almaguer 1994). Exclusionary zoning and rampant discrimination were inescapable in the first half of the twentieth century. Consider the case of Los Angeles. These practices made 95 percent of available Los Angeles residential areas off-limits for minorities as of World War II, forcing minorities into isolated and marginal spaces such as East Los Angeles, Watts, and Little Tokyo (Dymski and Veitch 1996). Eventually, political agitation by local leaders such as Ernest Roybal, together with the pressure of growing Hispanic, African American, and Asian American populations and the changing parameters of federal policy as detailed below, forced open more areas. East Los Angeles broadened to encompass Lincoln Heights on the west and Whittier on the east. As Horne (1995) documents, the Watts uprising in 1965 resulted in the definition of "South-Central Los Angeles" as a minority space, including neighborhoods that previously were primarily white.

After the Watts uprising and the end of racial covenants because of changing state and federal policy, racial exclusion was inverted: no longer did local political jurisdictions and associations keep minorities out through explicit "white only" policies; instead, some spaces were informally designated as areas in which whites were no longer expected to live. Several Los Angeles County cities, notably Compton and Inglewood, became known as centers of minority population. Through the 1990 U.S. Census, the segregation indices for the city of Los Angeles rivaled those of other U.S. cities (Denton 1994).

The interaction of housing affordability and racial exclusion also created distinctive racial and social fault lines in the other counties of Southern California. The latest development trends involve planned cities, often set at a far remove from other urban spaces—examples are Temecula and Murrieta in Riverside County, Santa Clarita in Los Angeles County, and virtually the entire emerging residential grid of Ventura County. These new growth areas not only significantly worsen the region's urban sprawl pattern, they also largely deepen the checkerboard pattern of racial/income polarization in the region.

How did federal housing-related policies affect these patterns? Here we focus on the period after World War II. Immediately after the war, federal housing policies privileged white households seeking housing in largely white neighborhoods (Isenberg 2001). Minority households and minority and lower-income areas received virtually no federal housing support. There were two primary channels for federal housing policy. One channel involved federal efforts to build or subsidize units for lower-income households. This program was extremely small prior to the 1960s, and it was linked to slum clearance. The second and larger channel involved efforts to encourage "mainstream" home ownership. A key here was FHA mortgage underwriting, a program set up in the 1930s to stabilize and subsidize mortgage lenders; a smaller Veterans Administration (VA) mortgage program was also established after World War II. Another strand of this policy consisted of tax expenditures: mortgage interest and property taxes were made deductible on federal income taxes. Conventional and VA/FHA mortgage loans alike are eligible for this tax deduction. The criteria for deciding which homes would qualify for FHA underwriting were explicitly racist (Squires 1992; Vandell 1995). Given that more than half the home-purchase loans made in the 1950s in Southern California were FHA loans, and that VA and other mortgage lending largely followed FHA criteria, federal tax expenditures for mortgage interest, property taxes, and mortgage underwriting commitments flowed almost exclusively to residential areas that excluded nonwhite households. The criteria explicitly discouraging FHA mortgage underwriting in areas with minority residents remained in force through the mid-1960s.

These two channels of federal housing policies shaped the growth of Southern California housing markets in the 1950s and early 1960s. Public housing units built in these years were almost entirely located in lower-income, heavily minority areas. Meanwhile, FHA and VA housing fueled the growth of Southern California's residential grid during this period of explicitly racist underwriting practices. Minorities were largely restricted to inner-core areas, because of the location of explicitly discriminatory compacts, because of prevailing housing-industry practices, and because of location decisions about public and subsidized housing units. FHA/VA loans were made with greater frequency in suburban than in inner-city areas, so these federal policies promoted racial separation. And because population pressures pushed the suburbs ever outward, while expanding the space ceded to minorities, these policies also underwrote urban sprawl.[1]

The explicit federal role in residential racial discrimination ended in the 1960s. The Civil Rights Act of 1963 and widespread episodes of urban unrest led to the War on Poverty, which included a wide array of social programs and several housing initiatives. In particular, federal expenditures on public housing were expanded dramatically, and various federal tax incentives for low-income housing were put into place. Continuing the established postwar trend, subsidized housing projects were located disproportionately in inner-core, heavily minority areas. Urban renewal programs targeted these same areas, clearing out dilapidated buildings and housing units and destabilizing inner-core neighborhoods. Consequently, downward pressure was exerted on the value of minority-area housing.[2] These patterns played out in the central-city and older inner-suburban areas of Los Angeles County. Low-income housing programs in the 1970s were also concentrated in these areas, in precisely the "marginalized" areas that minorities and lower-income people have occupied throughout the twentieth century.[3] This same pattern held in the region's other counties.

Meanwhile, the changing fabric of federal laws and policies, including the Fair Housing Act of 1968, together with sustained pressure by community activists, forced an end to overt racial discrimination in FHA policy. The federal commitment to access to housing was broadened with the passage of the Home Mortgage Disclosure Act in 1975 and the Community Reinvestment Act in 1977. These acts, respectively, require lenders to disclose the locations of their residential real estate loans and mandate banks and savings and loan associations to meet credit and banking needs throughout their market areas. In effect, these two acts broadened the scope of federal housing policy; the federal government now has regulatory authority to ensure that home mortgage loans are being made available to applicants in lower-income and minority areas, and that minority applicants also have equitable access to home mortgages.

These social and political reforms led to the reinvention of the FHA as a financing vehicle aimed at first-time home buyers, a disproportionate number of whom are minorities. FHA underwriting, however, was no longer the predominant financing vehicle for home purchases. Conventional loans—not supported by FHA underwriting or bound by FHA rules regarding property appraisal—became the primary housing-finance mechanism. And conventional loans were used to support "white flight" to new suburban areas surrounding the central cities. Indeed, the cycle of suburban sprawl and white flight that was originally underwritten by biased FHA policies remained the definitive model of urban growth for most U.S. cities. However, conventional loans replaced FHA loans as the workhorse of this expansion; conventional loans result in tax expenditures for mortgage interest and property taxes just as FHA loans do.

There is no doubt that FHA loans swung dramatically toward inner-core and heavily minority areas. Home Mortgage Disclosure Act (HMDA) data for Los Angeles County during the 1981–89 period provide some insight into the balance between the spatial distribution of FHA and conventional loans. As a measure of this distribution, Los Angeles County's census tracts are first ranked by median income, from highest to lowest. These rank-ordered tracts are then sorted into five quintiles of equal size, and statistics on the relative number of FHA and conventional loans are computed for each quintile. This procedure shows that FHA loans constituted only 0.82 percent of all 1981–89 home-purchase and refinancing loans in the highest-income quintile, but 4.8 percent of all such loans in the lowest-income quintile. When the same procedure is used to rank census tracts by their percentage minority populations, the distribution of FHA loans is similarly unbalanced: FHA loans constitute 0.95 percent of all home-purchase and refinancing loans in the lowest-minority quintile, but 6.3 percent in the highest-minority quintile.[4]

What is the net effect of these federal housing-related policies on urban sprawl in Southern California through 1990? In principle, there are contrary forces at work. The reorientation of FHA housing and expansion of federal investments in low-income housing in inner-core areas on one hand partially compensated for the suburban bias of home owner tax expenditures on the other. Data on lower-income housing expenditures are not available, but Table 3.1 presents some estimates of 1990 tax benefits in five Southern California counties.[5] The second column in the table contains estimates of home owners' mortgage interest and property tax deductions in 1990, by county. The next two columns show the impacts of these tax benefits on urban sprawl in each county through comparisons of the percentage of 1990 housing units and 1990 home-ownership tax benefits in inner-core areas. Inner-core areas consist of those tracts in which the median year for housing unit construction is 1960 or earlier. These figures clearly show that inner-core areas have systematically higher shares of housing units than of federal home owner tax benefits.

The data in Table 3.1 suggest that outlying areas receive a disproportionate share of home owner tax expenditures, indirectly supporting urban sprawl. No figures on federal lower-income housing expenditures are available, but undoubtedly these are far less than those for home owners. The symbiotic interaction of market and federal policies is evident: location decisions for federally subsidized housing, together with historical patterns of bias in FHA housing, reinforced a dynamic of poverty concentration and racial separation that itself fueled further suburban flight and expansion of the urban fringe.

What, then, are the net effects of federal housing-related policies and market dynamics on racial segregation in Southern California prior to 1990? The 1990 U.S. Census can be regarded as a compendium of net effects through that point in time. According to 1990 census data, all the Southern California counties have larger percentages of white households and home owners in suburban areas than in inner-core areas. Throughout the region, blacks and Latinos are far more likely to live in inner-core areas, with Los Angeles, Orange, and San Bernardino Counties showing the largest gaps; Asian Americans are more evenly distributed.

Federal Housing Policies and Access to Housing Credit since 1990

What has changed in this picture since 1990? We consider three dimensions of federal housing policy in this section: subsidized lower-income housing, home owner tax expenditures, and FHA housing. We then consider evidence concerning access to housing credit, relying on data collected under the Home Mortgage Disclosure Act.

After a hiatus in the 1980s and earlier 1990s, the U.S. Department of Housing and Urban Development began making comprehensive data on the location of subsidized housing units available to the public in the late 1990s. Figure 3.2 depicts the distribution of subsidized lower-income housing in the Los Angeles region in 1997 and 1998. These spatial patterns clearly indicate the concentration of subsidized housing units in lower-income and heavily minority areas. The fact that these units are disproportionately occupied by lower-income and minority residents reinforces income polarization and racial separation in the region. And as Massey and Denton (1993) have shown, concentrating low-income households in areas with high unemployment and low educational attainment reinforces these households' separation from access to social and personal resources.

Table 3.1. Estimated federal expenditures for owner-occupied and assisted housing, Southern California, 1990

County	1990 property tax and mortgage interest tax deductions ($)	Percentage of 1990 housing units in inner-core areas	Percentage of 1990 home-ownership-related tax deductions in inner-core areas
Los Angeles	3,670,843,029	29.2	17.1
Orange	1,547,740,910	13.8	8.5
Riverside	675,332,801	8.2	6.0
San Bernardino	664,847,100	18.1	11.0
Ventura	453,503,479	14.3	7.5

Source: Authors' calculations based on data from the Federal Financial Institutions Council and U.S. Census data.

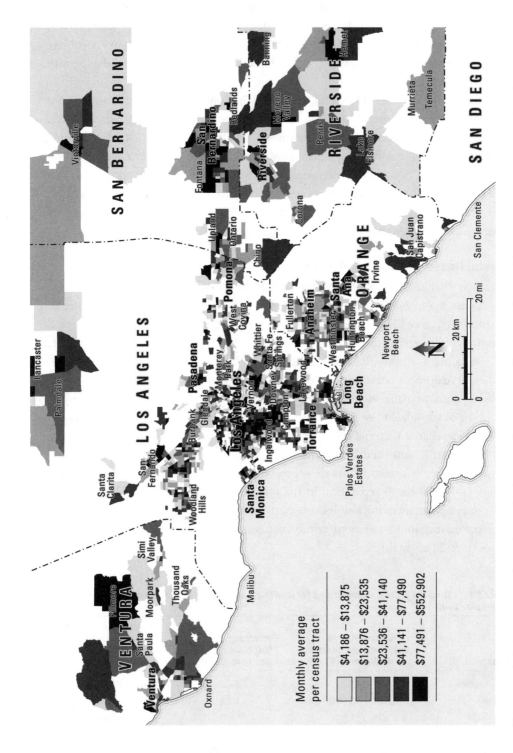

Figure 3.2. U.S. Department of Housing and Urban Development spending in Southern California, 1997–98. Areas in white depict no data.

Table 3.2 depicts federal lower-income units and dollar outlays in 1998 more systematically. The tracts in each county are divided into quartiles based on the percentage of their populations in poverty in 1990; thus the first line of data for each county in the table depicts that 25 percent of all census tracts with the lowest percentage of 1990 population in poverty, and so on. The four columns presenting data on federal lower-income housing outlays show that in three of the four counties listed, lower-income units and outlays are highest in the quartile with the highest-poverty population. The exception is Orange County, in which lower-income subsidized housing is spread evenly throughout the third and fourth poverty quartiles.

This brings us to federal home owner tax expenditures, which are shown by poverty quartile in the last two columns of Table 3.2. This table depicts the distribution of 1998 mortgage interest tax deductions for 1997 home purchases. As might be expected, the flow of mortgage interest deductions is disproportionately weighted toward the lowest-poverty (i.e., highest-income) quartile. Further, the imbalance in the locus of federal dollars by program type is remarkable. In Los Angeles County, the lowest-poverty quartile receives the bulk of the federal tax expenditures and outlays shown here in the form of mortgage deductions; the highest-poverty quartile has a larger volume of subsidized housing expenditures than of mortgage deductions.

Table 3.2. Distribution of federal housing expenditures in Southern California, 1998

Percentage of population in poverty, 1990	Lower-income housing units		Outlays		Morgage interest tax deduction 1998 home purchases	
	Number	%	$	%	$	%
Los Angeles County						
3.5	6,288	5.9	3,265,705	5.8	166,813,393	45.3
7.8	15,587	14.5	7,969,107	14.3	103,968,560	28.2
15.2	32,361	30.2	17,752,259	31.8	63,858,566	17.3
31.4	53,014	49.4	26,896,140	48.1	33,427,102	9.1
Total	107,250	100.0	55,883,211	100.0	368,067,621	100.0
Orange County						
2.2	2,145	12.7	1,120,588	12.8	82,644,786	47.1
4.4	1,705	10.1	970,564	11.1	36,774,948	20.9
7.6	6,809	40.3	3,327,384	38.0	38,956,575	22.2
18.6	6,254	37.0	3,329,515	38.0	17,227,644	9.8
Total	16,913	100.0	8,758,051	100.0	175,603,953	100.0
Riverside County						
5.1	1,020	12.4	355,843	11.2	27,701,625	47.0
8.8	2,270	27.7	804,754	25.4	15,016,722	25.5
13.8	2,050	25.0	853,990	26.9	9,959,859	16.9
25.0	2,860	34.9	1,155,865	36.5	6,301,344	10.7
Total	8,200	100.0	3,170,452	100.0	58,979,550	100.0
San Bernardino County						
3.9	1,611	13.9	707,091	13.8	20,488,122	37.9
9.3	2,489	21.5	1,052,405	20.6	15,182,826	28.1
14.9	3,001	26.0	1,392,679	27.3	12,541,983	23.2
30.1	4,462	38.6	1,956,653	38.3	5,884,915	10.9
Total	11,563	100.0	5,108,828	100.0	54,097,846	100.0

Note: Figures are distributed by U.S. Census tract quartiles based on 1990 percentage of population in poverty.

It should be noted that this remarkable result is based solely on the estimated value of mortgage deductions for homes purchased in 1997 alone and thus reflects only a portion of the total interest subsidy. We do not estimate the value of mortgage deduction tax expenditures for homes purchased in previous years; doing so with accuracy would require detailed information on home turnover. Clearly, however, mortgage-based tax expenditures utterly dwarf lower-income subsidies in all Southern California counties.

Table 3.3 also contains some comparative spatial data on federal outlays for home owners and for lower-income housing. Tax expenditures for homes purchased in 1997 with conventional home loans are weighted disproportionately toward suburban areas. In San Bernardino County, for example, note that 18 percent of all housing units are in inner-core tracts (see the third column in the bottom section of the table) versus only 4 percent of tax expenditures on homes purchased with conventional loans in 1997 (second column). Again with the exception of Orange County, a disproportionate amount of federal lower-income housing outlays are made in inner-core areas.

How does the FHA loan program, as reformulated, affect these trends? We have already noted the historical role of FHA loans in promulgating urban sprawl and racial separation, the subsequent efforts to overturn this legacy, and the shift of FHA loans to lower-income and minority areas in the 1980s. Table 3.3 shows that tax expenditures on FHA-financed homes purchased in 1997 were far more heavily weighted toward inner-core areas than were tax expenditures for conventionally financed homes. Overall, throughout the 1990s, the share of FHA loans among all home-purchase loans increased in lower-income and high-minority areas.

The expanded reporting by lenders under the HMDA for loans in the 1990s makes it possible for us to look deeper into the relationship between the FHA loan process

Table 3.3. Estimated federal expenditures for owner-occupied and assisted housing, Southern California, 1998

| County | 1998 mortgage interest tax deductions for homes purchased in 1997 | | 1998 HUD housing assistance expenditures ($) |
	All loans	FHA (% of total)	
Los Angeles	368,067,621	20.3	55,883,211
Orange	175,603,953	13.0	8,748,051
Riverside	58,979,550	43.6	3,170,452
San Bernardino	54,162,292	51.9	5,108,828
Ventura	43,005,819	13.2	3,482,313

| County | Share of federal tax benefits and expenditures in inner-core areas (%) | | |
	1997 conventional home-purchase loans	1997 FHA home-purchase loans	1998 HUD housing assistance expenditures
Los Angeles	22.8	25.8	48.4
Orange	3.2	18.8	17.8
Riverside	4.8	6.0	14.2
San Bernardino	4.0	18.0	41.9
Ventura	6.5	12.9	22.0

Source: Authors' calculations based on data from the Federal Financial Institutions Council and U.S. Census data.

Table 3.4. Total and FHA-approved home loans by race and area, 1992–98

County	All home-purchase loans					All FHA-insured home-purchase loans				
	Total Loans	% White	% Black	% Latino	% Asian	Total Loans	% White	% Black	% Latino	% Asian
Los Angeles	616,705	50.9	6.4	28.6	14.2	54,390	24.5	10.5	61.4	3.6
Inner core	116,858	41.1	9.6	41.5	7.8	12,265	5.7	12.6	80.3	1.4
Suburbs	499,847	53.2	5.6	25.5	15.7	42,125	30.0	9.9	55.9	4.3
Orange	136,957	72.8	1.3	13.4	12.5	28,534	49.0	2.3	43.6	5.1
Inner core	12,042	37.6	1.7	43.8	17.0	6,668	22.1	1.8	71.8	4.2
Suburbs	124,915	76.2	1.2	10.5	12.1	21,866	57.2	2.4	34.9	5.4
Riverside	131,411	65.9	5.5	24.7	3.9	44,324	47.7	6.3	43.1	2.9
Inner core	6,673	59.0	5.3	32.1	3.7	3,281	45.5	5.1	47.1	2.3
Suburbs	124,738	66.3	5.5	24.3	3.9	41,043	47.9	6.4	42.8	2.9
San Bernardino	81,441	52.4	6.8	35.6	5.3	52,208	40.5	8.0	48.6	2.9
Inner core	10,014	34.2	7.8	54.7	3.3	10,921	24.4	8.6	64.5	2.5
Suburbs	71,427	54.9	6.7	32.9	5.6	41,287	44.8	7.8	44.3	3.1
Ventura	37,721	78.5	1.5	15.3	4.7	36,983	30.4	8.9	57.4	3.3
Inner core	3,769	62.5	2.1	31.6	3.8	14,236	28.6	11.4	56.9	3.2
Suburbs	33,952	80.3	1.4	13.5	4.8	22,747	31.6	7.3	57.7	3.4

Source: Home Mortgage Disclosure Act data from the Federal Financial Institutions Examination Council for 1992, 1994, 1996, and 1998.
Note: Loans with no racial identification were excluded from calculations. Percentages reflect row totals.

and racial separation in Southern California. Throughout the region, FHA loans have been made to white applicants in far higher proportions in suburban and upper-income areas than in inner-city and lower-income areas. Table 3.4 illustrates this pattern for home-purchase loans reported under HMDA in the years 1992, 1994, 1996, and 1998. For example, 41 percent of *all* inner-core home-purchase loans in Los Angeles County were made to whites, but whites got just under 6 percent of all FHA-insured loans made in Los Angeles's inner-core area. In suburban tracts, white borrowers got 53 percent of all home-purchase loans, but 30 percent of those that were FHA insured. That is, FHA loans are used disproportionately as a vehicle for permitting white applicants to purchase suburban homes. This same pattern is found in San Bernardino and Ventura Counties.

Table 3.4 contains other evidence of the racialized character of contemporary loan markets. Most notably, the overrepresentation of Latinos among those obtaining FHA-insured loans is remarkable in all of these five counties. Further, Latinos are especially likely to obtain FHA-insured loans in inner-core areas of Los Angeles, San Bernardino, and Ventura Counties. Less distinct trends are found for black borrowers. In the two counties in which they are numerically most significant, Los Angeles and Orange, Asian American borrowers are substantially more likely to use conventional than FHA-insured loans.

This evidence suggests that minority applicants may be at a special disadvantage in seeking out housing in upper-income areas. Whether this is so can be ascertained by an additional empirical test: a probit model that investigates whether those seeking home loans are more or less likely to be approved if they are members of a racial minority. Probit models are a standard regression technique. Social scientists often use such techniques to determine whether an outcome of interest (in this case, the probability of loan approval) is systematically affected by another variable of interest (applicant race) after the values of other variables that may also influence the value of the outcome variable are controlled for. Probit models investigating whether minority applicants are less likely to obtain loans typically control both for variables correlated with applicant creditworthiness and for the economic and social characteristics of the area in which the home is located. The model deployed here includes applicants' income levels and also their loan/income ratios. It also includes several neighborhood variables, such as median income, population density, percentage of home owners, and level of minority residents.

The appendix to this chapter sets out the full model and explains the data used to estimate it. A healthy list of variables is incorporated, suggesting that if applicant race is found to be significant, racial discrimination may exist in this market. At the same time, this model—like most regression models—is incomplete: it does not control for home values, for individual applicants' credit and employment histories, or for wealth levels. This leads to some ambiguity about how to interpret a finding that applicant race has a statistically significant impact on the probability of loan approval. Some argue that if applicants of color are at a statistically significant disadvantage relative to others in equations like those run here, then proof of racial discrimination has been shown. Others are more skeptical, pointing out that racial discrimination is not proven because the "race variables" could be picking up differences in the credit-worthiness of minority and nonminority applicants. The estimated equation may not have a large enough list of variables on applicant characteristics, and some of the excluded variables, if their values vary systematically with race, could influence the value and significance of the (included) race variables.[6]

In part, these differing interpretations arise because experts in this field have different definitions of what racial discrimination is. Some analysts view racial discrimination as a situation in which significant structural differences in resources and opportunities exist between two groups—for example, whites and minorities, or women and men. A broad measure of racial disadvantage is then an appropriate investigative approach.[7]

As of this writing, no regression model yet designed has been accepted as proving the existence of racial discrimination to the satisfaction of all experts. The model used here does not have variables that identify the behaviors of possible racial perpetrators, and thus is not designed to unearth personal discrimination. It is instead a model that tests structural discrimination without sufficient detail to distinguish the specific sources of any racial differentials it identifies. This lack of precision is relatively unimportant here because of how this equation is used in this setting.

Here, we run some tests for the impact of applicant race on access to home-purchase loans in the years 1992, 1994, 1996, and 1998; these equations are run separately for each county. These equations differentiate between conventional and FHA loans, and they also differentiate between inner-core and suburban areas within each county. That is, we use this model to identify differences in the level of racial disadvantage in conventional and FHA Southern California home-loan markets, in different counties, in inner-core and suburban areas, and in different years.

Dymski (1996) ran several similar equations for Southern California counties—without differentiating between conventional and FHA loans or between inner-core and suburban areas—and found that minority applicants are almost invariably at a statistically significant and sizable disadvantage in winning home-purchase loan approval. The results of the probit model constructed for this study are shown in Table 3.5 and in Figures 3.3 and 3.4. Table 3.5 displays the coefficients for African American and Latino/Chicano applicants, by county, year, and area, as well as statistics on the number of applications included in each estimation. The model also incorporated coefficients for Asian Americans and Native Americans. The coefficients for African Americans and Latino/Chicano applicants are shown because they contain the most dramatic results. They indicate that blacks and Latinos are frequently at a statistically significant structural disadvantage in seeking home-purchase loans in Southern California. In Table 3.5, coefficients that are significant at the 1 percent (most robust) level are shown in boldface type and are underlined, those significant at the 5 percent level are shown in boldface, and those significant at the 10 percent level appear in italics. Social scientists often use the 5 percent level as a rough-and-ready cutoff for what variables significantly affect a given outcome variable.

Table 3.5. Loan approvals and denials and applicant race coefficients, home-purchase loans in Southern California, 1992–98

County	Loan approved	Loan denied	Coefficients for African American applicants				Coefficients for Latino/Chicano applicants				Coefficients for white applicants			
			1992	1994	1996	1998	1992	1994	1996	1998	1992	1994	1996	1998
Inner-core conventional loans														
Los Angeles	49,102	15,689	-0.392	-0.376	-0.438	-0.559	-0.008	-0.017	-0.126	-0.093	0.074	0.087	0.128	0.100
Orange	6,123	1,891	-0.745	-0.787	-0.664	-0.695	-0.348	-0.044	-0.246	-0.342	0.257	-0.058	0.011	-0.086
Riverside	1,836	525	-1.048	-1.341	-1.413	-0.798	-0.749	-0.212	-0.181	-0.727	0.738	0.542	0.197	0.649
San Bernardino	3,341	1,549	-0.319	-0.532	-0.303	-0.077	0.028	0.019	0.195	-0.035	0.055	0.086	-0.112	0.024
Ventura	2,664	573	-0.206	13.200	-0.813	-0.743	-0.402	-0.206	-0.252	-0.826	0.366	0.169	0.270	0.790
Suburban conventional loans														
Los Angeles	214,551	51,944	-0.463	-0.547	-0.603	-0.690	-0.180	-0.250	-0.223	-0.388	0.075	0.135	0.122	0.190
Orange	118,435	23,175	-0.594	-0.457	-0.600	-0.705	-0.211	-0.408	-0.362	-0.633	0.108	0.163	0.109	0.207
Riverside	43,237	10,270	-0.554	-0.718	-0.561	-0.734	-0.298	-0.419	-0.374	-0.628	0.323	0.442	0.408	0.592
San Bernardino	34,200	9,262	-0.570	-0.459	-0.881	-0.536	-0.263	-0.246	-0.226	-0.313	0.275	0.274	0.379	0.288
Ventura	32,462	6,246	-0.563	-0.230	-0.735	-0.901	-0.512	-0.318	-0.176	-0.417	0.341	0.210	0.188	0.361
Inner-core FHA loans														
Los Angeles	12,947	2,140	0.459	0.078	0.105	-0.060	1.395	0.851	0.685	0.071	-1.182	-0.627	-0.547	-0.039
Orange	2,883	660	NA	NA	NA	-0.243	0.020	0.403	0.790	-0.141	1.173	0.694	0.510	1.121
Riverside	2,086	167	NA	-1.464	-0.415	-1.370	-0.559	-0.124	0.360	-0.751	0.668	0.206	-0.126	0.846
San Bernardino	6,617	707	-0.661	-1.175	-0.912	-0.802	-0.164	0.217	0.647	-0.191	0.259	0.094	-0.211	0.303
Ventura	588	43	NA	NA	NA	NA	NA	NA	NA	NA	NA	NA	NA	NA
Suburban FHA loans														
Los Angeles	43,878	5,632	-0.565	-0.577	-0.315	-0.366	0.349	0.159	0.256	-0.166	0.349	0.058	-0.098	0.213
Orange	14,545	1,364	-1.081	-0.143	-0.299	-0.649	0.374	-0.241	0.171	-0.202	0.374	0.241	-0.052	0.257
Riverside	25,265	2,780	-0.690	-0.919	-0.731	-0.494	0.122	-0.090	-0.054	-0.020	0.122	0.268	0.198	0.136
San Bernardino	25,455	2,816	-1.033	-0.509	-0.691	-0.354	0.504	0.128	0.053	-0.198	0.504	0.047	0.118	0.250
Ventura	2,909	305	NA	-1.740	NA	0.423	0.005	0.332	0.577	-0.133	0.005	0.050	-0.619	0.125

Note: Data shown here are drawn from logit equations for probability of loan approval incorporating various measures of applicant credit worthiness and area characteristics. One set of equations incorporates coefficients for minority applicants, including Native Americans and Asian Americans (not shown here); another set incorporates separate coefficients for white applicants. Home Mortgage Disclosure Act data are used. Equations include all lenders and exclude non-race-identified borrowers. Boldface and underlined coefficients are significant at the 1 percent level, boldface coefficients are significant at the 5 percent level, and coefficients in italics are significant at the 10 percent level. NA = not available.

The equations for conventional home-purchase loans, for each county, almost invariably find African Americans at a statistically significant disadvantage in obtaining loan approval. For example, the −0.559 obtained for black applicants in Los Angeles in 1998, because it is significant at the 1 percent level, implies that blacks applying for loans were 56 percent less likely to be approved for loans than nonblack applicants, all else being equal (with several other factors related to creditworthiness controlled for, as discussed in the appendix).

A closer inspection of these results finds a disturbing trend: black applicants are more likely to be at a statistically significant disadvantage in *suburban* than *inner-core* areas when seeking conventional loans, and the degree of their disadvantage is almost invariably greater in suburban areas. Further, there is no evidence that this disadvantage improved from 1992 to 1998 (a period of sustained economic growth). For Latino applicants, there is little evidence of statistically significant disadvantage in seeking conventional loans in inner-core areas. On the other hand, Latinos exhibit a virtually uniform pattern of statistically significant disadvantage for conventional loans in suburban areas. The degree of measured disadvantage is less than that for blacks. Again, there is no evidence of improvement from 1992 to 1998.

The equations for FHA-insured home-purchase loans generate less extreme patterns of racial exclusion. The pattern of disadvantage for Latino applicants reaches statistically significant levels only sometimes in the five counties, with little difference between inner-core and suburban areas. However, a quite different pattern emerges for black applicants. Coefficients for black applicants for home loans in inner-core areas are statistically significant and negative for FHA-insured loans only in Riverside and San Bernardino Counties. However, when seeking FHA-insured loans in suburban areas, black applicants are virtually certain to face statistically significant levels of disadvantage that are just slightly less than for conventional loans in suburban areas. The sole exception is Ventura County, which has very few black home-purchase loan applicants.

These results can be represented dramatically in graphical terms. Figures 3.3 and 3.4 illustrate the main points from our model of access to housing credit. Instead of reproducing the coefficients from Table 3.5, we use statistical transformations of these coefficients that are termed *odds ratios*. An odds ratio for a given applicant category depicts the effect on the probability of loan approval of being in that category as opposed to being a white applicant. An odds ratio of 2 means that being in this category doubles an applicant's probability of loan approval (relative to white applicants, all else being equal), an odds ratio of 0.5 means an applicant's probability of approval is half what it would otherwise be, and an odds ratio of 1 indicates that being in this category has no systematic effect on loan approval.

The figures shown here use large and small markers to denote statistically significant and insignificant coefficients, respectively. Using 1998 as the sample year, Figure 3.3 demonstrates clearly that African American applicants throughout Southern California have odds ratios just over 0.5 of obtaining conventional suburban home-purchase loans, with the highest odds ratio in San Bernardino County. Although the graph does not show it, this disadvantage is very stable throughout the loan periods examined. Figure 3.3 also shows that Latinos applying for conventional suburban loans also exhibit some disadvantage, except that estimated odds ratios cluster around 0.75 instead of 0.5. The diverse character of Asian American experience is shown in this figure. Asian American applicants for conventional suburban loans are at a statistical advantage in Los Angeles and Orange Counties and at a statistical disadvantage in Riverside and San Bernardino Counties. This difference in outcomes may reflect two special factors in the first two counties: the emergence of a robust Asian American banking sector and the recent influx of a wave of Asian immigrants with relatively high wealth and skill levels. These results are consistent throughout the loan periods examined.

When our focus shifts from conventional suburban loans to inner-core loans, the systematic pattern observed for suburban areas largely disappears. For minorities seeking FHA home-purchase loans in suburban areas, a clear pattern emerges only for African Americans. Figure 3.4 shows that, for 1998, odds ratios for these applicants are stable and higher than those for conventional suburban loans. However, Figure 3.4 also shows that no systematic pattern appears for either Asian Americans or Latinos applying for FHA home-purchase loans in suburban areas. Although Asian American and Latino odds ratios appear higher than those for African Americans, in Riverside

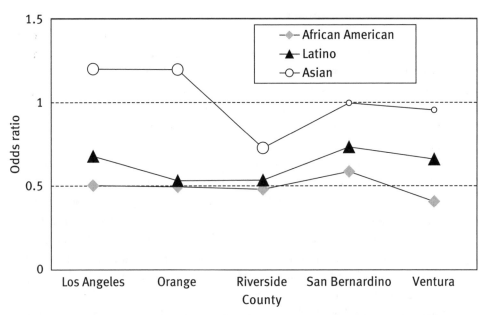

Figure 3.3. Odds ratios for conventional home-purchase loan applicants in suburban tracts, Southern California counties, by race, 1998. Odds ratios are derived from the coefficients shown in Table 3.5. An odds ratio of 1 means that applicants in this category have the same odds of approval as white applicants, all else being equal. An odds ratio of 2 means applicants in this category have twice the probability of approval of white applicants, and an odds ratio of 0.5 means half the probability of approval. Large markers are for differences statistically significant at the 5 percent level or better; small markers indicate statistical insignificance.

and Ventura Counties, the ratios are statistically insignificant. Also, unlike for conventional loans in the suburban areas, Asian Americans exhibit some disadvantage in applying for FHA loans.

The idea of the equations discussed to this point is this: How does being in one of the minority categories affect an individual's chances of home-loan approval? Implicitly, each minority is measured against "white" experience, which is considered the "normal case" (null hypothesis). Because we include four categories of minority, the impact of minority status is spread across several categories. An alternate way of measuring home-purchase loan status suggests itself: What is the effect of being white on the probability of loan approval, all else being equal? We ran equations of this type, which invert the usual logic of credit-market discrimination models, and the findings suggest that there is little or no systematic advantage associated with being white in applications for home-purchase loans in inner-core areas. However, there is a uniformly significant advantage for whites seeking conventional loans in suburban areas, and there is a pattern of partial advantage for whites seeking FHA loans to purchase suburban homes.

Taken as a whole, the results discussed here suggest that despite the termination of explicitly racist practices in federal home-ownership subsidies, federal housing policies follow a racialized logic. Lower-income areas are far more likely to have federally subsidized housing outlays than home owner tax expenditures, whereas the opposite

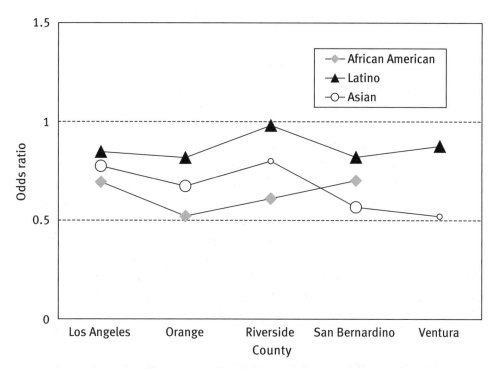

Figure 3.4. Odds ratios for FHA home-purchase loan applicants in suburban tracts, Southern California counties, by race, 1998. (See Figure 3.3 for an explanation of the meanings of these odds ratios.)

is the case for upper-income areas. FHA loans are far more likely to be used for whites in suburban areas, but for minorities in inner-core areas. And black and Latino applicants are far more likely to be at a disadvantage in suburban than in inner-core loan markets, no matter whether they are applying for conventional or FHA-insured loans. Given this racialized logic, it is not surprising that the home-purchase loan market tends to maintain or even worsen preexisting patterns of racial separation.

Conclusion

Scholars across the nation have in the past several years mounted an increasingly serious challenge to the idea that cities and urban form are best viewed as resulting from the operation of self-interested agents in decentralized market processes. Molotch (1993) has famously referred to the contemporary city as an urban growth machine. It may be that, but this machine operates unevenly over space. In this chapter, we have shown that the flow of federal expenditures for housing in Southern California is weighted heavily toward suburban and upper-income areas. Lower-income housing is located in areas that have historically absorbed marginalized minority populations, and this pattern has been stable over time. Each year's increment of tax deductions and federal housing subsidy outlays simply deepens the long-established pattern of differential access to different kinds of federal expenditures for housing. In the case of the home-ownership market, these outlays continue to fuel urban sprawl and social separation; in the case of subsidized lower-income housing, these outlays reinforce the concentration of regional poverty. Minority households, especially black and Latino/Chicano households, face unique challenges in seeking access to housing. Blacks and Latinos are far more likely to be at a structural disadvantage in home-purchase loan markets than are other applicants. This disadvantage becomes slightly worse if they seek conventional financing rather than FHA financing, but it becomes significantly worse if they seek loans of either type for homes in suburban, as opposed to inner-core, areas. Results for dissimilarity indices indicate both that there is widespread racial separation in Southern California and that home-purchase loan markets either maintain or worsen this separation. The home-acquisition/housing-finance process has to be viewed both as one source of increasing racial wealth disparities over time (Oliver and Shapiro 1995; Conley 1999) and as one source of urban sprawl. Federal policies once explicitly sanctioned—indeed, encouraged—this dual dynamic. This policy thrust has been reversed, at least in principle, due to pressures exerted by generations of inner-core community residents. However, given that federal subsidies in the form of tax expenditures are the silent partners to new subdivision development on the urban fringe, and that whites have systematic advantages (and minorities have systematic disadvantages) in obtaining home-purchase loans in such areas, federal policies now implicitly sanction this outward spatial thrust of the urban growth machine.

Appendix: A Model of the Determinants of Home-Purchase Loan Approval

The Home Mortgage Disclosure Act requires that virtually all lenders of home mortgages report application-level data annually; these data are reported at the census tract level. HMDA data encompass a range of residential loan types: home purchase, re-financing, and rehabilitation; single family and multifamily; owner occupied and absentee owned. The determinants of loan decisions for these different loan types may be quite different. To ensure uniformity, our sample is restricted to single-family home-purchase loans. The model estimated here for each county in our sample is as follows:

Probability of loan approval in the period 1992–98 =
  Intercept term,
  Year 1992 dummy variable,   [*controls for year effects*]
  Year 1994 dummy variable,
  Year 1996 dummy variable,
  Applicant's loan/income ratio,   [*applicant characteristics*]
  Log of applicant's annual income,
  Dummy variable for female applicants,
  Dummy variable for Native American applicants for 1992, 1994, 1996, and 1998,
  Dummy variable for Asian American applicants for 1992, 1994, 1996, and 1998,
  Dummy variable for African American applicants for 1992, 1994, 1996, and 1998,
  Dummy variable for Chicano/Latino applicants for 1992, 1994, 1996, and 1998,
  [or, in lieu of the above four minority dummy variables:
  Dummy variable for white applicants for 1992, 1994, 1996, and 1998],
  [Census tract] Median 1990 income,   [*census tract characteristics*]
  Median 1990 income squared,
  Residential density (average population per residential unit),
  Proportion of owner-occupied residential units,
  Dummy variables for high-minority areas (those 25 percent of each city's census tracts
      with the highest proportion of minority residents) for 1992, 1994, 1996, and 1998.

Equations that use the dummy-variable method measure race effects relative to the level of the intercept term. The relatively simple equations implemented here aim at unearthing baseline information concerning the impact of applicant race on credit-market outcomes. More refined tests would be required to identify the extent to which personal discrimination on the part of lenders may account for significant race dummy variables.

Notes

1. Voith (1999) has found statistical evidence that federal tax benefits are one factor explaining suburbanization and central-city decline.

2. Newman and Schnare (1997) provide evidence that housing projects may worsen neighborhood quality. Lee, Culhane, and Wachter (1999) show that public housing projects have adverse effects on housing prices in urban neighborhoods.

3. Goetz (1993) provides a useful history of public housing in Los Angeles.

4. These figures undoubtedly undercount FHA loans. In the 1980s, HMDA data were collected only from depository institutions, not from mortgage companies, and fewer lenders

with small loan volumes provided data than after the 1989 revisions in HMDA reporting requirements.

5. Data on mortgage interest and property-tax-based tax expenditures are not made publicly available, and detailed data on subsidized housing are available only for the 1970s and the late 1990s. The method used to estimate the spatial distribution of home owner tax expenditures is based on that used by Gyourko and Voith (1997), with differences in calculation due to data limitations. Details of the calculations reported here are available on request.

6. Other analysts view racial discrimination as a specific, malign act by an institution or individual that is not linked to any legitimate business objective. These analysts look for evidence of racial perpetrators or of economically irrational practices.

7. Cloud and Galster (1993) and Dymski (1996) provide recent reviews of the vast literature on this topic.

Works Cited

Almaguer, Tomás. 1994. *Racial Fault Lines: The Historical Origins of White Supremacy in California.* Berkeley: University of California Press.

Becker, Gary S. 1971. *The Economics of Discrimination.* Chicago: University of Chicago Press.

Clark, William A. V. 1993. "Measuring Racial Discrimination in the Housing Market." *Urban Affairs Quarterly* 28(4):641–50.

Cloud, Cathy, and George Galster. 1993. "What Do We Know about Racial Discrimination in Mortgage Markets?" *Review of Black Political Economy* 22(1):101–20.

Conley, Dalton. 1999. *Being Black, Living in the Red: Race, Wealth and Social Policy in America.* Berkeley: University of California Press.

Denton, Nancy A. 1994. "Are African Americans Still Hypersegregated?" In *Residential Apartheid: The American Legacy*, ed. Robert D. Bullard, J. Eugene Grigsby III, and Charles Lee, 49–81. Los Angeles: Center for AfroAmerican Studies.

Diamond, Douglas B., and Michael J. Lea. 1992. "Housing Finance in Developed Countries: An International Comparison of Efficiency." *Journal of Housing Research* 3(1):1–271.

Downs, Anthony. 1985. *The Revolution in Real Estate Finance.* Washington, DC: Brookings Institution.

Dymski, Gary A. 1996. "Why Does Race Matter in Housing and Credit Markets?" In *Race, Markets, and Social Outcomes*, ed. Patrick L. Mason and Rhonda Williams. Boston: Kluwer Academic Press.

Dymski, Gary A., and John M. Veitch. 1996. "Financing the Future in Los Angeles: Great Depression to 21st Century." In *Rethinking Los Angeles*, ed. Michael J. Dear, H. Eric Schockman, and Greg Hise. Thousand Oaks, CA: Sage.

Goetz, Edward G. 1993. "The Politics of Housing in Los Angeles." In *Shelter Burden: Local Politics and Progressive Housing Policy.* Philadelphia: Temple University Press.

Gordon, Peter, and Harry W. Richardson. 2000. "Defending Suburban Sprawl." *Public Interest* 139:65–71.

Gyourko, Joseph, and Richard Voith. 1997. "Does the U.S. Tax Treatment of Housing Promote Suburbanization and Central City Decline?" Working paper 97-13. Federal Reserve Bank of Philadelphia.

Horne, Gerald. 1995. *Fire This Time: The Watts Uprising and the 1960s.* Charlottesville: University of Virginia Press.

Isenberg, Dorene. 2001. "U.S. Housing Policy Transformation: The Challenge of the Market."

In *Seeking Shelter on the Pacific Rim: Financial Globalization, Social Change, and the Housing Market,* ed. Gary A. Dymski and Dorene Isenberg. Armonk, NY: M. E. Sharpe.

Lee, Chang-Moo, Dennis P. Culhane, and Susan M. Wachter. 1999. "The Differential Impacts of Federally Assisted Housing Programs on Nearby Property Values: A Philadelphia Case Study." *Housing Policy Debate* 10(1):75–94.

Massey, Douglas S., and Nancy A. Denton. 1993. *American Apartheid: Segregation and the Making of the Underclass.* Cambridge, MA: Harvard University Press.

McWilliams, Carey. 1973. *Southern California: An Island on the Land.* Salt Lake City, UT: Peregrine Smith. (Orig. pub. 1946.)

Molotch, Harvey L. 1993. "The Political Economy of Growth Machines." *Journal of Urban Affairs* 15(1):29–53.

Newman, Sandra J., and Ann B. Schnare. 1997. "'. . . And a Suitable Living Environment': The Failure of Housing Programs to Deliver on Neighborhood Quality." *Housing Policy Debate* 8(4):703–41.

Nivola, Pietro S. 1999. *Laws of the Landscape: How Policies Shape Cities in Europe and America.* Washington, DC: Brookings Institution.

Oliver, Melvin L., and Thomas M. Shapiro. 1995. *Black Wealth, White Wealth: A New Perspective on Racial Inequality.* New York: Routledge.

Ondrich, Jan, Alex Stricker, and John Yinger. 1998. "Do Real Estate Brokers Choose to Discriminate? Evidence from the 1989 Housing Discrimination Study." *Southern Economic Journal* 64(4):880–901.

Squires, Gregory. 1992. "Community Reinvestment: An Emerging Social Movement." In *From Redlining to Reinvestment,* ed. Gregory Squires, 1–37. Philadelphia: Temple University Press.

Vandell, Kerry D. 1995. "FHA Restructuring Proposals: Alternatives and Implications." *Housing Policy Debate* 6(2):299–393.

Voith, Richard. 1999. "Does the Federal Tax Treatment of Housing Affect the Pattern of Metropolitan Development?" *Business Review* (Federal Reserve Bank of Philadelphia), March/April, 3–16.

Wachter, Susan. 1990. "The Limits of the Housing Finance System." *Journal of Housing Research* 1(1):163–85.

PART II

Up against the Sprawl

4 | From the Barrio to the 'Burbs? Immigration and the Dynamics of Suburbanization

Enrico A. Marcelli

As public concern and academic research on the consequences of suburbanization increased during the 1990s, restrictionist immigration groups were quick to suggest that immigrants were the primary culprits. For instance, the authors of a recent study claim that 95 percent of "urban sprawl" between 1970 and 1990 in California was driven by population growth rather than increased per capita land consumption, and that if the federal government does not alter immigration policy, by 2025 "Californians will be living more densely than do today's residents of China" (Kolankiewicz and Beck 2000, 25).[1] Immigration scholars, on the other hand, have only begun to ask whether recent immigrants are directly contributing to suburbanization (Alba et al. 1999) and to investigate whether linkages exist between local labor market opportunities and the availability of antipoverty public assistance on the one hand and the arrival of recent immigrants on the other (Allen and Turner 1996; Zavodny 1999). Accordingly, the concentrated geographic distribution of recent immigrants (Frey and Liaw 1998a, 1998b), as contrasted with the diffused aging baby-boom generation (Frey and Devol 2000), has led to questions concerning the legitimacy of traditional spatial assimilation theory, which links socioeconomic assimilation with city-suburb mobility (Massey 1985).

Although historically immigrants may have been more likely to settle first in urban areas and then migrate to the suburbs with the passage of time and across generations (Fong and Shibuya 2000; Gans 1967; Jackson 1985), fully 43 percent of immigrants to the United States who arrived during the 1980s and resided in metropolitan areas were not located in central cities (U.S. Bureau of the Census 1993). In short, the increasing tendency of new immigrants to leapfrog over urban core areas and settle initially in the historically more ethnically homogeneous (e.g., white) suburbs could short-circuit the assimilation process (Alba et al. 1999; Logan and Golden 1986) and contribute to regional environmental stress despite evidence indicating that population dispersal remains "largely a product of internal migration" (Frey and Liaw 1998b, 399).

Some scholars have studied whether immigrants stimulate suburbanization indirectly by displacing others (Frey and Liaw 1998b; Kritz and Gurak 2001), but there has been scant research on recent immigrants' direct contribution (Alba et al. 1999; Alba, Logan, and Crowder 1997; Allen and Turner 1996). The Southern California region is a particularly useful place to study the economic and environmental consequences of recent immigrants because the majority of new arrivals continue to reside in the region (Passel and Zimmerman 2000). Thus I have two main objectives in this chapter. First, I investigate the extent to which recent immigrants directly affected urban sprawl in Southern California between 1990 and 1998. Second, I estimate how various individual demographic characteristics, as well as local (1) labor market conditions, (2) antipoverty public assistance availability, (3) foreign-born concentration, and (4) rental prices help explain the probability that recent legal immigrants settled in suburban areas. I accomplish this by linking data geographically from four sources at the Public Use Microdata Area (PUMA) level: (1) individual-level Immigration and Naturalization Service (INS) settlement data for newly legalized immigrants, (2) group demographic characteristics and rental price information from the 5 percent 1990 Public Use Microdata Samples (PUMS), (3) labor market demand information from the Southern California Association of Governments (SCAG), and (4) antipoverty expenditures from the Consolidated Federal Funds Report (CFFR).

Knowing whether immigrants contribute directly to suburbanization and whether job growth, cultural affinity, antipoverty assistance, or rental costs across PUMA "neighborhoods" help explain this is important for understanding whether the link between immigration and sprawl is real or imagined. The analysis, however, also goes beyond this popular debate and can provide both regional and federal-level policy makers with valuable information. At a regional level, planners are likely to be interested in the institutional determinants of residential settlement for anticipating and planning for new foreign-born arrivals (Zavodny 1999). At the federal level, it may be useful for politicians and legislators to know whether current U.S. immigration policy contributes to suburbanization and its attendant fiscal and spatial challenges.

Finally, the findings of this study have important theoretical implications. After all, spatial assimilation theory posits that against the collective tide of urban ethnic-enclave building run individual-level interests motivating outward residential mobility (Alba et al. 1999, 447). Institutional forces such as local labor market conditions and public assistance availability are generally viewed as providing only a contingent dissuasive influence (Massey 1985). The analysis that follows directly challenges this perspective and suggests that spatially specific economic factors and public policy can augment as well as dissuade suburbanization, and may have more than a minor influence on where recent immigrants reside.

Individual and Institutional Determinants of
Residential Location of Legal Immigrants

The Chicago school's explanation of residential organization was premised on a plant ecology model that stressed "the competitive process of invasion and succession whereby different income groups attained a dominance in different concentric zones around the city center" (Ward 1971, 126). It posited that ethnic group movement away from the city and toward the suburbs occurs across generations and is motivated by individual aspirations for upward socioeconomic mobility. From this perspective, collective or group interests act as constraints on outward residential and upward pecuniary mobility (Burgess 1967). Massey (1985) formalized this spatial assimilation model and added that regional factors such as the housing market and the geographic distribution of economic activity, not only ethnic enclaves, may also mediate individual residential settlement. This broader choice-within-constraint conceptualization is consistent with Ward's (1971) seminal study, which, while noting that "the increasing pressure of newly arrived immigrants and the unsatisfactory living arrangements of most tenements pushed families . . . from central areas" and that "very few outer suburban developments designed for large families were built for lower middle-income people" (143), mainly emphasized the importance of improved local transportation systems to an understanding of residential patterns. From the earliest scholarly discussions of city growth, then, both individual and institutional explanations of settlement choice have been offered.

Alba et al. (1999), who built on the work of Alba and Logan (1991), note that "despite high levels of suburban residence among recent immigrants from many groups, the distinction between urban and suburban space underpinning the spatial-assimilation model continues to function in important respects" (453). But because they found time of arrival to have played only a modest role in explaining urban versus suburban settlement—and found evolving institutional factors in the suburbs to be altering the shielding effect for the dominant ethnoracial group and the acculturation effect on newer immigrants—they suggest that the model is in need of some revision. Specifically, cultural affinity, economic opportunity, the availability of public resources, and cost-of-living differences may influence settlement behavior.

The findings of previous research on stimulants of suburban settlement indicate that the geographic concentration of earlier immigrant cohorts is the most important determinant of newer immigrants' residential settlement patterns. And although there is little evidence suggesting that most groups of foreign-born persons become more dispersed over time (Bartel and Koch 1991), Bartel (1989) found that the probability of a new male immigrant's settling in a metropolitan area is positively correlated with the percentage of that individual's ethnic group residing in the area. Buckley (1996), Dunlevy (1991), and Zavodny (1999) provide corroborating evidence at the state level.[2] None of this research, however, has focused on the relationship between immigration and suburbanization. Additional evidence that ethnic or cultural affinity plays an important role in directing immigrant settlement patterns comes from the internal migration of foreign-born persons. Belanger and Rogers (1992) found that when foreign-born persons migrate within the United States, they tend to gravitate toward areas with relatively high levels of coethnic geographic concentration. Likewise, Kritz and Nogle (1994) and Neuman and Tienda (1994) have shown that residing in an area with a high concentration of foreign-born persons can dissuade out-migration. Consequently, in addition to individual, family, and household characteristics (Alba et al. 1999), being near other immigrants can have a magnetic effect on migratory activity.

Economic opportunity is a second major factor that is important for understanding international migration (Easterlin 1961, 1982, 26–28) and for helping to explain the inter- and intrastate out-migration of lower-skilled U.S.-born workers (Frey and Liaw 1998a, 1998b; Muller 1993, 83, 89). However, although the demand for labor is a theoretically appealing migration force, empirical evidence on this topic is mixed, and to date no study has estimated whether spatially based job growth has an independent migration pull effect. Whereas Filer (1992) found that general local labor market conditions do not affect the locational choices of the foreign-born, Bartel (1989) found the opposite. Specifically, she found that foreign-born adult men are more likely to reside in metropolitan areas with higher wages and higher general-assistance payments, and foreign-born Latinos are less likely to live in areas where unemployment is relatively high. Bartel and Koch (1991) and Kritz and Nogle (1994), however, have found that higher state and metropolitan area unemployment does not stimulate out-migration among the foreign-born. And Zavodny (1999) has reported that although state-level economic conditions are significant for explaining the residential decisions of new family- and employment-based entrants, they are not important explanatory factors for all remaining admission groups (e.g., Immigration Reform and Control Act legalizations, refugees/asylee adjustments, and new refugees) or for all new immigrants taken together. One potential drawback of these studies is that the researchers did not adequately measure those economic conditions likely to attract new immigrants. For instance, if new immigrants are more likely than U.S.-born persons to accept lower-paying jobs (many of which are located in the service sector) and less likely to access welfare, then data on unemployment rates, manufacturing wages, and public assistance payments may not capture the most important economic factor attracting immigrants, namely, relatively low-wage jobs. Furthermore, recent research suggests that job growth rather than the number of jobs per resident may be a better proxy for labor demand (Raphael 1998a, 1998b; Pastor and Marcelli 2000), although Stoll and Raphael (2000) also provide evidence indicating that blacks and Latinos search for jobs primarily in low-growth areas.

Given the disagreement concerning the effect of labor market conditions on city-suburb migration and the fact that foreign-born concentration has historically been viewed as having a dissuasive impact on suburban immigrant settlement, researchers have increasingly emphasized welfare's magnetic effect on immigrant settlement (Borjas 1999b) and immigrants' local fiscal effects (Clark 1998). In other words, although concern about immigrants' negative fiscal effects is not new (Clune 1998), this is increasingly being expressed in geographic terms. Three types of welfare "magnets" have been identified: (1) those stimulating international migration, (2) those impeding return migration, and (3) those motivating interstate residential mobility (Borjas 1999a). Although there is virtually no empirical evidence that the availability of welfare represents a significant pull effect on those contemplating migrating to the United States, or that interstate differences motivate interstate residential mobility among the U.S.-born, there is some indication that receiving public assistance may dissuade return international migration and influence interstate residential patterns among the foreign-born. Exceptions exist, however. Buckley (1996), for instance, found that although immigrants are less likely than U.S.-born persons to receive welfare benefits, newer immigrants are more likely to settle in states with higher welfare benefits; therefore, cutting such benefits is likely to be an effective way of discouraging unskilled individuals' migration to the United States. Similarly, Zimmerman and Fix (1994) found evidence that secondary migration to states with higher levels of public assistance during the 1980s was more likely among refugees, although in the 1990s job opportunities and familial/cultural factors showed greater influence. Zavodny (1999) concurs, but is careful to note that the earlier positive correlation may have been influenced by government decisions concerning the states in which refugees may initially settle, and that the estimated impact of "welfare" may also pick up unmeasured aspects of a state's willingness to provide other services that refugees desire, such as language classes and job training. It is important to note that Zavodny did not find welfare to be a significant explanation for interstate migration of nonrefugee foreign-born persons.

In addition to cultural affinity, labor market conditions, and welfare availability, a fourth and final local institutional factor that may stimulate or dissuade suburban settlement is the expense of housing. Alba et al. (1999) have conducted the only study to date that has directly examined whether newer immigrants are more likely to settle in suburban areas, but, although they controlled for some of the metropolitan spatial-institutional factors discussed above, they unfortunately do not report whether or how these influence residential settlement patterns. Zavodny (1999), alternatively, found that the concentration of other foreign-born residents, rather than welfare generosity or general labor market conditions, helps determine immigrants' residential settlement. Zavodny's analysis was performed at the state level, however, and made no distinction between urban and suburban areas. Thus Zavodny did not examine differentials in intrametropolitan foreign-born concentration, job opportunities, welfare availability, and housing prices or how these influence whether immigrants directly contribute to suburbanization. The present study builds on the work of Alba et al. (1999), Allen and Turner (1996), and Zavodny (1999) by incorporating new measures of local labor demand (Pastor and Marcelli 2000) and local federal antipoverty expenditures (Joassart-Marcelli and Musso 2001) to investigate the significance of local institutional factors likely to influence the probability that recent immigrants will settle initially in a suburban area of Southern California.

Connecting Immigration, Employment, Housing, and Welfare Data at a Local Level

The primary data employed in this study are obtained from the Immigration and Naturalization Service data files and contain information on the demographic characteristics of the 911,266 aliens who became legal permanent residents (LPRs) (or simply legal immigrants) of the United States and reported that they intended to settle in the five-county Southern California region between fiscal years 1990 and 1998.[3] Recent research indicates that *intended* (reported) and *initial* (observed) settlement patterns are highly similar (Newbold 2000), thus reported intended residential location is likely to be a reasonable proxy for initial legal immigrant settlement.[4]

There were four main categories of immigrant legalization during the 1990s: (1) family sponsored, (2) employment based, (3) refugee and asylee adjustment, and (4) Immigration Reform and Control Act (IRCA) amnesty. The INS data employed here do not include IRCA legalizations, but the new immigrants from the remaining three categories represented from 10 to 16 percent of those who upgraded their status each year in the United States, and 13 percent on average across all nine years (see Figure 4.1). It is important to note that the exclusion of those who were legalized through IRCA does not significantly alter these percentages, given that after 1992 relatively few individuals obtained legal immigration status through amnesty. Further, given that all IRCA-adjusted immigrants selected settlement locations before

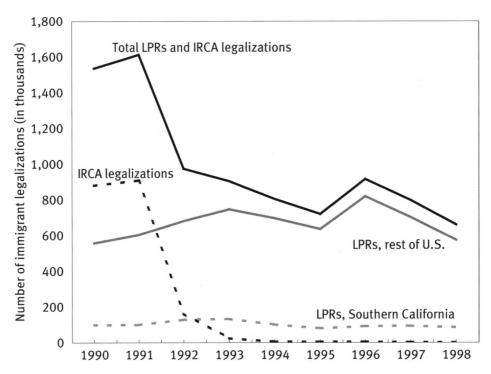

Figure 4.1. Traditional new legal permanent residents (LPRs) and Immigration Reform and Control Act (IRCA) legalizations, United States, 1990–98.

legalization means that their inclusion would bias the analysis of factors affecting settlement decisions.[5]

A foreign-born person could become a legal immigrant either by arriving in the
United States with a valid immigrant visa issued by the U.S. Department of State
in the source country (new arrival) or, for those who were already residing in the
United States with temporary visas, by petitioning the INS to be adjusted to permanent status (adjustments).[6] What Figure 4.1 reveals is that although there was notice-
able fluctuation in the number of new legal immigrants who came to the United States
each year during the 1990s and there was a downward trend overall, the supply to
Southern California was considerable and constant, hovering close to 100,000.

Although the INS data provide valuable information about country of origin, date
of admission, age, occupation, marital status, sex, and zip code of intended residence,
we must link these data with other data if we wish to learn something about how
nonindividual factors—such as the demand for labor, public assistance availability,
foreign-born geographic concentration, and rental prices—influence residential settlement patterns. Three secondary data sources provide the needed additional information. First, the 5 percent 1990 PUMS are used to construct demographic variables
at the PUMA or "neighborhood" level to serve as a proxy for foreign-born geographic
concentration and to distinguish urban from suburban neighborhoods (in 1990,
PUMAs in Southern California were geographic areas that had approximately 150,000
residents and 75,000 employed persons). Because (1) "no uncontested operational definition of 'suburbia' exists" (Alba et al. 1999, 448–49), (2) Los Angeles does not conform to the traditional central-city versus non-central-city (or city-suburb) dichotomy
that has been employed elsewhere (Alba et al. 1999; Guest and Nelson 1978; Massey
and Denton 1987, 1988; Schnore 1963), and (3) the pace of noncore urban development rose considerably after 1960 in Southern California, a suburban PUMA is defined here as one that had a higher percentage of houses built between 1960 and 1990
than was the case for the entire five-county region according to the 1990 PUMS.[7]

Although a PUMA is not the most desirable proxy for a neighborhood, it is
employed here because it is the only local geographic level at which we may connect
immigration, employment, housing, and welfare data to examine how these factors
may influence suburban settlement during intercensal years. And although the housing development definition at the PUMA level used here is not as convenient as the
traditional Census Bureau central-city/suburb dichotomy, because residents of the Los
Angeles metropolitan area tend to be more scattered into pockets of densely populated areas, it is also more likely to reflect the region's underlying geographic reality.[8]
In short, the multicentric character of the Southern California region requires a more
nuanced approach to the study of suburbanization, one suggested by Figure 4.2.

Although the 1990 PUMS permit us to construct static proxies for cultural affinity,
such as percentage of the population who are foreign-born or from a specific ethnic or
racial group by PUMA, they do not enable the construction of a job growth variable.
Raphael (1998a, 1998b) has shown that job growth is a better proxy for labor demand
than jobs per resident, thus it is more likely to capture the economic opportunity that

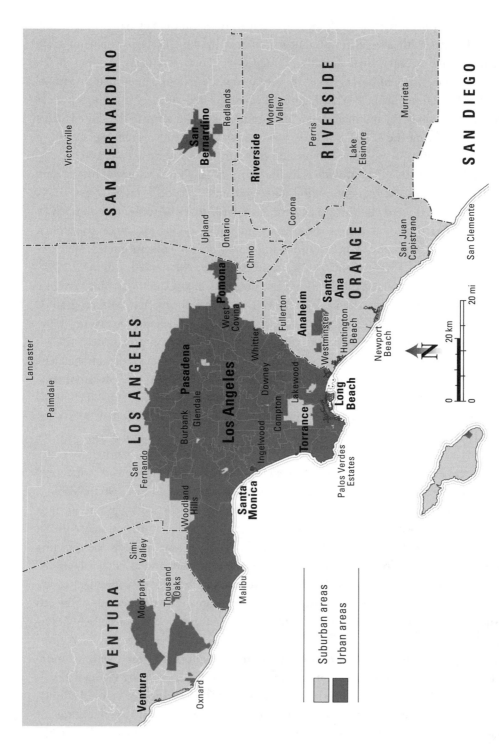

Figure 4.2. Urban and suburban areas, per Public Use Microdata Area (PUMA), 1998. Suburban PUMAs are classified as areas with a share of housing stock built between 1960 and 1990 that is higher than the regional share.

may attract potential in-migrants. With Dun & Bradstreet data obtained from the Southern California Association of Governments, Pastor and Marcelli (2000) followed Raphael's lead by creating a job growth variable for Los Angeles County from 1980 to 1990 by PUMA and found that it had an independent positive effect on hourly earnings among male workers. Given that 1980 data are available only for Los Angeles County, in the present study I rely on 1990 and 1994 data to compute job density and job growth variables for each PUMA in Southern California.

A third and final secondary data source, the Consolidated Federal Funds Report, is used to generate a proxy for federal antipoverty public expenditures per poor person by PUMA from the 1988–90 period (ANTIPOV). Specifically, estimates of total antipoverty expenditure were computed following the methodology developed by Joassart-Marcelli and Musso (2001) and detailed in chapter 7 of this volume.

With the INS data partitioned by zip code and the cultural affinity, labor demand, public assistance, and rent data separated by PUMA, the remaining task was to match zip codes to PUMAs.[9] This was accomplished through the overlapping of zip code and PUMA boundary files; similar to how cities were matched to PUMAs, when a zip code spanned multiple PUMAs, the zip code was assigned to that PUMA that enveloped the largest share of the zip code's territory. Aggregating the INS data (originally at the zip code level), the CFFR data (initially at the city level), and the SCAG and PUMS data (categorized at the PUMA level) at the PUMA level—again, although not as desirable as having all data categorized initially at the same geographic level—enables us to investigate how individual demographic characteristics and spatial-institutional factors influence new immigrants' settlement choices.

In the first phase of the regression analysis, a logistic regression model is employed to investigate the individual demographic determinants of initial suburban settlement for the five-county Southern California region. Each non-IRCA legal immigrant's PUMA of settlement—or, more precisely, its designation as either urban or suburban (SUBURB)—is regressed on individual demographic characteristics (AGE, FEMALE, MARRIED, LATINO, ASIAN); the within-PUMA foreign-born geographic concentration (FBPCT), proxies for the density of and change in the demand for labor (JOBDNSE and JOBGROW, respectively),[10] public assistance spending (ANTIPOV), and average rental price (RENT). We also control for year of entry (Y_t is a vector of eight dummy variables representing 1991 through 1998, with 1990 excluded).

$$
\begin{aligned}
\text{SUBURB}_{ipt} = {} & \alpha + \text{AGE}_{ipt}\beta_1 + \text{FEMALE}_{ipt}\beta_2 + \text{MARRIED}_{ipt}\beta_3 + \text{LATINO}_{ipt}\beta_4 \\
& + \text{ASIAN}_{ipt}\beta_5 + \text{FBPCT}_{ip,\,90}\beta_6 + \text{JOBDNSE}_{ip,\,90\text{--}94}\beta_7 \\
& + \text{JOBGROW}_{ip,\,90\text{--}94}\beta_8 + \text{ANTIPOV}_{ip,\,88\text{--}90}\beta_9 \\
& + \text{RENT}_{ip,\,90}\beta_{10} + Y_t + \varepsilon_{ipt}.
\end{aligned}
\tag{1}
$$

Thus SUBURB_{ipt} is a dichotomous variable equal to one if individual i intended to settle in a suburban PUMA, p, or to zero if in an urban PUMA, in year t. Equation (1) is estimated using individual-level INS data from 1990 to 1998, which include 588,964 (or 65 percent) of the 911,266 newly legalized aliens and adjusters who reported Southern California as their new intended place of settlement.[11]

Each explanatory variable is defined in Figure 4.3, and the anticipated directional influence on SUBURB is indicated by the sign inside the parentheses immediately following each variable name. For instance, relatively younger (e.g., working-age) recent adult immigrants are expected to be less likely to settle initially in the suburbs given (1) that employment opportunities are more abundant in cities and (2) their relative lower income combined with higher suburban housing prices. Among the four remaining individual demographic variables, being FEMALE, MARRIED, or ASIAN is likely to have a positive impact on the probability of newer immigrants settling in the suburbs. It has been argued, for instance, that the ideal of suburban domesticity is more appealing to women than to men (Marsh 1990). And although married persons are more likely than singles to settle in the suburbs for a number of reasons (e.g., larger families require more space and pooled incomes), and cultural affinity in the suburbs may be stronger among Asian immigrants as they have begun to concentrate in various noncore locations (Li 1997, 1998), being Latino is expected to have a negative impact on suburban settlement given this group's historic urban concentration and relatively low skill endowment. In sum, recent female adult immigrants who are older, married, and Asian are expected to be more likely to settle in the suburbs.

Although we control for specific spatial-institutional characteristics of suburban neighborhoods, using FBPCT, JOBGROW, ANTIPOV, and RENT, coefficients on these variables in the logistic regression model merely intimate differences between urban and suburban PUMAs rather than show how these characteristics influence individual suburban settlement. A more traditional locational choice model, as developed

---

Dependent variables

    SUBURB   Dummy variable set to 1 if new LPR intended to setle in a suburban Public Use Microdata Area (PUMA)

    NL_LPR   Natural log of the number of new LPRs who intended to settle in a suburban PUMA

Individual characteristics

    AGE (+)   Age of LPR
    FEMALE (+)   Dummy variable set to 1 if LPR is female
    MARRIED (+)   Dummy variable set to 1 if LPR is married
    LATINO (−)   Dummy variable set to 1 if LPR is from a Latin American nation
    ASIAN (+)   Dummy variable set to 1 if LPR is from an Asian nation

Spatial-institutional factors

    SUBURB (?)   Dummy variable set to 1 if new LPR intended to settle in a suburban PUMA
    FBPCT (+)   Percentage foreign-born by PUMA, 1990
    JOBDNSE (+)   Number of jobs per 100 residents by PUMA, 1990
    JOBGROW (+)   Percentage change in number of jobs by PUMA, 1990–94
    MANDNSE (+)   Number of manufacturing jobs per 100 residents by PUMA, 1990
    MANGROW (+)   Percentage change in number of manufacturing jobs by PUMA, 1990–94
    SERVDNSE (+)   Number of service sector jobs per 100 residents by PUMA, 1990
    SERVGROW (+)   Percentage change in number of service sector jobs by PUMA, 1990–94
    ANTIPOV (+)   Mean monthly antipoverty expenditure per poor person by PUMA, 1980–90
    RENT (−)   Average median monthly rent by PUMA, 1990

Residual

    ε   Error term

Figure 4.3. Variables in logistic and ordinary least squares regression analyses of legal permanent resident (LPR) suburban settlement.

below, is needed to determine how extraindividual factors influence residential choice. FBPCT, reflecting cultural affinity or immigrant networks, is expected to have a neighborhood pull effect, given that many new immigrants desire to reside near their compatriots for economic and psychological reasons. A similar effect is anticipated for employment growth, because this may provide immigrants with work opportunities. But the type of employment growth (e.g., manufacturing versus service sector employment) by neighborhood may be a more important predictor of residential settlement. Giuliano and Small (1991), for instance, identified five types of production subcenters across twenty-eight production agglomerations (clusters) in Los Angeles and Orange Counties in 1980. And Swartz (1992) found that more than one-half of all suburban firms patronize central-city firms. Thus, in the analysis that follows, we investigate not only total net job growth by PUMA (JOBGROW) but manufacturing (MANGROW) and service sector (SERVGROW) job growth as well. Because job growth may not capture job turnover effects, we also investigate the impact of job density (employment in an area normalized by number of residents in that area) for all jobs (JOBDNSE) as well as for the manufacturing (MANDNSE) and service (SERVDNSE) sectors. ANTIPOV is also likely to increase immigrants' probability of settling in the suburbs for two reasons: first, public assistance may provide relatively impecunious individuals with more disposable income, and second, recent evidence regarding antipoverty public spending in the Southern California region shows that antipoverty spending per poor person is higher in relatively wealthy suburban areas (Joassart-Marcelli and Musso 2001). Finally, a higher average rental price (RENT) is expected to decrease the probability of settling initially in a particular location.

Equation (2) represents such a locational choice model. Here we regress the natural log of the total number of recent non-IRCA adult legalized immigrants (LN_LPR) on our spatial-institutional variables, controlling for settlement year (Y_t) from 1990 to 1998 by PUMA. We do this first for all eighty-eight PUMAs for which we have data (four PUMAs lack sufficient CFFR antipoverty data), and then separately for the remaining fifty urban and thirty-eight suburban PUMAs.

$$\mathrm{LN\_LPR}_{pt} = \alpha + \mathrm{SUBURB}_p \beta_1 + \mathrm{FBPCT}_{p,\,90} \beta_2 + \mathrm{JOBDNSE}_{p,\,90-94} \beta_3$$
$$+ \mathrm{JOBGROW}_{p,\,90-94} \beta_4 + \mathrm{ANTIPOV}_{p,\,88-90} \beta_5$$
$$+ \mathrm{RENT}_{p,\,90} \beta_6 + Y_t + \varepsilon_{pt}. \tag{2}$$

Because there are nine values for LN_LPR per PUMA (one for each year from 1990 to 1998), there are a total of 792 observations (eighty-eight PUMAs multiplied by nine years). Thus $\mathrm{LN\_LPR}_{pt}$ is equal to the log of the number of new legal immigrants who settled in PUMA, p, in year t.

After summarizing suburban settlement trends among new immigrants in Southern California during the 1990s, we proceed with multivariate logistic and ordinary least squares (OLS) analyses of initial suburban settlement, highlighting the differential impact of individual characteristics and four institutional factors at the neighborhood level.

The Legal Immigrant Trickle into Southern California Suburbs

Analysis of regional origin reveals that foreign-born Asians (44 percent) and Latinos (38 percent) led immigration to Southern California from 1990 to 1998. European immigrants represented only 14 percent of the 911,266 new immigrants, and foreign-born persons from other regions of the world represented merely 4 percent. Further, whereas Latino immigration rose from 27 to 51 percent of the LPR flow, European immigration fell from 18 to 8 percent and Asian immigration fell from 51 to 36 percent (Figure 4.4). Although not shown here, more Mexicans (23 percent) obtained legal immigrant status between 1990 and 1998 in Southern California than any other national origin group. Only by summing the figures from the next three largest source nations, the Philippines (10 percent), Vietnam (7 percent), and El Salvador (6 percent), do we reach the number equal to that of Mexico.

Los Angeles County continued to attract the largest proportion of the 911,266 new immigrants in the 1990s, but the remaining four counties became increasingly popular (Figure 4.5). The proportion of new immigrants who settled in Los Angeles County, for instance, was 76 percent in 1990, but this figure had fallen to 68 percent by 1998. Meanwhile, Riverside County experienced the largest rise (3.2 percent), San Bernardino County saw a modest rise of 1.8 percent, and Orange and Ventura Counties gained about 1 percent each.

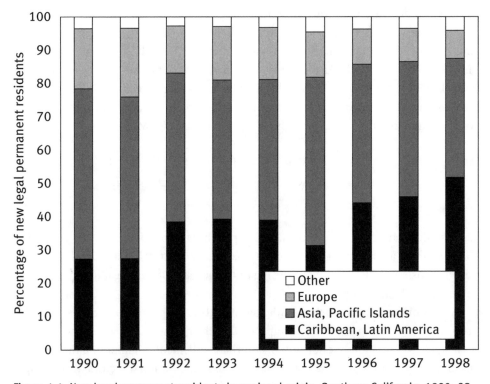

Figure 4.4. New legal permanent residents by regional origin, Southern California, 1990–98.

Applying our housing development definition of a suburban area to the entire Southern California region, we find that the proportion of new immigrants who settled initially in a suburban rather than an urban PUMA rose from 29 to 37 percent. Overall, 33 percent settled in the suburbs over the entire 1990–98 period. Consequently, although Los Angeles remains the dominant destination for most immigrants legalized during the 1990s, and two of every three new immigrants decided to live in urban areas, it is also the case that the proportion of new immigrants leapfrogging over cities for suburbs has been rising. We may tentatively conclude, therefore, that newer legal immigrants are indeed contributing to suburbanization in the greater Los Angeles region, but a trickle rather than a stream is perhaps the appropriate metaphor for the inflow to date.

Figure 4.6 illustrates why the slight rise in the proportion of new immigrants going to the suburbs should be interpreted with caution. Indeed, this trend is the result of fewer settling in urban areas and the number headed for the suburbs remaining fairly constant throughout the 1990s, rather than substantially more choosing the suburbs over the city. Still, an additional 30,000 to 40,000 new immigrants moving to the suburbs annually is likely to have increased the demand for housing and contributed to the need for greater public investment in infrastructure.[12] Figure 4.7 shows the geographic distribution of the new immigrants who settled in Southern California by PUMA.

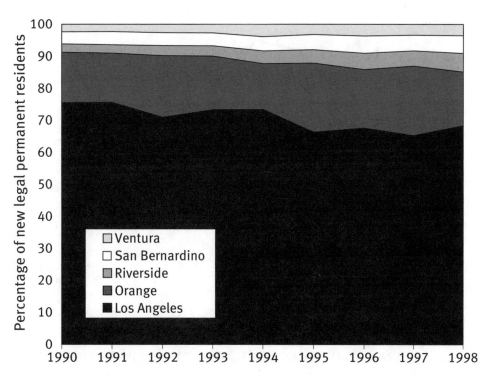

Figure 4.5. New legal permanent residents by intended county of residence, Southern California, 1990–98.

Table 4.1 provides descriptive statistics for the individual demographic and spatial-institutional explanatory variables that are used to investigate variations in immigrants' intent to settle in suburban PUMAs upon receiving legal immigrant status. Except for regional origin, there are few demographic differences between urban and suburban immigrant settlers. The mean age of immigrants entering either urban or suburban areas is thirty-one, and the percentages female or married are almost identical. Likewise, regardless of urban or suburban destination, very similar proportions were likely to report service, professional, or management occupations (e.g., lower-skilled occupations) and to have obtained their new immigrant status through family-related (family-sponsored or immediate relative) rather than employment-based or refugee provisions. Conversely, those from Asian nations were more likely than others to settle directly in suburban PUMAs—a dynamic that has led to the development of the "ethnoburb" (Li 1997, 1998)—and those from European nations were more than twice as likely to settle in urban neighborhoods.

The spatial-institutional factors hypothesized to influence urban/suburban differences in initial residential settlement vary more significantly than individual characteristics, however. But first, as a second check on whether the criterion used here for separating urban from suburban PUMAs is reasonable, note that the forty-one PUMAs (45 percent of those in the region) tagged as suburban represented approximately 60 percent of Southern California's population.[13] Although there exist no perfectly comparable estimates of the proportion of Southern California residents who

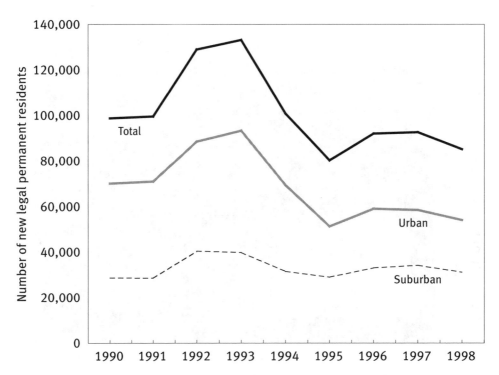

Figure 4.6. Numbers of new legal permanent residents by intended urban or suburban residence, Southern California, 1990–98.

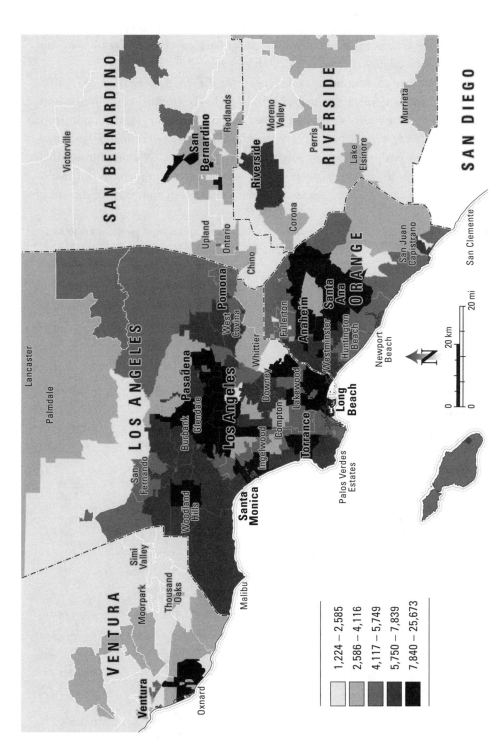

Figure 4.7. New adult legal permanent residents, per Public Use Microdata Area, 1990–98.

	1,224 – 2,585
	2,586 – 4,116
	4,117 – 5,749
	5,750 – 7,839
	7,840 – 25,673

were suburbanites, as of 1990 approximately 40 percent of the region's population resided outside of Los Angeles County. Assuming, conservatively, that at least one-third of the remaining residents of Los Angeles County live in suburban rather than urban areas, the estimate that about 60 percent of Southern Californians live in suburbs has some credibility (Fulton et al. 2000; Wolch et al. forthcoming).

When we turn to examining differences in the four categories of spatial-institutional variables, we see that the suburbs had a lower proportion of foreign-born residents (30 percent versus 47 percent). They also had lower aggregate employment concentration (forty-two jobs versus fifty-three jobs per hundred residents) and experienced weak but positive aggregate job growth (1 percent vs. −9.4 percent in urban areas). Similarly, when we analyze job density and job growth separately for manufacturing and the service sector, we see greater concentration and negative growth of

Table 4.1. Descriptive characteristics by urban and suburban area, new legal permanent residents (LPRs), Southern California, 1990–98

Characteristic	Urban area	Suburban area
Individual demographic characteristics		
Age (mean)	31	31
Female (%)	54.7	55.6
Married (%)	50.0	50.8
Regional origin		
Latin America	38.9	36.6
Asia	40.7	51.0
Europe	17.2	8.4
Other	3.2	4.0
Occupation of persons aged 16 or older (%)		
Professional and Management	22.2	21.7
Technical and administrative support	10.9	9.1
Service	43.1	46.5
Farming, forestry, and fishing	2.1	2.8
Higher-skilled labor	6.6	5.8
Lower-skilled labor	15.2	14.2
Immigrant class of admission (%)		
Family sponsored	28.8	32.1
Employment based	15.0	12.8
Immediate relative	27.9	33.5
Refugee/asylee	13.6	11.7
Other	14.9	9.9
Number of LPR observations, 1990–98	615,167	296,099
Percentage LPRs by area, 1990–98	67.5	32.5
1990–98 LPRs as % of area's 1990 population	10.8	3.5
Spatial-institutional factors		
Number of Public Use Microdata Areas (PUMAs)	51	41
PUMAs, % of urban-suburban area	55.4	44.6
Population, 1990	5,721,839	8,498,174
Population, % of urban-suburban area	40.2	59.8
Foreign-born, 1990 (%)	47.3	29.6
Total job density, 1990 (jobs per 100 residents)	53.2	41.7
Total job growth, 1990–94 (%)	−9.4	1.0
Manufacturing job density, 1990 (jobs per 100 residents)	10.1	7.1
Manufacturing job growth, 1990–94 (%)	−15.8	10.1
Service sector job density, 1990 (jobs per 100 residents)	22.6	17.2
Service sector job growth, 1990–94 (%)	−3.1	11.1
Antipoverty expenditure per poor person (mean), 1988–90 ($)	1,924	1,900
Rent, 1990 (mean) ($)	654	703

Sources: 1990–98 Immigration and Naturalization Service Legal Public Use Tapes; 1990 Public Use Microdata Samples; 1990–94 data from Southern California Association of Governments; 1988–90 data from Consolidated Federal Funds Report.

employment in urban neighborhoods. Conversely, although suburban neighborhoods were characterized by relatively lower manufacturing and service sector employment concentration, they experienced a 10 percent rise in the number of such jobs.

Furthermore, whereas suburban neighborhoods required renters to pay about fifty dollars more per month on average than urban neighborhoods, mean monthly antipoverty expenditure per poor person was almost identical. From these simple descriptive characteristics it seems reasonable to suspect that certain geographically circumscribed institutional factors may have had more than a modest influence on where new immigrants settled during the 1990s.

The first column in Table 4.2 intimates that married females were more likely to settle in suburban neighborhoods, but that age and ethnoracial group identity had no influence on their settling in the suburbs. Specifically, females were more than twice as likely as males and married persons were almost five times more likely than single persons to settle in suburban neighborhoods, but this is before differences in the spatial-institutional characteristics of urban and suburban areas are controlled for.[14]

Table 4.2. Logistic and ordinary least squares (OLS) regression analyses of intended legal permanent resident (LPR) settlement, Southern California, 1990–98

Characteristics	Logistic regressions of individual LPR settlement		OLS regressions of numbers of LPRs settling in urban or suburban neighborhoods		
	Model 1	Model 2	Model 1	Model 2	Model 3
Individual Characteristics					
AGE	−0.001	−0.001			
	(0.001)	(0.001)			
FEMALE	0.059 ***	0.041 **			
	(0.012)	(0.018)			
MARRIED	0.166 ***	0.078 ***			
	(0.030)	(0.029)			
LATINO	0.072	0.411 **			
	(0.296)	(0.180)			
ASIAN	0.359	0.566 ***			
	(0.250)	(0.162)			
Spatial-Institutional Factors					
SUBURB			0.080		
			(0.101)		
FBPCT		−10.696 **	1.908 ***	1.673 ***	3.051 ***
		(4.121)	(0.384)	(0.473)	(0.428)
MANDNSE		0.081 **	−0.011 *	−0.013	0.001
		(0.038)	(0.007)	(0.008)	(0.011)
MANGROW		2.329 **	−0.550 ***	−0.769 *	−0.185
		(1.085)	(0.186)	(0.366)	(0.141)
SERVDNSE		−0.046 **	0.010*	0.007	0.017 *
		(0.022)	(0.006)	(0.006)	(0.008)
SERVGROW		2.684 *	−0.250 *	−0.423	−0.164
		(1.472)	(0.145)	(0.388)	(0.156)
ANTIPOV		−0.001	0.000	0.000	0.000
		(0.001)	(0.000)	(0.000)	(0.000)
RENT		0.002	0.001 *	0.001 *	0.000
		(0.003)	(0.000)	(0.001)	(0.000)
Percentage concordant pairs	67.5	80.8			
R^2			0.51	0.40	0.63
N	574,318	567,823	792	450	342

*$p < .10$ **$p < .05$ ***$p < .01$

Two notable things happen once we control for differences in spatial-institutional factors such as foreign-born concentration, job growth, antipoverty expenditures, and rental prices (see the second column). First, although being female and married remain statistically robust predictors of the probability of having intended to settle in a suburban area, substantively they become weaker. Females are now slightly less than twice as likely as males, and married persons are slightly less than three times more likely than single persons, to have indicated that they were planning to settle in the suburbs. Second, persons who migrated from Asian or Latin American countries become 10 and 12.5 times more likely, respectively, than those who hailed from European or other nations to have reported suburban destinations.

The coefficients on the spatial-institutional variables indicate that the foreign-born (FBPCT) were less concentrated and that job growth in both manufacturing (MANGROW) and service (SERVGROW) sectors was greater in the suburbs vis-à-vis cities. Further, although manufacturing employment was more concentrated in the suburbs (MANDNSE), service sector employment was more concentrated in urban neighborhoods (SERVDNSE). Although the coefficients on antipoverty spending (ANTIPOV) and rental prices (RENT) are not significant, these findings confirm that the spatial-institutional differences between urban and suburban areas reported in Table 4.1 hold under multivariate scrutiny. Unfortunately, however, they tell us nothing concerning how these factors may have influenced the decisions of new immigrants to settle initially in the suburbs.[15] To approach the question of how spatially conditioned institutional factors may affect settlement decisions, we employ a traditional locational choice model that estimates factors influencing the total number of immigrants intending to settle in particular neighborhoods.

In the third column in Table 4.2, we employ OLS and regress the log of the total number of recent immigrants on our four categories of spatial-institutional variables across eighty-eight PUMAs from 1990 to 1998. From the coefficient on SUBURB, we see that recent immigrants were not drawn to particular neighborhoods simply because they were tagged as suburban by our housing development definition. Rather, other characteristics of PUMAs seem to have had greater influence on the residential settlement locations in Southern California during the 1990s.[16] First, the cultural affinity hypothesis finds substantive and statistically significant support. A 10-point increase in the percentage of foreign-born residents within a given PUMA (FBPCT) at the mean had the independent effect of attracting approximately 161 additional immigrants.[17] Alternatively, and contrary to the employment growth hypothesis, a 10-point increase in number of manufacturing jobs within a PUMA (MANGROW) was associated with 41 fewer immigrants intending to settle there, and a 10-point increase in the number of service sector jobs by PUMA (SERVGROW) was associated with 19 fewer immigrants. Although counterintuitive at first glance, these results may reflect the fact that immigrants are more likely to (1) move to neighborhoods less likely to have experienced recent job growth and (2) target larger geographic areas (e.g., a region or the suburbs) rather than a specific neighborhood (PUMA) to capitalize on employment opportunities.[18] Similarly, a neighborhood having experienced an increase of 10 manufacturing jobs per 100 residents (MANDNSE) could have expected 80 fewer new immigrants from 1990 to 1998, but on average a PUMA with 10 additional service sector jobs per 100 residents would have expected approximately 1,300 additional immigrants (or 144 per annum). Thus, although job growth (regardless of industry sector) and manufacturing job concentration appear to have been negatively associated with the settlement intentions of new legal immigrants in Southern California during the 1990s, this was not the case for service sector job density. New immigrants were more likely to migrate toward neighborhoods with higher proportions of service sector employment.

And finally, for all new immigrants regardless of urban/suburban settlement intention, the level of federal antipoverty assistance apparently had no effect, but an increase in rent of one hundred dollars was associated with approximately 80 additional immigrants desiring to settle there. In sum, these results suggest that our four spatial-institutional hypotheses (cultural affinity, employment conditions, welfare availability, and rental prices) explain about half of the variation in the number of new immigrants settling in Southern California neighborhoods during the 1990s.[19]

When we analyze how the various spatial-institutional factors influenced settlement choice by neighborhood within urban areas (fourth column) and suburban areas (fifth column) separately, all coefficients are signed similarly. Several differences, however, are worth highlighting. First, the impact of FBPCT on neighborhood choice was almost double in the suburbs compared with urban areas. One possible explanation for this is that when selecting specific neighborhoods in which to reside, new immigrants who settled in the suburbs relied more heavily on cultural/social networks than did those who settled in the more traditional urban core. A 10-point rise in the percentage foreign-born in an urban (or suburban) neighborhood was associated with 140 (273) additional immigrants intending to settle there.

The only job growth impact occurred within urban neighborhoods, and it was negative. Specifically, a 10 percent increase in the number of manufacturing jobs within urban PUMAs resulted in 56 fewer immigrants intending to reside there. However, augmenting the number of jobs per 100 residents within suburban PUMAs by 10 would have resulted in more than 3,000 additional immigrants. These results indicate that new immigrants may be drawn to areas where a large number of service sector jobs already exist, rather than to those areas where job growth is occurring. A possible explanation for this is that job turnover is higher where jobs are more highly concentrated than where new jobs are being created. Neither of our proxies for neighborhood employment conditions, however, permits us to investigate this possibility. Alternatively, a second hypothesis that may be pursued in subsequent research is that neighborhoods with higher concentrations of service sector employment are poorer, and more recent immigrants migrate to such areas to secure affordable housing.

Finally, although welfare availability does not appear to be an important determinant of settlement destination at the neighborhood level within cities or suburbs, and rental prices were unrelated to the settlement of immigrants headed for the suburbs,

RENT had a positive impact on those who were city bound. Although we may expect higher rents to dissuade neighborhood in-migration, it is important to note that our rent variable does not control for household or apartment size or density. If new immigrants are more likely to live with relatives or friends in urban areas, then the positive correlation makes sense.

Summary and Implications for Future Research

Immigration scholars have recently announced that "suburban settlement is emerging as a hallmark of contemporary immigration in the United States" (Alba et al. 1999, 446). And although the present analysis indicates that a rising proportion of newer immigrants settled initially in the suburbs during the 1990s in Southern California, one caveat is indispensable. This finding was driven exclusively by a decrease in the number of new immigrants settling in urban areas; there was no increase in the number of immigrants settling in the suburbs. Still, almost one-third (or 300,000) of all new immigrants who came to Southern California in the 1990s settled in suburban neighborhoods.

Controlling for individual demographic characteristics within a multivariate framework, this study has investigated the impacts of four spatial-institutional factors (foreign-born concentration, labor market conditions, welfare availability, and rental prices) on the probability of recent immigrants' settling in suburbs within the five-county Southern California region between 1990 and 1998. Like most previous research (Bartel 1989; Belanger and Rogers 1992; Buckley 1996; Dunlevy 1991; Kritz and Nogle 1994; Massey 1986; Neuman and Tienda 1994; Zavodny 1999), it has found that the desire to reside near other foreign-born persons is the most important factor influencing where newer immigrants initially settled during the 1990s in Southern California. Although foreign-born concentration (still highest in urban areas) may have represented a powerful drag on the probability of immigrants' settling initially in the suburbs, among those who headed for suburban neighborhoods, cultural or social ties were almost twice as important for explaining this. Not only does this lend support to Li's (1997, 1998) concept of the ethnoburb and suggest the appropriateness of a multi-versus monocentric analytic framework for studying factors influencing immigrants' local settlement destinations within Southern California, it highlights how cultural affinity can both encourage and dissuade suburban settlement.

Employing several industry-specific job density and growth variables to estimate labor market conditions, we have seen that among newer immigrants who settled in urban areas, manufacturing job growth had a repellent effect, but among those who settled in the suburbs the concentration of service sector jobs had a magnetic effect. We can conclude from these mixed results that the availability of service sector jobs may have had a positive influence on the probability of immigrants' settling initially in suburban neighborhoods. I want to caution, however, that neither the job growth variable nor the job density variable used here permits us to focus directly on job turn-over, and this may be a more important labor market indicator of what attracts new immigrants. Nonetheless, the mixed results of this analysis suggest that discouraging or encouraging certain types of industries is likely to have differential effects on the number of recent immigrants intending to reside in the suburbs. Service sector, but not manufacturing, job creation is likely to augment incentives for immigrants to settle outside the urban core. This is supportive of Heer's (2000) urban labor market saturation hypothesis as well as previous research findings suggesting that labor market conditions may influence immigrants' residential choices (Bartel 1989). It is inconsistent, however, with other evidence that labor market conditions are relatively unimportant (Bartel and Koch 1991; Filer 1992; Kritz and Nogle 1994; Zavodny 1999).

Similar to findings reported by Zavodny (1999) but contrary to those of Borjas (1999a, 1999b) and Buckley (1996), this study has found that welfare availability does not appear to have affected new immigrants' settlement patterns in Southern California. One explanation for this is that this analysis has examined residential settlement among new immigrants at too small a geographic level and therefore has missed required variation in poverty spending. This does not appear to be the case, however. The annual antipoverty expenditure variable constructed here from various Consolidated Federal Funds Report programs ranges from about $900 to $6,300 per poor person. A more feasible explanation is that refugees and asylees were intentionally excluded from the above regression analyses, and past work suggests these two groups may be more likely than other foreign-born entrants to use welfare (Zavodny 1999; Zimmerman and Fix 1994).

Consistent with the estimated impact of cultural affinity and labor market conditions (but unlike antipoverty spending), rental prices also seem to have influenced whether recent legal immigrants settled in the suburbs. Within urban areas, higher rents and the number of new immigrants intending to settle there were positively related. One possible explanation for this is that immigrants who decide to settle in urban areas are more likely to live with relatives or friends and to share expenses, which allows them to pay higher rents.

Of course, certain individual characteristics influenced newer legal immigrants' decisions to settle in the suburbs as well. Specifically, being female, married, and Asian or Latino had a positive impact on the probability of settling initially in the suburbs, a result consistent with the individual-level emphasis in Massey's (1985) well-known model of spatial assimilation and in Alba et al.'s (1999) research. Still, the finding that foreign-born and suburban service sector employment concentration had a magnetic rather than a constraining effect on newer immigrants' initial settlement in the suburbs calls into question the notion that collective forces only constrain individual-level motivations. Thus, although the present study found some support for the original spatial assimilation model at the individual demographic level, as did Alba et al.'s (1999) study, these results suggest the need for some modification in the existing theory to allow for more effective consideration of collective institutional forces.[20]

One useful direction for future research would be to incorporate a neighborhood population density variable to estimate more directly whether immigrants are contributing to "urban sprawl." Randomly selecting a member from each household rather than including all newer immigrants would also reduce any concern that migrating is a household-level rather than an individual-level decision. Another promising direction for future research would be to investigate further, with different data from other regions in the United States, whether and to what extent lower institutional barriers to suburban settlement (Alba et al. 1999) and the saturation of economic opportunity in urban areas (Heer 2000) influence immigrants' suburban settlement decisions in various parts of the country.

On the policy side, the results of the present study suggest for Southern California that generating attractive employment opportunities and affordable housing in urban areas could reduce the probability that newer legal immigrants will settle in the suburbs. Although this study has not employed multivariate analysis to investigate differences in the probabilities of suburban settlement between employment- and family-based entrants, by occupation, or by industry directly, descriptive statistics suggest that there are few such differences between immigrants settling in urban and suburban areas. Consequently, simply shifting emphasis in immigration policy toward employment-based preferences is unlikely to alter the patterns of surburbanization already under way. It also seems clear that federal welfare spending is neither an attraction nor a repellent to immigrant residents. In sum, if the goal is to slow the current trickle of recent new legal permanent immigrants to the suburbs in Southern California, changes in employment and housing policy are more likely to be effective than changes in immigration or welfare policy. Those who suggest that restrictionist immigration policies would constrain sprawl seem to be barking up the wrong policy tree: "smart growth" strategies are likely to be a good recipe for immigrants and native-born alike.

Notes

1. Alternatively, William Julius Wilson (2000) argues that although sprawl increased between 8 percent and 15 percent from 1970 through 1990 across U.S. metropolitan areas, population growth has been much slower.

2. Kritz and Gurak (2001) also show, contrary to the displacement thesis, that an increase in the number of recent immigrants affects the out-migration of native-born persons and those from previous foreign-born entry cohorts similarly at the state level.

3. The Southern California region includes Los Angeles, Orange, San Bernardino, Riverside, and Ventura Counties.

4. Readers may wish to see Greenwood, McDowell, and Trabka (1991) for a discussion of problems associated with the use of INS data.

5. Although I include all non-IRCA-adjusted immigrants in the following descriptive analysis, I exclude refugees and asylees from the regression analyses also, because upon their entry the INS may determine where these individuals initially settle (Zavodny 1999, 1023). Also, because initial residential locations of immigrant children are dependent on their parents' settlement, I exclude children from the regression analyses.

6. Again, the data employed in this study do not include the two million persons granted LPR status under the amnesty (or legalization) provisions of the 1986 Immigration Reform and Control Act during these years (shown in Figure 4.1 by the dark dashed line), the six million LPRs who settled outside the Southern California region, or any nonamnestied unauthorized immigrant residents.

7. Approximately 42 percent of all houses were built between 1960 and 1990 in the region, and forty-one (or 45 percent) of all ninety-two PUMAs had a percentage of their respective housing units that were built during this thirty-year period that exceeded the regional average. Los Angeles County had approximately 16 percent (or nine) of its fifty-eight PUMAs, Orange County had 93 percent (or thirteen) of its fourteen PUMAs, Riverside County had 100 percent of its six PUMAs, San Bernardino County had 89 percent (or eight) of its nine PUMAs, and Ventura County had 100 percent of its five PUMAs tagged as suburban. Alternatively, Alba et al. (1999) coded a metropolitan-area PUMA in the 1990 PUMS as urban when 95 percent of its population resided in a central city and as a suburb when 95 percent of its population did not. They did so because, unlike the 1980 PUMS, the 1990 PUMS does not provide a dichotomous central-city/suburban variable.

8. I also investigated how the urban-suburban dichotomous variable would change were one to use the 1970–90 period to represent suburban development, and only five PUMAs were not categorized as suburban that were using the 1960–90 selection criterion: PUMAs 4805 (Fullerton), 4807 (Buena Park, Cypress, La Palma, Los Alamitos, Seal Beach, Stanton), 6000 (Carson), 6515 (Los Angeles City: Sylmar, parts of Mission Hills and Granada Hills), and 6516 (Los Angeles City: Canoga Park, Woodland Hills). The 1960–90 threshold conforms better to known residential patterns and confirms that suggested to me by John Landis, whom I would like to thank.

9. P.O. box numbers are excluded because they are not attached to residences.

10. In addition to investigating the impacts of overall job density and job growth on the probability of an immigrant's settling in a suburban PUMA, we also examine the effects of manufacturing and service sector job density (MANDNSE and SERVDNSE) and growth (MANGROW and SERVGROW).

11. Among those who are dropped are 233,597 children, persons for whom age data were not available (150 persons), and 88,705 adult refugee and asylee adjusters. Adult refugee adjusters represented 25.6 percent and adult asylee adjusters represented 9.7 percent of all Southern California immigrants who legalized from 1991 to 1998. Two-thirds (385,784) reported valid occupational titles.

12. Heer (2000) argues that one possible explanation for the decline in the proportion of new immigrants choosing to reside initially in Southern California during the 1990s is that labor market saturation countered the forces of cumulative causation.

13. The first check was simply to observe the list of PUMAs falling into the suburban category and verify with regional experts that these categorizations are reasonable. Four PUMAs were questionable using the 1960–90 housing development criterion (Santa Ana, Anaheim, Fullerton, and Riverside), but, as we shall see below, redefining these as urban has little effect on the regression results. Most studies distinguish the suburbs from central cities (using the census definition) and from rural areas. In short, by 1990 approximately one-half of the U.S. population resided in suburbs—defined as "municipalities and places in metropolitan areas outside of the political boundaries of the large central cities" (Baldassare 1992, 476).

14. Probability interpretations of these coefficients are computed by multiplying the coefficient for a specific explanatory variable by the mean of the dependent variable (0.3295) and one minus this mean. For instance, multiplying the coefficient generated for the FEMALE variable (0.059 in the first column in Table 4.2) by 0.3295 (the mean of the dependent variable, or of having intended to settle in a suburban neighborhood) and (1 − 0.3295) converts the coefficient into a value of 1.30. This number implies that females were 130 percent more (or more

than twice as) likely than males to have preferred to settle in a suburb. This computation converts logistic regression coefficients into probabilities and is used to interpret all remaining coefficients in the first and second columns. Marcelli and Cornelius (2001) also found that female Mexican migrants were more likely than their male compatriots to settle permanently in the United States using data collected in San Diego and Los Angeles Counties in the early 1990s.

15. This is because each of the ninety-two PUMAs is assigned a value of one or zero for the dependent variable (suburb), and each PUMA has a unique value for each of the four categories of spatial-institutional factors. Thus reported coefficients indicate simply whether differences in these characteristics are statistically significant.

16. An indication that our dependent variable (SUBURB) is independent from our four spatial-institutional variables is that the highest correlation is between SUBURB and FBPCT (−0.59). The next-highest correlation is with JOBGROW (+ 0.44), and the two lowest were with ANTIPOV (−0.005) and RENT (+ 0.17). Thus we have some confidence that these factors are contributing information independent of the proportion of houses that were built between 1960 and 1990. Further, to check whether our regression results are period specific, we reran all models with a JOBGROW variable created from 1980–90 data for L.A. County only. Results were very similar, as they were when we redefined the four "questionable" PUMAs that were defined as suburban.

17. The figure of 161 is computed in the following way. The coefficient of 1.908 in the third column represents the impact of a unit change in FBPCT on LN_LPR. A one-unit change (plus 1.0) in this case is not useful given that our independent variable (FBPCT) ranges from 0.1 to 0.8. To arrive at the number of additional LPRs that would have settled in a PUMA in a given year resulting from a 10 percent rise in FBPCT requires taking the exponential of the mean of LN_LPR (6.6417) to obtain the number of LPRs (766) and then adding the equivalent of a 10 percent change (0.1908, which is 10 percent of the coefficient) to the mean of LN_LPR (thus giving 6.8325), computing its exponential to obtain the new number of LPRs (927), and subtracting (927 − 766 = 161).

18. Recent research in Los Angeles County indicates that poorer immigrants tend to be relatively more flexible in their use of various modes of transportation (Ong and Houston 2001).

19. Given that there are only eighty-eight independent data points in this regression after one employs a geographic cluster correction technique (StataCorp 1998), this level of explanatory power is encouraging. See Mason (2001) for a comprehensive overview of when to employ multilevel methods of statistical analysis.

20. Logan and Molotch (1987) and Massey and Denton (1993) have recognized that African Americans and other nonwhite minorities may be exceptions to the original spatial assimilation model, and Pastor and Marcelli (2000) have recently argued that job opportunities may provide incentives for individuals to reside in or near the suburbs.

Works Cited

Alba, Richard D., and John R. Logan. 1991. "Variations on Two Themes: Racial and Ethnic Patterns in the Attainment of Suburban Residence." *Demography* 28(3):431–53.

Alba, Richard D., John R. Logan, and Kyle Crowder. 1997. "White Ethnic Neighborhoods and Assimilation: The Greater New York Region, 1980–1990." *Social Forces* 75:883–912.

Alba, Richard D., John R. Logan, Brian J. Stults, Gilbert Marzan, and Wenquan Zhang. 1999. "Immigrant Groups in the Suburbs: A Reexamination of Suburbanization and Spatial Assimilation." *American Sociological Review* 64:446–60.

Allen, James P., and Eugene Turner. 1996. "Spatial Patterns of Immigrant Assimilation." *Professional Geographer* 48(2):140–55.

Baldassare, Mark. 1992. "Suburban Communities." *Annual Review of Sociology* 18:475–94.

Bartel, Ann P. 1989."Where Do the New U.S. Immigrants Live?" *Journal of Labor Economics* 7(4):371–91.

Bartel, Ann P., and Marianne J. Koch. 1991. "Internal Migration of U.S. Immigrants." In *Immigration, Trade, and the Labor Market*, ed. John M. Abowd and Richard B. Freeman, 121–34. Chicago: University of Chicago Press.

Belanger, Alain, and Andrei Rogers. 1992. "The Internal Migration and Spatial Redistribution of the Foreign-Born Population in the United States: 1965–70 and 1975–80." *International Migration Review* 26(4):1342–69.

Borjas, George J. 1999a. *Heaven's Door: Immigration Policy and the American Economy*. Princeton, NJ: Princeton University Press.

———. 1999b. "Immigration and Welfare Magnets." *Journal of Labor Economics* 17(4):607–37.

Buckley, Francis H. 1996. "The Political Economy of Immigration Policies." *International Review of Law and Economics* 16:81–99.

Burgess, Ernest W. 1967. "The Growth of the City: An Introduction to a Research Project" (orig. pub. 1925). In *The City: Suggestions for Investigation of Human Behavior in the Urban Environment*, ed. Robert E. Park and Ernest W. Burgess, 47–62. Chicago: University of Chicago Press.

Clark, William A. V. 1998.*The California Cauldron: Immigration and the Fortunes of Local Communities*. New York: Guilford.

Clune, Michael S. 1998. "The Fiscal Impacts of Immigrants: A California Case Study." In *The Immigration Debate: Studies on the Economic, Demographic, and Fiscal Effects of Immigration*, ed. James P. Smith and Barry Edmonston, 120–82. Washington, DC: National Academy Press.

Dunlevy, James A. 1991. "On the Settlement Patterns of Recent Caribbean and Latin Immigrants to the United States." *Growth and Change* 22:54–67.

Easterlin, Richard A. 1961."Influences in European Overseas Emigration before World War I." *Economic Development and Cultural Change* 10(3):331–51.

———. 1982. "Economic and Social Characteristics of the Immigrants." In *Immigration*, ed. Richard A. Easterlin, David Ward, William S. Bernard, and Reed Ueda, 1–34. Cambridge, MA: Belknap.

Filer, Randall K. 1992. "The Effect of Immigrant Arrivals on Migratory Patterns of Native Workers." In *Immigration and the Workforce: Economic Consequences for the United States and Source Areas*, ed. George J. Borjas and Richard B. Freeman, 245–69. Chicago: University of Chicago Press.

Fong, Eric, and Kumiko Shibuya. 2000. "Suburbanization and Home Ownership: The Spatial Assimilation Process in U.S. Metropolitan Areas." *Sociological Perspectives* 43(1):137–57.

Frey, William H., and Ross C. Devol. 2000. *America's Demography in the New Century: Aging Baby Boomers and New Immigrants as Major Players*. Santa Monica, CA: Milken Institute.

Frey, William H., and Kao-Lee Liaw. 1998a. "Immigrant Concentration and Domestic Migrant Dispersal: Is Movement to Non-Metro Areas 'White Flight'?" *Professional Geographer* 50(2):215–32.

———. 1998b. "The Impact of Recent Immigration on Population and Redistribution within the United States." In *The Immigration Debate: Studies on the Economic, Demographic, and*

Fiscal Effects of Immigration, ed. James P. Smith and Barry Edmonston, 388–448. Washington, DC: National Academy Press.

Fulton, William, Madelyn Glickfeld, Grant McMurran, and June Gin. 2000. *A Landscape Portrait of Southern California's Structure of Government and Growth*. Claremont, CA: Claremont Graduate University Research Institute.

Gans, Herbert. 1967. *The Levittowners: Ways of Life and Politics in a New Suburban Community*. New York: Pantheon.

Giuliano, Genevieve, and Kenneth Small. 1991. "Subcenters in the Los Angeles Region." *Regional Science and Urban Economics* 21(2):163–82.

Greenwood, Michael J., John M. McDowell, and Eloise Trabka. 1991. "Conducting Descriptive and Analytical Research with the Immigration and Naturalization Service Public Use Tapes." *Journal of Economics and Social Measurement* 17:131–53.

Guest, Avery M., and George H. Nelson. 1978. "Central City/Suburban Status Differences: Fifty Years of Change." *Sociological Quarterly* 19:7–23.

Heer, David M. 2000. "When Cumulative Causation Conflicts with Saturation of Economic Opportunity: Recent Change in the Hispanic Population of the United States." Paper presented at the meeting of the Population Association of America, Los Angeles, March 24.

Jackson, Kenneth T. 1985. *Crabgrass Frontier: The Suburbanization of the United States*. New York: Oxford University Press.

Joassart-Marcelli, Pascale, and Juliet Musso. 2001. "The Distributive Impact of Federal Fiscal Policy: Federal Spending in Southern California Cities." *Urban Affairs Review* 37(2):163–83.

Kolankiewicz, Leon, and Roy Beck. 2000. "Sprawl in California: A Report on Quantifying the Role of the State's Population Boom." Paper presented at the Californians for Population Stabilization conference "Waking from the Dream: Population and the Environment at the Millennial Edge," University of Southern California, August 13.

Kritz, Mary M., and Douglas T. Gurak. 2001. "The Impact of Immigration on the Internal Migration of Natives and Immigrants." *Demography* 38(1):133–45.

Kritz, Mary M., and June Marie Nogle. 1994. "Nativity Concentration and Internal Migration among the Foreign-Born." *Demography* 31(3):509–24.

Li Wei. 1997. "Anatomy of a New Ethnic Settlement: The Chinese *Ethnoburb* in Los Angeles." *Urban Studies* 35(3):479–501.

———. 1998. "Los Angeles's Chinese *Ethnoburb*: From Ethnic Service Center to Global Economy Outpost." *Urban Geography* 19(6):502–17.

Logan, John R., and Reid M. Golden. 1986. "Suburbs and Satellites: Two Decades of Change." *American Sociological Review* 51:430–37.

Logan, John R., and Harvey L. Molotch. 1987. *Urban Fortunes: The Political Economy of Place*. Berkeley: University of California Press.

Marcelli, Enrico A., and Wayne A. Cornelius. 2001. "The Changing Profile of Mexican Migrants to the United States: New Evidence from California and Mexico." *Latin American Research Review* 36(3):105–31.

Marsh, Margaret. 1990. *Suburban Lives*. New Brunswick, NJ: Rutgers University Press.

Mason, William M. 2001. "Multilevel Methods of Statistical Analysis." In *International Encyclopedia of the Social and Behavioral Sciences*, ed. Neil J. Smelser and Paul B. Baltes. Amsterdam: Elsevier Science.

Massey, Douglas S. 1985. "Ethnic Residential Segregation: A Theoretical Synthesis and Empirical Review." *Sociology and Social Research* 69(3):315–50.

———. 1986. "The Settlement Process among Mexican Migrants to the United States." *American Sociological Review* 51:670–84.

Massey, Douglas S., and Nancy A. Denton. 1987. "Trends in Residential Segregation of Blacks, Hispanics, and Asians: 1970–1980." *American Sociological Review* 52:802–25.

———. 1988. "Suburbanization and Segregation in U.S. Metropolitan Areas." *American Journal of Sociology* 94:592–626.

———. 1993. *American Apartheid: Segregation and the Making of the Underclass.* Cambridge, MA: Harvard University Press.

Muller, Thomas. 1993. *Immigrants and the American City.* New York: New York University Press.

Neuman, Kristin E., and Marta Tienda. 1994. "The Settlement and Secondary Migration Patterns of Legalized Immigrants: Insights from Administrative Records." In *Immigration and Ethnicity: The Integration of America's Newest Arrivals*, ed. Barry Edmonston and Jeffrey S. Passel, 187–226. Washington, DC: Urban Institute Press.

Newbold, K. Bruce. 2000. "Intended and Initial Settlement Patterns of Recent Immigrants to the U.S., 1985–1990: A Comparison of PUMS and INS Public Use Files." *Population and Environment* 21(6):539–63.

Ong, Paul M., and Douglas Houston. 2001. "Welfare Recipients and Public Transit." Working paper. University of California, Los Angeles, Lewis Center for Regional Policy Studies.

Passel, Jeffrey S., and Wendy Zimmerman. 2000. "Are Immigrants Leaving California?" Paper presented at the meetings of the Population Association of America, Los Angeles, March 23–25.

Pastor, Manuel, Jr., and Enrico A. Marcelli. 2000. "Men 'n the Hood: Skill, Spatial, and Social Mismatches among Male Workers in Los Angeles County." *Urban Geography* 21(6): 474–96.

Raphael, Steven. 1998a. "Inter and Intra-ethnic Comparisons of the Central City Suburban Youth Employment Differential: Evidence from the Oakland Metropolitan Area." *Industrial and Labor Relations Review* 51(3):505–24.

———. 1998b. "The Spatial Mismatch Hypothesis and Black Youth Joblessness: Evidence from the San Francisco Bay Area." *Journal of Urban Economics* 43(1):79–111.

Schnore, Leo. 1963. "The Social and Economic Characteristics of American Suburbs." *Sociological Quarterly* 61:453–58.

StataCorp. 1998. *Stata Statistical Software: Release 6.0.* College Station, TX: StataCorp.

Stoll, Michael A., and Steven Raphael. 2000. "Racial Differences in Spatial Job Search Patterns: Exploring the Causes and Consequences." *Economic Geography* 76(3):201–23.

Swartz, Alex. 1992. "Corporate Service Linkages in Large Metropolitan Areas: A Study of New York, Los Angeles, and Chicago." *Urban Affairs Quarterly* 28:276–96.

U.S. Bureau of the Census. 1993. *1990 Census of Population: Social and Economic Characteristics, Metropolitan Areas.* Washington, DC: U.S. Bureau of the Census.

Ward, David. 1971. *Cities and Immigrants: A Geography of Change in Nineteenth Century America.* New York: Oxford University Press.

Wilson, William Julius. 2000. Keynote address delivered at the conference "Prismatic Metropolis: Inequality in Los Angeles," October 19, University of California, Los Angeles.

Wolch, Jennifer, Manuel Pastor Jr., Pascale Joassart-Marcelli, and Peter Dreier. Forthcoming. "Region by Design: Public Policy and the Making of Southern California." In *Forging Metropolitan Solutions*, ed. Janet Pack and Bruce Katz. Washington, DC: Brookings Institution.

Zavodny, Madeline. 1999. "Determinants of Recent Immigrants' Locational Choices." *International Migration Review* 33(4):1014–30.

Zimmerman, Wendy, and Michael Fix. 1994. "Immigrant Policy in the States: A Wavering Welcome." In *Immigration and Ethnicity: The Integration of America's Newest Arrivals*, ed. Barry Edmonston and Jeffrey S. Passel, 287–316. Washington, DC: Urban Institute Press.

5 | Where Is the "Region" in Regional Transportation Planning?

Genevieve Giuliano

Transportation is often cited as the one area of planning where regional planning actually exists. Transportation planning and budgeting take place in a highly structured regional process mandated by state and federal law. However, this formal structure belies the reality of political decision making. In the Los Angeles region, transportation planning is regional in name only. There is no regional consensus on how growing congestion and mobility problems should be met, nor is there a viable institutional structure for developing consensus. Rather, transportation decision making is becoming increasingly decentralized and therefore dominated by local concerns. Although there are many advantages to local decision making, there are also some serious disadvantages. These include costly and ineffective investment decisions, distributional disparities, political conflicts between jurisdictions, and paralysis on key regional transportation issues.

In this chapter, I present a short history of the evolution of transportation planning in the Los Angeles region. I explain how economic conditions, local politics, and federal policy have interacted to generate today's fragmented process of planning and financing the region's transportation system. I then illustrate the consequences of regional fragmentation with three case studies.

Transportation in the Los Angeles Region, Today and 2025

To understand the L.A. area's transportation planning problems, one needs some basic information on the region. The vastness and diversity of the region is difficult to overstate:[1]

- It contains 17 million people and 7.3 million jobs spread over 38,000 square miles. These figures are expected to increase to 21.3 million people and 9.6 million jobs by 2020.

- It has experienced consistent growth—annual average population growth rate of 3 percent—over an entire century.
- It has the twelfth-highest GNP equivalent in the world.
- It has no majority race/ethnic group. Hispanics are expected to reach majority status sometime between 2020 and 2025.
- It has relatively high population density, especially in some areas of Los Angeles County, and vast areas of uninhabited desert in Riverside and San Bernardino Counties.

Given the region's population and employment numbers, it is no surprise that consumption of transportation services is also enormous. In 1998, the region's 9.6 million drivers traveled nearly 70 billion miles on state highways while consuming 6.4 billion gallons of gasoline and involving themselves in 90,000 injury accidents, of which 1,200 included fatalities (California Department of Transportation 1998). Traffic congestion is extensive and costly. The Southern California Association of Governments (SCAG 2000) estimates that the road system carries about 350 million vehicle miles per day and about 9 million vehicle hours. Delays account for 1.5 million hours, or 82 hours per driver per year, at an estimated cost of $1,370 per driver—the highest in the United States, and twice as high as New York. The region's public transportation systems carried more than 550 million passengers in 1997—87 percent of them in Los Angeles County—yet this accounts for just 2 percent of all person-trips, about the same share as bicycle trips.

Los Angeles's growing international trade has generated a sixfold increase in trade volume through area ports and airports, from $30 billion in 1979 to $180 billion in 1998. Container cargo through the ports doubled between 1989 and 1998, and heavy truck vehicle miles increased 30 percent over the same period, to more than 13 million. And the region's six major airports handled almost 82 million commercial passengers in 1998, a one-third increase since 1987.

As astonishing as these numbers are, SCAG predicts future increases of similar magnitude. The 2025 SCAG modeling forecast estimates 480 vehicle miles per day, 13 million vehicle hours, and 2.9 million hours of delay with the "preferred" investment plan, which carries an estimated price tag of $130 billion over the twenty-five-year plan period.[2] Air passengers are expected to increase to 157 million annually, and air cargo annual tons are expected to grow from 2.6 million (1997) to 9.5 million.

The transportation challenges facing the region are difficult to exaggerate. Past patterns of growth suggest that these future projections of travel demand are not unrealistic, as they derive directly from data on anticipated population and job growth. However, like past plans, the current one is held together by optimistic assumptions regarding revenues, transit use, and population and employment distributions; it is also rife with internal contradictions.

A Brief History of Regional Transportation Planning

In the United States, regional transportation planning has a long history. Early in the twentieth century, states and the federal government recognized the regional nature of transportation infrastructure. Regional planning became official in 1962, when the federal government mandated that transportation plans meet the "3C" criteria—comprehensive, coordinated, and cooperative—in order to receive federal transportation funds. It was from this legislation that metropolitan planning organizations (MPOs) were established, with regional transportation planning their main task. Subsequent federal and state legislation reinforced regional transportation planning; all federal funding for transportation is contingent on plans approved by both state and region (Weiner 1997).

However, transportation planning in practice was and continues to be another matter. MPOs were charged with putting plans together and conducting the associated technical work, but these organizations had no real authority. Regional planning was a consensus exercise, in which multiple stakeholders pushed (or opposed) their projects. Regional transportation plans were largely collections of projects determined at the local level. And because federal funding was so important, the regional plan inevitably adapted to what could bring in the most outside funding—that is, highways and, later, rail mass transit.

Major changes in funding policy took place in the 1980s. First, the Reagan administration significantly reduced federal transit subsidies, shifting the burden of supporting transit to state and local governments. Second, the federal fuel tax increase of 1982 for the first time earmarked a portion of the fuel tax for public transit. Third, additional rules gave regions increasing flexibility to use highway funds for public transit. Fourth, the growing scarcity of federal funds for transportation placed more financial burden on local governments.

The Los Angeles region was strongly affected by these policy changes. The major regional transit operator, the Southern California Rapid Transit District (SCRTD)—which in 1992 merged with the Los Angeles County Transportation Commission (LACTC) to form the Los Angeles County Metropolitan Transportation Authority (LACMTA, or MTA)—was in serious financial trouble in the late 1970s. Threats of massive service cutbacks and fare increases led to L.A. County voters' passage of Proposition A in 1980, a one-half-cent local sales tax measure that supported a basic bus fare of fifty cents for five years, capital funding for transit, and other transportation expenditures. In addition, the suburban counties had experienced rapid growth (the combined population of Orange, Riverside, and Ventura Counties more than doubled between 1960 and 1980) even though major highway construction had virtually halted by 1970. The combination of rising congestion and continued growth pressure resulted in the passage of local sales tax measures in Orange, Riverside, and San Bernardino Counties by 1990. Los Angeles County passed a second, additional sales tax measure (Proposition C) in 1990. As we shall see, such local tax measures are the de facto transportation plans for this region.

The 1991 Act

The 1991 Intermodal Surface Transportation Efficiency Act (ISTEA) marked a new beginning in transportation funding and planning. Under this act, the interstate highway system was deemed completed and the entire system of highway finance was restructured. Major elements of ISTEA included the following:

- It provided for flexible funding between transportation modes.
- It linked transportation planning with air quality management, for the first time requiring that a region's transportation plan be consistent with its air quality improvement plan (the "conformity" provision).
- It required that conformity be based on realistic future funding estimates.
- It required that the regional transportation plan (RTP) and the short-range regional transportation improvement program (RTIP) be developed *and approved*, meaning found to be in conformity and in fiscal balance by the MPO (SCAG in the Southern California region).

ISTEA was heralded as representing the beginning of a new era in transportation planning because of these new provisions. In practice, ISTEA was more evolutionary than revolutionary, except for regions with severe air quality nonattainment problems, such as Southern California. ISTEA was evolutionary in that it made an already complex system of funding even more complicated by establishing new funding categories, each with its own requirements and restrictions, by devolving certain responsibilities to states, and by increasing the states' role in planning and fund allocation. The challenge for regional planners had been to put together packages that best met local needs while capturing the maximum amount of nonlocal dollars. In practice, the objective under ISTEA is no different.

The passage of ISTEA placed Southern California in a challenging position. The region had to develop a regional plan that would meet the act's conformity requirements, operate within the constraints of requirements associated with all funding sources (federal, state, and local), and somehow address the enormous anticipated increase in travel demand associated with projected population and employment growth.[3]

One might argue that here was a real opportunity for SCAG. Rather than becoming a powerful force for regional transportation planning, however, SCAG took the opposite approach: it devolved much of the transportation planning process to its constituent counties and major operating agencies (e.g., LACMTA for transit and Caltrans for highways). Through the individual county transportation commissions, SCAG gave the counties the authority to program all funds accruing to their jurisdictions (including federal and state funds allocated to the region). In addition, SCAG divided Los Angeles County into eight subregions, each designated a council of government, and each subregion submits its own plan to LACMTA. The RTP and the associated short-range RTIP are therefore developed through a "bottom-up" process, and SCAG's role is to broker disagreements and ensure consistency when the county plans are put together.

Explaining Devolution in the Region

This decentralized process of transportation planning is explained by two major factors. First, regional planning has never had significant support in California. SCAG, an association of governments, was established in 1965 in part to avoid the possibility that a regional government with decision-making authority would be created (Lewes and Sprague 1997). As an association of governments, SCAG must work by consensus. The Regional Council, SCAG's decision-making body, and its seventy-one members are local elected officials. SCAG encompasses a region that is larger and more diverse than many entire U.S. states. The suburban counties within SCAG have historically had little in common with Los Angeles County. The establishment of county transportation commissions in the 1970s was in part an effort to control transportation decision making on a local level. As transportation problems have become more costly and severe, and conformity and budget limitations have imposed ever more stringent constraints, intraregional conflicts have increased.

It is important to note that this resistance to regional decision making goes far beyond transportation in Southern California. Conflicts over how (or if) the region's growth should be accommodated over the past two decades have intensified differences within the region. Issues such as affordable housing, facility location, and air quality are debated across highly diverse geographies, as other chapters in this volume describe.

Second, the increased importance of local funding inevitably translates to increased local control. Most of the local funding available comes from sales tax measures that were approved by voters. In Los Angeles County, proponents managed to get these measures on the ballot by promising a large "local return" share to cities (25 percent of the revenues from each proposition), and these are the only measures that have allocated a substantial share for discretionary use. The funds resulting from the Riverside, Orange, and San Bernardino County measures are earmarked for specific projects, modal categories, or locations, and each measure has built-in monitoring and reporting requirements. These sale tax measures reinforced the power of the county commissions and made the commissions legally responsible for carrying out the measures' provisions. In addition, many of the local sales tax projects require matching funds from federal or state sources, further committing future funds to local projects. Moreover, as state and federal funds become relatively less important (although they remain very important funding sources), higher levels of government have less control over local decision making.

Another factor affecting transportation planning in Southern California is the bewildering complexity of funding. My colleagues and I collected RTIP data for all available years for the five counties that make up the SCAG region from 1982–83 through 1998–99 and summarized budgeted expenditures by mode and funding source (modes are transit, state highways, and local arterials). We were able to verify that the data were relatively complete for twelve years within this period. Using these data, we identified 263 funding sources: 78 for transit, 93 for highways, and the remainder for local arterials. By government level, the numbers are 121 federal, 45 state, and 97 local sources. Several funding sources overlapped (e.g., a single fund was used for both state highways and local arterials). Some funding sources were renamed and others were replaced or eliminated over the years, so in any given year there were far fewer than 263 entries. Nevertheless, the task of managing such a budgeting and planning exercise is formidable.

What are the consequences of such a process? First, it is so complicated that only a few longtime agency staff members have any understanding of the details of the RTIP, which means that the programming process is really a "black box." Second, manipulating the plan to conform to funding priorities becomes planners' primary objective. Third, there is little accountability for transportation funding programs other than the sales tax measures that earmark funds for specific purposes. If it is almost impossible to figure out where the money went, it is also impossible to hold anyone accountable for how it was spent. It is little wonder that the local sales tax measures have included such strong accountability provisions.

Finally, funding complexity has contributed to the politicization of the planning process. Plans become artifacts of funding provisions rather than means for accomplishing objectives. Given the fragmented political structure of the region, it is not surprising that the debate often turns on which jurisdiction gets what instead of on how common problems might best be solved.

Consequences of Devolution and Fragmentation

What are the consequences of the decentralization of transportation planning? In this section, based on analysis of RTIP data, I discuss the direct effects of changes in funding patterns and then provide some examples of policy consequences.

Consequences of ISTEA and Devolution

The first consequence is that local residents in Southern California are paying an increasingly large share of transportation infrastructure costs, as illustrated in Figure 5.1. In the 1980s, federal funds (largely formula funding for highways and transit) made up the largest share of funds in most years. In the 1990s, local funds clearly dominated. It is worth noting that total funding increased from about $1.3 billion in 1982–83 to $8.8 billion in 1998–99 (inflated dollars). The local share was $620 million in 1982–83; it was $5.7 billion in 1998–99.

Shifting infrastructure costs to local residents has both benefits and costs. As costs become more coincident with users, subsidies are reduced, and users therefore pay more of their "fair share" of these costs. However, the major source of local funds in Southern California is the sales tax, which has little relationship to how much or where people travel. Although shifting costs to local residents shifts those costs away from the general U.S. taxpayer, the sales tax is a regressive form of taxation.

Lower-income households pay a larger share of their income in sales taxes than do other households, but lower-income households travel less. Hence the effect of this shift in financing is to place a relatively greater net burden on lower-income households in the region.

The second consequence is that the five counties have been able to pursue very different transportation investment programs, as illustrated in Figures 5.2 and 5.3, which show funding by mode for Los Angeles and Orange Counties, respectively. (Orange County serves here as a representative suburban county; the modal allocations are quite similar for the four suburban counties.) Clearly, these counties have invested in very different transportation systems. Los Angeles County is dominated by transit investment, especially in the 1990s, with highway investment very small in some years. In contrast, Orange County has invested almost exclusively in highways and local roads. The surge in Los Angeles County spending occurred earlier due to both federal contributions to the rail program and the county's earlier passage of the first sales tax measure.

Growing reliance on local funds has also had the effect of increasing differences between budget patterns across counties. Table 5.1 shows the average annual percentage share for transit, by county, before and after ISTEA. Reduced formula funding allowed more flexibility and resulted in more variation across the five counties.

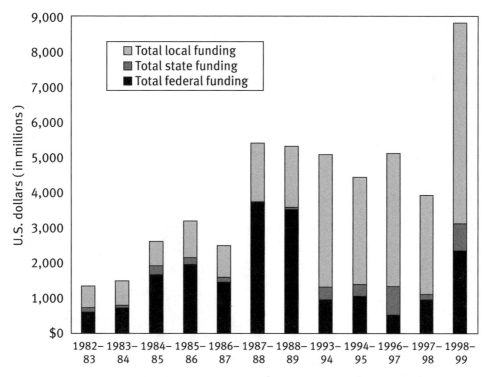

Figure 5.1. Transportation funding by source for Southern California (SCAG region), 1982–83 to 1998–99.

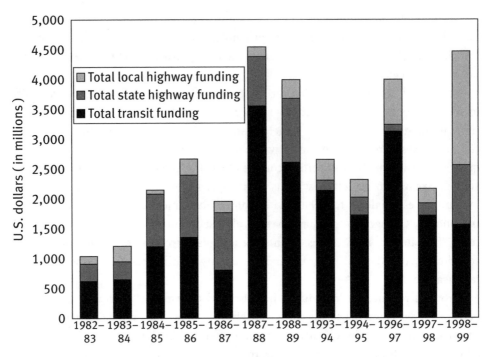

Figure 5.2. Transportation funding by mode for Los Angeles County, 1982–83 to 1998–99.

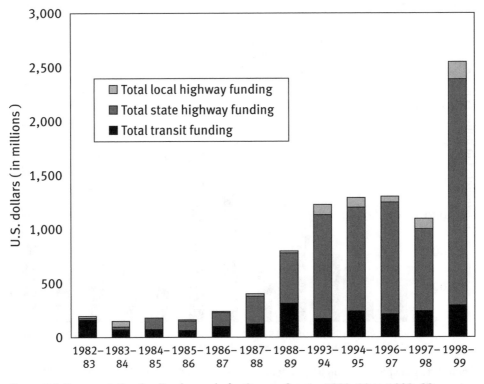

Figure 5.3. Transportation funding by mode for Orange County, 1982–83 to 1998–99.

The differences in investment strategies across counties also have both benefits and costs. Clearly, suburban voters' transportation preferences are different from those of Los Angeles County voters, and these preferences are being met. However, the transportation system is a regional system; flows do not stop at county borders. Local preferences are being accommodated at the price of the development of an integrated transportation system.

The lack of state and federal funds for transportation has also motivated a search for creative financing in Southern California counties, meaning a search for new revenue sources primarily from the private sector. Orange County's toll roads, jointly financed by users, new home buyers, and local taxpayers, are the result of such efforts. Projects funded in this way place more of the cost on users and hence promote more efficient transportation. However, these added costs also increase the price of housing, adding to already serious affordability problems in the region.

Conclusions on ISTEA

ISTEA has been implemented in the Los Angeles region in a manner consistent with historical trends. Both fiscal responsibility and decision-making authority have devolved to the local county level. Devolution continues with SCAG's establishment of subregions within Los Angeles County. The federal role is increasingly limited, because funding flexibility allows (and funding constraints require) regions to develop plans appropriate to local conditions.

On the other hand, conformity imposes severe constraints on the region. SCAG's one new source of power from ISTEA is that SCAG ultimately must decide on the RTP's conformity. SCAG officially has veto power over any project that does not conform (e.g., a project that would prevent the region from meeting air quality emissions reduction requirements). This is what makes it possible for SCAG to broker disagreements among its constituents.

Declining resources in a period of rapid regional growth caused local decision makers to turn to local revenue sources. In doing so, they not only established a major new funding source, they further solidified a long-standing tradition of highly localized planning. The conformity requirement has not been enough of a threat to change things, and the flexibility of ISTEA has had the effect of facilitating increased intraregional differences. Somehow the RTP numbers add up, and somehow the region is meeting its air quality requirements.

Table 5.1. Average annual transit budget share, in percentages, by county, before and after passage of the Intermodal Surface Transportation Efficiency Act (ISTEA)

County	Before ISTEA (1980s)	After ISTEA (1990s)
Los Angeles	61	72
Orange	46	16
Riverside	25	34
San Bernardino	16	12
Ventura	17	21
All counties	53	46

Case Studies: Consequences of Fragmented Transportation Planning

In this section, I use three case studies to demonstrate the consequences of highly localized and politicized transportation planning: public transit policy in Los Angeles County, private toll roads in Orange County, and the regional debate on airport capacity.

Public Transit Policy in Los Angeles County

Despite many billions of dollars invested in rail transit, the market share of transit within L.A. County continues to decline. This decline is explained in large part by economic and demographic trends common to metropolitan areas throughout the United States, including the decentralization of population and jobs; high rates of car ownership, even among the poor; and the array of federal policies that generally favor the private auto over other modes. However, the particular problems of Los Angeles are not adequately explained by these trends. Los Angeles has experienced more population growth and more growth from immigration than other large metropolitan areas, which suggests that transit demand should be increasing. Unfortunately, transportation policy in Los Angeles has focused on a specific mode rather than on serving transit demand.

The market for public transit is concentrated in the central portion of the region. Outside the central core, public transit carries about the same share of person-trips (less than 2 percent) as bicycles. Los Angeles County accounts for the overwhelming majority of transit ridership (87 percent), and within the county buses carry 93 percent of transit trips (1997 data). Figure 5.4 shows total public transit ridership in the region from 1983 to 1997. The high point is 1985, the cumulative result of the fifty-cent fare instituted as a result of Proposition A. Recent increases reflect both economic expansion (more commuting) and service expansions (rail in Los Angeles County, bus in other counties). However, on a trips per capita basis, transit use continues to decline.

Public transit in Los Angeles County has a turbulent history. The 1979 economic recession and inflation placed SCRTD on the verge of bankruptcy. Faced with the threat of service reductions and a doubling of fares, county voters were persuaded to pass Proposition A in 1980, which, among other provisions, guaranteed a fifty-cent transit fare for five years. The reduced fare generated a large increase in ridership, as noted above. However, SCRTD chose to shift Proposition A revenues to the rail transit capital fund at the end of the five-year period. The subsequent fare increase had the predictable effect, and transit ridership gradually declined: ridership was 422 million in 1991 and 357 million in 1997. Overall, the system lost nearly 71 million riders, or about 17 percent.

The new rail lines attracted additional passengers, but not in the numbers anticipated, and not from private autos. Most rail passengers are former bus riders, hence there has been a net decrease in transit ridership despite rail transit investment. To make matters worse, operating subsidy costs for the rail lines are very high, given the low passenger volume and high operating costs. Rubin, Moore, and Lee (1999, 59) have estimated total cost per passenger (using 1993 data) to be $1.73 for bus, $11.90 for light rail, $26.83 for heavy rail, and $46.09 for commuter rail.[4] By 1997, MTA had spent or was committed to spending almost $7 billion on rail construction; it is currently carrying another $3.66 billion in debt.

Disappointing results in attracting new transit passengers, construction problems, finance and management problems, and deterioration of the MTA bus system have led to serious political problems. Construction of the Red Line segment of the planned subway system encountered many difficulties, delays, and cost overruns. Defects in the lining of subway tunnels, a large construction-related sinkhole that damaged several buildings, and other problems led to accusations that MTA was using unqualified contractors and exercising poor oversight. Construction problems became so severe that in 1994 the U.S. Department of Transportation placed a freeze on federal funds designated for the rail line until MTA could demonstrate that the problems were being resolved. Construction problems generated large cost overruns: the first Red Line segment, originally estimated to cost $1.5 billion, ultimately cost $4.3 billion. Cost overruns were endemic to the entire project, making it increasingly difficult for planners to retain the rail system in the RTP. This proved to be a serious political problem, as public support was based on each subregion's getting its "fair share" of rail investment.

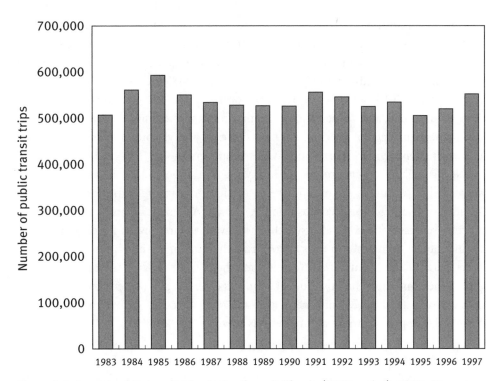

Figure 5.4. Annual public transit trips in Southern California (SCAG region), 1983–97 (unlinked trips).

Fiscal problems increased as more rail service came online, because operating costs were significantly higher than estimated at the same time fare revenues were lower. Hence the need for subsidies to keep the rail system operating increased. Facing increasing costs and stagnant revenues (the 1990s recession reduced sales tax revenues, a key source of MTA funds), MTA reallocated resources, essentially disinvesting in the bus system in order to continue investing in the rail system. Bus service was reduced, and all capital funds were earmarked for rail (e.g., bus replacements were delayed).

In 1996, MTA proposed bus and rail fare increases as a way of raising more revenues. The Bus Riders Union, an advocacy group for bus riders, sued MTA, arguing that the fare increase was discriminatory. The additional fare would be paid mostly by bus passengers, who are predominantly poor and minority, but the benefits would go to rail passengers, who are predominantly white and not poor. The lawsuit went beyond fares and attacked MTA's general bias toward the rail system. The Bus Riders Union, joined by the NAACP and other advocates, prevailed in court; MTA was found in violation of federal civil rights laws (Taylor and Garrett 1998). MTA was prevented from raising fares and furthermore was eventually placed under court order to increase bus service on overcrowded routes, to increase the bus fleet, and to apply the same levels of maintenance and passenger security for buses and rail lines.

The federal court order forced MTA to shift resources to the bus system, making it impossible to continue the rail expansion and nearly pushing the authority to insolvency. The fragile political consensus that had held the rail program together fell apart. In 1998, county voters passed Proposition 1A, which prohibited MTA from any further use of Proposition A funds for rail construction. The entire rail construction program was frozen, and a much-reduced rail transit plan was placed in the RTP.

Despite these problems, MTA continues to see rail as the best option for dealing with L.A. County's future transportation problems. MTA's current long-range plan (target year is 2015) allocates its $72.5 billion budget as follows: 38 percent to rail, 35 percent to bus, and 27 percent to all other modes. These numbers are difficult to comprehend in light of the shares of person-trips the various modes are expected to carry under even the most optimistic assumptions.

Nor is rail advocacy limited to LACMTA. Local politicians in Pasadena have succeeded in forming a separate joint-powers authority in order to proceed with the Pasadena rail line despite Proposition 1A and MTA's financial problems.[5] East Los Angeles representatives are also searching for ways to circumvent Proposition 1A or to find money from other sources to construct their rail line. And representatives from other parts of the county are advocating for their "fair share" of the rail investment pie. At the same time, the Bus Riders Union has emerged as a powerful political force, supported by the NAACP and many local minority advocacy groups in its efforts to force MTA to provide more and better bus service.

EXPLAINING OUTCOMES

Much has been written about the current fascination with rail transit and about the perverse incentives to invest in rail provided by federal funding policy (e.g., Kain 1999;

Pickrell 1992; Smerk 1991; Wachs 1989). However, Los Angeles transit policy is not explained simply by these factors. The geography of Los Angeles is such that only a few corridors have the density of population and activity approaching that required for reasonably successful rail transit. Most of the county is characterized by low to moderate density and by highly decentralized patterns of travel—clearly unsuitable to rail transit. But a rail plan could not pass political muster unless it promised something to everyone. Rail proposals for the Wilshire corridor failed in 1968, 1974, and 1978. It was not until 1980, with an expanded proposal that included rail to the suburbs and the promise of lower bus fares, that the tax proposal passed. In order to keep the political coalition together, the rail plan continued to expand; the 1992 county plan included a 400-mile, $180 billion system (Fulton 1997). There was no viable way to fund such a system, however, and once the budget requirements of ISTEA went into effect, this fiction could no longer remain in the region's long-range plan. LACMTA is making every effort to retain as much of this ambitious plan as possible (the agency's political mandate depends on it), and local politicians are becoming more aggressive in their battles for a piece of an ever-shrinking pie.

Lost in this struggle are transit passengers, particularly the poor and minority bus users of central Los Angeles. Although the federal court order has forced MTA to purchase some new buses and increase service on the most crowded routes, it has not persuaded the authority's board to reorient MTA to serve the people who actually rely on public transit. Rather, MTA continues to claim that only rail transit will someday get middle-class drivers out of their cars and hence solve the county's transportation problems.[6]

Private Toll Roads in Orange County

The Los Angeles region has led the nation in developing innovative solutions to lack of highway capacity. As noted earlier, the end of freeway building in the 1970s left the region with a growing problem as population and economic growth continued through the following decades. The 1980s economic expansion generated rapidly rising levels of congestion, and a variety of public and private stakeholders were motivated to find ways to expand existing highway facilities and fund new highways in developing areas. Among these innovations is the SR-91 private toll road, the nation's first experiment with congestion pricing.[7]

In 1988, the California State Legislature passed a measure that allowed the construction of four private highways. These were to be demonstration projects, designed to show whether private financing and user fees are a viable way to provide road capacity in high-demand corridors. Private investors were attracted to two of the four projects, one of them the toll lanes located in the median of the SR-91 freeway, which connects job-rich Orange County with the moderate-income suburbs of Riverside County.[8] SR-91 is heavily used and is congested for many hours every day. The geography of the area is such that there are no good alternate routes to SR-91, and consequently demand is relatively inelastic. It was therefore an ideal candidate for testing the private road concept.

The California Private Transportation Company (CPTC) obtained a franchise agreement in 1990 and completed approvals in 1992. Construction of the ten-mile private highway began in 1993. It was financed by a private consortium, with most of the funding coming from bank debt, construction companies, and a French company that specializes in private toll roads. The finished highway has two lanes in each direction, and entry points are limited to the two ends of the road. It is linked with high-occupancy vehicle (HOV) lanes at each end. When it opened in 1995, it became the first congestion-priced road in the United States.

CPTC had the freedom to set tolls on the road; its only constraint is a limitation on profits. Tolls have increased from $0.25 to $2.50 in 1995 to the current range of $0.75 to $4.25. Until 1998, car pools with three or more passengers could use the road for free; now they pay half price. Tolls are collected electronically; toll road users must have transponders and open accounts with CPTC.

The SR-91 private toll road was very controversial from the beginning. Orange County was a strong advocate for building the road, whereas Riverside County was strongly opposed. The entire SR-91 highway was planned to have HOV lanes, allowing Riverside County commuters to carpool to jobs in Orange County. Riverside officials argued that their county's citizens, many of whom work in Orange County for low or moderate wages, are "forced" to live in Riverside County because of the high costs of housing in Orange County and would be additionally penalized by having to pay to use the new lanes. They asserted that Orange County officials were exploiting every opportunity to get roads built, no matter the consequences. Riverside County sued Orange County over this issue in 1994, and the conflict was resolved through the agreement that car pools would be allowed to ride free.

There was broader opposition throughout California to the concept of private highways. Many people feared that a private operator would be able to charge monopoly prices and make excess profits at the expense of the traveling public. This opposition was strong enough to kill two proposed private roads in Northern California. Concerns were heightened when it was revealed that the CPTC franchise agreement included a "noncompetition" clause. This agreement prohibited Caltrans, the state transportation agency, from adding capacity in the corridor for a period of thirty-five years.

When the toll road opened, the addition of two lanes of capacity in each direction had the expected result, and all travelers in the corridor enjoyed travel-time savings. For the first few years, the private road appeared to be a great success. As the road is private, the company is not obligated to reveal financial information, and observers could only speculate on the financial success of the project. However, the reduction in congestion in the regular lanes was soon eliminated as demand in the corridor increased. Now the SR-91 is as congested as it was before the toll lanes opened.

The opening of the Eastern Corridor—one of three new high-capacity roads funded through a combination of developer fees, state and local highway funds, and user fees—created new problems. First, according to CPTC, it took business away from the toll lanes, decreasing CPTC's revenues. The company used this drop in revenues to justify ending the free car pool policy in 1998, rekindling the concerns of Riverside County. Second, according to Caltrans, new traffic merge patterns had increased accidents on the SR-91. Caltrans therefore decided in 1998 that auxiliary lanes were required to solve the merge problem. CPTC countered that the addition of lanes constituted an increase in capacity, and therefore violated its franchise agreement. When Caltrans continued with its construction plans, CPTC threatened to sue. Caltrans then backed off and abandoned the plan to add lanes.

Around the same time, CPTC proposed to sell the toll road and asked the state to approve approximately $350 million in bonds to finance the sale. Investigation by the state legislature revealed that the sale was a strategy for the consortium to receive payment on its loans while the management team operating the toll road would remain the same.

The controversies over the proposed sale and the auxiliary lanes launched a political firestorm. State representatives and others accused CPTC of trying to use the state government to bail the company out of a bad investment. Caltrans was accused of allowing dangerous traffic conditions to exist for the sake of private profits. Riverside County officials resumed their opposition to the toll road. In the face of such strong public opposition, CPTC abandoned its sale plan. However, controversy over the road continued. Riverside County once again instituted a lawsuit, this one claiming that the franchise agreement is unconstitutional and that the toll road should be opened to general traffic.

In 2001, the Orange County Transportation Authority expressed interest in purchasing the toll road. Officials saw this as the best strategy for eliminating the problems associated with the road, allowing the county to widen the highway and reduce tolls. A purchase agreement of $207 million was announced in 2002.

The SR-91 controversy, together with the poor performance of the San Joaquin Hills Toll Road, one of the three newer Orange County toll roads, has called into question the whole notion of privately financed roads and congestion pricing.

EXPLAINING OUTCOMES

The SR-91 private toll road, inevitably controversial as the first such road in California and as the first congestion-priced road in the country, was approved and constructed during a very short and fragile window of opportunity. Orange County officials were under great pressure to respond to rapid growth. A countywide antigrowth ballot measure was just barely defeated by voters. Several major development projects were being held up due to public opposition, much of it around the issue of traffic congestion. There was growing opposition to the Orange County Board of Supervisors, long dominated by development and business interests, and several communities were seeking incorporation in order to control growth within their borders.

As job growth continued in Orange County, housing demand pushed prices up. Efforts to slow development, together with the front-loading of development costs and the imposition of more stringent requirements on new development, increased housing scarcity and further inflated prices. Riverside County, with plentiful developable land

and a prodevelopment climate, became the escape valve. Many moderate-wage Orange County workers chose to buy single-family homes in Riverside and commute to their jobs via SR-91. By the mid-1980s, SR-91 traffic congestion had become legendary.

Both counties had to find a solution. Businesses in Orange County were threatening to leave because of difficulties in attracting workers. Residents in Riverside County were lobbying for traffic relief. Each county passed its own local funding proposition, and each had its own list of projects to fund, based on its own forecasts and planning objectives.[9] Riverside was committed to a system of HOV lanes (among other things); Orange County was also committed to HOV lanes, but also to the three new toll roads. Given the scarcity of highway funds, Orange County was disposed to explore every opportunity to stretch resources. Furthermore, having already accepted the concept of joint public-private funding, county officials did not find the idea of a fully private facility to be revolutionary. They saw the private toll road as one more strategy to get the needed capacity built.

One could argue that the SR-91 private toll road is a qualified success. It brought some relief to a heavily congested corridor, and the tolls meter demand. It is clear that if the tolls were removed, all traffic lanes would be congested and the number of car pools would drop. On the other hand, it is also clear that the traffic demand in this corridor is a function of housing prices and development policies. Affordable housing could be accomplished in Orange County only through high-density building—something few local jurisdictions (or home buyers) would find acceptable. Finally, the toll road has been a constant source of conflict between the two counties and has affected their cooperation on other regional issues.

Expanding Airport Capacity

It would be difficult to identify a more controversial transportation issue in Southern California than that of expanding airport capacity. Air travel is increasing even more rapidly in the region than auto travel. In the period from 1992 to 1997, air passenger traffic increased 24 percent, and air cargo traffic increased 52 percent. Figure 5.5 shows the numbers of air passengers annually for the region's six commercial airports. Economic restructuring, globalization, and rising incomes will continue to generate increases in air transport demand in the coming years. As noted earlier, Southern California's air transport demand is expected to double by 2020.

The region's three largest airports (Los Angeles, John Wayne, and the recently renamed Bob Hope Airport in Burbank) are nearing capacity (John Wayne due to legal constraints rather than physical capacity). The region's planners and policy makers are acutely aware of this approaching problem. Major expansion plans for Los Angeles International Airport (LAX) and Bob Hope Airport have been discussed, and a new international facility was proposed for the El Toro Marine Corps Air Station facility. However, local opposition to all of these plans is strong. In Burbank, a recent proposal to build a new terminal was ultimately defeated as a result of local political opposition. Residents feared that the new terminal would result in further increases in airport volume, despite assurances to the contrary from the Burbank City Council.

Expansion plans for LAX have been under study for several years. Plans to construct a new runway and increase capacity from the current 70 million annual passengers to 86 million have encountered strong opposition from nearby residents. The current mayor, elected in 2001, has proposed a new plan that focuses on increasing security rather than expanding capacity.

By far the most heated battles have taken place in Orange County, where, in 1994, county voters narrowly approved a measure to convert the former El Toro Marine base into a major international airport. El Toro, which is located in the southern portion of the county, is surrounded by affluent suburban residential communities. Approval of the plan was the result of unique conditions. The county was in the throes of an economic recession, and the airport was billed as an economic development strategy. The county has long been divided along north-south lines: the older, northern part is ethnically and economically diverse, whereas the southern part is overwhelmingly white and affluent. The vote on El Toro was split along these lines.

The opposition organized quickly after the measure passed: a coalition of south-county cities worked almost immediately to place an initiative on the next county ballot to withdraw zoning approval, while local advocacy groups sued the county. It took emergence from the recession, continued population shifts in the county from north to south, several lawsuits, and three ballot measures before opponents finally defeated the airport proposal. The 1999 anti-airport measure, which mandated a two-thirds

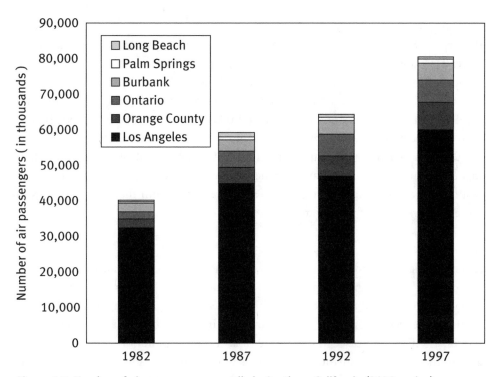

Figure 5.5. Number of air passengers annually in Southern California (SCAG region), 1982–97.

majority vote for approval of any airport, dump, or toxic waste site, won in a land-slide. The county then sued to challenge its constitutionality, and the measure was set aside by the courts. In response, airport opponents launched another initiative drive and placed a measure on the March 2002 ballot that would rezone the base as per-manent open space. This measure passed easily, and it is expected to withstand court challenge.

The debate over El Toro has spilled over to airport debates throughout the region. After being unsuccessful in wooing Newport Beach to oppose El Toro by promising in return to support Newport Beach's efforts to limit growth at John Wayne Airport, El Toro opponents proposed increasing capacity at John Wayne as a way of handling future demand. Opponents of LAX expansion are claiming that Orange County is not accepting its "fair share" of airport traffic and are advocating that conversion of El Toro go forward.

Meanwhile, proponents of a new San Bernardino airport (also a former military base) and a proposed airport in Palmdale are arguing that air demand should be shifted in their direction. They see new airports as economic development opportu-nities that will bring good jobs to these now economically depressed areas.

Where is SCAG in this debate? For more than two decades, SCAG planners have considered El Toro the best location for a future airport, and it has been a part of the long-range plan for many years. Because SCAG's long-range plan was not taken seri-ously, and because the increase in airport demand is a relatively recent phenome-non, there was little debate on the issue. However, once the ballot measure passed in 1994, airport advocates seized on the long-range plan as one of many justifications for the airport. SCAG facilitated and supported local airport advocates with their model forecasts. Using rather standard models, SCAG planners have produced a series of forecasts that show LAX, El Toro, and Ontario drawing the most passengers. Airports in more remote areas will not draw many passengers, even if El Toro is not built and the other urban airports are under growth limits. Thus SCAG planners argue that El Toro must be built if regional airport demand is to be accommodated.

Although SCAG planners are committed to El Toro, the SCAG board is another matter. Debates on the issue have been fierce, and a recent decision to approve a plan that includes El Toro has resulted in threats to withdraw from the organization from representatives of southern Orange County.

EXPLAINING OUTCOMES

It is not difficult to understand why local residents are opposed to airport expansion. Airports are known growth generators. In strong markets, their growth-inducing effects are so powerful that attempts to limit growth through zoning or other restric-tions are ineffective. Intensive growth around airports is beneficial for commercial interests, but the increased traffic, noise, and localized pollution generated by this growth make the areas surrounding airports unpleasant places for residents. Individ-uals who live near airports suffer most of the negative impacts and enjoy few of the benefits of these facilities.

Metropolitan areas around the world have long been faced with this problem. Some have solved it by locating new airports far from population concentrations (e.g., Washington, D.C., Denver, Paris, Hong Kong). Indeed, not one international airport has been constructed within a heavily populated area in the past thirty years. Given the experiences of other metropolitan areas, one may wonder why plans to locate an airport at El Toro, an already developed area, have been pursued for so long. The answer is that there is no effective institutional structure to resolve such difficult regional problems. Airports generate both enormous costs and enormous benefits, and these costs and benefits are unequally distributed. When such decisions become localized, the political process becomes little more than a power struggle between municipalities, each one trying to avoid the costs (no more airplanes in my backyard) and reap the benefits (cheap and accessible air travel). Fundamental questions, such as how local residents might be compensated, or how total impacts might be reduced, or whether it is reasonable policy to build capacity to meet projections that do not consider prices or costs, are never asked.

Conclusion

This chapter began with some information on the current and expected future magnitude of transportation problems in the Southern California region. Public transit policy in Los Angeles County, highway policy in Orange County, and airport planning policy in the region as a whole demonstrate the consequences of pursuing policies based on local interests and agendas. In Los Angeles, transit policy has become a tool of political expediency rather than a way to address and solve urban transportation problems. Orange County ultimately paid a very high price for a private toll road. The region's airport problems are likely to be mired in controversy and lawsuits for years to come. In all of these cases, a regional perspective is conspicuously missing. Over the past twenty years, the region's funding structure, with its growing reliance on local revenue sources, has reinforced decentralized and fragmented transportation planning. The regional planning institution, SCAG, reflects this fragmentation in its "bottom-up" planning, which begins with cities and subregions.

There is a great deal to be said for local decision making. Residents have more control over neighborhoods, cities have opportunities to foster unique development policies, and the variety that such decision making generates provides more choices for everyone. However, travel flows do not respect municipal boundaries. Most people shop in one place, work in another, and visit friends and family in still others. We might consider travel as the glue that holds the many separate places in a region together. There is no way for any given area to avoid the impacts of neighboring areas' transportation decisions. Los Angeles's transportation problems have been exacerbated by local decision making that has ignored this fact.

Notes

1. The information in this list comes from the Southern California Association of Governments (2000).

2. The proposed 2001 regional transportation plan includes $35.5 billion for committed projects (those already included and budgeted in previous plans), $63.7 billion for operations and maintenance, $11.3 billion for bonding costs, and $24.9 billion for new capital projects.

3. The 1998 federal transportation bill, the Transportation Equity Act for the Twenty-first Century, or TEA-21, did not substantially change any of the planning or conformity provisions of ISTEA.

4. These numbers would not be as disparate if calculated on the basis of passenger-miles, because rail trips are longer than bus trips, but bus trips remain the least costly by any measure.

5. The Pasadena Gold Line opened in 2003.

6. A new MTA CEO was appointed in 2001. One of his initiatives is Rapid Bus, an "express" bus service that was deployed on two routes in 2002 and is planned for several additional routes. Nevertheless, the rail transit program remains the cornerstone of MTA's long-range plan.

7. In congestion pricing, the toll varies in response to traffic conditions. The toll is higher at times of peak demand in order to manage demand and maintain traffic speed and flow.

8. The second project is SR-125 in San Diego County, which has not yet started construction.

9. There are technical implications to subregional planning. Transportation planning models focus on travel patterns within the area of analysis. Trips emanating outside the study area are "external trips" and are treated in a very rudimentary manner. Thus the modeling itself ignores interarea impacts.

Works Cited

California Department of Transportation. 1998. *Travel and Related Factors in California Annual Summary.* Sacramento: Caltrans Transportation System Information Program.

Fulton, W. 1997. *The Reluctant Metropolis: The Politics of Urban Growth in Los Angeles.* Point Arena, CA: Solano.

Kain, J. 1999. "The Urban Transportation Problem: A Reexamination and Update." In *Essays in Transportation Economics and Policy,* ed. J. Gomez-Ibanez, W. Tye, and C. Winston. Washington, DC: Brookings Institution.

Lewes, P., and M. Sprague. 1997. *Federal Transportation Policy and the Role of MPOs in California.* San Francisco: Public Policy Institute of California.

Pickrell, D. 1992. "A Desire Named Streetcar: Fantasy and Fact in Rail Transit Planning." *Journal of the American Planning Association* (spring):158–76.

Rubin, T., J. Moore, and S. Lee. 1999. "Ten Myths about US Urban Rail Systems." *Transport Policy* 6(1):57–73.

Smerk, G. 1991. *The Federal Role in Urban Mass Transportation.* Bloomington: Indiana University Press.

Southern California Association of Governments. 2000. *RTP Draft Community Link 21.* Los Angeles: SCAG.

Taylor, B., and M. Garrett. 1998. "Equity Planning in the 90s: A Case Study of the Los Angeles MTA." Paper presented at the annual meeting of the Association of Collegiate Schools of Planning.

Wachs, M. 1989. "US Transit Subsidy Policy: In Need of Reform." *Science* 244:1545–49.

Weiner, E. 1997. *Urban Transportation Planning in the United States: An Historical Overview.* 5th ed. Report no. DOT-T-97-24. Washington, DC: U.S. Department of Transportation.

6 | Metropolitan Fiscal Structure: Coping with Growth and Fiscal Constraint

Juliet Musso

This chapter examines the changing patterns of metropolitan finance in Southern California between 1982 and 1997. These patterns have shifted dramatically in response to a number of changes in local financing authority. The passage of state initiative Proposition 13 in 1978 reduced the fiscal choices available to local lawmakers by limiting the local property tax to 1 percent, capping the allowable growth in the taxable value of property, and requiring the approval of two-thirds of voters for any new special-purpose taxes. Revenues from the fixed 1 percent property tax rate are allocated among localities based primarily on state formulas created in 1978. Subsequent initiative measures have made the taxing environment even more restrictive; for example, between 1978 and 1986 a city council could, with a majority vote, pass a nonearmarked tax; since 1986, a majority vote of the people has been required for general-purpose tax increases.

The passage of Proposition 13 resulted in an effective shift of fiscal power from local governments to the state level (Musso and Quigley 1996; Shires 1999). As Table 6.1 shows, between 1978 and 1995, total public revenues in California increased from $125.2 billion to $204.6 billion, or 63.6 percent (in 1995 dollars). During the same period, the share of California public revenues controlled by the state increased from $52.2 billion (41.6 percent) to $112.1 billion (54.6 percent) (Shires 1999, ix, tab. S.1).[1] The county share of the state's public revenues declined in real terms from $10.4 billion to $10.3 billion, reflecting a steep drop in percentage share from 8.3 percent to 5 percent. While revenues controlled by cities increased in real terms from $13.7 to $18.9 billion, the city share of the total state fisc dropped from 11.0 percent to 9.2 percent (Shires 1999, ix, tab. S.1).

As a result of these changes, California counties experienced fiscal stress, finding it more difficult to balance the provision of state-mandated services (e.g., welfare and

Table 6.1. Level of government controlling public revenues in California (1995 U.S. dollars)

Level of government	1978	1981	1988	1992	1995	Percentage growth
Federal	28,718,587,092	28,014,807,776	28,935,040,344	40,871,762,942	45,675,769,771	3.6
%	22.9	22.3	17.3	20.2	22.3	
State	52,195,741,179	72,570,727,778	100,268,938,674	116,641,923,621	112,131,400,939	3.2
%	41.7	57.8	60.0	57.8	54.8	
Counties	10,396,960,009	4,789,937,712	6,974,929,495	9,745,519,354	10,292,417,931	5.6
%	8.3	3.8	4.2	4.8	5.0	
Cities	13,718,378,820	10,592,939,382	15,367,778,963	18,102,845,130	18,916,213,236	4.2
%	11.0	8.4	9.2	9.0	9.2	
Special districts	6,006,919,713	5,747,343,812	9,494,609,411	8,788,892,644	8,933,480,218	3.2
%	4.8	4.6	5.7	4.4	4.4	
Schools	10,520,228,076	1,257,546,643	1,292,355,641	1,445,664,495	1,733,385,972	2.3
%	8.4	1.0	0.8	0.7	0.8	
College	3,323,531,088	2,119,931,907	3,210,648,445	4,087,174,793	4,670,347,000	5.8
%	2.7	1.7	1.9	2.0	2.3	
Unspecified	353,800,450	418,376,128	1,444,462,446	2,178,883,231	2,231,578,497	12.7
%	0.3	0.3	0.9	1.1	1.1	
Total	125,234,146,428	125,511,611,137	166,988,763,421	201,862,666,212	204,584,593,564	3.6

Source: Shires (1999).

criminal justice) with municipal service provision to populations residing outside of city limits. Cities, which retained more fiscal discretion than counties, reacted by diversifying revenue sources and relying more heavily on contract services. Proposition 13 also hastened the formation of new cities within unincorporated areas of the state's counties. The restrictions on property taxes, and the manner in which revenues were allocated to newly formed cities, created incentives for communities to incorporate to capture revenues and localize service delivery.

Given that Southern California continues to experience rapid economic and population growth, there are serious questions about whether the region's fiscal structure can sustain increasing infrastructure and service demands. The problems of congestion, pollution, and land absorption fueled growth management measures in the late 1980s and during the 1990s economic expansion. Desires to localize land-use and fiscal policies have resulted in the creation of thirty new cities since 1980 and fueled active secession proposals among three areas of the city of Los Angeles—San Fernando Valley, Hollywood, and the harbor area.

In the post–Proposition 13 era, the region confronts two major issues regarding the structure of urban finances within metropolitan areas. The first is the extent to which the fiscal structure of cities promotes efficient and effective public service provision. The second is the equity of financing, in terms of both the extent to which fiscal structures rely on regressive taxing sources and the extent to which there are disparities in local fiscal capacity. As defined by Chernick (1998), fiscal capacity is "the ability of a governmental jurisdiction to translate economic activity within its geographic borders into public spending" (531).

The principles for evaluating financing structures include the extent to which public financing allows localities to provide service packages that respond to residential preferences, the extent to which the costs of services are paid by users rather than exported outside of the locality, the extent to which financing tools provide perverse incentives affecting land use or other activities, and the fairness of how costs are distributed among different income groups. Cities in Southern California rely on diverse portfolios of revenue sources. The traditional municipal finance source, the property tax, represents less than 10 percent of regional revenues; the most significant sources of finance are fees and taxes other than sales and property taxes, most notably, utility user taxes. This suggests an equity/efficiency trade-off with respect to urban finance. Increased reliance on fees likely promotes greater efficiency through the benefit principle, but the utility tax is a highly regressive form of taxation.

The patterns of both revenues and expenditures vary across the region, with transportation spending particularly high in Los Angeles County cities and proportionately more spending on culture and leisure in cities in Orange County and Riverside County. Between 1982 and 1997, proportionate spending in the region on police services declined somewhat, while proportionate spending on sanitation, health and housing, and general government increased slightly. There was an increase in contracting out during this period, largely as a result of the creation of new cities that contract out with counties for service provision or rely on independent service provision by special districts. Hence the trend during the period appears to be increased fragmentation of institutional form and heavier reliance on lower-cost service production mechanisms, such as contracting out.

We also find growing disparities with regard to city fiscal capacity. The distribution of fiscal capacity among the region's cities runs counter to conventional wisdom in two respects. First, there is a common perception that newly incorporated cities form around wealth and hence have higher fiscal capacity than older cities. We find no difference in fiscal capacity between older and recently incorporated cities, suggesting that other motivations, such as tax avoidance or land-use control, also motivate municipal incorporation.[2] Second, conventional wisdom has it that the inner core is fiscally ailing and suburban communities are fiscally advantaged. We find a much more complex distribution, with many relatively low-fiscal-capacity, low-service communities on the urban fringe. Fiscal advantages enjoyed by older coastal and hillside communities increased between 1982 and 1997, while interior cities attracted middle- and working-class residential growth. Orange and Los Angeles Counties tend to have much higher fiscal capacity than the regional average, whereas more rapidly developing San Bernardino and Riverside Counties have lower fiscal capacity. This leads one to question whether newly developing cities have adequate fiscal capacity to provide necessary services and infrastructure to support population growth.

Metropolitan "Fiscal Federalism"

The industrial restructuring that occurred during the latter half of the twentieth century has posed particular challenges for cities, as evolution toward a service economy contributed to increased income polarization and geographic concentration of poverty. Cities faced heightened competitive pressures in attempting to retain ever more mobile businesses. As Chernick and Reschovsky (1997) describe, cities that cannot compete, often older industrial cities, lose jobs and middle-income residents, leading to diminished tax resources and concentrated poverty populations that require higher investment in social services and other public services targeted to the nonpoor (Pack 1998). Chernick and Reschovsky characterize the resulting structural problems facing many cities as "malignant cycles of city decline . . . referred to as cumulative deterioration" (132).

This economic restructuring has occurred during an era characterized, both in California and nationally, by "tax revolt" politics that has played out through the enactment of initiatives restricting local revenues or expenditures. California has been a key battleground for fiscal politics as voters have approved a variety of tax limitation measures during the past two decades. Given the challenges posed by economic restructuring and globalization, it is important for a region to have a fiscal structure that is capable of responding efficiently to demands for public services and infrastructure investment. In Southern California, as in much of the United States, the regional governance structure resembles what Ostrom characterizes as a "polycentric federalism," a system in which services and financing powers are held by a fragmented overlapping system of governments. The fiscal federalism literature argues that such decentralization allows for greater administrative flexibility and efficiency of resource allocation, improved responsiveness to heterogeneous citizen demands, and innovation in providing services (Aronson and Hilley 1986; Musso 1998; Oates 1972; Wallis and Oates 1988).[3] The general wisdom is that redistribution policy is more efficiently carried out by higher levels of government because localized income redistribution will both attract the poor from other states or jurisdictions and drive away higher-income taxpayers, leading to suboptimal levels of welfare provision (Hamilton 1975; Gramlich 1990; Musgrave 1959; Musso 1998; Oates 1972).

Within a polycentric regional governance system, the choice of financing mechanisms is particularly important. Allocative efficiency requires that provision of local services achieve a benefit principle, a link between the financing and consumption of public services.[4] This benefit principle is more likely to function to the extent that local agencies rely on fee financing or on revenue sources that are difficult to export, such as the property tax. Taxes that may be transferred outside of the jurisdiction, such as the retail sales tax, motel or hotel taxes, and income taxes, are less likely to support allocative efficiency in service provision. As I discuss in more detail below, such decentralized financing typically results in trade-offs between efficiency and equity. Although it may promote allocative efficiency, it also leads poorer cities to have reduced fiscal capacity because they tend to have less valuable real estate and fewer economic transactions on which taxes can be imposed (Ladd and Yinger 1989).

From an economic standpoint, local competitive pressures posed by residential mobility limit the extent to which localities can rely on progressive taxation to redistribute income. A related equity issue is the variation throughout the region of fiscal capacity, or ability to leverage local economic resources to provide services. As Chernick (1998) notes, the concept of fiscal capacity is "both hypothetical and comparative, reflecting the differing amounts of revenue jurisdictions could raise, rather than what they actually raise" (531). Fiscal capacity can vary for a variety of reasons, including variation in economic activity and economic constraints such as surburban locational substitutes (Chernick 1998). In addition, localities may have differing authority to tax particular types of transactions. In California, for example, counties cannot impose taxes on sales or hotel stays within the jurisdictions of cities. In Southern California, cities do not vary in tax authority; both general law and charter cities have essentially the same taxing authority. Consequently, most of the variation in fiscal capacity occurring within the region is related to differences in wealth between cities or to structural fiscal factors, such as the allocation of property tax revenue and other state and federal revenue streams.

Low fiscal capacity can contribute to disinvestment in physical infrastructure and human capital, which in turn contributes to a cycle of economic decline. Within a metropolitan region, fiscal disparities can contribute to exurbanization, the flight of firms and wealthier residents from high-tax or service-poor cities to the fiscally advantaged suburbs. Substantial fiscal disparities within a region also can be "horizontally inequitable," meaning that individuals with similar characteristics may be subject to higher tax burdens or receive inferior services simply by virtue of residing within a city with low fiscal capacity (Bradbury et al. 1984). The migration of the wealthy into suburban enclaves can be of particular concern in fragmented metropolitan areas such as Southern California.

Rusk (1993) maintains that the solution to the problems of class stratification and service inequities is to foster "elastic cities" that promote integration through unified local governance structures. Given the lack of such consolidated regional governance structures in Southern California, equity of service provision is strongly influenced by the extent to which fiscal capacity varies throughout the region. The consolidated regional governance structures that exist typically are functional in orientation rather than being general service providers, such as the Metropolitan Transportation Authority or the South Coast Air Quality Management District. Although these agencies may facilitate regional planning around certain issues, their functional orientation does not support an integrated regional approach to resource allocation.

Changing Urban Finance in Southern California

Methodology

The primary source of data for this analysis is the information on city revenues and expenditures collected by the California Office of the State Controller for the years 1982 and 1997. These data are augmented as needed with data from the 1990 and 2000 U.S. censuses. Fiscal effort can be measured in several ways. The representative revenue structure approach developed by the Advisory Commission on Intergovernmental Relations (1971) consists of an average tax rate computed for each tax base in the region. One can then compare the effective tax rate imposed by a local government with the representative revenue structure for all localities to determine the extent to which a city is using its fiscal capacity. Yinger (1986) and Ladd and Yinger (1989) developed another method based on the fraction of income that local taxpayers pay in taxes. These measures have limitations, however, because they often ignore the institutional constraints imposed by state-local fiscal regimes (Musso 1998).

For purposes of this analysis, fiscal capacity is assessed using a modification of the "representative" income burden measure, multiplying aggregate residential income within a city by a standard tax burden, effectively the percentage of income paid in taxes across all jurisdictions. Intergovernmental grants, sales tax revenues, and property tax revenues are then added to get a measure of fiscal capacity. Conceptually, this index measures the amount of revenue a city would raise if it were to collect taxes, fees, and other revenues such that they represented the regional average proportion of residential income, adjusted upward for the intergovernmental grants, sales tax, and property tax allocated to the municipality under state law. Thus the measure takes into account both revenue sources that are subject to municipal discretion (e.g., transient occupancy taxes, utility taxes, municipal fees) and those that are less subject to local control (sales and property taxes, state and federal aid).

Population Growth and Institutional Change

Figure 6.1 summarizes estimates of city and county population prepared by the California State Department of Finance for 1982 and 1997. Particularly rapid growth occurred during this period in the eastern counties of San Bernardino and Riverside, the populations of which doubled. Figure 6.1 also hints at the institutional change that occurred to accommodate this growth—in 1997 about 90 percent of the regional population resided within city limits, as opposed to 80 percent in 1982. This was a result of both annexation and incorporation occurring in the 1980s and early 1990s. During the 1980s and 1990s, in part to control growth and in part to provide public services to newly developed areas, thirty new cities formed in unincorporated county areas of the region. Many of these cities contract with their counties for police services and share service provision responsibilities with overlapping special districts.

In 1997, the most recent year for which fiscal data are available, there were 177 cities in the five-county region (Table 6.2). It should be noted that services also are provided by more than 1,100 special districts, and that the five counties also continue to provide municipal services to roughly 1.6 million people, or 12 percent of the population, who reside outside incorporated city limits. The pattern has been rapid growth in unincorporated areas, which tend to be less restrictive with respect to growth, followed eventually by residentially initiated incorporation. However, the single largest

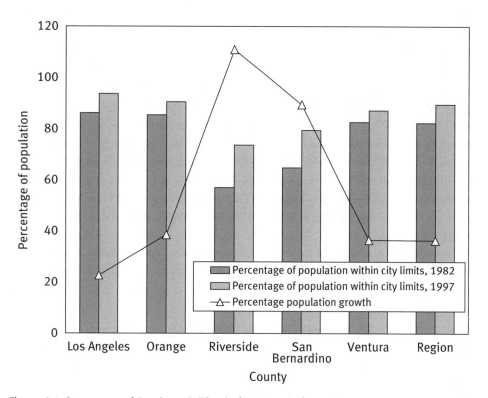

Figure 6.1. Percentage of Southern California (SCAG region) population residing within city limits and population growth by county, 1982–97.

unincorporated community in the region is not in the fringes, but in the core of Los Angeles: the community of East Los Angeles, with well over 100,000 residents, would be the third-largest city in Los Angeles County were it to incorporate.

Patterns of Metropolitan Finance and Spending: An Equity/Efficiency Trade-off

Composition of City Revenues

Table 6.3 summarizes 1997 city revenues by sources for the five counties in the Southern California metropolitan region. In 1997, cities collectively received $13.04 billion in municipal revenues, an increase of 80.5 percent over their 1982 collections of $7.22 billion (1997 dollars). In per capita terms, this represented a 27.5 percent increase over the fifteen-year period. Cities in the region have diverse revenue portfolios, with property tax revenues, the traditional municipal financing source, representing only a small share, less than 10 percent in 1997. The most significant sources of finance are fees and taxes other than sales and property taxes, which collectively represent approximately one-third of the city fisc.

Figure 6.2 illustrates relative reliance on particular sources for cities within the various counties. Cities in Los Angeles County, which might be considered the core of the region, have slightly more revenue per capita than cities in surrounding counties and are somewhat *less* reliant on sales tax revenues and state-local intergovernmental transfers and *more* reliant on other taxes, property taxes, and federal transfers. Cities located in the counties of Orange, Ventura, and San Bernardino, where much of the region's growth has been concentrated, are proportionately more reliant on sales taxes than are cities in Los Angeles County, suggesting that sales tax reliance poses an incentive for retail competition, particularly on the urban fringe. Land-use decisions may become "fiscalized" in the sense that they will reflect desire to capture fiscally lucrative developments, such as big-box retail, rather than attention to balanced planning to respond to needs of local residents. Orange County cities are the clear winners in the sales tax game, receiving $135 per capita from this source in 1997. Fee financing is a particularly important component of city finance in San Bernardino and Ventura Counties, representing almost one-third of all city revenues collected by cities in these two counties.

Figure 6.3 displays the changes in the composition of city financing that occurred between 1982 and 1997. Two particularly dramatic trends can be identified: reduced reliance on sales and property taxes, and increased reliance on fees and on taxes other

Table 6.2. Number of cities and special districts in Southern California by county

County	Number of cities	Number of special districts
Los Angeles	88	361
Orange	31	185
Riverside	24	284
San Bernardino	24	191
Ventura	10	97
Region	177	1,118

Table 6.3. City revenue composition in Southern California by county, 1997

Revenue source	Los Angeles	Orange	Riverside	San Bernardino	Ventura	Region
Total revenues ($)	8,862,369,416	2,203,107,834	738,382,029	824,481,659	412,377,722	13,040,718,660
Total city population	8,592,142	2,421,613	1,029,630	1,346,961	629,288	14,019,634
Per capita revenues ($)						
All sources	1,031	910	717	612	655	930
%	100	100	100	100	100	100
Property tax	107	84	53	44	64	91
%	10.4	9.2	7.4	7.3	9.7	9.8
Sales tax	93	135	94	89	99	100
%	9.1	14.8	13.1	14.5	15.1	10.8
Other tax	205	105	124	88	80	165
%	19.9	11.5	17.2	14.3	12.2	17.7
Fee-based finance	226	130	164	199	209	201
%	21.9	14.3	22.9	32.4	31.8	21.7
State and local transfers	95	93	101	77	69	92
%	9.2	10.2	14.1	12.6	10.5	9.9
Federal transfers	99	43	22	25	30	74
%	9.6	4.8	3.0	4.0	4.6	7.9
Other revenues	205	320	159	91	105	206
%	19.9	35.2	22.2	14.9	16.1	22.2

Note: This table excludes data on revenues from populations residing in county unincorporated areas, for which the distribution of revenues and expenditures cannot meaningfully be calculated. Electricity, water, port, and airport enterprise fees, which are disproportionately large, concentrated in few cities, and restricted with respect to use, are also excluded, as are redevelopment agency revenues not reported in the data used for this analysis.

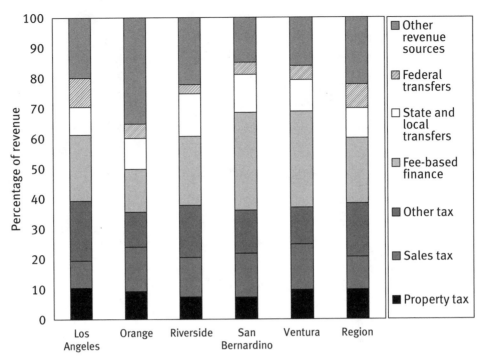

Figure 6.2. Composition of municipal revenue base in Southern California (SCAG region) by county, 1997.

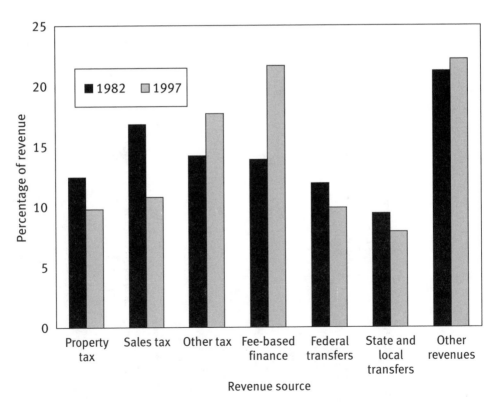

Figure 6.3. Changing revenue composition of five-county SCAG region, 1982–97.

than sales and property taxes. During this period, cities in the region became *less* reliant on traditional municipal financing sources, sales and property taxes, in large part because state law governs tax rates on these sources. For example, state law establishes a uniform sales tax of 6 cents on the dollar, of which 4.75 cents is retained by the state and 1 cent is distributed either to the city or the county, based on the location of sale. Given that sales taxes are distributed based on site of sale, cities and counties have an incentive to compete for land uses, such as malls, that generate regionally oriented retail sales.

Despite cities' somewhat reduced reliance on the sales tax, such competition over regional retail is likely to continue given that the sales tax is one of few city sources that can be "exported" to individuals outside the city. Interior counties tend to be more reliant on the sales tax while also experiencing relatively low fiscal capacity and high needs to support population growth. Consequently, sales tax competition is particularly fierce in the interior counties.

At the same time, cities have become considerably more reliant on fees and a wide array of other taxes, particularly utility taxes. Figures 6.4 and 6.5 illustrate the types of fees and sources of taxes other than sales and property tax in 1997 for the five-county region. Figure 6.4 shows that almost 40 percent of taxes collected in the region outside of sales and property taxes were from utility taxes—that is, taxes imposed on gas and electricity usage. Other taxes came from business and retail activity, including business franchise and license taxes (collectively 28 percent of other taxes) and the transient occupancy tax (13 percent). As Figure 6.5 illustrates, the single largest area for fees in 1997 was health and sanitation (primarily sewage treatment and solid waste disposal) at 42 percent. All fees are targeted revenues, as they are earmarked to support the particular services for which they are collected. As Proposition 13 reduced general fund revenues, cities have responded by reducing general fund support for services that can be funded with fees.

The shift in reliance on sales and property taxes to reliance on fees and utility taxes suggests that municipal financing in the region may be characterized by an efficiency/equity trade-off. Although fees and utility taxes are more efficient than sales taxes in that they cannot be "exported" to nonresidents and do not create perverse land-use incentives, they are regressive and as such may exacerbate income disparities in the region. Such fees are regressive because payments for utility use and basic services such as sanitation represent a much larger share of the income of poorer households than of better-off households, and, as a consequence, taxes and fees based on these sources are also disproportionately experienced by lower-income households.

Composition of City Expenditures

Table 6.4 summarizes city expenditures by function for the five counties in the region for 1997. The single largest area of expenditure was public safety, which includes police protection as well as fire protection, emergency medical services, street lighting, and related expenditures. In 1997 the share of spending in this area ranged from 27.5 percent of city expenditures in Ventura County to 40 percent of expenditures in

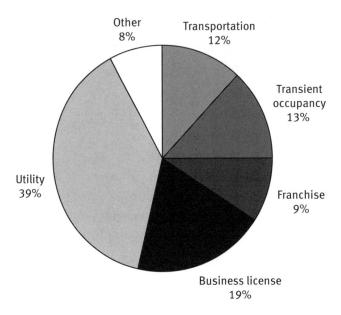

Figure 6.4. Composition of taxes other than sales and property taxes, Southern California (SCAG region), 1997.

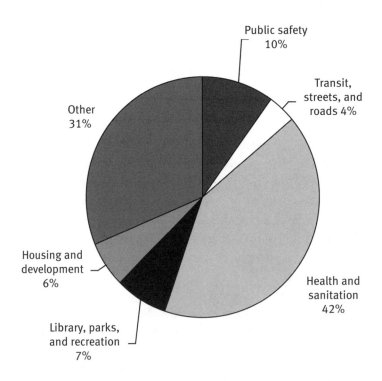

Figure 6.5. Composition of fees and assessments, five-county SCAG region, 1997.

Table 6.4. City expenditure composition in Southern California by county, 1997

Expenditure	Los Angeles	Orange	Riverside	San Bernardino	Ventura	Region
Total expenditures ($)	8,348,572,740	1,630,057,130	700,748,211	795,283,548	380,461,379	11,855,123,008
Total city population	8,592,142	2,421,613	1,029,630	1,346,961	629,288	14,019,634
General government ($)	93.03	54.89	86.53	65.14	69.33	82.22
%	9.6	8.2	12.7	11.0	11.5	9.7
Public safety ($)	367.43	271.07	225.59	205.87	166.15	315.81
%	37.8	40.3	33.1	34.9	27.5	37.3
Transportation ($)	115.95	100.99	119.16	106.23	118.52	112.78
%	11.9	15.0	17.5	18.0	19.6	13.3
Economic development ($)	138.99	98.56	61.18	50.40	58.01	114.15
%	14.3	14.6	9.0	8.5	9.6	13.5
Health and sanitation ($)	131.05	47.18	93.42	115.96	132.68	112.42
%	13.5	7.0	13.7	19.6	21.9	13.3
Culture and leisure ($)	97.93	99.61	85.37	45.72	55.14	90.36
%	10.1	14.8	12.5	7.7	9.1	10.7
Other ($)	27.27	0.82	9.33	1.11	4.76	17.86
%	2.8	0.1	1.4	0.2	0.8	2.1
Total ($)	971.65	673.13	680.58	590.43	604.59	845.61

Note: This table excludes data on electricity, water, port, and airport enterprise expenditures, which are disproportionately large, concentrated in few cities, and restricted with respect to use. Also excluded are redevelopment agency expenditures not reported in the data used for this analysis.

safety-conscious Orange County. Cities in Los Angeles County spend proportionately somewhat more on transportation-related public services relative to the rest of the region, and Orange County cities spend somewhat less on sanitation, perhaps because such services tend to be privatized. Orange County and Riverside County cities spend proportionately more on culture and leisure, which includes parks and recreation and libraries.

Between 1982 and 1997, total municipal expenditures in the five-county region increased by 77 percent, from $6.7 billion to $11.9 billion (1997 dollars). In per capita terms, this represented a 25 percent increase over the period. Figure 6.6 illustrates how the composition of city expenditures across the region changed during this period. The major change was that cities devoted a relatively smaller proportion of spending to public safety in 1997 than in 1982. In 1982, city expenditures on public safety were $2.9 billion (1997 dollars), or 43.7 percent of total city expenditures. In 1997, public safety expenditures were $4.4 billion. Although this represented a 52 percent increase in expenditures, the proportionate share of city expenditures devoted to public safety actually declined to 37.3 percent. There were small increases in proportionate spending on sanitation, health and housing, and general government during the same period. One explanation for the changed composition in expenditure is that the pressing demands of growth on infrastructure and basic municipal services such as sanitation caused public safety to become a proportionately smaller share of the

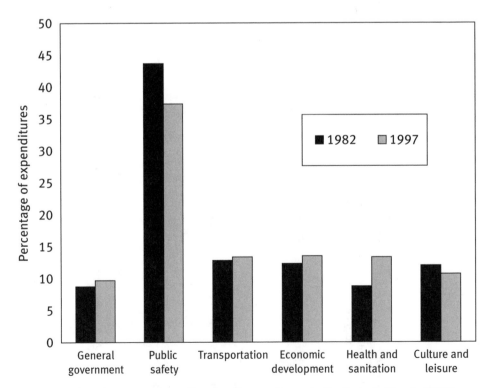

Figure 6.6. Changing composition of regional expenditures in Southern California (SCAG region), 1982–97.

urban fisc. As I discuss in more detail below, it is also the case that most new cities formed in the region contract out for public safety, suggesting that increased reliance on contract police services may have allowed the provision of public safety services at lower cost.

Contracting Out

One of the ways in which Southern California cities have coped with a constrained fiscal environment has been to rely heavily on outsourcing of public services to public or private agencies. Table 6.5 summarizes the percentages of cities relying on five different arrangements in key service areas: providing services completely in-house, contracting with a public agency, contracting with a private agency, combinations of public and private agency contracting, and provision by another government.[5] Over the period from 1982 to 1997, there was a general trend away from in-house service provision toward outsourcing of public services to public or private agencies. The major explanation for this shift is the creation of new cities mentioned previously; these new cities all rely heavily on county contracts for service provison. In some cases, they rely on independent service provision by special districts.

Table 6.5. Service provision arrangements in Southern California cities by service type, 1982 and 1997 (in percentages)

Service	Year	In-house	Public agency contract	Private agency contract	Mixed outsourcing	Other government	Number of cities
Police protection							
	1982	65	34	0	0	1	153
	1997	55	45	0	0	0	176
Fire Protection							
	1982	52	32	0	0	16	153
	1997	38	39	0	0	23	176
Emergency medical services							
	1982	24	24	16	10	27	147
	1997	22	27	12	5	34	176
Libraries							
	1982	32	31	0	1	36	143
	1997	28	17	0	1	53	172
Parks and recreation							
	1982	76	3	2	10	9	150
	1997	69	3	6	9	13	174
Planning							
	1982	85	3	8	1	3	153
	1997	78	3	15	2	2	176
Transit							
	1982	11	25	10	6	48	132
	1997	11	19	13	10	47	171
Water							
	1982	46	11	12	0	30	149
	1997	35	10	8	3	44	176
Garbage disposal							
	1982	16	11	57	1	15	146
	1997	9	6	63	2	20	176
Sewer treatment							
	1982	33	33	10	3	22	147
	1997	23	37	9	5	36	175

Cities are particularly reliant on contracting with public agencies for police enforcement; in 1997, 45 percent of cities in the region contracted out with counties for police services. Cities that contracted out for police services were generally those that were relatively small in size; in 1997, only 23 percent of city residents were served by contract police forces. Other service areas in which there is substantial regional reliance on interagency contracting are fire and emergency services. The most common area for contracting with private sector firms is garbage disposal; in 1997, 63 percent of cities, housing 45 percent of city residents, contracted out for solid waste disposal. Cities also tend to outsource emergency medical services, transit services, and sewer treatment. In the case of libraries, there has been a general decline in reliance on county contracts and an increase in reliance on provision by other local governments, in this case library districts.

In sum, the recent trend has been toward reduced sales tax dependency overall and greater reliance on more efficient, nonexportable tax sources such as utility taxes. This overall trend masks inter- and intraregional differences, however. For example, cities in Orange County receive a somewhat higher share of revenue from sales taxes than do cities in other counties, and sales tax dependency is much more variable in Los Angeles County. The region has seen increased reliance on outsourcing of public services, with cities either contracting such services out to public or private agencies or leaving the provision of services to other local governments, generally special districts.

Patterns of Fiscal Capacity Defy Conventional Wisdom

We now turn to an analysis of fiscal disparities in the region using the income burden approach discussed above. Between 1982 and 1997, per capita fiscal capacity in the Southern California region increased from $852 to $1,088, or 27.7 percent (1997 dollars). However, this fiscal capacity was not evenly distributed throughout the region. Figure 6.7 is a Lorenze curve showing the distribution of per capita fiscal capacity among cities in the five-county region. If fiscal capacity were evenly distributed among all cities in the region, the distribution would take the form of a straight 45-degree line. The larger the area between the distribution of fiscal capacity and such a 45-degree line, the greater the disparity in fiscal capacity among cities. The index of fiscal disparity is the Gini coefficient, which varies from zero (if fiscal capacity is completely evenly distributed) to one (if one city captures all of the fiscal capacity for the region). Figure 6.7 and a corresponding Gini coefficient of .20 suggest that the regional revenue distribution is somewhat inequitable. Although the average per capita fiscal capacity was $1,167 in 1997, the gap between low and high was more than ten to one, from a low of $340 (in the city of Gardena) to a high of $4,079 (in the city of Rolling Hills). The interpretation of this is that if income within each city were taxed at the regional average, Gardena would be able to provide only $340 in services to each of its residents, whereas Rolling Hills would be able to provide $4,079 in services. Moreover, intraregional fiscal capacity increased during the study period, as the Gini coefficient increased from .16 in 1982 to .20 in 1997.

A fiscal effort index, computed as the ratio of local revenues over fiscal capacity, is also useful for clarifying the extent to which cities' revenues can differ from cities' ability to raise revenues; that is, it illustrates which cities are making a more substantial "fiscal effort." Table 6.6 summarizes three measures of fiscal strength by incorporation era, contrasting per capita revenue, fiscal capacity, and "fiscal effort" for cities incorporated before 1950, from 1950 through 1977, and after the passage of Proposition 13 in 1978. Cities that formed in the middle period were by and large the "cities by contract" described by Gary Miller (1981), who found that incorporation was motivated in large part by a desire to avoid county property taxation. Many of these cities have no or extremely low property taxes because they incorporated to avoid property taxes, and their lack of property taxes was locked in by the revenue allocation formulas that were enacted following Proposition 13. Proposition 13 preserved a fiscal incentive to incorporate because a portion of county property taxes, and all sales taxes, within a jurisdiction are transferred to the new city upon incorporation.

The conventional wisdom is that cities that incorporated more recently have higher fiscal capacity than older cities within the region. For example, incorporation allowed the city of West Hollywood to capture substantial sales tax revenues and parking fees because of the concentration of retail and entertainment activity within its boundaries. It should be noted, however, that other nonfiscal factors, such as regulatory issues, also

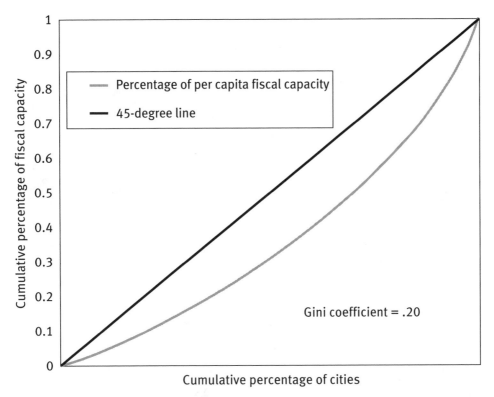

Figure 6.7. Distribution of per capita fiscal capacity among Southern California (SCAG region) cities, 1997.

drive incorporation. In West Hollywood, residents' concern about police treatment of the gay community and desire for stricter rent control were mobilizing issues. The Malibu incorporation was driven by residents' desire to restrict housing development by preventing construction of a large water treatment plant.

As Table 6.7 shows, there are no significant relationships among cities from the three eras with regard to fiscal capacity, although cities that incorporated before 1950 do raise more revenues per capita than their counterparts that incorporated later (this difference is marginally significant: $p = .09$). The cities do differ, however, in per capita

Table 6.6. Per capita revenue and fiscal capacity of Southern California cities, 1997, by era of city incorporation

	Era of incorporation			
Measure of fiscal strength	Before 1950	1950–77	1978–97	All cities
Per capita revenue[a]				
Mean	1107.88	898.00	627.75	951.52
N	83	61	30	174
Per capita fiscal capacity				
Mean	1107.32	1278.49	1077.02	1166.75
N	83	61	21	165
Fiscal "effort"[b]				
Mean	1.05	0.67	0.60	0.85
N	83	61	21	165

[a] Difference in means is marginally significant ($F = 2.46$; $DF = 2,171$; $p = .089$).
[b] Fiscal effort is ratio of per capita revenue to fiscal capacity; difference in means is highly significant ($F = 7.34$; $DF = 2,162$; $p = .001$).

Table 6.7. Characteristics of Southern California cities with highest and lowest fiscal capacity, 1997

City	County location	Per capita fiscal capacity ($)	Estimated population, 1997	Median household income, 1990 ($)	Percentage white, 2000
High fiscal capacity					
Rolling Hills	Los Angeles	4,065.93	1,999	150,001	79.8
Hidden Hills	Los Angeles	3,609.74	1,919	150,001	94.0
Beverly Hills	Los Angeles	3,572.23	33,700	54,348	85.1
Indian Wells	Riverside	3,355.24	3,143	87,942	96.3
Irwindale	Los Angeles	2,797.27	1,162	33,000	47.0
Newport Beach	Orange	2,757.94	70,098	60,374	92.2
San Marino	Los Angeles	2,729.43	13,561	100,077	47.7
Palos Verdes Estates	Los Angeles	2,654.25	14,163	101,320	78.3
Garden Grove	Orange	2,630.22	57,415	39,882	46.9
Laguna Beach	Orange	2,532.34	24,253	53,419	92.0
Low fiscal capacity					
Lynwood	Los Angeles	519.52	66,675	25,961	33.6
Bell	Los Angeles	512.49	36,790	22,515	48.5
Maywood	Los Angeles	459.63	29,469	25,567	43.0
San Jacinto	Riverside	436.20	24,197	20,810	69.3
Cudahy	Los Angeles	417.22	24,711	22,279	43.1
Bell Gardens	Los Angeles	401.64	44,227	23,819	48.1
Adelanto	San Bernardino	390.96	13,613	18,835	50.5
Blythe	Riverside	387.97	20,556	22,847	55.4
Coachella	Riverside	386.34	21,038	23,218	38.8
Gardena	Los Angeles	339.32	153,824	33,063	23.8

fiscal effort, with older cities raising more revenue per dollar of fiscal capacity than their newer counterparts. This may be due to higher costs of services among older cities (which tend to be full-service cities with older infrastructure and potentially greater proportions of poor). It also could be evidence of "Tiebout" sorting around service preferences, where the newer cities have formed around populations with preferences for lower taxes and lower levels of service provision.

There is a marked coastal/valley gap in fiscal capacity within the five-county region. The highest fiscal capacity cities are concentrated along the coast, in Los Angeles and Orange Counties, whereas cities with low fiscal capacity tend to be found in the industrial core of Los Angeles County and in the interior of San Bernardino and Riverside Counties. Table 6.7 lists the ten cities with the highest fiscal capacity and the ten with the lowest fiscal capacity to give an idea of the variation between these groups. The ten cities with high fiscal capacity are predominantly white and wealthy; four had median household incomes in excess of $100,000 in 1990. In contrast, cities with low fiscal capacity fall into two groups: poor minority communities within the urban core of Los Angeles County and moderate-income suburban communities in Riverside and San Bernardino Counties.

Figure 6.8 categorizes cities in terms of their level of fiscal capacity and fiscal effort, the ratio of actual revenues raised over fiscal capacity. Cities in the coastal corridor of Los Angeles County tend to be characterized by both high fiscal capacity and high fiscal effort, whereas those in the industrial core of the county pair low fiscal capacity and high effort. Along the coast of wealthy, more conservative Orange County, cities tend to combine high fiscal capacity and low fiscal effort. This may reflect greater reliance on contracting out as well as preferences for lower levels of public services. Many of the fiscally constrained suburbs in the interior of the region are characterized by low fiscal capacity and high effort.

Table 6.8 summarizes a county comparison of city fiscal measures for 1997, again including per capita revenue, fiscal capacity, and fiscal effort. The pattern of results here suggests that although cities do not differ significantly across counties in terms of per capita revenues, fiscal capacity does differ, again with San Bernardino and Riverside Counties having much lower fiscal capacity due to lower aggregate residential incomes. The implication is that cities in these two counties must make significantly more effort than those in the coastal counties to raise the same revenues.

This pattern would appear to defy the conventional wisdom of exurbanization, in which newly developing suburban communities, those on the urban fringe, are understood to be wealthier and to have higher capacity to provide urban services. Municipal incorporation during the past several decades has promoted the creation of low-tax, relatively low-service communities in the urban fringe. During the study period, older coastal and hillside communities increased in income while the interior counties of San Bernardino and Riverside attracted middle- and working-class residential growth. Orange and Los Angeles Counties tend to have much higher fiscal capacity than the regional average, and more rapidly developing San Bernardino and Riverside Counties have lower fiscal capacity. This leads one to question whether newly

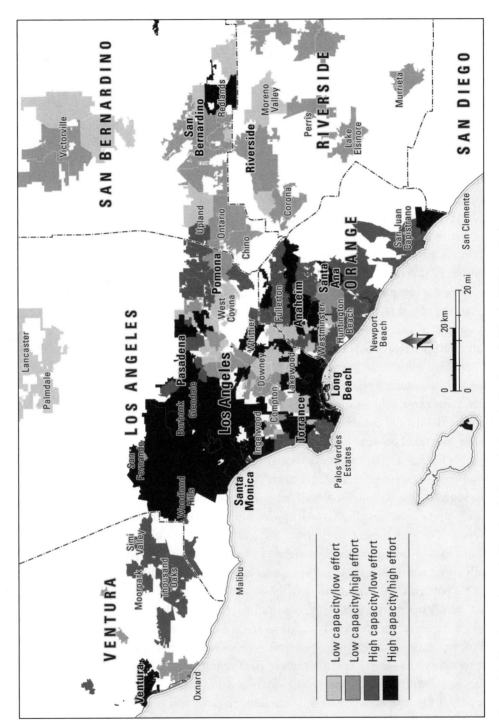

Figure 6.8. Fiscal capacity and effort for designated places in Southern California (SCAG region).

developing cities have adequate fiscal capacity to provide necessary services and infrastructure to support population growth.

Finally, Table 6.9 summarizes a model that explains the fiscal effort ratio in terms
of a number of city characteristics. Explanatory factors included in this simple model
are median household income, median housing value, population and population
squared (modeling the city production function as U-shaped), city age (years since
incorporation date), whether the city is a charter city (1 = yes), and an index expressing the number of eleven city services produced in-house rather than contracted out
or provided by another unit of government. The model has relatively good explanatory power, with an adjusted R^2 of .28, respectable for a cross-sectional analysis. The
joint significance and direction of the two population measures (population and population squared) are consistent with findings reported in much of the urban finance
literature, which suggests that costs of service provision are U-shaped with respect
to population size, initially declining as population increases, until economies of scale
are exhausted and congestion leads to increasing costs as a function of population. For
example, up to some population level the municipality can provide a chosen amount
of police protection at declining average cost. However, past that level, the city will

Table 6.8. Fiscal capacity measures for Southern California cities by county, 1997

Measure of fiscal strength	Los Angeles	Orange	Riverside	San Bernardino	Ventura	All Cities
Per capita revenue						
Mean	1022.5	807.91	1017.15	916.64	719.58	951.52
N	85	31	24	24	10	174
Per capita fiscal capacity[a]						
Mean	1279.58	1357.51	942.84	786.93	982.82	1166.75
N	83	29	21	22	10	165
Fiscal "effort"[b]						
Mean	0.79	0.64	1.09	1.18	0.78	0.85
N	83	29	21	22	10	165

[a] Difference in means is statistically significant ($F = 4.09$; $DF = 4,169$; $p = .003$).
[b] Fiscal effort is ratio of per capita revenue to fiscal capacity; difference in means is statistically significant ($F = 2.92$; $DF = 4,160$; $p = .023$).

Table 6.9. Determinants of city fiscal effort

Variable	Coefficient	T statistic	Significance level
Median housing value, 1990	−2.02E-06	−2.977	0.003
Median household income, 1989	−3.49E-07	−0.088	0.930
Population, 1997	−2.44E-06	−2.556	0.012
Population squared	6.59E-13	2.588	0.011
Age of city	2.26E-03	1.172	0.243
Number of city services produced in-house	5.07E-02	1.961	0.052
Charter city	0.548	4.259	0.000
(Constant)	1.02	6.345	0.000
Model characteristics			
Number of observations	265		
Adjusted R^2	0.277		
F statistic	9.96		

Note: Dependent variable = effort ratio.

need to add more patrols, leading to increased average costs. This would suggest that very small and very large cities may be characterized by higher fiscal effort due to economies of scale. As one would expect, median housing values are inversely related to fiscal effort, and fiscal effort is higher for charter cities and those that produce more services in-house.

Conclusions and Policy Recommendations

This analysis of municipal finance in Southern California suggests three main conclusions. First, in several respects, cities in the post–Proposition 13 era may have become more administratively efficient but less equitable. For example, since 1982, Southern California cities have become *less* reliant on property taxes, sales taxes, and federal aid, and *more* reliant on alternative financing sources such as utility taxes and fees. This would appear generally to be "good news" from an efficiency standpoint, as fees and utility taxes are not exportable and do not create the potentially perverse land-use incentives associated with some revenue sources, such as sales taxes. From an equity standpoint, replacing the property tax with utility taxes and fees may be less desirable, as these tend to be highly regressive revenue sources. Moreover, a number of new cities formed during the past couple of decades, most of which rely heavily on outsourcing of service delivery, either by contracting out with county government or private firms or by relying on special districts to provide services. Although this outsourcing likely reduces the costs of service delivery, the cost savings from contracting out may come at the expense of lower-paid labor.

Second, disparities exist across the region with regard to city fiscal capacity. Although one might expect to find higher-capacity cities in the wealthier suburbs and a fiscally hollow urban core, there are actually many relatively low-fiscal-capacity, low-service communities on the urban fringes. Fiscal advantages enjoyed by older coastal and hillside communities increased between 1982 and 1997, while interior counties attracted middle- and working-class residential growth. Orange and Los Angeles Counties tend to have much higher fiscal capacity than the regional average, in contrast to the more rapidly developing San Bernardino and Riverside Counties. Thus some newly developing cities may not have adequate fiscal capacity to provide necessary services and infrastructure to support population growth.

Although cities have responded to fiscal constraints through diversification of revenue sources, these tax increases for the most part preceded the 1986 passage of Proposition 62, which required that any new general taxes be approved by a two-thirds city council vote followed by a majority vote of the electorate. Moreover, a state initiative enacted in 1999 restricts somewhat local governments' ability to impose new fees. These stricter fiscal regulations may make it particularly difficult for cities to service economic and population growth in the future. In addition, the California State Legislature has a history of responding to budgetary shortfalls by shifting revenues away from cities and counties. The lack of a substantial revenue base that is controlled locally, rather than by the legislature, increases the fiscal uncertainty facing cities.

Cities' heavy reliance on utility taxes is also of concern, given the instability of the California energy sector. The dramatic increases in costs during California's recent energy crisis imposed pressure on cities to reduce utility rates; these rate reductions may be difficult to reverse if energy costs fall. Southern California cities need to achieve additional fiscal stability and independence, preferably by means of revenue sources that are reasonably progressive and do not create perverse land-use incentives. Unfortunately, the fiscal constraints imposed by Proposition 13 and other initiative measures make reforming local finance in California an extremely difficult task, because most local revenue sources are effectively fixed, making fiscal reform a zero-sum game.

Notes

1. Note that the series available from Shires does not correspond to the series utilized elsewhere in this paper. Unless otherwise specified, tables and figures rely on demographic data from the U.S. Census of Population and fiscal information from *Financial Transactions Reports*, California State Controller's Office (1982–1997).

2. This confirms findings I have discussed elsewhere (Musso 2001).

3. However, these gains must be balanced against potential economies of scale in the production of public goods (Hirsch 1970), interjurisdictional externalities or spillover costs (Oates 1972; Greene and Parliament 1980), and the effects of intergovernmental competition and migration pressures (Peterson and Rom 1989; Gramlich and Laren 1984).

4. As defined by Rubinfeld (1985), within a jurisdiction, an optimal or efficient allocation is one that maximizes the net willingness to pay for public goods, given a fixed population. Across a system of jurisdictions, efficiency in public goods provision requires provision of a public goods level that satisfies the aggregate of individual demands and is produced at minimum cost.

5. The difference between "other government" and public agency contracting is that the former involves independent financing and service provision, typically by a special district.

Works Cited

Advisory Commission on Intergovernmental Relations. 1971. *Measuring the Fiscal Capacity and Effort of State and Local Areas*. Washington, DC: U.S. Government Printing Office.

Aronson, J. Richard, and John L. Hilley. 1986. *Financing State and Local Governments*. Washington, DC: Brookings Institution.

Bradbury, Katherine L., Anthony Downs, and Kenneth A. Small. 1984. *Urban Decline and the Future of American Cities*. Washington, DC: Brookings Institution.

Chernick, Howard. 1998. "Fiscal Capacity in New York: The City versus the Region." *National Tax Journal* 51(3):531–40.

Chernick, Howard, and Andrew Reschovsky. 1997. "Urban Fiscal Problems: Coordinating Actions among Governments." In *The Urban Crisis: Linking Research to Action*, ed. Burton A. Weisbrod and James C. Worthy. Evanston, IL: Northwestern University Press.

Gramlich, Edward M. 1990. "A Policymaker's Guide to Fiscal Decentralization." *National Tax Journal* 43:39–52.

Gramlich, Edward M., and Deborah S. Laren. 1984. "Migration and Income Redistribution Responsibilities." *Journal of Human Resources* 19:489–511.

Greene, Kenneth V., and Thomas J. Parliament. 1980. "Political Externalities, Efficiency, and the Welfare Losses from Consolidation." *National Tax Journal* 33:209–17.

Hamilton, Bruce W. 1975. "Zoning and Property Taxation in a System of Local Governments." *Urban Studies* 12:205–11.

Hirsch, Werner Z. 1970. *The Economics of State and Local Government.* New York: McGraw-Hill.

Ladd, Helen, and John Yinger. 1989. *America's Ailing Cities: Fiscal Health and the Design of Urban Policy.* Baltimore: Johns Hopkins University Press.

Miller, Gary. 1981. *Cities by Contract: The Politics of Municipal Incorporation.* Cambridge: MIT Press.

Musgrave, Richard A. 1959. *The Theory of Public Finance: A Study in Public Economy.* New York: McGraw-Hill.

Musso, Juliet Ann. 1998. "Fiscal Federalism as a Framework for Governance Reform." In *Handbook of Public Finance*, ed. Fred Thompson and Mark T. Green, 347–96. New York: Marcel Dekker.

———. 2001. "The Political Economy of City Formation in California: Limits to Tiebout Sorting." *Social Science Quarterly* 82(1):139–53.

Musso, Juliet Ann, and John Quigley. 1996. "Intergovernmental Fiscal Relations in California: A Critical Evaluation." In *Infrastructure and the Complexity of Economic Development*, ed. David Batten and C. Karlsson. New York: Springer-Verlag.

Oates, Wallace E. 1972. *Fiscal Federalism.* New York: Harcourt Brace Jovanovich.

Pack, Janet Rothenberg. 1998. "Poverty and Urban Public Expenditures." *Urban Studies* 35(11):1995–2019.

Peterson, Paul E., and Mark C. Rom. 1989. "American Federalism, Welfare Policy, and Residential Choices." *American Political Science Review* 83(3):711–28.

Rubinfeld, Daniel L. 1985. "The Economics of the Local Public Sector." In *Handbook of Public Economics*, vol. 2, ed. Alan J. Auerbach and Martin Feldstein, 571–645. Amsterdam: North-Holland.

Rusk, David. 1993. *Cities without Suburbs.* Baltimore: Johns Hopkins University Press.

Shires, Michael A. 1999. *Patterns in California Government Expenditures since Proposition 13.* San Francisco: Public Policy Institute of California.

Wallis, John Joseph, and Wallace E. Oates. 1988. "Decentralization in the Public Sector: An Empirical Study of State and Local Government." In *Fiscal Federalism: Quantitative Studies*, ed. Harvey S. Rosen, 5–32. Chicago: University of Chicago Press.

Yinger, John. 1986. "On Fiscal Disparities across Cities." *Journal of Urban Economics* 19:316–37.

7 | Federal Expenditures, Intrametropolitan Poverty, and Fiscal Disparities between Cities

Pascale Joassart-Marcelli, Juliet Musso, and Jennifer Wolch

Over the past two decades, Southern California cities have experienced both an increase in poverty concentration and a drastic shift in fiscal responsibilities generated by the devolution of the welfare state. As a consequence, local ability to finance antipoverty efforts has become increasingly important, challenging cities with low fiscal resources, high concentrations of poor people, or both. The devolution of federal income support programs is particularly difficult for cities experiencing rapid population growth, large-scale immigration, economic decline and restructuring, aging infrastructure, and environmental problems linked to natural hazards and pollution.

Despite devolution and some curtailment in federal funding in specific program areas, the federal government continues to provide localities with billions of dollars for antipoverty and related expenditures. For example, between 1994 and 1996, the federal government spent an average of $77.4 billion per year in Southern California—more than 25 percent of the region's economy. Of these funds, $12.3 billion were allocated to antipoverty programs, including individual transfers as well as locally based housing, education, and health projects. Consequently, it is increasingly important that federal funds are allocated on an effective and equitable manner in order to reduce poverty and provide the best possible life chances to all people in the region.

Do federal dollars go to the cities that are most in need of assistance, as indicated by their weak fiscal capacity and disadvantaged populations, helping them to provide critical urban services and invest in job development and infrastructure necessary to economic growth? Or, in the absence of explicit efforts to take fiscal differentials into account in the allocation of federal funds, do these resources disproportionately benefit communities that are already more affluent? In this chapter we focus on the

195

allocation of federal funds to Southern California cities and the impact of those funds on the regional geography of poverty. More specifically, we analyze whether federal expenditures alleviate fiscal disparities across cities and thus help reduce urban poverty, and we identify the determinants of federal funding flows to Southern California's cities.

We first provide a summary of recent trends in antipoverty policies, review the fiscal federalism literature on fiscal equalization, and highlight the context of Southern California. We then focus on the data and methodology issues associated with the allocation of federal funds and the measurement of local fiscal capacity. Following that discussion, we describe the distribution of federal funds throughout the region and over the period from 1983 to 1996. We identify both historical and geographic trends and explain these trends on the basis of socioeconomic, demographic, and fiscal characteristics of cities where federal funds are allocated. We also provide a model that identifies the key factors determining the allocation of federal funds to cities. Finally, in our conclusion we highlight some important policy considerations for a more equitable distribution of regional fiscal responsibilities.

Welfare State Devolution, Fiscal Federalism, and Southern California Cities

Since the New Deal, the federal government has traditionally been responsible for antipoverty programs. The Social Security Act of 1935 created a framework for old-age pensions and social insurance. Throughout the 1930s and after World War II, these programs expanded in scope (e.g., to provide support for surviving dependents, disabled workers, retirees in need of medical care) and new ones were created (e.g., food stamps, Medicaid, subsidized housing, Supplemental Security Income). However, in the 1970s, political forces mounted against concentration of authority in the hands of the federal government and began to shift the balance of power toward the states (Skocpol 1995). Under Nixon's administration, "categorical" grants were transformed into "block" grants, giving states more control over the ways federal funds were spent. As a consequence, general revenue sharing increased from less than $500 million in 1970 to more than $8.6 billion in 1980 (Donahue 1999). During the Carter administration, federal funding to state and local governments began to decline (Musso and Quigley 1996). This decline accelerated during the Reagan years, which also saw a massive attack on social spending. By the early 1990s, a major transformation of U.S. social policy had taken place, with responsibilities shifted from federal to state and local governments. As a consequence, federal grants to state and local governments had increased, but the share of self-funded state and local spending had also risen (Fisher 1996).[1] More recently, the welfare reform legislation enacted in 1996 reduced federal control over traditional welfare programs by creating block grants to the states and capping future federal funding. Other legislation expanded state discretion over transportation spending, drinking water standards, and highway safety (Hovey 1999). Thus the shift of policy control as well as financial responsibility from the federal government to state and local governments has remained a dominant trend in U.S. politics.

Fiscal Federalism and Income Assistance

The conceptual case for leaving the lead to state and local governments has been emphasized in studies of fiscal federalism focused on the optimal allocation of fiscal responsibilities among subnational governments. Arguably, decentralization allows for greater administrative flexibility and efficiency of resource allocation, improved responsiveness to heterogeneous citizen demands, and innovation in providing services (Aronson and Hilley 1986; Musso 1998; Wallis and Oates 1988). However, these gains must be balanced against potential economies of scale in the production of public goods (Hirsch 1970), interjurisdictional externalities or spillover costs (Oates 1972; Greene and Parliament 1980), and the effects of intergovernmental competition and migration pressures (Peterson and Rom 1989; Gramlich and Laren 1984).

The general view is that stabilization and redistribution policies are best carried out at the federal level because of state and local governments' limited ability to affect either one without generating externalities and migration movements that would cancel most benefits (Musgrave 1959; Oates and Schwab 1991; Musso 1998). With regard to redistribution policy, it is argued that local attempts to redistribute income may both attract the poor from other states or jurisdictions and drive away higher-income taxpayers, leading to suboptimal levels of welfare provision (Hamilton 1975; Oates 1972).

Despite the conventional notion that redistribution is best handled by the federal government, state and local governments are involved in numerous redistribution and antipoverty activities. First, state governments administer several important income redistribution programs, including Temporary Assistance for Needy Families (TANF, formerly Aid to Families with Dependent Children, or AFDC) and Medicaid. Second, state and local tax structures and other financing arrangements have redistributive implications. Finally, locally provided public services such as education, urban development aid, and infrastructure also affect redistribution.

Fiscal Federalism and Cities

A major issue resulting from the devolution of federal responsibilities is that states and cities vary immensely in their ability to raise the revenues necessary to carry out these functions. These fiscal disparities raise concerns about efficiency as well as present both vertical and horizontal equity problems.[2] The equity and efficiency problems associated with fiscal disparities in lower levels of government provide a rationale for efforts by the federal government to redistribute funds to state and local entities in an effort to reduce or eliminate disparities. The majority of intergovernmental flows, however, are determined by statutory formulas or administrative processes and are not explicitly aimed at reducing fiscal disparities. Thus it is doubtful that current flows of funds from the federal government to state or local governments equalize fiscal capacities among jurisdictions.

In this context of fiscal disparity, poor states and cities may find themselves in a challenging position to fight poverty. First, compared with wealthier areas, their ability to raise tax revenue is limited. By most measures of fiscal effort, cities with high poverty concentration are already overextending their tax base.[3] Second, both need for public services and the costs of such services tend to be higher in poorer communities, requiring disproportionate levels of spending. This static problem of making ends meet is further complicated by a dynamic phenomenon in which poorer communities are unable to invest many resources to promote economic growth and thus remain in poverty. In contrast, states and cities with higher fiscal capacities can afford lower business taxes while providing superior public services such as schools and infrastructure. Doing so, they are more successful at attracting businesses and promoting private sector employment, which in turn improves economic opportunities and reduces poverty. In short, cities do not compete on a level playing field, and unless fiscal equalization reduces disparities, inequality and poverty are likely to increase.

In the United States, fiscal disparities among cities form a unique geographic pattern. Poorer cities are typically concentrated in the older center of a region, and wealthier cities tend to be located in outlying areas. This pattern is reinforced by the dynamics of interurban migration, in which firms and wealthier residents have incentives to leave the older and poorer cities characterized by higher taxes and inferior services for newly developed suburbs with higher tax capacities. Aside from the reproduction of poverty and inequality, exurbanization leads to a number of environmental problems linked to traffic congestion, air pollution, and destruction of open space and natural habitat. Moreover, suburbanization requires the development of expensive infrastructure, which can potentially decrease the federal funds available to support antipoverty policies.

The Southern California Context

As in other areas of the United States, state, county, and city governments in California have seen an increase in their responsibility to provide public services accompanied by rising flows of federal funds since the late 1970s. However, California has a unique intergovernmental fiscal structure that severely restricts local governments' ability to raise revenues. This has been especially true since 1978, when Proposition 13 limited the amount of property tax revenue allocated to local governments, restricted adjustments in assessed property values, and required the approval of a supermajority of voters for any new special-purpose taxes. Other initiatives have imposed further limitations on state and local spending. To cope with reduced property tax revenues, cities have had to rely on alternative sources of income, such as sales taxes and user fees (Musso and Quigley 1996). In this context, fiscal disparities among cities are seriously exacerbated.

At the same time, Southern California has experienced dramatic changes in its economic and employment structure and in the population's demographic characteristics, with important implications for the geography of poverty. We now turn to an examination of 170 cities within the Southern California region during the period from 1983 to 1996 to better illustrate the implications of these dynamics for fiscal disparities and poverty.

Tracking Federal Expenditures and Their Urban Fiscal Impacts

Our analysis relies on three major data sources. First, the Consolidated Federal Funds Reports (CFFR) from 1983–84 to 1996–97 provide federal expenditure information by city, county, and state. (We have estimated additional expenditures using 1996 data from the Internal Revenue Service and 1990 U.S. Census data.) Second, we have used the Annual Reports of Financial Transactions Concerning Cities of California for 1981–82 and 1996–97 to calculate local fiscal capacity measures. Finally, we obtained data on socioeconomic and demographic variables from the 1980 and 1990 U.S. Censuses. We describe below the methodology we used to select, aggregate, and organize the data.

Federal Expenditure Data

The CFFR provide data on federal expenditures and obligations by states, counties, and cities for more than two thousand government programs, including grants, salaries and wages, procurement contracts, and payments to individuals. However, in order to use the data, we had to perform several steps to create estimates of federal expenditures for Southern California cities.

The first step consisted of organizing the large number of programs into manageable categories. Following the example set by Persky (1999) and Summers (1999), we created thirty-two subcategories and organized these into five general groups: retirement, nonspatial redistribution, spatially related redistribution, other spatially related programs, and all programs not otherwise categorized (see Table 7.1). Hence redistribution programs are divided into nonspatial (i.e., individual-level transfers such as food stamps, medical assistance, and unemployment benefits) and spatial programs (i.e., federal expenditure targeting specific areas such as housing projects, community development, health, and education). Other spatially related programs include those allocated to specific areas but the purpose of which is nonredistributive (e.g., infrastructure, transportation, crime reduction, and housing-related tax benefits). Given that the identification codes of programs changed over time, this categorization had to be done separately for each year. Also, loans and insurance programs were dropped because they do not represent direct payments to localities.

The second step consisted of allocating undistributed funds to each city and adding them to directly allocated funds. There are approximately 350 undistributed programs that are allocated to counties rather than cities. This represents approximately 60 percent of all expenditures. For example, these programs include food stamps, medical assistance, and other important poverty-related programs as well as retirement programs. Unfortunately, there are no other generally available data on the number of people in each city receiving specific federal transfers. Consequently, an allocation methodology was required. In Summers's (1999) study of Philadelphia, funds were allocated to each city based on the following variables: (1) the city's share of the county's population age 65 and over for retirement categories, (2) the city's share of population below the federal poverty level for redistribution categories (both spatial and nonspatial), and (3) the city's share of the county population for all other categories. However, this methodology relies on restrictive assumptions regarding the way federal moneys are distributed. This is especially problematic for redistribution categories because it assumes that federal funds are allocated perfectly to poor households.[4]

A more reliable method is to allocate the funds based on a set of predictors obtained through logistic regressions performed on a larger sample (Persky 1999). Using 1992 Current Population Survey (CPS) data (Annual Demographic Files) for a sample of individuals from the Los Angeles, Orange, and Riverside-San Bernardino metropolitan areas, which provide detailed information on a wide range of programs, we computed separate regressions for each of the broad categories as well as for specific programs. In the case of retirement programs, the fact that a person was 65 years old or more predicted fairly well whether he or she would receive any type of retirement funds (such as Medicare and Social Security funds).[5] This finding gives support to the method used by Summers (1999) described above. For redistributional

Table 7.1. Real per capita federal spending, Southern California, 1983–85 and 1994–96

Expenditure	1983–85 ($)	1994–96 ($)	Percentage change
Retirement	1,689.76	1,832.11	8.42
Social Security and other retirement	1,070.56	1,028.37	−3.94
Medicare and related	469.02	703.48	49.99
Retirement for veterans and families	150.18	100.26	−33.24
Redistribution-transfers	288.02	798.75	177.33
Food stamps	26.34	85.08	222.94
Redistributional grants	94.22	220.90	134.45
Medical assistance	92.98	285.34	206.88
Unemployment	5.64	13.85	145.74
Supplemental security income	62.53	115.49	84.68
Redistribution to veterans	6.30	0.00	−99.96
Earned income tax credit	0.00	78.08	—
Redistribution—spatial	80.69	183.33	127.21
Housing and other space-related transfers	6.00	122.92	1948.92
Housing and community development	59.51	36.96	−37.89
Education	3.82	4.55	19.05
Health	11.36	18.91	66.43
Other spatial	608.98	1,392.96	251.95
Highways and related	41.59	53.98	29.77
Other infrastructure	35.49	17.22	−51.48
Assistance for disaster and environment	318.04	642.26	101.94
Crime	0.66	5.26	697.56
Housing-related tax benefits	213.20	674.25	216.25
All other	3,238.95	1,457.66	−55.00
Transfers to families and veterans	1.71	2.27	32.65
Direct business	6.91	12.48	80.50
Direct payments—post office	0.00	0.00	0.00
Procurement—defense	2,293.99	722.27	−68.51
Procurement—civilian	357.78	214.26	−40.11
Procurement—post office	13.48	32.72	142.72
Salaries and wages—military and defense	261.08	150.75	−42.26
Salaries and wages—other civilians	100.30	99.76	−0.54
Salaries and wages—post office	151.80	146.38	−3.57
Research	37.30	56.79	52.25
Arts	0.04	0.39	863.01
Other health	14.13	15.96	12.98
Other grants	0.43	3.62	739.36
Total	203.70	4,912.47	−13.71

programs, however, poverty alone does not seem to explain a large share of the variation in transfers. In fact, when the official poverty level is used as an explanatory variable for receiving poverty-related federal transfers, only 51.1 percent of pairs are concordant.[6] However, the predictive power of the model increases when we define poverty at 150 percent of the official level instead and add gender and age variables.[7] Although the percentage of concordant pairs decreases for specific programs such as SSI, it actually increases for larger programs such as food stamps and medical assistance, giving us some confidence in using poverty, gender, and age as predictors. Hence, by using 1980 and 1990 census data on the number of females, persons in poverty, and adults (18 to 64 years old) by city, we can predict with 76.3 percent confidence the number of people who receive poverty-related transfers in each city.[8] We then used these predicted values to calculate the share of each county's undistributed poverty-related federal expenditure to be allocated to each city.

The last broad category includes all other programs, most of which are not related to each other and are distributed in the form of larger grants for research, procurements, and salaries. For lack of a better alternative, like Summers (1999) we used a city's share of the county population (in 1984 and 1995 for each period, respectively) as the allocating factor. Nevertheless, more than 80 percent of these programs are directly distributed to cities and do not need to be allocated by any estimation method.

Finally, a third adjustment step was needed because of large annual differences in certain programs. To dampen such variation, we computed a three-year average for two periods: one ranging from 1983 to 1985 and another from 1994 to 1996. We also adjusted all the numbers for the thirty-two subcategories to real per capita figures, using 1996 as the base year in order to facilitate comparisons.[9]

The CFFR data are augmented by data on two categories of expenditure that play a very important role in shaping the geography of poverty. First, the earned income tax credit provides income relief through the federal tax code. Reforms in 1986 and 1994 increased benefits, making EITC one of the most important federal antipoverty measures, especially in the context of devolution. Because outlays were not reported until 1997, it was necessary to estimate benefits for the 1994–97 period based on IRS and CPS data. Information from 1996 IRS data on the number of people filing for EITC by zip code was aggregated by city and combined with 1996 CPS data on average EITC amounts for the five-county region to obtain total EITC expenditure by city.

Second, the fact that owners occupying their own homes fail to pay taxes on the implicit income they receive from their investment represents a tax subsidy to home owners that is not included in CFFR data.[10] As Gyourko and Sinai (2000) argue, these indirect housing-related tax benefits tend to favor wealthier suburban residents and may contribute to the socioeconomic gap between central cities and suburbs. We used census data from 1980 and 1990 on home ownership and property values to estimate these benefits for each period. More specifically, for each census tract, we estimated the annual household income of property owners by dividing median property values by three.[11] We then estimated the imputed income on home ownership investment as a 5 percent return on the median value of properties. Using the marginal tax rate applicable to the annual income level estimated, we were then able to compute the tax break obtained on this imputed income. We multiplied this average figure by the number of owner-occupied housing units in order to generate a total amount of tax benefit for each tract. In turn, we aggregated tract amounts by city. Like the other expenditures from CFFR data, EITC and housing-related tax benefits by city were adjusted to 1996 dollars and computed on a per capita basis to facilitate comparisons.

Measuring Fiscal Capacity

As noted above, there are several measures of fiscal capacity, most of which require extensive data and time-consuming computations. One common measure, developed by the Advisory Commission on Intergovernmental Relations (1971), calculates fiscal capacity by estimating the amount of revenue each local government would raise based on a hypothetical representative tax system (RTS) for the region. The RTS is a list of effective average tax rates for each tax base in use. This requires detailed information regarding sources of revenues and tax bases (e.g., sales, property values, income). A simpler approach is to calculate local fiscal revenues as a fraction of aggregate income and apply this average rate to each city's income to estimate fiscal capacity (Ladd and Yinger 1989). This second method, often called the "income burden" approach, is distinguished from the first by the fact that it uses income rather than a vector of sources to calculate the average tax rate. In the present study, we rely on the income burden approach.[12]

Several related measures of fiscal capacity can be devised, depending on the types of revenues included:

- *Total fiscal capacity* relies on all revenue sources.
- *Local fiscal capacity* excludes federal and state intergovernmental aid over which local governments have no control.
- *Discretionary local fiscal capacity* excludes also property taxes, which have been limited since the passage of Proposition 13, and sales taxes, which are based on the sale site and are relatively constant and hard to adjust in the short run.

This last measure also excludes enterprise revenues from production of electricity, which tend to be highly concentrated in a few cities and risk distorting the results. In Southern California, discretionary local fiscal capacity is a better indicator of the amount of revenues a city is able to control, and we use that measure throughout the rest of this chapter. For example, since Proposition 13, cities have relied heavily on user fees and other types of revenues over which they have adjustment powers.

Dynamics of Federal Expenditure Flows to Southern California Cities

On average, between 1983 and 1996, real per capita spending decreased by almost 14 percent. However, as Table 7.1 shows, this was mostly driven by sharp cuts in the broadest category, labeled "all other," which includes defense spending. Redistribution categories more than doubled, driven partly by the fact that in the 1994–96 period the economy had not fully recovered from the early 1990s recession and so the proportion of the population living in poverty was higher than in 1983–85.[13] It is likely that the 1996 welfare reforms and the continued expansion of the economy both served to lower these figures in more recent years. "Other spatial programs," which include housing-related tax benefits, infrastructure, environment, and crime, increased by more than 250 percent.

Changes in specific programs are more drastic and often explain the variation in the broader categories. For example, within the retirement category, Social Security represented the largest outlay but decreased by 4 percent. In the nonspatial redistribution category, food stamps showed the fastest growth in spending, but still represented a very small part of overall spending. Interestingly, both Medicare and medical assistance increased significantly, pointing to the rising real cost of health care provision and the health insurance crisis facing Southern California. Spatial redistribution programs represent a very small part of federal expenditures. However, the huge increase in housing and other spatially targeted programs is noteworthy. It is primarily due to short-term increases in federal funds allocated to specific areas following the 1992 urban Los Angeles uprising as well as indirect tax subsidies to home owners and disaster assistance mostly linked to the 1994 Northridge earthquake and annual flooding. Finally, changes in defense spending explain the massive decline in the "all other" category noted above. Whereas in 1983–85 defense spending clearly represented the largest subcategory, by 1994–96 it had been surpassed by Social Security. Per capita defense and military procurements decreased from $2,294 to $722, and per capita wage and salary payments were cut from $261 to $151.

Overall, redistribution programs continue to represent the smallest federal expenditure categories. In 1994–96, despite a dramatic increase, spatial and nonspatial redistribution programs constituted a mere 18 percent of federal spending in the five-county region. Moreover, the bulk of federal antipoverty efforts consists of nonspatial programs or individual transfers such as medical assistance, SSI, and food stamps (almost 80 percent of redistribution programs) rather than spatially based programs aimed at improving jobs, education, and health services (approximately 20 percent). This is partially explained by the dominant discourse against direct government intervention in the economy.[14] Moreover, "universal" programs such as Social Security, medical assistance, unemployment benefits, and the EITC typically receive more support than do policies targeted solely for specific groups, such as housing projects and community redevelopment efforts. According to Wilson (1987), this is explained by the fact that public programs perceived by members of the wider society as benefiting only certain groups (e.g., black families in urban ghettos) receive less support than do more universal programs.

As Joassart-Marcelli and Musso (2001) note, there are substantial disparities in funding throughout the region, and that variation has changed over time, with Orange County recently surpassing other counties in federal receipts. Although Los Angeles County received the largest part of federal funds channeled to the region, on a per capita basis in 1994–96, Orange and Ventura County residents received much higher amounts than those in Los Angeles. In contrast, Riverside and San Bernardino County residents received lower averages. As Figure 7.1 illustrates, however, these differences have not always been constant over time. In the early and mid-1980s, Los Angeles County enjoyed the highest per capita average and Ventura County had the lowest. Per capita averages remained low in San Bernardino and Riverside Counties throughout the whole period and actually declined slightly.

The higher averages in Orange and Ventura Counties are driven mostly by the "other spatial" category, which includes home-ownership tax benefits and infrastructure projects.[15] Overall, Los Angeles County receives a higher per capita average for redistribution programs (both spatial and nonspatial). Again, this is not surprising given the greater proportion of poor households in the county. Similarly, Riverside has a higher figure for retirement funds because it has a greater proportion of retirees than the other counties.

County patterns, however, often obscure sharp intracounty differences. Within each county, there are important differences between cities. As Figure 7.2 illustrates, per capita redistributive spending (i.e., spatial and nonspatial redistribution categories) in 1994–96 varied drastically from one place to another. The cities of Los Angeles,

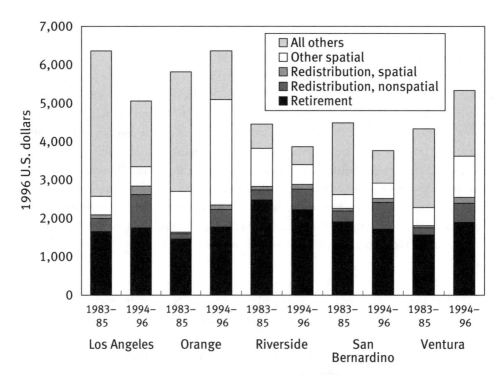

Figure 7.1. Per capita federal expenditure by category, Southern California counties, 1983–85 and 1994–96. Earned income tax credit and home-ownership tax credits are excluded from this chart because annual figures are not available.

Riverside, and San Bernardino, as well as a large number of cities east of Los Angeles, received higher averages than did cities in the southern part of Orange County or in Ventura County. For example, cities such as Cudahy, Bell Gardens, Maywood, and Huntington Park had significantly higher per capita averages (approximately $1,200) than cities such as Laguna Niguel, Mission Viejo, and Villa Park (about $350).

Larger variations are observed for the residual category (i.e., all other spending categories, including retirement, nonredistributive spatial, and other). Figure 7.3 shows the relatively low amounts of funding received by cities located to the east of Los Angeles and in San Bernardino and Riverside Counties compared with those in Orange County. For example, in 1994–96, the city of El Segundo received an average of $37,565 in "other" funds per person, whereas Hawaiian Gardens received only $1,549.[16]

These patterns seem to be closely related to the geography of poverty in the region. Although poor cities tend to receive larger amounts of redistributive funds, they benefit from fewer nonredistributive expenditures. This, in turn, is in part due to the distribution of defense installations and defense-dependent communities that receive the bulk of procurement-related expenditures.

In 1983–85, the patterns are almost identical. Cities that received more funds in 1994–96, were already receiving larger amounts in the first period. Some of the poorest cities in the region, such as Huntington Park, Lynwood, South Gate, and Paramount, received less in 1983–85 than they did in 1994–96. Cities in the central and northern parts of Orange county also received fewer redistributive funds in the first period, with the most striking example being the city of Orange itself. This is most likely related to the changes in poverty levels in the region.

Nonredistributive expenditures were more evenly spread throughout the region in 1983–85 than in the later period. In 1994–96, they had begun to move out of Los Angeles County and to concentrate in Orange County.

Explaining Urban Variations in Federal Expenditures

One of the central questions of this research is whether antipoverty programs are targeting poor communities or communities characterized by other sorts of features. For purposes of examining this question, we have grouped spending categories into two broad types: redistributive (or antipoverty) and other. The former includes the spatial and nonspatial redistribution categories defined above, and the latter includes retirement, other spatial, and all other categories. With a few specified exceptions, we use these two general categories in the remaining analyses in this chapter. Table 7.2 defines the variables used in the following analyses and indicates their sources.

Poverty, Race/Ethnicity, and Federal Expenditures

In an attempt to see whether federal funds are directed to poor communities with limited fiscal capacity, we categorized cities into poverty quintiles and calculated average per capita spending for each quintile (Table 7.3).[17] In both 1983–85 and 1994–96, cities in the poorest quintile received fewer federal funds (on a per capita basis) than

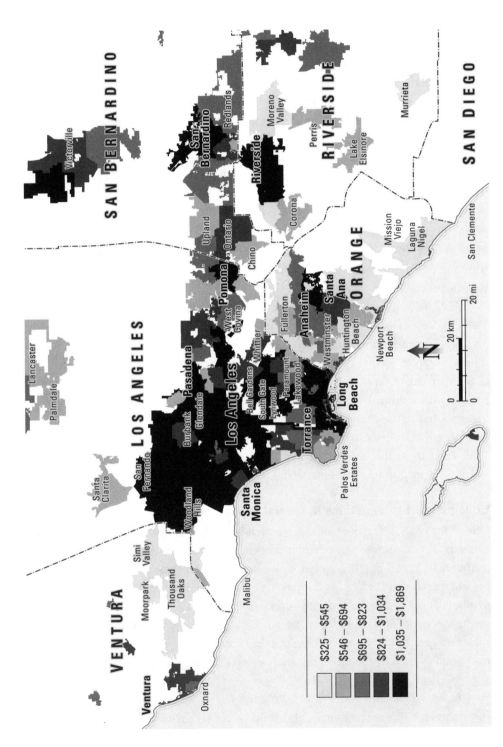

Figure 7.2. Per capita redistributive expenditures in Southern California, 1994–96, in U.S. dollars.

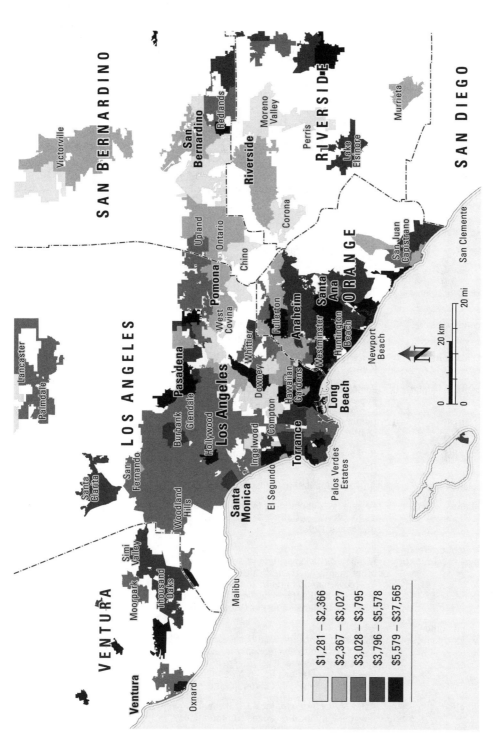

Figure 7.3. Per capita nonredistributive expenditures in Southern California, 1994–96, in U.S. dollars.

Table 7.2. Variable definitions and expected regression coefficient signs

Variable	Definition (source)	Redistributive expenditure	Non-redistributive expenditure
Dependent variables			
Per Capita Redistributive Federal Expenditures	Estimated city redistributive expenditure (food stamps, medical assistance, other transfers, housing, etc.) per capita annual average, by city (CFFR 1983–85, 1994–96; IRS 1996; CPS 1996)		
Per capita other federal expenditures	Estimated city nonredistributive expenditure (retirement, infrastructure, defense, etc.) per capita annual average, by city (CFFR 1983–85, 1994–96; Census 1980, 1990 STF3)		
Independent variables			
Percentage in poverty	Percentage of city population below 150 percent of official poverty level (Census 1980, 1990 STF3)	+	?
Percentage Latinos	Percentage of Latinos in city population (Census 1980, 1990 STF1)	+	?
Percentage blacks	Percentage of African Americans in city population (Census 1980, 1990 STF1)	+	?
Percentage Asians	Percentage of Asians in city population (Census 1980, 1990 STF1)	?	?
Percentage immigrants	Percentage of foreign-born persons in city population (Census 1980, 1990 STF3)	−	?
Charter city	Dummy variable set to 1 if the city has its own charter (SCAG 1990)	+	+
Age of city	Number of years since city incorporation (SCAG 1990)	+	+
Population size	Total city population (Census 1980, 1990 STF1)	+	?
Population growth	Percentage population growth 1980–90 and 1990–98 (Census 1980, 1990; Department of Finance 1998)	+	+
Per capita discretionary local fiscal capacity	Estimated city capacity to raise revenues other than property and sales taxes, intergovernmental grants and electrical utilities (computations based on 1982 and 1997 Controller's Report of California Cities)	−	−
Per capita other revenue capacity	Estimated per capita total fiscal capacity minus per capita discretionary local fiscal capacity and federal-level intergovernmental grants (computations based on 1982 and 1997 Controller's Report of California Cities)	−	−
Fiscal effort	Ratio of discretionary local fiscal capacity over discretionary local revenues (computations based on 1982 and 1997 Controller's Report of California Cities)	+	+

Note: CFFR = Consolidated Federal Funds Report; CPS = Current Population Survey; STF = Summary Tape File; SCAG = Southern California Association of Governments.

did those in the more affluent quintiles. Indeed, cities in the richest quintile received almost 90 percent more funding than the poorest cities in 1983–85 and 80 percent more in 1994–96. These findings give support to the argument that federal programs fail to help the poorest groups.

However, if one distinguishes between redistributive and nonredistributive spending, two different stories emerge. Not surprisingly, the allocation of redistributive funds is closely associated with poverty levels. Indeed, in both periods, the per capita averages consistently increase with each poverty quintile, suggesting that poorer cities benefit from larger federal antipoverty expenditures. Interestingly, although the average increases in all quintiles between 1983–85 and 1994–96, the rate of increase becomes lower when one goes from low-poverty to high-poverty quintiles. Thus the most rapid increase in average per capita redistributive expenditure is taking place in cities with the lowest poverty levels. This suggests that the increase in antipoverty expenditures noted above has been disproportionately directed to poor individuals who live in nonpoor cities.

Other funds, in contrast, tend to go disproportionately to the wealthiest cities. In both periods, cities in the richest quintile received almost twice as much federal money as did cities in the poorest quintile. These figures suggest that poor cities may be hurt by a lack of federal funds for nonredistributive purposes such as infrastructure and procurement. This is of great concern if the funds they receive for antipoverty programs are insufficient, forcing them to reallocate local and state funds to these most pressing needs and further reduce spending on other important programs. This is especially problematic given that urban poverty generates uncompensated costs or

Table 7.3. Per capita real federal spending by poverty quintiles of cities, Southern California, 1983–85 and 1994–96

Poverty quintile	Total	Redistribution	Other
1983–85 per capita federal spending ($)			
1 (lowest poverty rate)	7,813.19	215.16	7,598.02
2	8,114.51	251.20	7,863.31
3	4,725.80	349.24	4,376.56
4	4,689.62	387.07	4,302.55
5 (highest poverty rate)	4,182.46	571.64	3,610.83
1994–96 per capita federal spending ($)			
1 (lowest poverty rate)	7,024.07	601.63	6,422.44
2	6,165.07	632.82	5,532.25
3	4,796.42	776.13	4,020.29
4	6,027.93	908.64	5,119.30
5 (highest poverty rate)	3,911.71	1,151.15	2,760.56
1983–85 to 1994–96 percentage change in per capita federal spending			
1 (lowest poverty rate)	−10.10	179.62	−15.47
2	−24.02	151.92	−29.64
3	1.49	122.23	−8.14
4	28.54	134.75	18.98
5 (highest poverty rate)	−6.47	101.38	−23.55

Note: The 1983–85 quintiles are based on 1980 city-level poverty rates, and the 1994–96 quintiles are based on similar 1990 data. There are 149 cities in the 1983–85 sample and 168 cities in the 1994–96 sample.

externalities linked to higher costs of providing law enforcement, education, and other services (Pack 1998).

The relationship between federal expenditures and the poverty level of a city can also be observed on an individual city basis. Analysis of the correlation between each city's poverty rates against its per capita average of antipoverty federal spending suggests a positive relationship between the two variables (see Table 7.4). In short, poorer cities benefit from greater federal funds designed to alleviate poverty. However, there is no clear relationship between a city's poverty status and its flow of federal funds. In fact, the correlation coefficients are smaller and negative, suggesting that poorer cities get fewer funds.

In Southern California, as in most urban areas of the United States, poverty is highly related to race and ethnicity. Communities of color often represent the poorest segment of society that federal policies fail to reach. As these groups tend to concentrate in specific areas, poorer cities often have large proportions of blacks, Latinos, or immigrants.[18] Nevertheless, "minority" status is not synonymous with poverty, and federal funds may be allocated differently among cities with different ethnoracial compositions, as suggested by the correlations between per capita federal expenditures and the percentage of ethnoracial and immigrant groups in each city shown in Table 7.4.

Antipoverty programs seem to target communities with large proportions of Latinos, immigrants, and, to a lesser extent, blacks. In contrast, cities with large representations of whites receive lower per capita flows of redistributive federal funds. This is not surprising given the differing statuses of these groups. On the other hand, other programs seem to be disproportionately allocated to cities with large proportions of whites, with fewer funds going to places with high proportions of immigrants,

Table 7.4. Correlation analysis between selected characteristics of Southern California cities and per capita federal expenditure, 1994–96 and 1983–85.

Characteristic	1994–96			1983–85		
	Redistribution	Other	Total	Redistribution	Other	Total
Poverty						
Poverty rate	0.6109	−0.2485	−0.2056	0.61	−0.07	−0.0584
Race/ethnicity						
Percentage foreign-born in city	0.5411	−0.1594	−0.0820	0.1731	−0.0661	−0.0628
Percentage Latinos in city	0.5684	−0.2032	−0.0889	0.275	−0.1309	−0.1258
Percentage blacks in city	0.2646	−0.1516	−0.0950	0.1886	−0.0122	−0.0087
Percentage Asians in City	0.0056	−0.0345	−0.0609	−0.1003	−0.0296	−0.0315
Percentage whites in city	−0.6125	0.2487	0.1339	−0.4029	0.1437	0.1362
Population						
Total population	0.1622	−0.0115	0.0002	0.0454	−0.0009	0.0000
Population growth	−0.1798	−0.1525	−0.1663	0.6833	−0.0641	−0.0513
Institutional/ Fiscal characteristics						
Charter city	0.1848	0.1068	0.1207	0.1030	0.1399	0.1418
Age of city	0.2929	0.0590	0.0805	0.0352	0.1258	0.1264
Total fiscal capacity	−0.2114	0.2747	0.2609	−0.2714	0.2597	0.2547
Discretionary local fiscal capacity	−0.2685	0.1482	0.2352	−0.3601	0.0686	0.0619
Fiscal effort	0.1825	0.0152	0.0283	0.0810	0.0735	0.075

Latinos, African Americans, and Asians. Because these other funds represent the biggest share of federal expenditure, on average, cities with larger white populations receive more federal funds.

It is interesting to note that the differences between ethnoracial groups were not as large in 1983–85 as they were in the 1990s. With regard to redistributive funds, this suggests that the number of poor minorities has increased and become more concentrated during the period and that the federal government has become more effective at targeting them. Concerning other funds, it suggests that the preferential status of white communities increased over the whole period at the expense of immigrant, Latino, and, to a lesser extent, Asian and African American communities.

Population Growth and City Size

One may expect cities with rapid population growth to receive more federal funds given their rising need for infrastructure, schools, and so on. However, the data suggest no clear relationship between the allocation of federal funds and population growth. Total expenditures were practically unrelated to population growth in both periods. Nevertheless, the correlation between redistribution expenditures and population growth was stronger and positive in the first period.

In general, the size of a city has very little influence on per capita spending. Nevertheless, cities with larger populations tend to receive slightly more redistributive funds. This is partially due to the fact that larger cities suffer from more severe poverty. For example, the city of Los Angeles had a population of 3,485,398 inhabitants in 1990—of whom 30.4 percent lived below 150 percent of the poverty threshold—and received an average of $1,395 per capita in antipoverty programs from 1994 through 1996. Indeed, Los Angeles has both the largest number of people and the most poor people; hence it had one of the highest rates of per capita antipoverty federal expenditure in that period.

Federal Flows and Fiscal/Institutional Characteristics of Cities

Both fiscal and institutional features of cities can be expected to influence their receipt of federal funds. With respect to the latter, we considered age and charter/general law status. Older cities received slightly more federal moneys than did younger ones. This is especially true for redistributive funds in 1994–96, suggesting perhaps that newly incorporated cities have a lower poverty rate or are less effective in attracting federal funds. Charter cities received slightly higher per capita funds than did general law cities. Although this is partially linked to age and poverty conditions, it may also reflect the strength of charter cities' local public and business institutions and their ability to attract more federal funds to finance specific projects—whether redistributive or not.

Turning to fiscal characteristics, in principle a redistributive tax system aiming at equalizing opportunities across cities ought to allocate more funds to areas with lower fiscal capacity. Under that system, poorer areas with lower property values, fewer retail centers, and lower household incomes would be compensated by the federal

government for their lack of local tax revenues. Thus we would expect cities with limited fiscal capacity to receive more federal funds than other cities. As Musso argues in
chapter 6 of this volume, cities vary substantially across the region with regard to fiscal
capacity, and these disparities have increased during the past decades.

The poorest cities, located east of Los Angeles and in Riverside and San Bernardino
Counties, had the lowest fiscal capacity in both periods, whereas the highest fiscal
capacity was found in the beach cities south of Los Angeles and in Orange County.
The correlation analyses reported in Table 7.4 reveal that although fiscal capacity is
negatively correlated with per capita antipoverty expenditure, it is positively correlated
with other types of expenditures. Thus, overall, flows of federal funds may exacerbate
fiscal disparities across cities in the region and favor wealthier cities, which are often
located in outlying areas.

To the extent that the allocation of federal funds does not take into consideration
fiscal needs and capacity, poorer cities often have to make a bigger "fiscal effort."[19] To
examine this phenomenon, we divided cities into quintiles based on their levels of
poverty and then calculated average discretionary local fiscal capacity and revenues
for each quintile. Figure 7.4 illustrates the results of these computations for the 1990s,
showing that discretionary local fiscal capacity declines drastically with rising poverty.
However, locally raised revenues per capita actually increase with poverty and thus

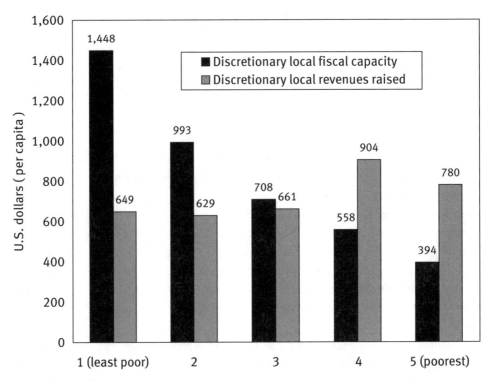

Figure 7.4. Per capita discretionary local fiscal capacity and revenues, by poverty quintile,
Southern California cities, 1997.

are not proportional to discretionary local fiscal capacity. This suggests that cities in the poorest quintile may be forced to raise higher revenues than other cities in order to provide adequate public services to residents, despite their lower fiscal capacity. In other words, residents of poorer cities tend to give a higher tax effort or pay a disproportionately higher share of their income for public services. A similar, although slightly more equitable, pattern was observed in 1982.

Correlation coefficients reported in Table 7.4 indicate that fiscal effort is positively related to federal expenditure levels. To investigate further the extent to which federal expenditures equalize or exacerbate the inequalities described above, we calculated fiscal equalization measures by adding per capita federal expenditure (redistributive and other) and capacity to raise other revenues to our discretionary local fiscal capacity measure.[20] Clearly, as illustrated for the 1994–96 period in Figure 7.5, federal expenditures do not equalize fiscal capacity across city poverty quintiles. This pattern of inequality increased from 1983–85 despite the overall increase in antipoverty expenditure noted above. This is primarily due to the rising gap in fiscal capacities among cities, which the federal allocation of funds does not take into account.

This reinforces the correlation analysis result that wealthier cities tend to be the recipients of larger federal expenditures. This is partly due to the fact that local project financing is often based on local resources combined with matching federal funds. In other words, cities with a stronger economic base may benefit from greater federal

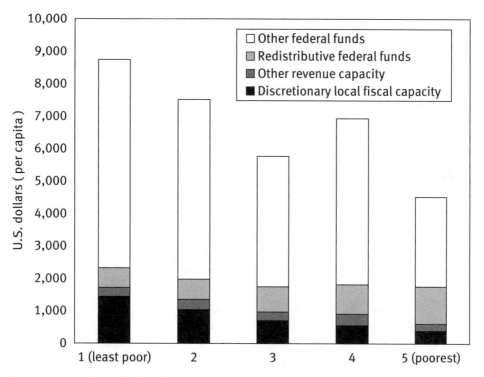

Figure 7.5. Fiscal equalization, by poverty quintile, Southern California cities, 1990s.

spending to the extent that they are able to allocate money toward commercial and infrastructure development and can apply for federal funds to match or complement local funds. Moreover, home-ownership tax subsidies disproportionately favor wealthier cities with larger proportions of home ownership and higher property values. This is especially true in wealthier suburban communities.

A less severe pattern can be observed across counties, although disparities between cities in San Bernardino and Riverside Counties and cities in Los Angeles and Orange Counties persisted in both periods. The latter not only have greater fiscal capacities but also receive greater amounts of federal funds. Hence fiscal equalization across counties does not occur.

Another way to estimate fiscal equalization is to compare coefficients of variation of fiscal capacity among Southern California cities with those of total figures including both capacities and federal expenditures.[21] Whereas the coefficient of variation of discretionary local fiscal capacity was over 55 percent in 1982 and 68 percent in 1997, it rose to 181 percent for the total figures in 1982 and 70 percent in 1997. Although adding the capacity to raise other revenues to discretionary local fiscal capacity did not affect disparity very much, adding federal expenditure had a huge impact. Indeed, disparity among cities is greater after one takes federal expenditure into account than it is before one does so.

In summary, our analysis highlights the extent of fiscal disparities across cities in Southern California and suggests that the allocation of federal funds exacerbates rather than reduces these disparities. Of course, a complete analysis would require us to take into account expenditure needs and to compare them with city capacity to raise revenues. Fiscal equalization, as measured here, focuses only on the revenue side and ignores the fact that some cities may have higher public services requirements and thus need more revenues. Indeed, one might expect cities with high levels of poverty to have higher expenditure needs. If this is the case, the disparities across cities may actually be more severe than suggested here.

Multivariate Analysis of the Determinants of Federal Funding

Descriptive statistics suggest that federal funds are allocated to each city based on a number of relevant variables, including poverty conditions, race/ethnicity of residents, population growth, size, age, institutional type, and fiscal characteristics. However, it is difficult to see which of these variables are most important and to what extent they explain variations in federal expenditure—either redistributive or nonredistributive. Thus we performed a series of regression analyses to test the importance of each factor while controlling for a number of other variables.[22]

The model is based on the following specification: $Y_c = \alpha + \beta X_c$, where Y_c is the dependent variable measuring either the per capita redistributive or other (i.e., non-redistributive) federal expenditure by city c and X is a vector of city-level characteristics, including a socioeconomic variable (poverty), race and ethnicity variables (proportions of Latinos, blacks, Asians, and whites), demographic variables (proportion of immigrants, proportion of population over age 65, population growth, population), institutional variables (city age, charter versus general law city), and fiscal variables (discretionary local fiscal capacity, other revenues capacity, and fiscal effort), as defined in Table 7.2.

Redistributive Expenditures

Because a significant proportion of redistributive expenditures is allocated to cities based on a prediction equation including poverty as one of the predictors, there is a potential endogeneity problem linked with regressing redistributive expenditure on poverty. In an attempt to solve this problem, we use two-stage least squares regressions with an instrumental variable for poverty. The poverty instrument is predicted using median income, proportion of African Americans, and proportion of Latinos. These variables seem to predict poverty rather well given the high R^2 obtained (0.7438 in 1990, and 0.7254 in 1980). Moreover, using the predicted value (instrument) instead of the actual value of poverty appears to be an appropriate way to control for endogeneity given the low correlation between the residuals from each stage.

Table 7.5 shows the regression results for the natural logarithm of redistributive per capita spending on a set of independent variables for 1994–96 and 1983–85.

Table 7.5. Two-stage least squares regression results: explaining city-level per capita redistributive federal expenditure in Southern California, 1983–85 and 1994–96

Characteristic	1983–85 Coefficients	1994–96 Coefficients
Percentage in poverty[a]	4.114388****	4.126874 ****
	0.762219	*0.7204496*
Percentage Asians	0.671485	0.6880148 ****
	0.690417	*0.331401*
Percentage immigrants	0.219980	−0.0683279
	0.477114	*0.3366363*
Charter city	0.942969*	0.1163104 ****
	0.070005	*0.0546538*
Age of city	0.000164	0.0009615 *
	0.001031	*0.000684*
Population size	0.000000	0.0000000
	0.000000	*0.0000001*
Population growth	0.601506****	−0.1815225
	0.064737	*0.2507585*
Per capita discretionary local fiscal capacity	0.000746****	0.0003638 ****
	0.000262	*0.0000836*
Per capita other revenues capacity	−0.000387*	−0.0004429 ****
	0.000262	*0.0001333*
Fiscal effort	0.019235	0.0526164 ****
	0.025290	*0.0230106*
Intercept	4.096776****	5.524471 ****
	0.179383	*0.1638155*
Number of observations	146	165
R^2	0.6187	0.5723
Adjusted R^2	0.5905	0.5446
Correlation of residuals	0.2388	0.2049

Note: Expressions in italics are standard errors; dependent variable is natural log of per capita redistributive federal expenditures.
[a] Instrumental variable.
* significant at the 20 percent level.
** significant at the 15 percent level.
*** significant at the 10 percent level.
**** significant at the 5 percent level.

According to these regressions, the most significant determinant of the allocation of redistributive federal funds is poverty. This suggests that the federal government does allocate antipoverty funds according to cities' poverty levels.

The proportion of Asians in a city is the only race and ethnicity variable used in the regression, given that whites represent the group of reference (i.e., the largest), which is typically left out, and that the proportions of blacks and Latinos are used in the prediction of the instrumental variable for poverty and consequently have to be dropped from the regression to avoid multicollinearity. The proportion of Asians did not play a significant role in the first period, but it seemed to be important in attracting redistributive funds in the second period. However, because city poverty was predicted using the share of Latinos and African Americans, it is likely that cities with large proportions of Latinos and African Americans receive disproportionate amounts of redistributive federal funds.

Surprisingly, population growth played a positive role in 1983–85 but a negative although less significant role in 1994–96. This may be linked to the fact that population growth was most rapid in the poorest cities during the 1980s but slowed down during the 1990s and shifted to suburban areas as wealthier residents moved away from urban areas.

The institutional strength of cities, measured by whether they have their own charter, seems to play a significant role in their ability to attract greater amounts of antipoverty funds. This finding reinforces the importance of considering institutional structural forces in the study of intrametropolitan poverty.

Finally, discretionary local fiscal capacity has a positive and significant influence on the allocation of redistributive federal funds to Southern California cities. This implies that antipoverty federal expenditures target cities with higher levels of fiscal capacity. This finding is not surprising given that we found little evidence of fiscal equalization across cities by federal spending policies.

In both periods, the capacity to raise other revenues (i.e., sales and property taxes, state and other nonfederal intergovernmental grants) had a negative impact on the amount of redistributive funds received. Moreover, cities with higher fiscal effort— even after poverty and other characteristics were controlled for—received more resources than others, especially in 1994–96.

NONREDISTRIBUTIVE EXPENDITURES

Regular ordinary least squares (OLS) technique can be employed for nonredistributive expenditures given the limited endogeneity problems associated with the allocation procedure.[23] Hence, in this case, actual poverty is used and all race and ethnicity variables can be included in the model (Table 7.6).

Overall, the significance of the model is less satisfying than in the case of redistributive expenditure, and fewer variables appear to play a role in explaining the allocation of federal resources. In both periods, the proportion of the population over 64 years old plays an important role. Undoubtedly, this is related to the retirement portion of nonredistributive expenditures.

In both periods, institutional characteristics of cities played an important role. Both older cities and charter cities were associated with higher levels of per capita nonredistributive expenditure. This suggests that cities characterized by stronger institutions and greater experience in dealing with upper levels of government have a better chance of receiving federal funds for general purposes.

Fiscally, cities with higher discretionary fiscal capacity received fewer funds in the first period, but discretionary fiscal capacity had an insignificant impact in 1994–96. However, the capacity to raise other revenues had a positive influence on the amount of nonredistributive funds allocated to a city in 1983–85. Thus cities with larger property and sales tax revenues were able to attract more funds, reflecting a lack of fiscal equalization.

Poverty was not a determining factor in the process of federal resource allocation in 1983–85, and it became a negative factor in 1994–96. This suggests that more recently cities with high proportions of people in poverty have received lower levels of

Table 7.6. Ordinary least squares regression results: explaining city-level per capita nonredistributive federal expenditure in Southern California, 1983–85 and 1994–96

Characteristic	1983–85 Coefficients	1994–96 Coefficients
Percentage in poverty	−0.551431	−1.140859**
	0.962216	0.7117025
Percentage blacks	−0.351874	−0.8514754**
	0.626903	0.5665278
Percentage Latinos	−0.901867***	−0.2791878
	0.539275	0.4391371
Percentage Asians	−1.061645	−0.4314741
	1.270713	0.6339968
Percentage immigrants	0.736678	−0.0708438
	1.002283	0.7240592
Charter city	0.389733****	0.1615589**
	0.124470	0.1069279
Age of city	0.003374***	0.0016776*
	0.001759	0.0012485
Population size	0.000000	0.000000
	0.000000	0.000000
Population growth	0.027091	−0.9067268***
	0.119718	0.4841309
Per capita discretionary local fiscal capacity	−0.000484*	0.000074
	0.000371	0.0000958
Per capita other revenues capacity	0.001482****	0.0002007
	0.000439	0.0002574
Fiscal effort	−0.052228	−0.0071916
	0.043955	0.0454535
Percentage 65 years old or older	3.579824****	3.452188****
	0.935519	0.7077677
Intercept	7.312485****	8.078668****
	0.238440	0.2002597
Number of observations	146	164
R^2	0.3988	0.4386
Adjusted R^2	0.3396	0.39

Note: Expressions in italics are standard errors; dependent variable is natural log of per capital nonredistributive federal expenditures.
* Significant at the 20 percent level.
** Significant at the 15 percent level.
*** Significant at the 10 percent level.
**** Significant at the 5 percent level.

nonredistributive federal expenditure than have wealthier cities after other factors are controlled for.

In 1983–85, a city's proportion of Latinos had a negative and significant impact on the amount of funds received, implying that federal resources were directed away from cities with such populations. However, this variable became insignificant in 1994–96.

The regressions also indicate the importance of population growth in determining the amount of nonredistributive funds in 1994–96. Cities with faster population growth in the 1990s received smaller per capita average expenditure than did slower-growing cities. This suggests that federal expenditures do not necessarily go to cities where public demands may be higher due to population increases and accompanying infrastructure needs.

The fact that poverty and fiscal capacity variables are not highly significant and that the R^2 is rather low suggests that other forces are at work. In short, the allocation of nonredistributive federal funds may be based on idiosyncratic factors such as voting patterns, numbers of projects proposed and approved, political stability, and other forces not captured in the data available here. Nevertheless, it does not seem to promote any attempt at fiscal equalization across Southern California cities.

Because nonredistributive expenditures include diverse types of spending that may be allocated by very different processes, we ran separate regressions (not shown here) for retirement, defense, and home-ownership benefits—the three largest components of other expenditures. Not surprisingly, we found that the retirement category is most influenced by the proportion of population over 64 years old, but is also negatively influenced by population growth. This suggests that fast-growing areas are characterized by larger proportions of young persons or immigrants, who are less likely to enjoy retirement benefits. Regarding defense spending, the most important variable was poverty, which had a negative impact, followed by the proportion of Latinos, which had a positive impact. This suggests that most federal defense spending takes place in middle-class industrial suburbs such as Pico Rivera, Azusa, and Anaheim, where a high proportion of Latinos now reside. Cities with high levels of poverty are often characterized by obsolete infrastructure and declining job bases, and thus are unlikely to benefit from large defense contracts. Finally, indirect spending associated with home-ownership tax relief is most positively associated with discretionary local fiscal capacity and negatively related to poverty rate and proportions of African Americans and Latinos. This confirms the findings of Aldana and Dymski (chapter 3, this volume), who, although they focus on other aspects of the housing tax benefits to home owners (i.e., mortgage interest deductions), suggest that federal housing favors wealthier suburban areas with high proportions of white residents at the expense of poorer urban neighborhoods with high proportions of Latinos and African Americans.

Conclusion

The extent to which federal funds effectively target poor communities and equalize cities' fiscal capacity has become an urgent issue in Southern California because of rising income disparities and concentrated poverty in the region combined with de-creasing federal responsibility for social welfare at the local level. As the fiscal federal-ism literature reveals, this may lead to both efficiency and equity problems, providing a rationale for fiscal equalization across cities to eliminate or reduce disparities. With-out at least some degree of fiscal equalization, poorer cities may find it difficult to fight poverty and continue to provide other public services to residents. Thus a down-ward spiral of increasing inequality and poverty is likely to result.

Analyses of CFFR data and data from additional sources reveal that federal spend-ing in the region decreased between 1983 and 1996. However, redistributive federal expenditures increased during this period, although they continue to represent less than a fifth of overall spending. The general decline in spending is mostly explained by drastic cuts in defense and military spending. Important variations are also found in the region across cities and counties. In general, cities in Orange and Los Angeles Counties receive more than do cities in San Bernardino and Riverside Counties. Al-though spending in most counties stabilized or declined, spending in Ventura County increased throughout the period. Cartographic analysis also suggests great disparities across cities in both periods.

The variations in levels of redistributive and nonredistributive federal expendi-tures seem to be linked to several important factors. First, although redistributive expenditures are positively related to city-level poverty, nonredistributive funds are moving in the opposite direction. Second, race and ethnicity play an important role in federal funds allocation. High proportions of ethnoracial minorities in a city have a positive impact on per capita redistributive expenditures, but a negative influence on nonredistributive expenditures, especially home-ownership tax benefits. Third, cities' age and institutional strength seem to influence their ability to attract either type of federal expenditures, with older cities and institutionally stronger cities attracting more funding. Fourth, cities with higher discretionary local fiscal capacity and higher fiscal effort are typically associated with higher levels of redistributive expenditures, but these factors do not significantly affect nonredistributive expenditures. Conse-quently, federal flows of expenditures do not equalize fiscal capacity across cities, counties, or poverty quintiles, and poorer cities have more limited resources than other cities both to fight poverty and to provide other public services. In fact, federal expenditures seem to exacerbate disparities in urban fiscal capacity, regardless of expenditure needs.

Under such circumstances, federal expenditures may alleviate some of the direct costs associated with poverty through redistributive expenditures, but they fail to give cities equal chances to compete in the provision of other public services by dis-proportionately allocating nonredistributive funds to fiscally healthier cities. Indeed, federal expenditure allocation patterns could exacerbate the gap between wealthier and poorer cities by promoting infrastructure and housing development and job creation in wealthier suburban areas while failing to address the problems of poorer cities, which are typically located in the urban core and older industrial suburban areas. Such fiscal policies allow residents with higher incomes to escape the higher tax burden and perhaps less desirable living conditions associated with poorer areas while trapping poorer residents in a cycle of poverty.

This uneven pattern is especially problematic if concentrated poverty imposes additional costs on poor cities. To the extent that antipoverty programs are insufficient to eliminate poverty, cities are faced with the residual costs associated with poverty and consequently may be forced to cut the funds they can allocate to other programs. The federal government does not take this into account in its allocation of other funds, and so poorer cities often fall behind in their ability to finance infrastructure projects and create jobs for local residents. Although further research is necessary to evaluate the extent of this "uncompensated cost" problem, this chapter has highlighted some of the important factors influencing the distribution of federal funds across cities in Southern California.

Notes

We would like to thank Alex Alonso, George Kivork, Julie Park, Lydia Thornton, Lili Wang, and Brooke Zobrist for their research assistance; Thomas W. Lester, Joseph Persky, Haydar Kurban, and Jerry Keffer for their advice on using CFFR data; and Michael Dear, Enrico Marcelli, Manuel Pastor, Chris Weare, and participants at the Southern California Studies Center's Building the Sustainable Metropolis Project for comments and suggestions. Special thanks go to the Southern California Studies Center and the National Science Foundation Program in Geography and Regional Science for funding this research. Earlier versions of these results were published previously in Joassart-Marcelli and Musso (2001).

1. To be sure, overall spending, including antipoverty expenditures, continued to increase during this period. However, real benefits per poor person barely rose at all (Burtless 1994). Although public spending as a share of GDP rose from 28.3 percent in 1970 to 31.3 percent in 1990, the federal government's share stayed around 20 percent and the state and local governments' proportion rose from 8 to 10 percent between 1970 and 1990. In 1996, the federal government's share remained at 20 percent, whereas the state and local governments' share had risen above 12 percent (Gottheil 1999).

2. Unequal distribution of public services may reduce the efficiency of private resource allocation by firms and individuals; wealthier areas may be able to attract businesses with lower taxes and better services, leading to reallocation of resources based on nonmarket forces and merely shifting economic activities and jobs from one area to another without generating any net economic benefit for society (Musso 1998; Bartik 1991; Lugar 1987). With respect to horizontal equity, under fiscal decentralization, poor people are not treated similarly throughout the country or even within a region; in 1992, for example, AFDC recipients in Vermont, Connecticut, and Hawaii received an average of almost $200 per month, whereas those in Alabama and Mississippi received less than $50 (Fisher 1996). Considering vertical equity, poor people who tend to be concentrated in urban areas often face higher tax rates and lower levels of quality of public services coupled with higher costs of living than do wealthier residents in suburban communities.

3. For a review of definitions of fiscal capacity, see Musso's discussion in chapter 6 of this volume. As Musso notes, most measures are problematic because they ignore the institutional constraints imposed by state-local fiscal regimes.

4. Redistribution or antipoverty categories include a wide range of programs, such as food stamps, school lunches, medical assistance, scholarships for low-income students, and job training. On average, only 20 to 25 percent of these expenditures are allocated directly to cities. The remaining 75 to 80 percent need to be allocated using an estimation procedure.

5. The percentage of concordant pairs for the logistic regression estimating the likelihood of receiving retirement funds based on whether a person was 65 years old or older was 84.6 percent (87.5 percent for Medicare and 78.6 percent for Social Security). The Somers's d was 0.823.

6. Poverty related transfers include AFDC, Supplemental Security Income (SSI), food stamps, medical assistance, energy assistance, housing assistance, and school lunch programs.

7. Because the official poverty level is very low, many people who qualify for government assistance are not officially considered poor. Raising the poverty level to 150 percent of the official threshold allows us to capture that share of the population. Moreover, age and gender variables permit us to target the recipient population better given the fact that women, children, and elderly people are most likely to receive aid.

8. This assumes that the predictors of receiving federally funded assistance (i.e., poverty, age, and gender) are the same in each city as they are for the whole region.

9. Real figures are computed in 1996 dollars based on the urban consumer price index for Los Angeles.

10. Although the tax benefits associated with home ownership include mortgage interest deductions, property tax deductions, and untaxed portion of imputed income from property, only the last of these is taken into account here. This is consistent with Musgrave and Musgrave's (1980) argument that all investments should be treated similarly for tax purposes. Mortgage interest and tax deductions represent costs of investing that are typically tax deductible for all other types of formal investment and thus do not represent unusual deductions as long as the net income generated by the "home" business is fully taxed. In contrast, the lack of taxation on imputed revenues from investment in home ownership (i.e., the rent a home would generate were it rented out instead of occupied by its owner) is a real subsidy to the extent that revenues generated by other types of investments (including real estate property rental) are typically taxed.

11. This is a common estimation procedure based on the assumption that people's ability to purchase a home is determined by their level of income and that, on average, a household spends a third of its income on housing.

12. The method we use varies from that used by Ladd and Yinger (1989) in that we do not adjust revenues for income exporting. This is because California cities are severely restricted in imposing revenues that are subject to exporting, such as sales, business, or income taxes.

13. CPS statistics for California indicate that between 1983–84 and 1994–96, the official poverty rate increased from an average of 13.9 percent to 17.2 percent.

14. To the extent that the government gives transfers to individuals, it allows them to purchase the goods and services they choose from private firms. However, if the government itself produces the goods and services, it interferes with the market system by competing for resources with private firms. For this reason, in a climate of governmental downsizing, public opinion often favors individual transfers over direct government intervention in the economy.

15. From 1994 through 1996, several Orange County cities (i.e., Huntington Beach, Fountain Valley, and Santa Ana) received very large amounts of federal money for flood control.

16. From 1994 through 1996, El Segundo received more than $30,000 per capita in defense-related contracts per year.

17. We ranked cities according to the proportion of households within them with income below 150 percent of the official poverty threshold. We use the 150 percent cutoff to measure poverty throughout this section.

18. Southern California cities' poverty rates are positively correlated with their proportions of Latinos (0.77), immigrants (0.56), and blacks (0.27) and negatively correlated with their share of whites (–0.72) and Asians (–0.23).

19. Fiscal effort is defined as the ratio of capacity over revenues. However, regional capacity is calculated by multiplying the income burden rate by the regional income, where the income burden rate is the ratio of regional revenues over regional income. Thus regional capacity is automatically equal to regional revenue, generating a fiscal effort index equal to one.

20. The capacity to raise other revenues is based on the difference between the total fiscal capacity measure discussed above and the discretionary local fiscal capacity measure used throughout this section. Thus it includes sales and property taxes and intergovernmental grants. However, we have excluded federal intergovernmental grants to avoid double counting, as such grants are reflected in the federal expenditure figures. All numbers are adjusted in 1996 dollars and are on a per capita basis.

21. The coefficient of variation is defined as the standard deviation over the mean. It is thus a relative measure that allows for comparisons by removing the influence of the magnitude of the data.

22. Again, some of the results of these analyses are also reported in Joassart-Marcelli and Musso (2001).

23. Two-stage least squares regressions were performed using an instrumental variable for the proportion of the population 65 years old or above. However, the results were almost identical to the OLS procedure, so we decided to use the actual value with regular OLS rather than the predicted value because it measures the impact of the elderly population more accurately. It is useful to remember that 55 percent of nonredistributive funds in 1994–96 and 68 percent of such funds in 1983–85 included nonretirement expenditures such as defense and infrastructure that are typically allocated at the city level, as well as home-ownership tax benefits directly estimated for each city.

Works Cited

Advisory Commission on Intergovernmental Relations. 1971. *Measuring the Fiscal Capacity and Effort of State and Local Areas.* Washington, DC: U.S. Government Printing Office.

Aronson, J. Richard, and John L. Hilley. 1986. *Financing State and Local Governments.* Washington, DC: Brookings Institution.

Bartik, Timothy J. 1991. "Federal Policy Toward State and Local Economic Development in the 1990s." *Research in Urban Economics* 9:161–78.

Burtless, Gary. 1994. "Public Spending on the Poor: Historical Trends and Economic Limits." In *Confronting Poverty: Prescriptions for Change,* ed. Sheldon H. Danziger, Gary D. Sandefur, and Daniel H. Weinberg, 51–84. Cambridge, MA: Harvard University Press.

Donahue, John D. 1999. *Hazardous Crosscurrents: Confronting Inequality in an Era of Devolution.* New York: Century Foundation Press.

Fisher, Ronald C. 1996. *State and Local Public Finance.* Chicago: Irwin.

Gottheil, Fred. 1999. *Principles of Macroeconomics*, 2d ed. Cincinnati, OH: South-Western College Publishing.

Gramlich, Edward M., and Deborah S. Laren. 1984. "Migration and Income Redistribution Responsibilities." *Journal of Human Resources* 19:489–511.

Greene, Kenneth V., and Thomas J. Parliament. 1980. "Political Externalities, Efficiency, and the Welfare Losses from Consolidation." *National Tax Journal* 33:209–17.

Gyourko, Joseph, and Todd Sinai. 2000. "The Spatial Distribution of Housing-Related Tax Benefits in the United States." Working paper. Brookings Institution, Center on Urban and Metropolitan Policy, Washington, DC.

Hamilton, Bruce W. 1975. "Zoning and Property Taxation in a System of Local Governments." *Urban Studies* 12:205–11.

Hirsch, Werner Z. 1970. *The Economics of State and Local Government.* New York: McGraw-Hill.

Hovey, Harold A. 1999. *Can States Afford Devolution? The Fiscal Implications of Shifting Federal Responsibilities to State and Local Governments.* New York: Century Foundation Press.

Joassart-Marcelli, Pascale, and Juliet Musso. 2001. "The Distributive Impact of Federal Fiscal Policy: Federal Spending and Southern California Cities." *Urban Affairs Review* 37: 163–83.

Ladd, Helen, and John Yinger. 1989. *America's Ailing Cities: Fiscal Health and the Design of Urban Policy.* Baltimore: Johns Hopkins University Press.

Lugar, Michael I. 1987. "The States and Industrial Development: Program Mix and Policy Effectiveness." *Perspectives on Local Public Finance and Public Policy* 3:29–63.

Musgrave, Richard A. 1959. *The Theory of Public Finance: A Study in Public Economy.* New York: McGraw-Hill.

Musgrave, Richard A., and Peggy Musgrave. 1980. *Public Finance in Theory and Practice.* New York: McGraw-Hill.

Musso, Juliet Ann. 1998. "Fiscal Federalism as a Framework for Governance Reform." In *Handbook of Public Finance*, ed. Fred Thompson and Mark T. Green, 347–96. New York: Marcel Dekker.

Musso, Juliet Ann, and John Quigley. 1996. "Intergovernmental Fiscal Relations in California: A Critical Evaluation." In *Infrastructure and the Complexity of Economic Development*, ed. David Batten and C. Karlsson. New York: Springer-Verlag.

Oates, Wallace E. 1972. *Fiscal Federalism.* New York: Harcourt Brace Jovanovich.

Oates, Wallace E., and Robert M. Schwab. 1991. "The Allocative and Distributive Implications of Local Fiscal Competition." In *Competition among States and Local Governments: Efficiency and Equity in American Federalism*, ed. Daphne Kenyon and John Kincaid, 127–45. Washington, DC: Urban Institute Press.

Pack, Janet Rothenberg. 1998. "Poverty and Urban Public Expenditures." *Urban Studies* 35(11): 1995–2019.

Persky, Joseph. 1999. "Chicago Metropolitan Case Study." Paper presented at the Case Study Meeting of the Center on Urban and Metropolitan Policy, Brookings Institution, Washington, DC.

Peterson Paul E., and Mark C. Rom. 1989. "American Federalism, Welfare Policy, and Residential Choices." *American Political Science Review* 83(3):711–28.

Skocpol, Theda. 1995. *Social Policy in the United States: Future Possibilities in Historical Perspective.* Princeton, NJ: Princeton University Press.

Summers, Anita A., 1999. "Update on Philadelphia Metropolitan Case Study." Paper presented at the Case Study Meeting of the Center on Urban and Metropolitan Policy, Brookings Institution, Washington, DC.

Wallis, John Joseph, and Wallace E. Oates. 1988. "Decentralization in the Public Sector: An Empirical Study of State and Local Government." In *Fiscal Federalism: Quantitative Studies*, ed. Harvey S. Rosen, 5–32. Chicago: University of Chicago Press.

Wilson, William Julius. 1987. *The Truly Disadvantaged: The Inner City, the Underclass, and Public Policy.* Chicago: University of Chicago Press.

8 | The Preservation of Nature at the Urban Fringe

Stephanie Pincetl

Over time, Southern Californians have engaged in a Faustian bargain—growth and prosperity at the expense of entire habitats and species, making the region the endangered species hot spot of the continental United States (Dobson et al. 1997). This situation has developed incrementally as a result of a conjunction of several factors: strong legal protection of private property rights, local home rule, a preference for single-family dwellings subsidized by state and federal policies, land speculation, the fiscalization of land use, and population growth. Recent studies indicate that sprawl is a leading cause of the rapid decline in the nation's biological resources (Czech, Krausman, and Devers 2000; Kostyack 2001; National Wildlife Federation 2001). Although species loss is not unique to the Southern California region, urbanization's impacts on natural systems in the region have been particularly severe because of the area's high level of biodiversity. This has created tension between continued land development and species preservation as required by the federal Endangered Species Act (ESA) of 1973, which protects species from becoming extinct.

In response to the impacts of urbanization, several parallel species and habitat preservation strategies have developed in Southern California. Innovative approaches to land development entitlements and preservation have been forged by emerging coalitions of interests, including governmental agencies at county, city, state, and federal levels; special districts; and nonprofit organizations. Together, these interested parties have developed new arrangements for habitat protection and management that are often "bottom-up" by jurisdiction.[1] The particular configurations of these arrangements are different from community to community, depending on the local mixture of institutional, socioeconomic, and cultural/attitudinal factors. The precise mix of these factors changes from community to community depending on the unique characteristics of each place (Press 1999), including the perceived threat of the finding

that a species is endangered and subsequent use of the federal ESA to stop development if a species becomes listed.

In this chapter, I place the struggle over land use that the Endangered Species Act engenders into an urban regime analytic framework in order to provide a better understanding of the emergence of local governance structures that develop and manage habitat protection. I first present an overview of the major structural constraints that have shaped local land use in California over time and the challenges that arise from the use of science to protect nature. I argue that the varied approaches to habitat preservation emerge from local political, economic, and institutional conditions in the various counties and localities in Southern California, and I present an initial typology of those approaches. Finally, I argue that local approaches have emerged as bottom-up solutions in response to conditions of scientific uncertainty, fiscal austerity, devolution of governmental authority, and the necessity of complying with the federal ESA. Although the programs being implemented are resulting in habitat preservation—given that some lands are indeed being set aside—it is too soon to know whether these programs will succeed in achieving coherent and long-term protection for endangered species.

Understanding Urban Growth in Southern California

Southern California has been and continues to be one of the fastest-growing regions in the United States. Scholars have been seeking to understand the evolving dynamics of urban growth since the late nineteenth century. More recently, urban regime theory has emerged to explain the growth and development of cities in the late-twentieth-century period of globalization, decentralization, and devolution (see, e.g., Elkin 1987; Stone 1989). Urban regime theory concerns the ways in which local governments tend to embrace the development agenda of downtown business interests in order to meet the need for tax revenue accumulation and the demands placed on public expenditures by the electorate in a governmental structure that restricts localities' governmental authority (Calavita 1992; Piven and Friedland 1984, in Jonas 1997; Elkin 1987). Urban regime theory examines the role that land-use planning plays at the local level as the fundamental building block for any local economic development agenda. Land-use planning is one of the principal prerogatives of local government, and for this reason urban regime theory gives primacy to how business interests and local governments allocate land in the pursuit of economic growth. Gibbs and Jonas (2000, 299) point out how existing urban regimes in Southern California are increasingly affected by environmental issues and regulations and thus must take them into consideration. The environment, these authors suggest, has become a particular object of regulation and focus of struggle. Their research findings indicate that not only is the environment a topic in policy and governance, but new actors at the local scale who represent the environment may in fact be emerging, depending on the specific context.

In fact, Jonas (1997) and others have pointed out that today in Southern California, at the territorial level of a county, for example, an actual governing coalition may need to go beyond traditional organizations and require the development of other tiers of government and governance agreements in order to ensure economic growth and vitality. The context for local decision making has changed dramatically due to changing economic, political, and fiscal conditions, including globalization, the taxpayers' revolt, and the devolution of governmental authority, responsibility, programs, and costs to localities. Such institutions, which emerge to manage important aspects of policy making or implementation parallel to the regular governmental institutional framework, can be called structures of *governance*, as they are a mix of traditional government entities but also include other, nongovernmental, players. Habitat conservation, for example, is managed in some cases by cooperating public, private, and nonprofit entities.

To date, theories of urban political power and development have tended to put analytic primacy on traditional coalitions organized to promote economic growth—chambers of commerce, real estate developers, builders, and bankers. It is now well understood that land-use decisions in the city and county of Los Angeles have been strongly influenced, over time, by development and water interests, leaving both jurisdictions intensively developed (see, e.g., Davis 1990, 1998; Gottlieb and FitzSimmons 1991; McWilliams 1979). But the current context of reduced public expenditures, continued pressure for and by growth, and the need to preserve habitat for endangered species has created opportunities for alternative approaches to local governance. These alternative approaches include the increasing participation of nonprofit organizations and strategic coalitions consisting of scientific experts, advocates, home owners, and local activists. Significantly, these coalitions too often couch their efforts in economic development terms, pointing to the positive correlations between real estate prices and environmental amenities such as parks and the economic efficiencies that can be derived from growing "smart."

The wide-ranging habitat protection efforts currently employed in Southern California represent an evolution from conventional growth-oriented local coalitions of interests (traditional booster coalitions organized to promote growth) toward sophisticated and complex coalitions that operate with a larger view and negotiate and compromise around land-use controls at a regional scale. They range from no-growth advocates to growth promoters and include everything in between.

Given California's continued and unrelenting population growth and concomitant urban development, the topics of growth and its management have preoccupied state leaders for more than forty years, starting with the governorship of Pat Brown (1958–65). Since then, numerous proposals have been put forward to rationalize the process of growth to ensure more equity, better environmental quality, and maintain the state's quality of life, including proposals to develop state-level institutions, regional institutions, and better inter- and intragovernmental arrangements (Pincetl 1999b). Growth and its pressures have incited hundreds of local and regional ballot initiatives aimed at stopping urbanization, controlling it, and/or managing its pace, shape, and location. However, for fundamental structural reasons, such as home rule, the fiscalization of land use, and special districts, among other factors reviewed elsewhere in this volume, these attempts have by and large resulted in only small, incremental improvements in the management of growth in the state.

Home Rule

Home rule was established in California during the Progressive Era in 1916. Under home rule, charter cities gained local fiscal autonomy; the ability to make and enforce laws and regulations with respect to municipal affairs; the right to the ballot initiative, referendum, and recall; and the ability to create special districts (this ability actually dates from the nineteenth century). Cities could thus enact local ordinances, such as building and zoning codes, without seeking state authority to do so, and until the 1960s municipal incorporations could take place with no state oversight. With the ability to raise money, communities had every incentive to incorporate as new cities. Local control over local land use and the power to raise revenues, combined with strong decentralist, local democratic control sentiments, created a patchwork of jurisdictions across the state, especially in Southern California, where population growth has been the greatest. The Southern California Association of Governments (SCAG) planning area encompasses 184 cities, six counties, and more than a thousand special districts. Each of these has its own geographic boundaries, structures of governance, and accountability mechanisms.

Home rule, with its local decision-making power over local land use, creates an incentive for fragmentation, a situation in which mechanisms for regional cooperation, coordination, and public discussion about how and where growth ought to occur are difficult to erect and to empower. SCAG, a regional agency, was established to serve as a regional forum for discussion and cooperation around land-use issues, but because it has no regulatory authority, it serves primarily to distribute funds received from the federal government to encourage better regional planning, particularly transportation planning.

The Fiscalization of Land Use and Open-Space Preservation

Prior to the passage of Proposition 13—the property tax reduction ballot initiative—in 1978, local property taxes provided an important share of city and county budgets in California. During the 1960s and until 1978, local, state, and federal funds for local open-space preservation grew tremendously (Press 1999). The state not only made money available, it also defined and expanded the scope of local powers for land preservation, motivated voluntary conservation efforts by private landowners (such as the Williamson Act), and helped cities, counties, and regions develop expertise for land-use—and, by extension, conservation—planning. This is exemplified by the state requirement that all cities and counties adopt "open-space elements" in their general plans. Localities, benefiting from inflation-driven property taxes as well as state money, could purchase parks and open-space lands. This was augmented by federal generosity: the Land and Water Conservation Fund and a grant program for open-space acquisition near urban areas funded by the Department of Housing and Urban Development (Press 1999).

The taxpayer revolt that ushered in Proposition 13 resulted in strict limits on property taxes, which had the immediate effect of cutting property tax receipts for local governments throughout the state. Proposition 13 also imposed limits on state and local governments' ability to raise new taxes. "Local governments such as counties, cities, school districts and special districts could not increase taxes without approval of the local electorate" (Baldassare 1998, 26). Approval of any new tax now requires a two-thirds supermajority vote. Since the passage of Proposition 13, local governments have faced serious shortfalls in the revenues they need to fund local services, yet they are under continuous pressure to deliver those services. Localities felt this pressure most acutely during the recession of the 1990s (Lyon 1998).

Proposition 13 and federal retrenchment abruptly changed the situation for localities. It undermined the doctrine of home rule—the state now collects property taxes and redistributes the funds to cities and counties, and only a small portion of these taxes returns to them (Silva and Barbour 1999). Because the approval of two-thirds of voters is required to enact any new taxes, cities and counties have had to rely on growth-related taxes, sales taxes, assessments, exactions, and impact fees for revenue, as well as outright negotiations with developers and/or nonprofit conservancies and other agencies. Jurisdictions now make trades with developers to provide open space, parks, schools, and other formerly city-provided social services before granting the right to build—yet another reason cites are motivated to approve development.

Special Districts

Special districts also play a role in urban growth and in habitat conservation arrangements with counties. For example, the Metropolitan Water District (MWD) board, which is made up of representatives from MWD client cities, voted to build Diamond Lake in the Domenigoni/Diamond Valleys in Riverside County, almost doubling Southern California's water surface storage and covering 4,500 acres. The construction of the lake solidified MWD's long-term drive to provide water for further growth in the eastern part of the region. Such decisions have significant long-term implications for future land development and growth in the region. Other special districts, particularly those related to infrastructure, can also have important growth-inducing effects by deciding to increase capacities.

Science, Preservation, and the Endangered Species Act

Concern about species disappearance is nothing new in the United States. The Endangered Species Act, passed in 1973 and signed into law by President Nixon, was the culmination of a century of concern about species extinction, starting with the disappearance of the bison in the 1890s. Alarm about species disappearance forms one of the cornerstones of the American movement to protect nature that emerged in the late nineteenth century and is integral to the rise of the nation's national park system and reserves. Implicit in the concern about species disappearance and the need to set aside protected lands is a belief that there is value in preserving nature for its potential importance to human survival as well as for aesthetic reasons. At the same time, the justification for the preservation of nature is grounded in science. Decisions about what to preserve and how are also based on scientific analyses and recommendations, thus science has a key role to play in nature preservation.

Still, when the ESA became law, it is unlikely those involved could have anticipated its application to the situation of urbanizing regions such as Southern California, where dozens of species have become threatened by the routine process of subdivision approval. Traditionally, state and federal resource agency professionals have focused on large tracts of wildlands, whereas land-use planners concentrated on zoning, permits, and capital facilities, categorizing wildlands as vacant (Scott and Sullivan 2000). This has led to a series of connected results: nature is largely seen as existing outside of the city, the wildland-urban interface remains unmanaged (Scott and Sullivan 2000), and neither resource professionals nor planning professionals can adequately plan for nature in urbanizing contexts or in the city (Beatley 2000). Michael Pollan's (1991) insight applies well to this all-too-common situation: "All or nothing says the wilderness ethic. . . . Americans have done an admirable job of drawing lines around certain sacred areas (we did invent the wilderness area) . . . [and] the only environmental ethic we have has nothing useful to say about those areas outside the line. Once a landscape is no longer 'virgin' it is typically written off as fallen, lost to nature, irredeemable" (188).

Indeed, the problems of habitat preservation and species survival today transcend the nature/culture divide and the urban/rural division of labor. Sprawl has created a jumbled landscape in which these categories no longer are useful—lands that fall between suburban developments are neither natural nor urbanized, and it is increasingly obvious that nature does not end at the edge of the city but is present in, and necessary to, all built environments.

The Role of Science

Originally, the ESA was designed to preserve individual endangered species—that is, species that were threatened with possible extinction. Such an approach proved frustrating, ineffectual, and inefficient in light of the dynamic relationship between species and habitats. Congress then added habitat conservation plans (HCPs) to the ESA in 1982 in an effort to conserve imperiled species facing the risk of habitat destruction. Congress viewed HCPs as a win-win situation for imperiled species because they took habitat into consideration, allowing a more encompassing approach. Along with HCPs, Congress created Incidental Take Permits, which allowed—for the first time— the taking of a limited number of listed plants or animals in exchange for a commitment to an HCP to protect and manage other habitat areas, ensuring endangered species' overall recovery chances. As Kostyack (2001) notes, "Facing the possibility of significant development restrictions due to the ESA's prohibition against taking of listed species and the possibility of liability for issuing permits in violation of this prohibition, local governments . . . have negotiated with federal agencies to ensure that their development plans are consistent with ESA standards," thus allowing development to go forward (10712).

However, habitat protection is fundamentally an issue of how much habitat is required and where it must be located to ensure the long-term viability of a species or an ecosystem. HCPs—or other species and habitat protection plans—must be scientifically defensible. The U.S. Department of the Interior, under the HCP provision of the ESA, is allowed to permit the "taking" (killing) of species as long as these takings are incidental to economic activities and their impacts are minimized or mitigated according to HCP agreements. The secretary of the Department of the Interior can issue a take permit only after finding that "the taking will not appreciably reduce the likelihood of the survival and recovery of the species in the wild" (ESA sec. 10 [a][2] B [iv]; see Smallwood 2000). Thus, in order to satisfy the ESA requirements, HCPs and other species protection plans must make use of the best available scientific data to ensure species survival.

Because land-use determination is a political process, profound and unresolvable issues arise among groups with differing interests, and science becomes a political tool, used to defend property values—the NIMBY phenomenon—or to justify smart growth based on better transportation planning or other planning. The science of HCPs and species protection and recovery under conditions of intense urbanization and anthropogenic environmental change is still fraught with uncertainty, and this further politicizes the context in which species protection and land planning take place.

Science and Preservation

For habitat preservation strategies to be successful ecologically in the long term, they should be proactive and should involve ecosystem-level planning that spans and crosses jurisdictions. Yet most habitat preservation planning is reactive, often confined to finding a solution to development impediments caused by a listed endangered species. In addition to being opportunistic and crisis driven, attempts to preserve habitat at the urban fringe raise profound and difficult scientific questions. Habitat preserve design itself is compelled by the ESA requirement that species be preserved and that preservation plans be based on the best available science. Thus the entire effort for habitat preservation is predicated on the ability of science to determine what remedies can be elaborated to prevent species' extinction.

One major difficulty in elaborating tailored land-use programs for species and habitat protection lies in unresolved scientific questions concerning such issues as the appropriate size and location of habitat preserves themselves, their connectivity, and how wildlife can move between habitat patches. Connectivity and corridors (a complex and controverted distinction itself) among habitat patches are recognized as often vital to the survival of species, as island biogeography studies have demonstrated (Scott 2001). At present, however, there are insufficient species- and site-specific data available to allow the design of corridors and habitats that will work for different species with different requirements, and the assumptions of island biogeography may not fully apply to Southern California ecosystems. Habitat designs are often built around "indicator species" that may or may not embody the characteristics of less well-studied species (Scott 2001; Andelman 2000). At the same time, corridors between habitats need to be planned in advance of development on the basis of how animals move to ensure that the animals will have adequate space to do so. For example, before a freeway is constructed, it is necessary to know where tunnels should be placed under the roadway to allow fauna to move. Today, wildlife corridors are being created despite a lack of good biological data on which to base their design.

The designing of habitat preserves themselves involves equally complex biological, political, and economic issues and trade-offs. For example, a plan can be designed to preserve *states* (land units or species assemblages) or *processes* (interactions among species and systems). Each approach has its own set of objectives (Scott and Sullivan 2000). And in the end, the process is voluntary for the landowner. Participants may delineate preserves to include as many or as few species, habitats, vegetation types, or other elements as necessary to reach consensus among interest groups. Thus the process that occurs among the participants is the determining factor, although participants frequently make their decisions based on biologically based ranking criteria—criteria that some observers consider to be highly questionable (Scott and Sullivan 2000).

Overall, the designs of habitat reserves have been criticized as based on insufficient information regarding the ecology and distribution of the species and ecosystems under consideration (Smallwood, Beyea, and Morrison 1999; Scott and Sullivan 2000; Smallwood 2000). Critics also note that, despite this inadequate science, such designs become the basis for long-term management. Habitat reserves do, however, provide certainty for land developers. Once land has been set aside through negotiation, developers are guaranteed certainty with respect to their other lands—they are free to develop them regardless of what might be found on them later. As Kareiva et al. (1999) have observed: "It is easy to identify what is given up from the viewpoint of a private landowner, because the dollar value of future development . . . is easily calculable. It is much harder to quantify what is given up in terms of a species' prospects for long-term survival. That is the challenge for the scientific component of HCPs" (7).

Because of the uncertainty of the science component, divergent expectations of interest groups on the ground result in habitat planning and preservation exercises driven by economic, amenity, aesthetic, and political values rather than scientific principles. Instead of habitat values, land values—which are based on potential buildability—can play a determinative role in land selection (Margules and Usher 1981, in Scott and Sullivan 2000), and existing land uses also constrain the size, shape, and linkages among wildlife habitats (Scott and Sullivan 2000).

In the end, protected habitats reflect the spatial division of labor set forth by Michael Pollan (1991). The messy terrain of suburbanization, with its mix of developed and undeveloped lands, different territorial jurisdictions, and states of nature, is not easily addressed with rules (the ESA) that have been developed to apply to lands more clearly identifiable as urban or rural, however artificial that distinction is in reality. When Congress passed the ESA, it did not have the preservation of species at the urban fringe in mind.

Habitat Preservation Strategies in Practice

Because the HCP approach (which remains in use) was developed to protect one species at a time, other habitat protection strategies have emerged, including Multiple Species Habitat Conservation Planning (MSHCP) and the state-led Natural Community Conservation Planning (NCCP) program, which is an attempt to encompass ecosystems. (The NCCP program became the habitat preservation framework for coastal sage scrub in Southern California for very specific reasons, as I discuss later in this chapter.)

NCCPs, HCPs, and MSHCPs approach habitat conservation from different starting points, although the results often end up looking quite similar. All of these approaches require landowner cooperation. They are nominally voluntary, but the threat of an ESA listing often forces landowners to the table. NCCPs are predicated on the following:

- *Coordination* "among public agencies, land owners, and other private interests" and a "mechanism by which landowners and development proponents can effectively participate in the resource conservation process"
- *Regional planning* that "can effectively address cumulative impact concerns, minimizes wildlife habitat fragmentation, promotes multi-species management and conservation"
- An *early planning framework* "for proposed development projects within the planning area in order to avoid, minimize, and compensate for project impacts to wildlife" (California Fish and Game Code, sec. 2800, quoted in Pollak 2001b, 15).

NCCPs are state programs that require local jurisdictions to coordinate among themselves to ensure consistency and agreement about land use.

HCPs, as discussed above, tend to be created for the protection of particular species. They allow flexibility in ESA implementation where the prohibition on "take" would otherwise bring a project to a halt. An HCP protects the habitat deemed necessary for the survival of a given species. MSHCPs and NCCPs work in much the same way, but MSHCPs are federal programs.

Each type of plan emerges within environmental review structures that are dispersed among different local, state, and federal agencies. Because of the ESA requirements, the federal Fish and Wildlife Service (FWS) must ultimately approve all plans. In Southern California, this means approval from one of two FWS regional offices, in Carlsbad or Ventura. Personnel working in different offices do not always apply the same standards, and they tend to be sensitive to organized, vocal interests in their own areas. One study found the degree of conflict over species protections to be a factor in recovery spending by the FWS (Simon, Leff, and Doerksen 1995). In addition, the federal Environmental Protection Agency, the state Environmental Protection Agency, the state Resources Agency, the state Fish and Wildlife Department and Commission, flood control districts, county governments, city governments, other special districts, councils of government, and regional associations of governments may be involved, creating bewildering agency overlaps and gaps in jurisdiction (Scott and Sullivan 2000). Each agency may operate independent of others and demand different types of remediation or programs; often, the various agencies do not communicate with each other (Scott, Wehtje, and Wehtje 2001).

Finally, nonprofit conservancies are emerging as habitat conservation actors. A conservancy may simply purchase a piece of land that is valuable for its biological diversity or for the links it provides between other habitats preserved under an HCP, MSHCP, or NCCP. Conservancies such as the Trust for Public Land (TPL) and the Nature Conservancy (TNC) employ their own staff scientists and conduct their own surveys of habitats to determine whether they should acquire lands for preservation. They may or may not use privately raised funds, but most frequently apply for state funds or use some combination of public and private funds. Conservancies may or may not act in conjunction with other agencies to purchase and manage lands. Their increased involvement in local land-use issues is a significant factor in the emergence of the new structures of governance discussed earlier. Conservancies represent a new set of actors in local urban regimes. Decision making within conservancies, however, is not subject to public accountability or even to independent scientific scrutiny.

Thus habitat preservation strategies are varied and involve different sets of institutional and nonprofit participants in habitat acquisition and management. The individuals and groups who use these strategies, however, share a common goal of preserving habitat for threatened or endangered species.

How the Counties Have Responded

By the late 1980s in Southern California, use of the Endangered Species Act as a means to set aside habitat in the face of land development had become unsatisfying for both environmentalists and developers. For environmentalists, the costs of scientific research, listing, and lawsuits were burdensome, and the outcomes were uncertain— although environmentalists saw slowing or even stopping development as desirable, this strategy did not lead to coherent long-term outcomes. For the development community, it meant time delays, uncertainty, and increased costs. In the early 1990s, the listing of the California gnatcatcher, a small songbird that lives in the coastal sage scrub ecosystem, as a threatened species in Orange County served as a warning about what could potentially happen throughout the region: a moratorium on all further land development. This event precipitated innovation in habitat protection strategies and put all local jurisdictions facing urban growth on notice.

As the following discussion demonstrates, not all localities responded to the threat of an ESA listing in the same manner. Local responses emerged from local cultures, planning traditions, fiscal capacities, past land uses, and other locally specific factors, including the degree to which there were potentially endangered species at risk. Local responses were predicated on the configuration of existing local urban regimes and the capacity of regime members to develop responses to the potential of a threatened or endangered species listing to halt further land development. Each county (and some cities) in the SCAG region, faced with potential ESA listings, has engaged in activities involving various constellations of participants, depending on who is present and active in local land-use politics and policies (Figure 8.1).

Orange County

Orange County could be termed the exceptional county in Southern California for the proactive role its urban regime constituents played when faced with the threat of an ESA listing. The reasons for the county's exceptional approach are complex and derive, in part, from the area's highly concentrated pattern of landownership. Outside of the cities, there are only a few large landowners in the entire county, a legacy of the Spanish land-grant era. The Irvine Ranch Company (IRC), the largest landowner, has prided itself on its planned-growth communities since its land development inception. The company culture has been committed to long-range planning and to planning itself. Its approach to planning seems to have been highly influenced by the garden city movement, which was itself a reaction to the chaotic and haphazard growth of urban industrial cities of the nineteenth century. IRC planners were influenced by the writings of prominent urban critics, and they attempted to develop a thorough and comprehensive planning approach. Orange County planning officials had no objections to this approach, given that they were concerned to avoid the "aimless urban sprawl" so characteristic of other parts of the county and the region as a whole (Schiesl 1995). Although Orange County was not the first area to attempt to craft land-use solutions to address the problem of endangered species, its Governor Wilson-backed innovation of the Natural Community Conservation Planning program in the early 1990s made its efforts renowned and, for a time, the desired template for the rest of the state.

The threat of a listing of the California gnatcatcher, a coastal sage scrub–dwelling bird, by the FWS, responding to a petition for listing by the Natural Resources Defense Council, led the state Resources Agency, in conjunction with the IRC and with the strong support of Governor Wilson (a Republican), to develop the NCCP approach. The NCCP process required action by the FWS to issue a rule so that the federal take prohibition on endangered species would not conflict with the NCCP program.

The NCCP process was predicated on volunteer landowner participation to construct preserves for coastal sage scrub habitat. It was intended to bring all stakeholders to the table in order to set aside coherent regional habitat preserves (Fulton 1997;

	Planning tradition			
County	Strong (historical commitment)	Evolving (growth-causing change)	Opportunistic (if politically and fiscally feasible)	Weak (pro-property rights)
Orange	X			
Riverside		X		
San Bernardino				X
Los Angeles			X	
Ventura	X			

Figure 8.1. A typology of local county planning traditions in Southern California.

Pincetl 1999a). Then-Secretary of the Interior Bruce Babbit also endorsed the NCCP program, due to fear that Congress might significantly weaken the ESA (which was coming up for reauthorization) because of the perception that it was a death knell for land development in many parts of the country. Development industry lobbyists were hard at work in Washington, and lawsuits were pending, all part of the concerted effort to weaken or abolish the ESA (Fulton 1997).

The NCCP process is similar to that for HCPs, in that it allows the taking of habitat and individual species in exchange for habitat set aside. It is different from the federal HCP in that it is a state-led program that is voluntary, locally initiated, potentially applicable at a county or regional scale, and initiated before the landscape becomes degraded to protect ecosystems at the landscape scale while accommodating compatible development.[2] It is a landscape-oriented approach that can potentially resolve habitat fragmentation while ensuring development too.

For the Wilson administration, the NCCP in Southern California was an experimental program for habitat preservation that could later be applied, if successful, to other areas in the state facing similar habitat preservation controversies. The NCCP, directed by the California Department of Fish and Game, was enacted in 1991 by the state legislature. Thus far, it has been applied in Southern California only to coastal sage scrub (starting in Orange County), but NCCP efforts are under way in other parts of the state, and the San Diego County MSHCP is termed an NCCP.[3]

The NCCP process has been under way since the early 1990s in Orange County, and it seems to have been relatively successful in central Orange County, preserving a substantial portion of the remaining coastal sage scrub ecosystem. This success is due to the cooperation and participation of the IRC, which is scarcely surprising given that the NCCP process itself was the brainchild of interaction between the IRC and the state Resources Agency (Pincetl 1999a). Consistent with the company's long-range approach, the IRC has earmarked the 63,000-acre Irvine Ranch for eventual public ownership to mitigate for future company development projects. It contracted with the Nature Conservancy to study ways to implement an open-space reserve, and this work resulted in a stewardship plan. The plan will develop long-term habitat management and restoration programs for land now set aside as a natural sanctuary and managed by TNC. This arrangement is an example of the new kinds of land preservation strategies that are emerging and the governance coalitions and structures that are beginning to both supplement and replace conventional federal and state land preservation approaches.

In contrast, with increased urban growth creeping south in Orange County, the Rancho Mission Viejo Company (formerly the Santa Margarita Company) has put off participating in an NCCP process, instead pushing to create "bubble developments" on its lands. The county has already approved at least one development—8,000 homes for 25,000 people on 2,400 acres—despite county staff studies showing it will cost the county $300,000 a year in services.[4] Rancho Mission Viejo Company has also unveiled a development plan for southern Orange County that encompasses 25,000 acres. The company has, however, recently expressed interest in revitalizing the NCCP process, so as of this writing it is too soon to know what will ensue. Also planned for southern Orange County is another major toll road, which would affect the watershed and have impacts on the habitats of six federally listed species (*Endangered Habitats League Newsletter* 2000).

Efforts for habitat preservation in Orange County have set a precedent in Southern California because the NCCP offered a path to habitat preservation that worked in advance of development and was state led rather than federally mandated. The Rancho Mission Viejo Company, the other large landowner in Orange County, has a different company culture than that of the IRC and seems to plan with a shorter-term horizon, proposing developments sequentially in a more conventional manner. The company has been more chary of the NCCP process, episodically expressing interest in participating.

The Orange County example illustrates the evolution of public/private and nonprofit cooperation in habitat preservation, as well as the ways in which approaches to habitat conservation may vary even within one county depending on landownership. Other counties with even more landowners have developed even more complex habitat preservation and management arrangements.

Riverside County

Riverside County offers perhaps the most complex set of programs for habitat conservation. The fastest-growing county in California, it is reputed to have entitled for future construction more than 100,000 units in its western portion. This situation has stimulated the growth of planning strategies at the county and municipal levels. Home of the Quino checkerspot butterfly, Stephens' kangaroo rat, and Delhi Sands flower-loving fly, among other listed species, the county is engaged in developing a county integrated plan to comprehensively and simultaneously plan for land use, habitat, and transportation to complement its HCP efforts. The plan articulates a new paradigm: efficient, coordinated planning influenced by the ideas of smart growth. Riverside County interprets smart growth as infrastructure-efficient growth—coordinating transportation planning with land-use planning in a proactive manner.

Due to intense development pressure owing to the need for affordable housing for Orange County workers, Riverside County's legacy of agricultural land use and relatively inexpensive land prices made it the ideal bedroom community for its affluent neighbor to the west. However, as the county urbanized it became increasingly clear that unplanned growth was causing tremendous traffic problems and degrading the quality of life in the area. Coupled with the county's need to plan for habitat preservation, a transportation-based planning effort gradually evolved. Yet, as I explain below, even within the county different strategies for habitat preservation are emerging, a result of sharp distinctions between the eastern and western parts of the jurisdiction.

In the rapidly urbanizing western area of Riverside County, a number of parallel and overlapping approaches to habitat preservation are under way. The county is concentrating its efforts on saving lands that are on the periphery of development— lands that are largely undevelopable because they are too steep or have some other constraints. These lands will ultimately constitute a western Riverside MSHCP. At the same time, nonprofits such as TNC, TPL, and other smaller organizations are also significantly involved in habitat protection. These efforts supplement and complement planning by the county, sometimes serving to realize plans for which the county's funding alone is inadequate. Consequently, habitat preservation in the west is being accomplished through the combined efforts of the county's land-use planning prerogatives and nonprofit land acquisition and management (Figure 8.2).

The Nature Conservancy has been involved in the creation of several reserves in Riverside County. The Santa Rosa Plateau Ecological Reserve is in the southern end of the Santa Ana Mountains, the site of a historic ranch. There are now 8,300 acres preserved here. TNC has been active here, purchasing key acres in the Tenaja Corridor, which stretches three miles from the Cleveland National Forest to the Santa Rosa Plateau Ecological Reserve, as a corridor for migration for bobcats, deer, mountain lions, and other species. Here TNC is reselling some properties with conservation easements, limiting subdivision and development, as well as protecting the fauna and flora by developing covenants with landowners, an emerging use of covenants in biologically sensitive areas. TNC is also active in preserving the Santa Margarita River watershed, having purchased the largest remaining privately owned parcel on the river.[5]

TPL has also been active in efforts to protect habitat, concentrating on key lands for wildlife connectivity. It recently purchased Johnson Ranch, which had been proposed for development and road building, to preserve habitat connections. TPL, like TNC, is intent on purchasing lands within the western Riverside planning area to assist in protecting endangered species and habitats.[6]

The MWD, the immensely powerful special district that delivers water to most of Southern California, is also a partner in habitat preservation efforts in western Riverside County. The Diamond Lake reservoir, mentioned earlier, was built on the habitat of the endangered Stephens' kangaroo rat. In exchange for a development permit, MWD created a plan to preserve habitat for the kangaroo rat and other species as a mitigation measure. MWD worked to create the Southwestern Riverside County Multi-Species Reserve, which consists of 9,000 acres surrounding and connecting Diamond Valley Lake with Lake Skinner via the 2,500-acre Dr. Roy Shipley Reserve, also purchased by MWD as part of its mitigation for the creation of Diamond Lake. The reserve's management committee is composed of representatives of MWD, the Riverside County Conservation Agency, the U.S. Fish and Wildlife Service, the California

Conservancy	Linkage purchase and management	Habitat preservation purchase and management	Collaborative participation, purchase and management
Trust for Public Land	X	X	
The Nature Conservancy	X	X	X

Figure 8.2. Nonprofit conservancies' involvement in habitat preservation in Southern California.

Department of Fish and Game, and the Riverside County Regional Park and Open Space District. Here, too, TNC is involved, having purchased the original 3,100-acre portion of the reserve in 1984 when residential development was beginning to boom in western Riverside County. In 1991, MWD joined Riverside County, the state of California's Wildlife Conservation Board, and TNC to purchase and protect 3,825 additional acres in the area, creating yet another reserve. MWD is providing almost $14 million for reserve management and research. The reserve management is governed by a multiagency group, creating a specific separate entity.[7]

Habitat protection efforts in eastern Riverside County are significant as well, but they reflect a different set of motivations and involve different actors. Eastern Riverside County, which includes the communities of Palm Springs, Cathedral City, Coachella, Desert Hot Springs, Indian Wells, Indio, La Quinta, Palm Desert, and Rancho Mirage, is not under the same kind of intense development pressure as western Riverside County. The establishment of the Coachella Valley MSHCP was led by the Coachella Valley Association of Governments (CVAG) and is seen by local leaders as vital to the local economy, which is dependent on resorts and retirement communities.[8] Yet it too demonstrates the institutional complexity that characterizes conservation planning. The Coachella MSHCP came out of a memorandum of understanding (MOU) that included the nine cities listed above, the county of Riverside, the U.S. Fish and Wildlife Service, the California Department of Fish and Game, the Bureau of Land Management, the U.S. Forest Service, and the National Park Service. The MOU was the first step in initiating the planning effort for the MSHCP. The overall plan area in the Coachella Valley and surrounding area mountains includes approximately 1,205,839 acres. Unlike in western Riverside County, this is a regionwide, integrated plan, possible because of the commitment of CVAG, which is composed of cities with like concerns and demographics.[9] It is important to note that the efforts of CVAG are not part of the county integrated plan, which, despite its name, is focused on western and southwestern Riverside County.

Further, despite all these efforts at habitat protection, development approvals continue apace as well. Recently, the Riverside County Board of Supervisors approved a 4,367-home development despite the negative recommendation of the Planning Commission. This development, which will also include shopping centers, schools, and parks, is planned for an area between Calimesa and Beaumont in the northern portion of the county. Environmentalists oppose it, claiming that at least thirty-eight endangered, threatened, or sensitive species currently live on the land slated for development (Gold 2001).

Riverside County's different and sometimes contradictory approaches to the protection of endangered species show the flexibility and bottom-up nature of habitat planning. The county itself is engaged in an integrated planning process, the result of legal pressure from the ESA, the first time land-use planning has been attempted on a regional level. The CVAG is initiating habitat planning too, but for its own jurisdiction, a subset of the county. Planning for the western portion of the county is shaped by the many decisions that have already been made, which create a vast patchwork of subdivisions and commuter suburbs for Orange County. Riverside County cities have large spheres of influence, and there is little or no coordinated planning occurring between the cities and the county in the west, where there is the most development pressure. The Johnson Ranch purchase by TPL shows how difficult it is for the county to succeed at habitat preservation—each city can approve developments in its own sphere, even if the county is developing habitat protection plans that might require inclusion of city-controlled lands, and the county too has been approving developments irrespective of habitat preservation concerns. At this point one of the greatest obstacles to habitat preservation for Riverside County, in addition to jurisdictional fragmentation, is a lack of sufficient resources to finance land purchases. Private conservancies have provided an alternative vehicle through which the county can participate in purchasing and managing habitat preserves, but this can only be supplemental.

San Bernardino County

By way of contrast, San Bernardino County has been the least active among Southern California counties in developing habitat preservation plans, partly because of the pro–property rights character of its political culture. Further, development pressure has not been as acute in San Bernardino as in Riverside County, thus there is less pressure for habitat conservation because development is not yet threatening sufficient numbers of species—although there are some important hot spots. Other than establishing the Chino Hills Dairy Preserve, a significant habitat area and preserve, the county has done little to advance species protection. There is no county-level MSHCP or any other habitat protection planning. And, notably, conservation planning for the endangered Delhi Sands flower-loving fly (a hummingbird-like insect) has not progressed. Of the 35,000 acres of Delhi Sands habitat in San Bernardino, only 330 acres of good habitat remain, most of which have been designated an "enterprise zone" and targeted for rapid development.

Due to fiscal pressure, cities and the county are engaged in legal battles over annexations and development in the race for scarce tax revenues. In 1998, the city of Ontario annexed and rezoned 8,000 acres of dairy preserves initially destined for habitat protection and authorized 31,000 units of uncoordinated residential sprawl as a means to encourage economic growth. The county is fighting this proposal on legal grounds, but the cities in the county have formed a consortium to fight the protection of endangered species.

Despite the county's designation of the area as a preserve, the city of Chino is annexing 5,000 acres of the Chino Hills Dairy Preserve. Most of the annexation area, perhaps two-thirds, is subject to flooding, and water agencies will be purchasing flood easements in the "inundation area." This will prevent residential development in the Santa Ana River watershed area, but will allow replacement of agricultural uses by golf courses, racetracks, off-road vehicle parks, parking lots, and other recreational uses, which can be sources of revenue. On the remaining acreage, the city is proposing a "new urbanist" development (*Endangered Habitats League Newsletter* 2001).

The Santa Ana River watershed is an important ecological feature in the county, and efforts are under way to support the enhancement of wetlands within the Chino Basin and to create a conservation program for the Santa Ana sucker, a fish that is proposed for listing as endangered. The county has not taken a proactive role in either case. Further, the county's rare alluvial fan sage scrub habitat is currently being developed, project by project. For example, the county has approved a development at the mouth of a Rancho Cucamonga canyon that would entail tearing down a Depression-era earthen embankment that currently protects hundreds of homes, several schools, and the nearby Ontario International Airport (Mozingo 2001). The approval for forty homes is representative of politics in San Bernardino County, where county officials were recently jailed for corruption associated with development permits.

In 1999, in the face of threats of endangered species listings, a consortium of San Bernardino County cities hired a Washington, D.C., lobbying firm with the goal of pressuring Congress to get the U.S. Fish and Wildlife Service to "ease up" on protecting endangered species. Individual cities in the county, beyond Chino, have also been knowingly destroying habitat—Rialto issued grading permits on habitat occupied by the Delhi Sands flower-loving fly with no federal permit to take any species. The city of Colton prepared a "negative declaration" in its environmental review of the impacts of a highway through the most intact remainder of the Delhi Sands flower-loving fly habitat and approved an industrial project in its heart (*Endangered Habitats League Newsletter* 1999).

Outside the urbanizing areas, a great proportion of lands in the county are federally owned—national forests, national scenic areas, or military lands. Compared with its neighboring counties, San Bernardino's attention to habitat preservation has been nothing but hostile or indifferent. The county's strategy seems to involve the refusal to acknowledge the authority of the Endangered Species Act. Jurisdictions in the county see questions of growth or growth management largely as a zero-sum game as they compete to provide the most attractive package to attract development. Significantly, neither TPL nor TNC appears to be involved in San Bernardino County, and participation by local environmental groups is weak. A regional organization, the Endangered Habitats League, has been fighting a lonely battle to preserve the Delhi Sands flower-loving fly, but with little success.[10] San Bernardino County's political culture might be seen as one that has not developed the new forms of governance exhibited in the surrounding high-growth counties. Instead, it has retained older forms developed during the period of high defense spending and investment that was the economic motor of the county. The county and city governments find common cause in fighting habitat conservation, and, because the urgency to do so is low at this point, those in the development community have not determined that it might be to their advantage to enter into habitat agreements in exchange for future certainty of development.

Clearly, San Bernardino County demonstrates how localities differ and how contemporary movements for habitat protection are place specific. The lack of habitat conservation efforts in the county also indicates that it contains no habitats compelling enough, either for their beauty or for their ecological significance (not easily determined), for nonprofit organizations such as TPL and TNC to get involved. With the gradual decline of state and federal park planning and purchases, places that lack local interest in such planning and the capacity to do it, such as San Bernardino County, simply continue to do business as usual.

Los Angeles County

Urbanized Los Angeles has been creeping north and northeast. There are already more than 500,000 people in the northern area, and SCAG predicts that the population will grow by 169 percent by 2020. The county as a whole is expected to grow by 33 percent in the same period. The Santa Clarita Valley, Palmdale, and the Tejon Ranch are expected to have thousands of new homes built in the near future. Newhall Land and Farming hopes to build 21,000 homes in the Santa Clarita Valley (current plans are held up by litigation over habitat and endangered species), and Tejon Ranch, which controls more than 200,000 acres, is in the process of planning a 4,000-unit community. As a representative of the development firm Kaufman and Broad has put it, "There are no geographic restrictions, there's an infinite amount of land that can be developed" (quoted in Sanchez 1999). Water availability, a familiar theme in California's development history, has become an important factor in this area. A recent court ruling held that there would be sufficient water for the Newhall Land and Farming homes, despite great concern expressed by some experts, and it is likely that further legal challenges will occur over water availability.

Los Angeles County has not engaged in any systematic habitat protection initiatives since 1972, when it designated a number of Significant Ecological Areas (SEAs), areas of "high biological resource value," in the county. Due to the weak protection for SEAs in the language of the county's general plan, residential uses consistent with adopted community, areawide, or countywide plans, commercial uses of a "minor" nature, compatible agricultural uses, and compatible extractive uses, including oil and gas recovery, have been allowed to occur on SEAs (Landis 1993). As demonstrated by developments in the northern portion of the county and in the Santa Monica Mountains, where development in excess of density limits set in the general plan has been allowed, Los Angeles County has done little to advance land and habitat preservation. SEA designations have been routinely ignored, as they do not have the force of law. In short, development in the county has proceeded in an opportunistic manner.

The county is under some pressure to reform the SEA designations to resemble a comprehensive habitat conservation plan. However, as there are no imminent threats of species listings, and species currently listed have not yet significantly impeded development on a large scale, the county has not moved in this direction. The federal threat of potentially shutting down development is not acting as an incentive for the county to develop enforceable regional habitat preservation plans. Nevertheless, the county is revising the SEAs in advance of the full general plan update (the state requires an update every ten years), indicating some concern for endangered species planning as a major component of what will be a full-scale land-use planning exercise.[11]

As it stands, the design of the new proposed county SEAs seems to be mostly influenced by the need for new housing. To date, the boundaries of the new SEAs conform to those of proposed developments. For example, the SEA for the area of the proposed Newhall Ranch development, in the northern portion of the county in the Santa Clarita Valley, is simply configured to accommodate that planned development.[12] Newhall Ranch proposes to build 21,600 homes on 12,000 acres, providing for 60,000 new residents. The plan has been held up for a number of reasons relating to habitat concerns, especially over the effects of development on the Santa Clara River (Chambers 2001) and water availability.

It is significant to note that Newhall Land, the developer of Newhall Ranch, in order to meet its water needs, has entered into an agreement with landowners in Kern County for their State Water Project entitlements and has also arranged for water storage capacity near the town of Wasco, northwest of Bakersfield, more than a hundred miles away (Chambers 2001). Resolving problems concerning water supply for housing in Los Angeles County by forging individual development-level agreements with distant water sources is an emerging trend in the state, with the rise of water marketing and water transfers. Water transfers build on and further the transfer of water across large geographic areas and different ecological regions. Current water exchanges via the State Water Project, Central Valley Project, and Los Angeles Aqueduct have had profound effects on the state's water regimen and on the regions from which water is collected. These infrastructures were built by the state and federal governments and are regulated by publicly accountable bodies. The arrangements made by Newhall Ranch represent an additional manipulation of the state's water, the long-term effects of which are still to be discovered. These arrangements also transcend any regional political regulating bodies and are far removed from public accountability. They, too, are a form of governance, just as are habitat protection arrangements, and they represent the creation of parastatal organizations—organizations that function to meet public needs in a semiprivate manner.

The only NCCP activity within Los Angeles County is the Palos Verdes Peninsula NCCP, in which only the city of Rancho Palos Verdes has opted to participate. (Other peninsula cities have chosen not to participate because they see their land as being built out and no development is inhibited by federally listed species.) Rancho Palos Verdes does face development limitations from the ESA and is indeed the site of the largest tracts of open land on the peninsula.

The Ventura County/Los Angeles County border has been an area of great controversy over development. On the Los Angeles County side, the Newhall Ranch was approved, creating increased traffic for the Ventura County side. On the Ventura County side, the Ahmanson Ranch development was approved, which was anticipated to aggravate traffic in Los Angeles County and, in addition, further threaten the red-legged frog, listed as endangered. The proposed Ahmanson Ranch development, the result of a compromise allowing Ventura County open-space lands to be purchased, would have consisted of 3,050 new homes and 10,000 new people (Fulton 1997; Brooks 2001). As a result of tremendous pressure from environmentalists, the landowner decided not to go through with the project and sold the land back to the state at the end of 2003.

Ventura County

Ventura County itself is an exception in the SCAG region. It continues to have a significant agricultural base while at the same time its urban population is more affluent on the whole than the populations of the other SCAG counties. Quality of life is of great concern for residents of Ventura County, and the county has shown a strong commitment to planning over time. The increased pace of agricultural land conversion, traffic, and growth in recent years has resulted in several attempts to control urbanization. In 1999 voters passed a ballot initiative known as SOAR (for Save Open Space and Agricultural Resources), which was sparked by a Moorpark development proposal for 3,200 homes and commercial development. SOAR requires any general plan amendment that would allow or encourage growth (for example, zoning changes or extension of the sphere of influence) to be subject to popular vote after review by local authorities. This essentially transfers land-use development authority from the cities and county directly to the voters. Under SOAR, a farmer who wishes to build on his or her land needs to get approval from the voters.

The SOAR initiative follows previous attempts in a three-decade-old movement to address sprawl in California (Pincetl 1999b). These efforts have ranged from state-level legislative proposals to city-level ordinances and rules, creating a patchwork of programs across the state that reflects local cultures and histories. The SOAR initiative represented an innovation in these long-standing approaches based on common concern about the pace and location of urban growth.

In early 2002, a developer planned to bypass the Moorpark City Council and put his development proposal directly on the ballot, seeking Moorpark voters' approval of a 1,500-home development (including a 2,117-acre preserve, 499 acres of open space, a greenbelt between Moorpark and Simi Valley, a 43-acre sports park, a man-made lake, and a new interchange and four-lane arterial road). It was difficult to anticipate how the voters would react to a development proposal that circumvented the conventional development process by going directly to the voters, potentially raising legal questions with respect to the land-use authority of cities and counties in the future. Developer-launched initiatives were not anticipated by the SOAR initiative, which, ironically, arose out of opposition to the same development proposal for Moorpark (although the original proposed development was somewhat larger).

The Emergence of a New Type of Urban Regime

As a result of constraints on the traditional urban growth regime as elaborated by Elkin (1987) and others—jurisdictional fragmentation, the long-term effects of Proposition 13, significant fiscal restructuring and devolution, and poor land-use planning for environmental protection locally and on a regional level—a new form of urban regime has emerged in Southern California to contend with the exigencies of the Endangered Species Act. The major participants in this new urban regime include private landowners, associations of governments, special districts, federal agencies, nonprofits, and local governments (Figure 8.3).

The key distinguishing feature of this emerging urban regime, shown schematically in Figure 8.4, is the active role played by nonprofits, which are involved in land purchase and management for habitat preservation, either on their own or in collaboration with complex sets of private property owners and/or local, state, and federal governmental partners. Nonprofits, just like private landowners, have no obligation for public accountability in their actions. This new urban regime negotiates land acquisition and develops land management strategies within the constraints of the ESA and property owners' interests. These arrangements, in turn, affect land planning in the region as well as in localities. The results on the ground vary in type from NCCPs, HCPs, and MSHCPs to county integrated plans. Processes and plans vary in scale, size, and complexity as well as in public involvement and transparency. Plans do, however, generally attempt to create conservation strategies that will ensure landowner certainty and cooperation, because landowner participation is voluntary. The scientific strengths of the plans vary widely.

Conclusion

Although open-space preservation occurred steadily throughout the twentieth century in Southern California, policies based on an urban/nature divide—including local open-space preservation efforts over time—have proven inadequate to protect

Participants	Regime roles
Local governments	Plan land use Negotiate boundaries Participate in developing management structures Purchase land
Nonprofit organizations	Identify habitats; purchase habitats Manage habitat or partner in habitat management Participate as experts Approve plans Leverage public funds to purchase land May purchase land
Federal agencies	Enforce Endangered Species Act; approve habitat plans May participate in habitat management
Special districts	Negotiate reserve boundaries Contribute lands Set up land management structures; manage lands May provide funding for management
Southern California Association of Governments	Develop boundaries Create memoranda of understanding and management structures May assist in finding funds for land purchase and management
Private landowners	Negotiate with federal, state, and local officials about endangered species habitat May hire own scientists Develop boundaries Contribute land May participate in land management strategies/funding

Figure 8.3. Regime roles of Southern California habitat preservation participants.

indigenous fauna and flora in the region. Open-space preservation and traditional park policies have not been sufficient to ensure species protection, nor have these policies adapted to the demands of the ESA. This is the case even with the current increased sensitivity to habitat conservation. In recent years, state-level structures have not provided the resources to protect endangered species at the local and regional levels, nor do they possess land-use allocation authority to do so, except by eminent domain. This leaves localities to comply with federal law and figure out innovative habitat protection strategies in a context of a sharply changed political and economic climate and low resources.[13] Communities in California, like elsewhere, have distinctive political cultures. As Press (1999) notes, "What is politically possible in one county might be unthinkable in another" (164).

Southern California remains the state's leader in population growth, both from internal reproduction and from immigration. Although the Los Angeles metropolitan area itself is relatively dense compared with other metropolitan regions in the country (Fulton et al. 2001), the wealth of species endemic to Southern California's unique geography and climate has meant that localities have had to develop habitat protection plans in order to meet the demands of the federal ESA. Endangered species protection has been added to the many factors to be considered in the planning of local land uses.

The varied approaches to conserving habitat in Southern California represent a bottom-up process developed place by place to deal with particular species or constellations of species that are threatened or listed as endangered. With the legal authority of the Endangered Species Act looming as a hammer, localities have cobbled together responses that are highly contingent on the specificities of their situations. Behind these plans is often the presence of the federal Fish and Wildlife Service, which

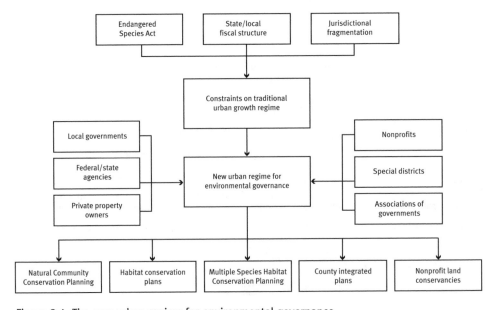

Figure 8.4. The new urban regime for environmental governance.

is ultimately responsible for the protection of species—it serves as the representative of the public interest in species preservation. But despite the involvement of the FWS, coordinated, systematic, and consistent species protection among counties, and even between counties and their cities, does not seem to be emerging. Even the two FWS regional offices in Southern California seem to have different approaches that reflect their leadership and the pressures they face.

Clearly, without the threat posed by the ESA, none of these activities would be taking place. Habitat preservation is required, but at the same time no clear and consistent approaches have been developed that ensure the application of a common standard, nor is there any reliable pool of funding available. Rather, the plans emerge from the conditions of the localities and are shaped by local coalitions of interests that have the capacity to participate. Because environmental protection is an issue, these coalitions of interests that normally come together at the local level to ensure there are favorable conditions for growth also include new players—land trusts, environmental organizations, and federal and state wildlife agencies. What emerges is a complex new layer of land-use management processes and agreements to address the specific problem at hand—species preservation—in a context of continued need, and pressure, for development.

Over the past three decades, California has seen waves of attempts to manage urban growth (Pincetl 1999b). Proposals have been put forth to create statewide agencies and/or regional agencies, and numerous local growth control and growth management ballot measures have been proposed. Smart growth proposals represent yet another approach to urban growth. Smart growth movements emerge from the realization that previous attempts to manage, slow, or even stop growth have been inadequate. Smart growth advocates accept the inevitability, and indeed the necessity, of growth given population increases and the fiscal structures of local jurisdictions that depend on growth to be able to meet their obligations. Smart growth plans aim for growth that is efficient and coordinated, growth that will not cause too many unforeseen and detrimental externalities. To date, some developments in Southern California have been touted as smart growth developments (such as Ahmanson Ranch), and counties in the region have initiated planning to encourage smart growth (such as the western Riverside County integrated plan). These smart growth initiatives emerged in parallel with habitat preservation efforts and might benefit those efforts. For example, there is hope that the western Riverside County smart growth plan will encompass habitat preservation planning in more than an opportunistic manner, integrating it fully, but this remains to be seen, especially given that habitat preservation planning has no obvious funding mechanism and will ultimately require land purchases. To date in western Riverside County, the lands targeted for habitat preserves have been those on which building would be difficult.

What remains entirely neglected in all of these efforts is a reconceptualization of the nature/culture divide and what is necessary for a new vision of the relationship of the city to its environment. As long as nature is seen as existing "out there," planning for species preservation will be difficult. Nature needs to be viewed as an integral element of the infrastructure of human activities, including urbanization and cities. It needs to be acknowledged as an equal partner that exists throughout—in already urbanized areas as well as urbanizing places. Smart growth may be an avenue for such a new approach to cities, but it will require a shift in thinking about how nature is planned for and planned with. Overcoming the nature/culture divide would also lead to improvements in the quality of human life in urbanized areas, as renaturalization of the city could increase public open space, improve water quality and groundwater recharge, and reduce air pollution, among many other benefits. Preserving endangered species at the periphery of urbanization over the long run will require an understanding that the way in which land is developed at the fringe has a strong link to what is possible in already urbanized areas.

Southern California, under the threat of the federal Endangered Species Act, is developing a number of different approaches to habitat preservation under difficult conditions of scientific uncertainty, fiscal austerity, development pressure, and uneven public support. It has been inventive and creative in doing so, developing new bottom-up governance arrangements that involve complex sets of self-designated partners, creating a new type of urban regime that includes the nonprofit sector. These processes are an example of what Desfor and Keil (1999) describe as "environmental policies [that] are made in a situation where no singular government structure exists, and governance structures and procedures have to be developed in a contentious process of brokering and negotiation" (330). The degree to which these efforts are successful in preserving species diversity—the ultimate goal for the long-term public interest—will not be known for a number of years. It is certain, however, that these new governance structures add to an already dense set of governmental structures at the local and regional levels, and are already daunting to understand. They represent another phase of attempts to control, manage, and direct urban growth in the state, but they lack transparency and democratic accountability and do not address the fundamental problem of building better cities.

Notes

My thanks to Travis Longcore and Robert Vos for their thoughtful comments and careful reading, to Dan Silver and Travis Longcore for firsthand information and for being sounding boards; and to Jennifer Wolch and Manuel Pastor for their valuable direction. This chapter was also immeasurably improved by my participation in a Pacific Coast Geographer's Association session organized by Jim Sullivan and including Tom Scott and Walter Wehtje. Finally, I would like to thank Andy Jonas for his long-term involvement in trying to understand the emerging processes around habitat protection and for creating a climate in which academic research about these issues can take place.

1. I use the term *bottom-up* deliberately to denote a process that occurs at the level of place.

2. Travis Longcore assisted me in identifying the subtle nuances that distinguish the HCP, NCCP, and MSHCP programs.

3. For an in-depth overview and analysis of the NCCP program, see Pollak (2001a, 2001b).

4. This information comes from a public meeting of the Orange County Board of Supervisors, October 17, 1995.

5. The Nature Conservancy Web site, http://www.tnccalifornia.org/preserves.

6. Trust for Public Lands Web site, http://www.tpl.org/tier3.

7. Metropolitan Water District Web site, http://www.mwd.dst.ca.us/mwdh2o/index02.html.

8. Personal communication with Jim Sullivan, director of environmental resources for the Coachella Valley Association of Governments, April 4, 2001.

9. Given the planning area's size and the numbers of agencies involved, the plan is too complex to be examined in detail here. More information is available on the Riverside County Web site, http://www.co.riverside.ca.us/cvag/mshcp.

10. Interview with Dan Silver, coordinator, Endangered Habitats League, Los Angeles, April 8, 2001.

11. Telephone interview with Terrell Watt, planning consultant, April 10, 2001.

12. Cities and counties in California are obliged, under state law, to accommodate growth and to build the housing necessary for that growth. Each city and county is allocated its "fair share" by the state Department of Housing and Community Development. Housing capacity in Los Angeles County (and the city of Los Angeles) is far below that needed for the existing and anticipated population. Hence it appears that the county is doing all it can to use new proposed suburban developments to comply with its "fair share" as determined by the state.

13. My thanks to Bob Vos for this crisp formulation.

Works Cited

Andelman, Sandy J. 2000. *Designing and Assessing the Viability of Nature Reserve Systems at Regional Scales: Integration of Optimization, Heuristic and Dynamic Models.* Seattle: Nature Conservancy of Washington.

Baldassare, Mark. 1998. *When Government Fails: The Orange County Bankruptcy.* Berkeley: University of California Press.

Beatley, Timothy. 2000. "Preserving Biodiversity: Challenges for Planners." *Journal of the American Planning Association* 66(1):5–20.

Brooks, Oakely. 2001. "How Green Is This Growth?" *High Country News*, April 9, 6.

Calavita, Nico. 1992. "Growth Machines and Ballot-Box Planning: The San Diego Case." *Journal of Urban Affairs* 14:1–24.

Chambers, Carol. 2001. "Study Finds Water Supply Adequate for Housing Plan." *Los Angeles Times*, April 20, B3.

Czech, Brian, Paul R. Krausman, and Patrick K. Devers. 2000. "Economic Associations among Causes of Species Endangerment in the United States." *Bioscience* 50:593–601.

Davis, Mike. 1990. *City of Quartz: Excavating the Future in Los Angeles.* New York: Verso.

———. 1998. *Ecology of Fear: Los Angeles and the Imagination of Disaster.* New York: Metropolitan.

Desfor, Gene, and Roger Keil. 1999. "Contested and Polluted Terrain." *Local Environment* 7:331–52.

Dobson, A. P., J. P. Rodriguez, W. M. Roberts, and D. S. Wilcove. 1997. "Geographic Distribution of Endangered Species in the United States." *Science* 275 (January): 550–53.

Elkin, Stephen L. 1987. *City and Regime in the American Republic.* Chicago: University of Chicago Press.

Endangered Habitats League Newsletter. 1999. "Delhi Sands Ecosystem Teeters on Brink." Vol. 9(summer):2.

———. 2000. "Where We Stand, 2000." Vol. 10(winter):1–4.

———. 2001. "City of Chino Planning on Track." Vol. 11(winter):1.

Fulton, William. 1997. *The Reluctant Metropolis: The Politics of Urban Growth in Los Angeles.* Point Arena, CA: Solano.

Fulton, William, Rolf Pendell, Mai Nguyen, and Alicia Harrison. 2001. *Who Sprawls Most? How Growth Patterns Differ across the U.S.* Washington, DC: Brookings Institution.

Gibbs, David, and Andrew E. G. Jonas. 2000. "Governance and Regulation in Local Environmental Policy: The Utility of a Regime Approach." *Geoforum* 31:299–313.

Gold, Scott. 2001. "Suit Seeks to Halt Huge Project." *Los Angeles Times,* September 17, B3.

Gottlieb, Robert, and Margaret FitzSimmons. 1991. *Thirst for Growth: Water Agencies as Hidden Government in California.* Tucson: University of Arizona Press.

Jonas, Andrew E. G. 1997. "Making Edge City: Post-suburban Development and Life on the Frontier in Southern California." In *Changing Suburbs: Foundation, Form and Function,* ed. Richard Harris and Peter. J. Larkham, 202–21. London: Spon.

Kareiva, Peter, Sandy J. Andelman, Daniel Doak, Bret Elderd, Martha Groom, Jonathan Hoekstra, Laura Hood, Frances James, John Lamoureux, Gretchen LeBuhn, Charles McCulloch, James Regetz, Lisa Savage, Mary Ruckelshaus, David Skelly, Henry Wilbur, Kelly Zamudio, and NCEAS HCP Working Group. 1999. "Using Science in Habitat Conservation Plans." Report, American Institute of Biological Sciences and National Center for Ecological Analysis and Synthesis, Santa Barbara, CA.

Kostyack, John. 2001. "NWF v. Babbitt: Victory of Smart Growth and Imperiled Wild Life." *Environmental Law Reporter* 31:10712–18.

Landis, Betsey, 1993. "Significant Ecological Areas: The Skeleton in Los Angeles County's Closet?" In *Interface between Ecology and Land Use in California,* ed. Jon E. Keeley. Los Angeles: Southern California Academy of Sciences.

Lyon, David W. 1998. "Representation without Taxation: Proposition 13 and Local Government in California." Speech presented at the Municipal Law Symposium, Hastings College of the Law, September 18.

Margules, C. R., and M. B. Usher. 1981. "Criteria Used in Assessing Wildlife Conservation Potential: A Review." *Biological Conservation* 43:63–76.

McWilliams, Carey. 1979. *Southern California: An Island on the Land.* Santa Barbara, CA: Peregrine Smith.

Mozingo, Joe. 2001. "Plan to Level Levee Alarms Residents." *Los Angeles Times,* May 20, B12.

National Wildlife Federation. 2001. "Smart Growth and Wildlife." White paper. http://www.nwf.org/smartgrowth.

Pincetl, Stephanie. 1999a. "The Politics of Influence: Democracy and the Growth Machine in Orange County, U.S." In *The Urban Growth Machine: Critical Perspectives, Two Decades Later,* ed. Andrew E. G. Jonas and David Wilson. Albany: State University of New York Press.

———. 1999b. *Transforming California: A Political History of Land Use and Development.* Baltimore: Johns Hopkins University Press.

Piven, Frances Fox, and Roger Friedland. 1984. "Public Choice and Private Power: A Theory of Fiscal Crisis." In *Public Service Provision and Urban Development,* ed. Andrew Kirby, Paul Knox, and Steven Pinch, 390–420. New York: St. Martin's.

Pollak, Daniel. 2001a. "The Future of Habitat Conservation? The NCCP Experience in Southern California." California State Library, California Research Bureau, Sacramento.

———. 2001b. "Natural Community Conservation Planning (NCCP): The Origins of an

Ambitious Experiment to Protect Ecosystems." California State Library, California Research Bureau, Sacramento.

Pollan, Michael. 1991. *Second Nature: A Gardener's Education.* New York: Atlantic Monthly Press.

Press, Daniel. 1999. "Local Open-Space Preservation in California." In *Toward Sustainable Communities: Transition and Transformations in Environmental Policy*, ed. Michael Kraft and Daniel A. Mazmanian, 153–83. Cambridge: MIT Press.

Sanchez, Jesus. 1999. "L.A. County's Growth Spurt Pushes North." *Los Angeles Times*, March 8, B3.

Schiesl, Martin J. 1995. "Designing the Model Community: The Irvine Company and Suburban Development, 1950–88." In *Postsuburban California: The Transformation of Orange County since World War II*, ed. Rob Kling, Spencer Olin, and Mark Poster, 55–91. Berkeley: University of California Press.

Scott, Thomas A. 2001. "Functional Connectivity in the Fragmented Landscapes of Southern California." Unpublished manuscript.

Scott, Thomas A., and James Sullivan. 2000. "Selection and Design of Multiple Species Preserves." *Environmental Management* 26(suppl.):S37–53.

Scott, Thomas A., Walter Wehtje, and Morgan Wehtje. 2001. "The Need for Strategic Planning in Passive Restoration of Wildlife Populations." *Restoration Ecology* 9(3):262–71.

Silva, Fred J., and Elisa Barbour. 1999. *The State-Local Fiscal Relationship in California: A Changing Balance of Power.* San Francisco: Public Policy Institute of California.

Simon, Benjamin M., Craig S. Leff, and Harvey Doerksen. 1995. "Allocating Scarce Resources for Endangered Species Recovery." *Journal of Policy Analysis and Management* 14(3):415–32.

Smallwood, Shawn K. 2000. "A Crosswalk from the Endangered Species Act to the HCP Handbook and Real HCPs." *Environmental Management* 26(suppl.)1:S23–35.

Smallwood, Shawn K., Jan Beyea, and Michael L. Morrison. 1999. "Using the Best Scientific Data for Endangered Species Conservation." *Environmental Management* 24(4):421–35.

Stone, Clarence N. 1989. *Regime Politics: Governing Atlanta, 1946–1988.* Lawrence: University Press of Kansas.

PART III
Which Way L.A.?

9 | Can Growth Control Escape Fiscal and Economic Pressures? City Policy before and after the 1990s Recession

Pascale Joassart-Marcelli, William Fulton, and Juliet Musso

The past two decades in the United States have witnessed a rapid increase in state and local government activities intended to influence future physical development within jurisdictions, and nowhere has this growth management movement been as widespread as in California. Beginning in the early 1970s, a rising number of city and county jurisdictions began to adopt policies and regulations to guide the rate, amount, type, location, quality, and timing of development. In Southern California, the late 1980s saw a surge of growth management activity, jumping from a low annual average of four measures per year between 1975 and 1985 to an average of twenty-six measures between 1985 and 1990 for the 116 cities in the sample examined in this chapter. These attempts to limit or shape growth were often undertaken under the banner of environmental protection and preservation of community character. Today, the popularity of "smart growth" initiatives reflects ambivalent public opinion regarding unregulated growth and its consequences, which include traffic congestion, pollution, loss of open space, destruction of historic buildings, and fiscal stress (see Gearin, chapter 10, this volume). On the one hand, many communities welcome growth as a source of income, jobs, and improvements, but on the other hand they reject development if they believe it will require additional expenditure, alter the lifestyle and appearance of their cities and towns, and threaten the environment (Warner and Molotch 1995).

Although the rise of growth management in the 1980s may suggest growing environmental consciousness, it could also reflect more mundane considerations. Indeed, several authors have emphasized the fiscal and exclusionary motives behind such policies (Bogart 1993; Briffault 1990; Fischell 1995; Ladd 1998; Pendall 1999; Platt 1997). For example, growth management regulations can be used as a way to limit or prevent growth of multifamily and rental housing, which tends to be associated with lower-income residents, who often require high levels of public expenditures while contributing little to local revenues. Similarly, land-use regulations and other local government policies can reflect a preference for revenue-generating activities such as shopping centers and business parks at the expense of more costly land uses such as affordable housing. Finally, communities can initiate growth controls to indirectly exclude ethnic and racial minorities, as well as low-income and even moderate-income households, in attempts to protect property values or to preserve racial homogeneity.

Despite the unconstitutional nature of such practices in some states, as illustrated by the Mount Laurel decisions of the New Jersey Supreme Court in 1975 and 1983 (Platt 1997), growth control measures motivated by exclusionary and fiscal purposes may be becoming more widespread for at least two reasons. First, the changing character of suburban development (including the creation of larger and more diverse job centers), as well as the demographic diversification of some suburbs, has met with resistance from older, wealthier, and more homogeneous suburbs. Second, the increased responsibility of local government to provide public services, linked to devolution of federal programs and mandates, has contributed to higher levels of local fiscal stress and promoted local policy responses designed to raise local revenues and reduce expenditures.

However, the impact of fiscal motives on growth control has not been studied systematically. As Ladd (1998) notes, more research is needed to "isolate fiscal considerations from other considerations that might affect land use and growth control [and] determine the characteristics of localities that lead to fiscally motivated zoning" (71). Moreover, despite the dynamic nature of urban growth control policies and the cyclical features of economic and fiscal conditions, studies that have attempted to explain the adoption of such policies have tended to be static. Researchers have typically focused on the use of growth controls in local jurisdictions and how this is influenced by demographic and socioeconomic characteristics (Bates and Santerre 1994; Levine, Glickfeld, and Fulton 1996) or how it affects housing market conditions and community composition (Donovan and Neiman 1995; Landis 1994; Pendall 1999; Wolch and Gabriel 1981) in a given period. To our knowledge, no researchers have looked at growth control from a historical perspective and attempted to explain adoption patterns using a dynamic approach that emphasizes changes both in jurisdiction characteristics and growth management strategies.

Our purpose in this chapter is to investigate the extent to which Southern California cities engaged in exclusionary or fiscally motivated growth controls during the expansionary and recessionary periods of the late 1980s and the 1990s. More specifically, we analyze what city characteristics explain the adoption of growth management measures, with a special emphasis on the role of the 1990 recession. If the motives for growth controls were simply to manage growth for environmental purposes, we would expect such policies to be adopted in areas with rapid population growth and rising density. However, if economic and exclusionary goals were dominant, we would be more likely to find growth management policies in wealthier and more homogeneous cities, regardless of population growth trends. Moreover, we would expect these fiscal or economic motives to be exacerbated by recessionary conditions and weakened by economic prosperity.

Southern California represents an ideal context in which to analyze this question. First, it comprises more than 170 cities in five counties, providing a large sample of jurisdictions in close proximity to each other.[1] Second, economic restructuring, globalization, and federal and state devolution and expenditure cutbacks have created a highly fragmented region with economically, fiscally, and demographically diverse cities likely to have a wide range of motives for adopting—or failing to adopt—growth management measures. Third, continuous population growth in Southern California has resulted in increased density in existing urban areas as well as rapid suburbanization, thus making effective growth management an urgent issue for many localities and the region as a whole. Finally, like the rest of the state, Southern California is limited by the tax rules imposed by Proposition 13 and faces other important fiscal constraints that may promote the use of alternative methods to reach fiscal objectives (see Musso, chapter 6, this volume).

Understanding the motivation behind growth management is a crucial issue for policy makers and scholars who are interested in preserving the environment, improving public services (especially to low- and moderate-income residents), and decreasing intraregional economic disparities. If specific cities independently choose to limit growth in an attempt to preserve or raise property values and maintain or improve fiscal conditions, it is unlikely that their actions will have a positive impact on restricting sprawl in the region as a whole. In fact, if growth is restricted in some cities, it may push new development to outlying areas and actually contribute to sprawl, as previous research has suggested (Glickfeld and Levine 1992). Moreover, such patterns may concentrate poor people and controversial land uses in already disadvantaged neighborhoods and exacerbate economic inequality among cities.

This is not to say that localities should not use growth management strategies, but that a concerted regional effort is preferable to independent and often conflicting local initiatives for the achievement of the broader goals of environmental protection and regional well-being. As in the "tragedy of the commons," self-interested individuals or localities may benefit from their own actions in the short run but undermine the well-being of all in the long run by ignoring the implications of their behavior for socioeconomic disparity and environmental degradation. Consequently, policy makers and scholars must understand the factors that influence growth management policies in order to suggest better alternatives.

In this chapter, we first discuss the data used in our analysis and summarize the findings of previous research. We then analyze the type of growth management measures enacted in pre- and postrecession periods (i.e., 1989–92 and 1995–98), focusing on geographic patterns. Finally, we examine the factors that explain (1) which cities adopted growth management and (2) why their behavior may have changed from the first period to the second.

Building on Recent California Growth Governance Survey Research

We base our analysis on previous work by Fulton, Glickfeld, Levine, and others (Glickfeld and Levine 1992; Levine and Glickfeld 1992; Levine et al. 1996; Fulton et al. 2000; Glickfeld et al. 1999). In 1988 and 1992, this team of researchers conducted surveys of California counties and cities in an effort to obtain information regarding growth governance. We rely here on data from the 1992 survey by Glickfeld and Levine, complemented by data from a 1998 survey conducted jointly by a team of researchers at the University of California, Berkeley, and the California Department of Housing and Community Development (UCB/CHCD), directed by John Landis. The UCB/CHCD survey included most of the questions pertaining to growth management found in the 1992 survey. Consequently, by combining these two data sets, we are able to obtain comparable information for two distinct periods.

The combined data constitute a sample of 116 cities (out of 168) for which growth management activity was measured in both periods. The data set contains twelve common growth management measures passed by Southern California jurisdictions by date and method of enactment for each period.[2] Figure 9.1 lists and defines these growth management measures. These data are complemented by a series of demographic and socioeconomic indicators obtained primarily from the 1980 and 1990

Measure	Definition
Residential building permit cap	Limits the number of residential building permits granted in a given time period
Commercial building permit cap and restrictions	Limits the number of commercial building permits granted in a given time period or imposes restrictions on their size/height or land requirements
Adequate public facilities requirement (residential)	Requires developers to finance local infrastructure, such as roads and sewers, associated with residential development
Adequate public facilities requirement (commercial)	Requires developers to finance local infrastructure, such as roads and sewers, associated with commercial development
Urban limit lines	Restricts development to areas within specific boundaries
Growth management element in general plan	Adapts the city's general plan to include specific growth management goals
Rezoning of residential development area	Assigns land previously identified for residential use to less dense uses, such as agriculture or open space
Downzoning of residential development area	Changes existing residential zoning laws to limit residential development
Residential building floor-area and height restrictions	Restricts the size of buildings on a given lot or imposes minimum lot size for a given building
Simple majority vote requirement	Requires simple majority vote for changes in existing zoning laws to allow further development
Supermajority vote requirement	Requires supermajority vote for changes in existing zoning laws to allow further development
Other measure to control development	Includes rezoning of commercial or industrial land use to less intense use, phased development, creation of environmentally sensitive areas, and other measures

Figure 9.1. Types of growth management measures.

U.S. Census of Population and Housing as well as fiscal capacity variables computed from the 1981–82 and 1996–97 Annual Reports of Financial Transactions Concerning Cities of California (see Musso, chapter 6, this volume, for details on fiscal capacity computation).

Previous work based on the 1988 and 1992 surveys highlighted several important conclusions. First, in California as a whole, the number of existing measures designed to affect growth increased by 50 percent between 1988 and 1992. Second, although Southern California jurisdictions used a variety of approaches to manage growth, they tended to favor measures designed to maintain low density and ensure appropriate provision by developers of infrastructure, public services, and facilities. These types of measures, as opposed to urban growth boundaries and other strict controls, tend to allow greater suburban sprawl. Third, there was some degree of variation among counties in approaches to growth governance. For example, whereas cities in Ventura County enacted stricter growth controls than did cities in other areas, those in Orange County typically attempted to promote growth rather than limit it. Fourth, the demographic and socioeconomic characteristics of cities explained the types of approaches they adopt to govern growth. Affluent communities with more highly educated residents tended to adopt more growth management measures than did communities with lower socioeconomic status and greater proportions of ethnoracial minorities.

In the following pages we update some of these earlier findings and examine whether the trends and relations observed previously still hold for the 1995–98 period. Moreover, we add a fiscal and economic dimension to the analysis.

Trends in Local Growth Management, 1989–92 and 1995–98

From 1989 through 1992, 54.3 percent of the 116 jurisdictions in the Southern California sample adopted at least one measure designed to manage growth. However, this proportion fell to 25.9 percent of jurisdictions for the 1995–98 period. This represents a considerable decline.

Among the jurisdictions that passed at least one measure in the first period, almost three-fourths did not adopt any new measure in the second period (see Table 9.1). Similarly, among those that did not adopt any measure in the first period, more than three-fourths continued to avoid using any policy tools to manage growth. Hence behavior in the first period cannot be used to predict behavior in the second period. As correlation analysis reveals, there is no clear relationship between the number of measures adopted by each locality in the first period and the number adopted in the

Table 9.1. Numbers of jurisdictions adopting growth management measures in Southern California, 1989–92 and 1995–98

	1995–98		
1989–92	Adopted at least one measure	Did not adopt any measure	Total (%)
Adopted at least one measure	16	47	63 (52.5)
Did not adopt any measure	13	44	57 (47.5)
Total (%)	29 (24.2)	91 (75.8)	

second period.[3] This suggests that cities do not necessarily follow consistent long-term strategies for growth management; rather, they may simply respond to short-term conditions.

The two periods considered in this analysis are part of a broader trend illustrated in Figure 9.2. Growth management activities seem to have been relatively moderate during the 1970s and early 1980s, but during the second half of the 1980s such activities accelerated rapidly. In 1988 alone, the 116 Southern California cities in the sample adopted forty-two measures. Although no data are available for 1993 and 1994, it is clear that by the mid-1990s the number of growth management measures adopted had decreased significantly. This decline is likely due to the 1990 recession, from which Southern California had only recently recovered. Hence the pattern observed in Figure 9.2 suggests the possibility of a "business cycle" effect, in which cities adopt growth measures following periods of rapid growth but put growth management activity on hold during or following recessionary times. We analyze the impact of the business cycle on growth management activity in greater detail in the following sections by comparing the prerecession period of 1989–92 and the postrecession period of 1995–98.[4]

Total numbers such as those reported in Figure 9.2, however, may hide variations in specific categories. Figure 9.3 shows the percentages of jurisdictions that adopted the twelve growth management measures examined here in both periods. As the figure indicates, Southern California jurisdictions reduced all types of measures passed,

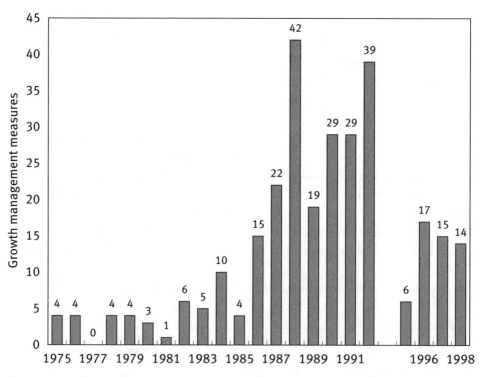

Figure 9.2. Total growth management measures adopted in Southern California jurisdictions, 1975–98.

except for rezoning of residential development areas and simple majority vote requirement. The former reflects a desire to change land use from residential use to other
purposes that may be linked to the economic hardship associated with the 1990 recession. The latter is related to the recent trend in California of bringing local policy decisions to the ballot box. Downzoning, despite its decline from the first period, became
the most commonly adopted measure in 1995–98, along with rezoning. The sharpest
declines were experienced in commercial building restrictions, residential floor-area
ratio limits, and growth management elements in the general plan.

To analyze these changes in more depth, we grouped the twelve growth management measures into three categories: commercial, residential, and other. *Commercial*
refers to measures directly aimed at reducing commercial activity (i.e., commercial
caps or infrastructure requirements), *residential* refers to activities directed at curb-
ing residential growth (e.g., residential caps and floor-area restrictions, rezoning and
downzoning of residential areas), and *other* includes a variety of approaches whose
targets could be both commercial and residential (e.g., urban limit lines, vote requirement). As Figure 9.4 illustrates, a shift from commercial to residential controls
occurred between the two periods under consideration. Although commercial restrictions represented the least popular approach in both periods, they dropped from 18
percent of the total in 1989–92 to only 11 percent in 1995–98. The drop in the raw
number of commercial measures was even more dramatic: twenty-three such measures were passed in the first period, compared with five measures in the second.

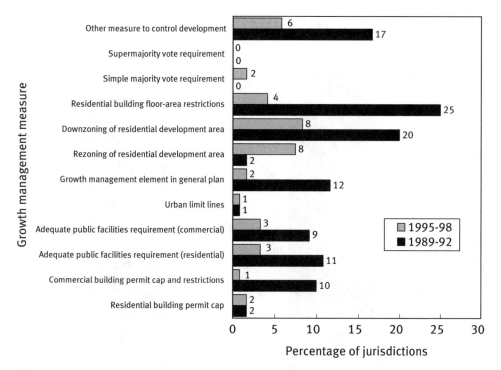

Figure 9.3. Growth management measures, Southern California, 1989–92 and 1995–98.

Perhaps this is not surprising given that commercial development tends to provide high tax revenues, especially sales taxes, while generating few service costs. Under recessionary conditions, it may be difficult for cities to forgo revenue opportunities associated with commercial development, especially when poverty and unemployment put greater pressure on local public resources.

Residential measures, however, showed the opposite trend. Almost two-thirds of all measures passed during the second period were related to residential development, with more than half being forms of zoning, as opposed to approximately 20 percent in the first period. Interestingly, the empirical research on the impact of growth management suggests that rising housing prices and exclusionary practices have more often been associated with zoning than with other types of growth management practices (Wolch and Gabriel 1981; Ladd 1998). Levine (1999) has also shown that downzoning particularly affects minorities and low-income households by discouraging construction of rental housing. Nevertheless, it is important to remember that the overall number of cities involved in growth management in the second period decreased dramatically, from sixty-three to thirty, so that even though the percentage of cities adopting residential measures increased, the actual number declined.

There are important variations within the region of Southern California, as Figure 9.5 illustrates. In the 1989–92 period, Orange County had the highest proportion of

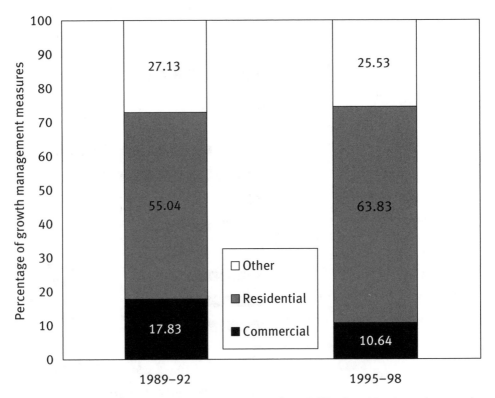

Figure 9.4. Growth management measure types, Southern California, 1989–92 and 1995–98.

cities passing growth management measures (i.e., 71 percent), followed by San Bernardino (60 percent) and Los Angeles (55 percent) Counties. Riverside and Ventura Counties experienced lower levels of participation, with 40 percent and 11 percent of cities, respectively, passing specific measures designed to curb growth. However, during the 1995–98 period, an almost complete reversal occurred. While all other counties experienced declines in the proportion of cities that passed growth control measures, jurisdictions in Ventura County began to regulate or manage growth actively. In this period, 56 percent of jurisdictions somehow participated in efforts to reduce or shape growth. This is best exemplified by the 1998 SOAR (Save Open Space and Agricultural Resources) initiatives, which created urban growth boundaries around six of the county's ten cities and required voter approval for subsequent boundary and zoning changes affecting agricultural and open-space land in unincorporated areas. In contrast, the sharpest declines took place in San Bernardino and Orange Counties, where growth management had been strongest in the previous period. It is noteworthy that the relative strength of growth management in Orange County in the first period was driven by the fact that twelve cities, mostly along the coast, added growth management elements to their general plans.

County aggregates can hide more specific local variations. In both periods, there were important differences among cities within each county. In either period, a given

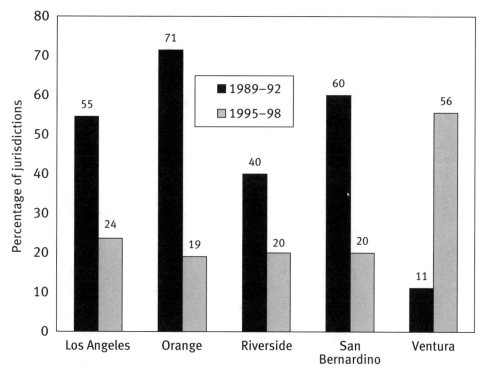

Figure 9.5. Percentage of jurisdictions involved in growth management by county, Southern California, 1989–92 and 1995–98.

city was likely to be adjacent to other jurisdictions pursuing conflicting—or at best different—approaches to growth management.[5] There is no consistency from one period to the other—a number of cities adopted new measures in the first period but failed to do so in the second period, and vice versa. One of the few consistencies, with no measures passed in either period, is found in southeastern Los Angeles County among the "hub cities"; farther south in Downey, Lynwood, Paramount, Lakewood, Artesia, and Cerritos; and to the east in Pico Rivera and South El Monte.[6] Not surprisingly, most of these cities are among the poorest in Southern California, and have been virtually transformed from white to Latino suburbs in the last generation. Throughout the region, no cluster of more than three adjacent cities was consistently involved in growth restriction during both periods.

Why Do Some Cities Pass Growth Management Measures?

Clearly, there is significant diversity in the approaches Southern California jurisdictions use to curb or redirect growth, both historically and geographically. In this section we examine the potential reasons for this wide diversity, focusing on the role of fiscal or exclusionary motives.

Modeling Growth Management Activity

Five broad sets of variables may be used to explain the growth measure activity of cities: demographic variables, housing variables, institutional variables, socioeconomic variables, and fiscal variables. We describe each kind briefly in turn below.

DEMOGRAPHIC VARIABLES

Changes in population are expected to increase density and affect the availability of resources for local residents and thus are likely to generate political pressure for growth restrictions. This is the argument most commonly used by policy makers and smart growth advocates. However, as noted earlier, this rhetoric may mask less benevolent goals. Moreover, the demographic composition of population growth, such as the race or ethnicity and immigration status of new residents, although highly correlated with socioeconomic status, can also affect growth measure activity through political and cultural processes. For example, one may expect cities with larger immigrant communities to be less likely to pass growth restriction measures given their lower level of political participation. In fact, in Southern California's recent history, politicians have been reluctant to enact growth restrictions unless such restrictions are supported by a large constituency (Fulton 1997). Moreover, cities with large constituencies of white residents may be more likely to engage in exclusionary policies than cities with large proportions of minorities (Wolch and Gabriel 1981; Shen 1996).

HOUSING VARIABLES

If growth controls are designed to manage excessive growth, then we would expect to find such policies in areas with low vacancy rates, high average number of persons per unit (reflecting crowding), and high proportions of new residents. However, if growth management is exclusionary or fiscally motivated, we might see the opposite and expect areas with high property values and lower proportions of renters to be more involved in growth management (Logan and Zhou 1989).

INSTITUTIONAL VARIABLES

The age and the type of government in a city may influence local ability to enact growth policy changes. For example, we expect recently incorporated cities, as well as general law cities, to be less able or inclined to restrict growth.[7] However, ceteris paribus, we expect suburban cities to be more likely to adopt growth management policies, given the dominant political attitude of self-governance in these areas, where the desire to escape the problems of older and more centrally located cities prevails (Logan and Zhou 1989; Levine et al. 1996).

SOCIOECONOMIC VARIABLES

The poverty and unemployment rates in a city are likely to influence its desire and ability to restrict growth. Although poorer areas may suffer fiscally from inflows of new residents (especially if the newcomers have low income levels and require subsidized services), they may be in a difficult position politically to restrict growth (Pincetl 1992), as further development is traditionally perceived as a solution to deteriorating and insufficient housing, lack of jobs, and poor fiscal conditions (Warner and Molotch 1995). On the other hand, wealthier communities may not need the extra income that new development—whether commercial or residential—could generate and consequently may choose to restrict growth. Indeed, in wealthier areas, residents are likely to perceive new development as altering the community composition and generating more costs.

FISCAL VARIABLES

Given the complexity of state-local intergovernmental relations in California, it is useful to distinguish among the different aspects of fiscal capacity. Here, we use per capita fiscal capacity to represent each city's ability to raise revenues. We compute this indicator by multiplying each city's aggregate income by a representative regional rate (i.e., the average share of aggregate income allocated to discretionary city revenues for all of Southern California) and adding actual revenues obtained from sales and property taxes and intergovernmental aid (see Musso, chapter 6, this volume). We expect cities with high discretionary local fiscal capacity to be more likely to restrict growth because they are able to raise sufficient revenues and are wary of extra costs associated with inflows of lower-income residents. However, cities that receive a high proportion of their revenues from sales taxes may want to maintain commercial development for fiscal reasons regardless of the potential social costs. For this reason, we also include a variable reflecting the proportion of revenues from sales taxes. This highlights the importance of distinguishing among the sources of city revenues in a context where such revenues are limited by institutional forces and retail is preferred over housing and manufacturing growth due to local reliance on sales tax revenues.

The model developed here attempts to explain whether a city adopted any growth management measures (GMM) based on the factors described above. Thus GMM can take the value of zero or one and is expressed as follows:

$$GMM = \alpha + \beta_1 D + \beta_2 H + \beta_3 I + \beta_4 S + \beta_5 F + \varepsilon,$$

Where D, H, I, S, and F are vectors of demographic, housing, institutional, socio-economic, and fiscal variables, respectively, β_i are vectors of regression coefficients, α is the constant term and ε is the error term.

Before we present the regression results, we focus below on the independent variables in greater detail and describe their variation across cities.

Contrasts between Growth Management and Non–Growth Management Cities

Table 9.2 shows the variables used here to proxy the effects of the five factors described above and compares their average values for cities involved in growth management and other cities in Southern California. Several important distinctions can be made between cities involved in growth management and those not involved. First, the socio-economic factors related to passage of growth measures changed during the two time periods. Race and ethnicity variables did not seem to differ significantly in the first period, except for the proportion of blacks and Asians being slightly higher in growth-restrictive cities. In the second period, however, cities involved in growth control had a higher proportion of white residents and a smaller proportion of immigrants and Latinos. Moreover, although in the region as a whole the proportion of whites decreased dramatically between 1980 and 1990, cities where growth management took place in the second period were characterized by below-average decreases in the representation of whites.

Thus in the second period growth management appears to have become more exclusionary or influenced by race/ethnicity. For example, ordinances restricting growth were passed in the cities of Hermosa Beach, San Clemente, Rancho Mirage, and Ventura during the 1995–98 period.[8] All these cities have proportions of white residents ranging between 78 percent and 91 percent, proportions of immigrants between 1 percent and 14 percent, and declines in the proportions of white residents of less than 8 percent—all of which are uncharacteristic of the region as a whole.

Surprisingly, cities that attempted to restrict growth in the first period were already characterized by relatively slow population growth. This suggests that either they did not use growth control primarily to restrict population growth or that they had passed other similar measures earlier, effectively reducing population growth between 1980 and 1990.

Second, the comparative housing characteristics of the two groups of cities became less important during the recession. In the first period, cities controlling growth had lower vacancy rates, higher property values, and larger proportions of renters, suggesting a tight housing market with a potential for quick turnover and demographic

Table 9.2. Characteristics of cities by growth control activity, Southern California, 1989–92 and 1995–98

Characteristic	1989–92			1995–98		
	Growth control		Significance of difference (from t test)	Growth control		Significance of difference (from t test)
	No	Yes		No	Yes	
Fiscal						
Per capita total fiscal capacity ($)	547.49	507.81		1,135.67	1,194.75	
Percentage of city revenue from sales taxes	21.28	19.76		15.24	11.96	*
Socioeconomic						
Poverty rate (%)	18.20	17.52		19.19	15.56	*
Unemployment rate (%)	14.28	14.58		18	13.10	*
Median annual income ($)	21,916.88	20,940.74		41,553.56	41,648.96	
Demographic						
Population	32,388	128,858	**	49,846.40	204,420.9	*
Population growth (%)	29.23	21.57	***	10.87	10.30	
Percentage blacks	3.13	5.36	**	4.73	4.56	
Percentage Asians	3.44	4.96	**	8.80	9.70	
Percentage Latinos	24.60	21.10		30.06	22.18	*
Percentage whites	77.08	76.50		55.09	62.81	**
Percentage immigrants	16.15	16.56		23.75	19.16	*
Housing						
Vacancy rate (%)	9.30	5.28	*	9.04	7.73	
Median property value ($)	93,562.50	100,572.00	***	231,469.60	244,675.00	
Median rent ($)	291.56	291.82		684.91	708.96	
Average number of persons per unit	2.84	2.76		2.88	2.56	*
Percentage of rental units	36.92	41.04	**	39.89	43.06	
Institutional						
Charter city (%)	11.54	40.35	*	25.61	32.14	
Age of city (years)	56.1	65.7	**	56.4	76.1	*
Suburb (%)	57.14	56.60		56.98	56.67	

* Difference significant with at least 95 percent confidence.
** Difference significant with at least 90 percent confidence.
*** Difference significant with at least 80 percent confidence.

change. For instance, growth measures were adopted in Rolling Hills and San Marino, where vacancy rates were below 3 percent and median property values reached $200,100.[9] These housing conditions contrast sharply with those in cities that did not pass growth management measures, such as Perris and Lake Elsinore, where more than 10 percent of units were vacant and property values were below $50,000. In the second period, however, housing conditions did not seem to be significantly different between cities controlling growth and others, except for the lower average number of persons per unit. This suggests that housing conditions may matter most during fast growth periods and housing market booms, but are not a driving force during recessionary periods.

Third, cities involved in growth control tend to be older and to have their own charters (at least in the first period), highlighting the importance of institutional characteristics and suggesting that growth management is a highly political issue. No clear differences were observed between suburban cities and others.[10] This last finding is surprising given the perception that suburbs have been more active in restricting growth and protecting their resources. This may be due to the fact that in Southern California suburbs do not represent a uniform group of jurisdictions but are characterized by heterogeneity. Hence it may be important to distinguish between suburbs by controlling for characteristics such as fiscal capacity and socioeconomic status, as we do in the regression analyses presented below.

Fourth, socioeconomic variables were not significantly distinguishable across growth-controlling cities and others in the first period but became significantly different in the postrecession period. In 1995–98, cities involved in growth management usually had lower proportions of residents in poverty and lower rates of unemployment. This supports the argument that the cities most negatively affected by the 1990 recession may have hesitated to restrict growth—if not choosing to promote it—because they wanted to attract jobs and raise revenues. For example, from 1995 through 1998, among the twenty cities in our sample with poverty rates over 30 percent, none passed growth management measures except for Los Angeles and South Gate. No measures were passed in the poorest ten cities.

Finally, cities involved in growth management could not be easily distinguished from others based on their fiscal characteristics in the first period. However, in the postrecession period, they became more differentiated. Cities that implemented growth controls typically had higher per capita city revenues and discretionary local fiscal capacity (i.e., ability to raise their own revenues regardless of property and sales taxes or intergovernmental flows) and received significantly lower proportions of their revenues from sales taxes. For example, no measures were passed in Costa Mesa, Montclair, or Santa Fe Springs—cities where sales taxes represent between a third and half of city revenues and fiscal capacity ranges between $500 and $800 per capita, a high number by regional standards. Hermosa Beach, San Clemente, and South Pasadena—where sales taxes contribute less than 10 percent to city revenues and per capita fiscal capacity is above $1,000—adopted new measures.[11]

Explaining Differences in Growth Management Practice

Although we have identified several important characteristics of growth-controlling cities, logistic regressions can be useful for determining which variables influence the likelihood of a city's adopting growth management measures while controlling for certain factors. Table 9.3 displays the results of such regressions for the pre- and postrecession periods.[12]

In the first period, the predictive power of the model—as measured by the percentage of concordant pairs—is not as high as in the second period. The results suggest that in the prerecession period, growth control activity was motivated mostly by housing and institutional characteristics as well as by population growth. Indeed, cities with higher population growth and more overcrowding (measured by the average persons per unit) were less likely to adopt growth management measures, as confirmed by the reduced-form model. This contradicts the argument that cities engage in growth management efforts in an attempt to slow population growth. Indeed, cities with overcrowded households may hesitate to limit growth because alleviating the housing shortage by building new units probably seems more useful and urgent than restricting growth. Cities with high proportions of renters were also less likely to restrict growth. Moreover, suburban and older cities were more likely to engage in growth management efforts. Fiscal and socioeconomic variables played no significant role in influencing growth management activity in this first period.

Consequently, we can conclude that in the first period, which was characterized by a growing economy, rapid population growth, and booming real estate markets, fiscal and socioeconomic characteristics did not seem to motivate growth management. Rather, growth management took place in suburban cities that had slower population growth, higher proportions of home owners, and lower levels of overcrowding.

During the second period, the power of the model increased as a greater number of variables became significant (see Table 9.3). However, housing characteristics and population growth no longer played a determinant role. Instead, socioeconomic and fiscal variables began to matter. Cities with high poverty rates became less likely to adopt growth management policies. Moreover, cities with high proportions of revenues from sales taxes were also less likely to do so.

Other things being equal, cities with high proportions of minorities were more likely to restrict growth. This may be due to the fact that cities experiencing dramatic shifts in their ethnic composition may attempt to slow these demographic trends by restricting growth.

Thus in the postrecession period socioeconomic conditions played a very important role in determining growth control activity. As we have argued above, cities with high poverty and unemployment rates may perceive growth as a potential solution to their problems and be reluctant to limit it. This is especially true if growth provides housing, jobs, and fiscal resources in a period when these are scarce.

In summary, Southern California cities followed different motives concerning

Table 9.3. Logistic regression results explaining the likelihood of a city's adopting any growth management measure, Southern California, 1989–92 and 1995–98

| Characteristic | 1989–92 | | 1995–98 | |
	Full model	Reduced model	Full model	Reduced model
Demographic				
Proportion Latinos	3.96657		8.83085 ****	
	3.91869		5.07285	
Percentage blacks	−4.88409		6.42335 *	
	5.29491		4.61693	
Percentage Asians	13.43529 **		10.26112 **	
	8.30739		6.60258	
Percentage foreign-born	3.34644		−5.74344	
	6.37849		9.30417	
Population	0.00000		0.00002 ****	
	0.00000		0.00001	
Population growth	−1.78041 **	−0.97818 *	−6.29813	−4.48795
	1.22446	0.74861	6.15908	3.68363
Socioeconomic				
Poverty rate (150%)	5.18307		−24.24438 ****	
	7.07728		11.47354	
Unemployment rate	−3.74083		−4.90031	
	6.05637		5.65335	
Institutional and fiscal				
Per capita fiscal capacity	−0.00093		−0.00039	
	0.00160		0.00129	
Percentage of city revenue	2.48653		−7.80805 **	
from sales taxes	3.01122		5.00115	
Charter city	−0.05839		−1.88924 ****	
	0.66622		0.90029	
Age of city	0.02810 ****		0.00786	
	0.01354		0.01267	
Suburb	1.19034 **		0.22327	
	0.77655		0.97402	
Housing				
Vacancy rate	−1.79510	−0.56158	3.97011	−2.85756
	3.71018	2.32575	4.93958	2.92594
Median property value	0.00001		0.00000	
	0.00001		0.00001	
Percentage of rental units	−7.03698 ****		1.74463	
	3.26204		4.37956	
Average number of persons	−2.60917 ****	−0.85685 ****	−1.81902	−0.70167 **
per unit	1.36202	0.49646	1.60547	0.43045
Percentage of long-term	−7.08811		−2.62149	
residents (more than	12.05094		7.38643	
20 years)				
Intercept	5.22885	2.59849 ****	7.61655 *	1.84312 *
	4.88942	1.49577	5.84247	1.40194
N	97	98	108	108
Pseudo-R^2	0.2349	0.0393	0.3544	0.0536
Concordant pairs (%)	69.07	62.24	84.26	72.22

Note: Expressions in italics are standard errors.
* Significant at 20 percent.
** Significant at 15 percent.
*** Significant at 10 percent.
**** Significant at 5 percent.

growth management in the pre- and postrecession periods. In the late 1980s and early 1990s, growth control policies were more likely to be adopted in suburban cities with low population growth and slightly better housing conditions, such as cities in the northeastern part of Los Angeles County and the coastal areas of Orange County. The lack of significance of other factors reveals the wide range and large number of cities involved in growth management at that time. However, in the period following the recession, growth management activity decreased, and cities' motives for restricting growth changed. Growth control became more exclusionary and economically or fiscally motivated. It took place in areas with better economic conditions and lower reliance on sales taxes.

Although the regression results discussed above suggest that different sets of variables explain cities' growth management activities during the first and second periods, they do not explain why cities may have changed their behavior from one period to the next. As hypothesized earlier, one may expect cities that suffered severely from the 1990 recession to be less likely to be involved in growth management activity during the mid-1990s. We originally ran multinomial logistic models in order to capture the diversity of choices made by cities from one period to the next. However, the number of observations in each category was so small that the results were practically insignificant. Instead, we opted for a simpler logistic model that analyzes the likelihood that a city having passed a growth management measure in the first period stopped doing so in the second period. The results are shown in Table 9.4.

As expected, given the regression results noted above, cities with high levels of poverty in 1990 and cities that relied heavily on sales taxes were more likely to have stopped growth management activity. Perhaps surprisingly, putting growth control policies on hold does not seem to be significantly related to housing characteristics or even population growth. Cities in which fiscal capacity improved (when poverty, unemployment, and other characteristics are controlled for) were more likely to have stopped growth management, whereas those whose capacity decreased continued growth management activities.

Clearly, the poverty level of a city has a very strong effect on the probability that the city would change its behavior. In other words, cities that suffered most severely from the recession were often unable to continue to adopt growth control policies. This also confirms the finding that cities' motives for growth control were more economically based in the postrecession period than in the first period. Thus not only did poor cities reduce their growth management activities, but wealthier cities became more likely to increase theirs.

Conclusion

Analyses of the urban landscape of the Los Angeles region indicate that it is both densifying and spreading outward. As the population continues to grow, it is also changing, putting new pressures on existing resources. In this context, several jurisdictions have adopted various measures to manage growth. However, as the data analyzed in this chapter suggest, the number of such measures adopted has decreased since the mid-1990s. Indeed, only about 25 percent of Southern California cities passed new growth management measures from 1995 through 1998, as opposed to more than 50 percent from 1989 through 1992. This is surprising given the trend toward greater growth management in the 1980s and the current popularity of "smart growth" approaches to urban development. We have argued here that this decline is explained by a shift in the motives behind growth control policy that parallels the economic recession of the early 1990s.

Between 1989–92 and 1995–98, several important changes took place. Not only did the total number of growth management measures adopted decline, but a shift occurred from general restrictions and mixed approaches to zoning methods, most often associated with exclusionary and fiscal motives. Geographically, growth management activity declined in all Southern California counties except Ventura, where it increased rapidly. The largest decreases took place in San Bernardino and Orange Counties, two fast-growing areas. Little consistency can be found within cities from

Table 9.4. Logistic regression results explaining the likelihood that a city having adopted any growth control in 1989–92 stopped doing so in 1995–98

Characteristic	Regression results
Socioeconomic	
Change in poverty rates	5.51749
	6.00395
Poverty rate	43.21091 **
	28.63495
Change in unemployment rate	−2.27342 *
	1.67363
Unemployment rate	16.36940
	16.67161
Demographic	
Population growth	−19.10580
	36.53950
Population	−0.00001
	0.00001
Percentage Latinos	−15.93506 *
	11.41434
Percentage blacks	−33.72009 ****
	19.43467
Percentage Asians	−14.43843 *
	10.23044
Housing	
Housing units growth rate	−0.72110
	13.83815
Fiscal	
Per capita fiscal capacity growth rate	3.57431 *
	2.55217
Per capita fiscal capacity	−0.00176
	0.00197
Percentage of city revenues from sales taxes	41.90678 ****
	24.31644
Intercept	−8.41202 **
	5.56252
N	42
Pseudo-R^2	0.4634
Concordant pairs (%)	85.71

Note: Expressions in italics are standard errors.
* Significant at 20%.
** Significant at 15%.
*** Significant at 10%.
**** Significant at 5%.

one period to the next, with the notable exception of the "hub cities" and neighboring jurisdictions where no measures were passed in either period.

Using logistic regressions, we have attempted to explain this dramatic change in behavior between the pre- and postrecession periods. In the first period, growth management was more widespread across Southern California cities and was not easily explained by specific variables. Nevertheless, it appeared that suburban cities with relatively good housing conditions but lower population growth were more likely than others to be involved in growth control. Such cities include Hermosa Beach, San Marino, San Clemente, and Rolling Hills. In the second period, however, socioeconomic and fiscal conditions—which had been insignificant in explaining growth control activity during the first period—became the dominant forces behind growth restriction. Following the 1990s recession, only cities with lower poverty and limited reliance on sales taxes were able to adopt new growth controls. In fact, the decline observed in the number of growth management measures adopted by Southern California jurisdictions is primarily explained by poverty and share of sales taxes, as cities in economic hardship were more likely to have stopped their growth management activity. This can be interpreted as a consequence of the recession, which made development a politically attractive solution to unemployment and dwindling local fiscal resources.

Planners often give support to growth management as a tool to maintain equilibrium between development and conservation of environmental quality, optimize the use of existing infrastructure, and equalize the fiscal and economic costs and benefits of growth across a region. But growth management in Southern California does not appear to be used primarily as a tool for equitably and efficiently guiding community development. On the contrary, wealthier cities often use it as a way to maintain their fiscal strength and identity by avoiding inflows of poorer residents and immigrants. These actions in service of parochial goals do nothing to promote broader regional objectives of environmental protection and shared prosperity and are likely to contribute to future problems by promoting the concentration of poverty and unemployment. Furthermore, they may actually increase sprawl by forcing exurbanization into ever more remote areas, such as southern Orange County and the Inland Empire of Riverside and San Bernardino Counties. As Levine (1999) and Shen (1996) suggest, growth controls contribute to the redistribution of housing production and population toward nonrestrictive areas and indirectly promote sprawl.

As the economy continues to grow and population increases, Southern California cities are likely to embark on new growth management policies. Indeed, in a recent report Myers and Puentes (2001) list seventy-eight growth-related measures that appeared on the November 2000 election ballots in California, a high proportion of which were in Southern California. Whether these new measures were designed primarily to protect open space and habitat is doubtful, given the evidence of economically and fiscally motivated growth control activity in the late 1990s. As long as growth control is motivated by NIMBYism and is not based on regionally set goals, it will continue to be ineffective in reducing sprawl and protecting natural resources. It will reduce opportunities for affordable housing and, in the long run, will hinder the sustainability of the region (Pincetl 1994).

Three types of policy are necessary to ensure more effective growth control in Southern California. First, local growth control activities need to be coordinated in a regional effort. This would promote the establishment of regional goals and prevent some cities from limiting growth at the expense of others. Housing, employment, and the environment are regional issues, and they require a regional land-use perspective.

Second, policy makers must address economic disparities and the concentration of poverty to reduce the economic incentives hidden behind growth controls. On the one hand, reduction of poverty will decrease political opposition to growth control in poor cities that are fearful of economic repercussions; on the other hand, if the costs linked to poor households are alleviated by regional, state, and/or federal policies, wealthier cities will be less likely to engage in exclusionary and fiscally motivated growth control activities. In short, growth controls are more likely to serve their intended purposes if economic disparities are reduced.

Third, fiscal reform is necessary to change cities' incentives to enact growth restrictions. Often local governments make land-use decisions based on fiscal considerations and thus promote commercial development over housing and industrial development. This contributes to urban sprawl by limiting affordable housing in the region's center, leading residents to move to outlying areas with cheaper housing. The revenues of local governments must be less dependent on sales taxes and sufficient to allow cities to pursue effective and equitable growth control. Unless these economic and fiscal considerations are addressed in a regional effort, growth management is likely to promote sprawl and exacerbate poverty and economic disparities within the region.

Notes

We would like to thank Madelyn Glickfeld and Ned Levine for permission to use their 1992 Growth Control Survey data and John Landis for access to the 1998 University of California, Berkeley, and California Department of Housing and Community Development's Growth Management Survey data. This research was funded in part by the Southern California Studies Center and the National Science Foundation's Program in Geography and Regional Science. Jennifer Wolch and Peter Dreier provided useful comments, and Alicia Harrison helped with the production of maps.

1. The Southern California metropolitan region includes the counties of Los Angeles, Orange, Riverside, San Bernardino and Ventura.

2. The data from Levine and Glickfeld's survey are more extensive than those from the UCB/CHCD survey. The former include information regarding eighteen types of growth management measures and a series of other detailed variables about the effectiveness of measures passed, infrastructure and public facilities, water, housing cost and affordable housing, and interjurisdictional arrangements and conflicts, whereas the latter include information about only fifteen growth control measures. In order to make comparisons between the two study periods, we kept only the twelve growth measures that were common to both surveys and dropped all other variables. For each of these twelve measures, we have information on whether

a jurisdiction passed the measure, when a measure was adopted, and how it was adopted (i.e., resolution, ordinance, initiative, or other). To limit the comparison further to two periods of similar length (four years), we kept only information about measures passed from 1989 through 1992 and from 1995 through 1998.

3. The correlation coefficient between the total measures passed in the first and second periods for the 120 jurisdictions in the sample is –0.0686.

4. Although the recession took place in 1990, the effect on the housing market began to be felt in 1992. Thus economic conditions influence housing and, potentially, growth management activities with a lag of two or three years. Consequently, growth management policies undertaken in the 1989–92 period still reflect the economic boom of the late 1980s, whereas those undertaken in the 1995–98 period are likely to reflect the recession of the early 1990s.

5. Statistical analysis of the spatial distribution of growth control measures reveals no spatial autocorrelation in either period. The Moran coefficients were not significantly different from zero (i.e., –0.036 in 1989–92 and –0.0038 1995–98), suggesting a completely random pattern of growth control adoption in the Southern California region, with no clustering or dispersion effects found.

6. The so-called hub cities are located directly east of South-Central Los Angeles between the Alameda corridor and the I-5 freeway. They include Bell, Bell Gardens, Commerce, Cudahy, Huntington Park, Maywood, South Gate, and Vernon. We have no data for Bell Gardens, Cudahy, or Huntington Park, but the other cities (with the exception of South Gate) did not pass any measures.

7. Under California law, cities may be either general law cities or charter cities. Charter cities have their own city charters and enjoy more freedom from state law than do general law cities, which must abide by all state laws. Any general law city in California can become a charter city simply through voter approval of a charter, but most cities are general law cities. Charter cities tend to be larger and/or older than general law cities.

8. According to our survey data, Hermosa Beach adopted floor-area ratio limits (1995); San Clemente passed a significant number of measures, including floor-area ratio restrictions and rezoning and downzoning of areas previously identified for residential development (1996), and added a growth management element to its general plan (1993); Rancho Mirage rezoned some land previously set for residential development (1997); and Ventura capped residential development (1997) and required adequate public facilities for residential and commercial development (1996).

9. Rolling Hills adopted height limits and floor-area ratios in 1988. San Marino also set floor-area ratio limits (1988) and downzoned land previously identified for residential use (1991).

10. We define suburban cities as cities that experienced above-average housing stock increases after 1960.

11. South Pasadena adopted a number of growth management measures in 1998, including rezoning and downzoning of land previously set aside for residential use. See note 8 for a description of the measures adopted by Hermosa Beach and San Clemente.

12. Because the variables used in these regressions are spatially distributed, we checked for the possibility of distortion introduced by spatial autocorrelation. In all cases, regression residuals were not significantly spatially correlated with each other, and thus no adjustments were made to the regressions. Moran coefficients are reported at the bottom of Table 9.3.

Works Cited

Bates, Laurie J., and Rexford E. Santerre. 1994. "The Determinants of Restrictive Residential Zoning: Some Empirical Findings." *Journal of Regional Science* 34:253–63.

Bogart, William T. 1993. "What Big Teeth You Have! Identifying the Motivations for Exclusionary Zoning." *Urban Studies* 30:1669–81.

Briffault, Richard. 1990. "Our Localism: Part I—The Structure of Local Government Law." *Columbia Law Review* 90:1–115.

Donovan, Todd, and Max Neiman. 1995. "Local Growth Control Policy and Changes in Community Characteristics." *Social Science Quarterly* 76:780–93.

Fischell, William A. 1995. *Regulatory Takings: Law, Economics, and Politics.* Cambridge, MA: Harvard University Press.

Fulton, William. 1997. *The Reluctant Metropolis: The Politics of Urban Growth in Los Angeles.* Point Arena, CA: Solano.

Fulton, William, Madelyn Glickfeld, Grant McMurran, and June Gin. 2000. *A Landscape Portrait of Southern California's Structure of Government and Growth.* Claremont, CA: Claremont Graduate University Research Institute.

Glickfeld, Madelyn, William Fulton, Grant McMurran, and Ned Levine. 1999. *Growth Governance in Southern California.* Claremont, CA: Claremont Graduate University Research Institute.

Glickfeld, Madelyn, and Ned Levine. 1992. *Regional Growth—Local Reaction: The Enactment and Effects of Local Growth Control and Management Measures in California.* Cambridge, MA: Lincoln Institute of Land Policy.

Ladd, Helen F. 1998. *Local Government Tax and Land Use Policies in the United States: Understanding the Links.* Williston, VT: Edward Elgar.

Landis, John D. 1994. "Do Growth Controls Work? A New Assessment." *Journal of the American Planning Association* 58:489–508.

Levine, Ned. 1999. "The Effects of Local Growth Controls on Regional Housing Production and Population Redistribution in California." *Urban Studies* 36:2047–68.

Levine, Ned, and Madelyn Glickfeld. 1992. *Follow-up Survey on Growth Control.* Sacramento: California State Association of Counties.

Levine, Ned, Madelyn Glickfeld, and William Fulton. 1996. "Home Rule: Local Growth . . . Regional Consequences." Report prepared for the Southern California Association of Governments.

Logan, John R., and Min Zhou. 1989. "Do Suburban Growth Controls Control Growth?" *American Sociological Review* 54:461–71.

Myers, Phyllis, and Robert Puentes. 2001. "Growth at the Ballot Box: Electing the Shape of Communities in November 2000." Discussion paper prepared for the Brookings Institution Center on Urban and Metropolitan Policy.

Pendall Rolf. 1999. "Do Land Use Controls Cause Sprawl?" *Environment and Planning B: Planning and Design* 26:555–71.

Pincetl, Stephanie. 1992. "The Politics of Growth Control: Struggles in Pasadena, California." *Urban Geography* 13(5):450–67.

———. 1994. "The Regional Management of Growth in California: A History of Failures." *International Journal of Urban and Regional Research* 18:256–74.

Platt, Rutherford H. 1997. "The Geographical Basis of Land Use Law." In *Geography, Environment, and American Law,* ed. Gary L. Thompson, Fred M. Shelley, and Chand Wije. Boulder: University Press of Colorado.

Shen, Qing. 1996. "Spatial Impacts of Locally Enacted Growth Controls: The San Francisco Bay Region in the 1980s." *Environment and Planning B: Planning and Design* 23(1):61–91.

Warner, Kee, and Harvey L. Molotch. 1995. "Power to Build: How Development Persists Despite Local Controls." *Urban Affairs Review* 30(3):278–406.

Wolch, Jennifer R., and Stuart A. Gabriel. 1981. "Local Land Development Policies and Urban Housing Values." *Environment and Planning A* 13:1253–76.

10 | Smart Growth or Smart Growth Machine? The Smart Growth Movement and Its Implications

Elizabeth Gearin

Pressures to address issues of managing growth and creating more livable communities are mounting in Southern California as the region's growth machine (Logan and Molotch 1987) continues its twenty-five-year slowdown (Fulton 1997; Soja and Scott 1996).[1] Land expansion is waning partly as a result of decreasing amounts of available land, increased appreciation of the environment, and broadened understanding of regional interdependence. In 1998, for example, Ventura County voters passed an initiative requiring voter approval for open-space and farmland rezoning. Initiation of habitat conservation planning through the state's Natural Community Conservation Planning and other programs has prompted some Southern California jurisdictions to mount large-scale regional planning efforts. Although the particular techniques for controlling or promoting growth may change, concern about sprawl is now widespread in Southern California.

Smart growth is widely favored as a solution to sprawl. It is practiced almost everywhere in the United States, from small towns and rural areas to large cities and some entire states, and has been endorsed by a wide variety of organizations, including some with traditionally competing goals, from the Sierra Club and the Urban Land Institute to Bank of America and the National Association of Home Builders (NAHB). The mounting sense that "the problems that we face will not be solved by the kind of thinking that created them" has led to a growing recognition that smart growth can somehow help solve problems of sprawl, congestion, and loss of open space.[2]

Perhaps because of, or maybe in spite of, this new emphasis on smart growth across the country, there is a need to make sense of this trend in planning practice. Is it really a progressive, even radical, movement? Despite virtually universal support for smart growth, there are few clear definitions of the concept and seemingly little consensus. The smart growth tools advocated by various jurisdictions and organizations represent a mix of old and new methodologies, from urban growth boundaries, implemented in Oregon in the early 1970s, to energy-efficient homes, as supported by Baltimore Gas and Electric in Maryland.[3] Some tools are designed specifically to control growth, such as limiting the number of new residential dwelling units approved for development at any given time (Lacayo 1999; O'Malley 1998), whereas others focus on increasing understanding about the natural environment, such as demonstrating the economic benefits of land preservation.[4] Still others urge regional cooperation (Froehlich 1998), recognizing the interconnectedness of private and public activities within metropolitan areas. The term *smart growth* connotes positive planning and development. Further confusing conceptualization comes from the frequent conflation of smart growth with two theoretically and practically very different trends in planning: new regionalism and urban sustainability. Most important, is smart growth just a growth machine in new and more stylish garb—a *smart growth machine*? Or can it address the critical problems of urbanization facing Southern California?

In this chapter, I provide a critical and conceptual analysis of smart growth and compare this tool-oriented approach with the broader goals and values of other recent planning trends. I present a typology of smart growth tools, illustrate the tools' underlying strategic mechanisms, and identify the geographic levels at which the tools are used. (A smart growth tool kit in the chapter appendix applies this typology to practical examples.) The chapter concludes with a discussion of the role of smart growth in Southern California, including its potential to address growth issues successfully.

What Is Smart Growth?

Definitions and Background

Maryland Governor Parris Glendening coined the term smart growth as a "political and marketing decision" to implement Maryland's strategy of simultaneously funding infrastructure in targeted growth areas while conserving land in targeted preservation areas.[5] Use of the phrase has since spread, and currently it is understood to refer to specific implementation tools and strategies that proactively direct growth as well as the processes retroactively undertaken in response to low-density exurbanization or sprawl. In other words, smart growth unites the traditionally separate and sometimes competing growth promotion techniques with growth management measures. In fact, attendees at the 1999 Annual Partners for Smart Growth Conference disagreed over whether it means growth restrictions, or greater freedom for the market to guide growth (see *Growth/No Growth Alert* 1999). The term *smart growth* has become a catchall for competing planning programs and policies.

One reason for these various and sometimes competing views is that the smart growth constituency is exceptionally diverse and broad. Smart growth has been lauded for saving taxpayer and developer money, for increasing property values, for conserving the environment, and for having positive impacts on the business climate. Smart growth tools address demands for historic preservation, farmland protection, protection of the environment, preservation of architecture, and land development. Many smart growth components, such as high-density or clustered development and city centers, parallel key aspects of the popular new urbanism approach to designing communities.[6] Proponents of the new urbanism increasingly emphasize the social and economic equity of some aspects of smart growth. But smart growth is not antigrowth. It tries to accomplish development in ways that improve the quality of life and protect the environment, rather than by fostering mere urban growth or economic expansion per se. Thus smart growth is still very much about growth.

Despite its broad application in the planning lexicon, smart growth's methods for directing growth in practice are actually narrow, involving only physical environment and land-use policies. Although smart growth tools are many and varied, the foundation for all of them is in land use. Smart growth fails to address issues of social equity, especially the problems facing the poor. Emerging critics underscore this when they argue that smart growth and its antisprawl development efforts worsen traffic congestion, ignore market preferences to expand into green space, and limit housing options by restricting the supply of developable land (DiLorenzo 2000; O'Malley 1998; Stroup 2000; Easterbrook 1999; Burchell, Listokin, and Galley 2000).[7]

Where did smart growth come from? Perhaps the primary impetus for the nascent smart growth movement has been the postwar growth machine—the political-economic coalitions of businesses, developers, local elected officials, and media that have promoted metropolitan-area growth. This power structure implicitly assumes the desirability of growth and bounds land-use debates within a spectrum of growth as inevitable, something that simply must be accommodated. Early challenges to the growth machine, in the 1950s and 1960s, came from urban community groups concerned with the negative effects of displacement and gentrification. In the 1970s pre–smart growth advocates critiqued the growth machine on environmental grounds (Logan and Molotch 1987).

Neither equity and social-based issues nor concerns for a healthy natural environment gained much political clout until the 1980s and 1990s, when a motley crew of interest groups threw their support behind various iterations of the generically named smart growth. Middle-class suburbanites noted the negative effects of decades of traditional land-use decisions on their lifestyle and seriously questioned the ideology of value-free development. Urban boosters, including businesses, sought to correct the balance of political power between suburbs and cities, by advocating regionwide interests. Land developers, responding to challenges to the growth machine, some sincerely concerned about the social costs of unchecked development and others motivated by the opportunity to take advantage of this new, palatable growth ideology to reframe themselves, shifted political grounds as development clout was challenged, increasingly successfully, by home owner groups, environmentalists, and community organizations. It is unsurprising, then, that different constituencies promote different interpretations of smart growth (Logan and Molotch 1987).

The long debates over Ahmanson Ranch and Playa Vista epitomize the changing land-use arena in Southern California. Home owners seeking to protect their investments, environmentalists spurred by habitat loss and environmental degradation, and bureaucrats assigned to ensure the application of laws designed to protect various interests challenge the waning influence of the regional growth machine. Supporters of the Ahmanson Ranch project declared that it represented smart growth, citing the transfer of nearly ten thousand acres as permanent, public open space, reduced reliance on automobiles through mixed-use development, creation of a nonprofit institute to study and protect the natural environment, and provision of much-needed housing in the region. In addition to environmental groups focused on dwindling open space and endangered species habitat, foes of the project noted access and traffic issues identified in environmental review documents and concerns about water availability.[8] The Playa Vista plan incorporates high-density, mixed-use buildings in a variety of configurations, from courtyard apartments and duplexes to single-family housing, with riparian and wetland preserves. Although the developer and proponents label this smart growth, opponents cry foul, noting the development's location on one of the last remaining large coastal wetlands in Southern California.[9] In both instances, the developers had to move beyond the historically surefire appeasement tactic of downsizing into deal making. Before the developer agreed to halt the project and sell the site to the state, Ahmanson Ranch's development agreement with Ventura County permitted the development of more than three thousand homes and two golf courses in exchange for preserving almost ten thousand acres of public open space. The Playa Vista project preserves more than half of the site as open space, including the restoration and expansion of the Ballona Wetlands, and is expected to receive substantial tax breaks from the city of Los Angeles based on the developer's promise to create thousands of new jobs.

Links to New Regionalism and Urban Sustainability

Two other broadly defined planning trends are linked to smart growth in the current literature and conceptually (Figure 10.1). *New regionalism* is based on the assertions that cities and suburbs are economically and in some cases environmentally interdependent and that regions are now the paramount actors in the global economy. Smart growth and new regionalism overlap in instances where given smart growth tools encourage regional planning and cooperation. *Urban sustainability*, the broadest of the three planning trends, encompasses components of both smart growth and new regionalism. It focuses on creating and maintaining patterns of urban development and everyday life that do not exceed regional carrying capacity, in order to address environmental problems and distribute natural resources equitably.

New Regionalism

Regionalism in planning evolved from attempts to balance city and countryside in response to crowded industrial cities in the early twentieth century, shifted to focus on regional economies and economic development in the late 1940s, expanded to encompass social movements in the 1960s, and reemerged as the new regionalism, incorporating economic development and equity with environmental issues (Wheeler 2002). Advocates cite the intertwined health of the city and its outlying areas and the negative implications of competition among interregional jurisdictions for limited resources and economic investment. Whether they believe that the relationship between central cities and suburbs is complementary or competitive, supporters of new regionalism represent varied aims. Business leaders assert that metropolis-wide labor markets provide more efficient and cost-effective delivery of services than do local labor markets (Harrison 1998), labor and community activists support new regionalism's redistributive properties (Pastor et al. 2000), and environmentalists believe new regionalism fosters rational regional planning and deters sprawl.

New regionalism is both narrower and broader than smart growth. It uses far fewer and different implementation tools, yet it has a broader application, with its three-part focus on equity, environmental protection, and economic growth. Whereas smart growth is limited in application primarily to land-use programs and policies, new regionalism necessarily employs a wider range of land-use and economic programs and strategies for political engagement and action. Moreover, although smart growth and new regionalism are often rhetorically supported for many of the same reasons—expectations of increased efficiency, greater social equity, and improved environmental protection—voters typically fail to support regionalized taxes and services (Summers 1998), whereas smart growth attracts broad political support. This may be because regionalism efforts affect more people in the short term and are predicated on interjurisdictional (or at least interorganizational) coalition building and cooperation, whereas smart growth tools rely on incremental steps to effect change mostly at the local level. Further, smart growth tools focus primarily on discrete land uses and goals, whereas regionalism implies politically unpopular redistribution. Smart growth is widespread in practice, but real-world examples of the new regionalism appear quite limited. Examples of overlap between the two are prominent, however: Minneapolis and St. Paul redistribute area taxes, and New Jersey uses tax-base sharing to compensate jurisdictions for losses due to regional land-use decisions. The flexible urban growth boundary in Portland, Oregon, is often cited as an example of smart growth,

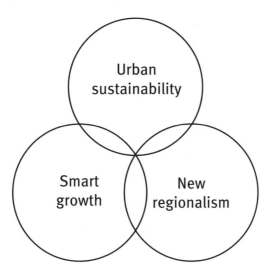

Figure 10.1. The nexus of smart growth, new regionalism, and urban sustainability.

yet it is only a component part of the region's twenty-five years of incremental, coalition-style regional transportation and land-use planning, made possible by joint political and public ideology favoring compact growth patterns (Abbott 1997; Downs, Nelson, and Fischel 2002). On the other hand, jurisdictions with any smart growth–style regional planning range from Cape Cod to San Diego, and from Vermont to Utah (Hollis 1998; Froehlich 1998; Porter 1998).

Urban Sustainability

Sustainability has been defined as the "need for humanity to live equitably within the means of nature" (Wackernagel and Rees, 1996, 33). Similarly, the urban sustainability approach to planning has evolved from biological and ecological arguments that a given area has finite resources and that, despite technological progress, the earth's ecosystem cannot support current economic development and consumption trends indefinitely (Wackernagel and Rees 1996). Proponents of urban sustainability assert that traditional unregulated development accelerates environmental deterioration and that densely populated Western nations, characterized by advanced technology and extensive development, consume quantities of natural resources and waste assimilation capacity that far exceed their geographic bounds. Despite ambiguity in the terminology, planners and policy makers generally agree that urban sustainability is a good thing.

Advocates for urban sustainability are diverse, and their approaches are both varied and far-reaching. Sustainability is a much more comprehensive concept than smart growth, recognizing the broad spectrum of impacts to the earth's resources, and advocates of sustainability attempt to mitigate these impacts by focusing on limiting resource consumption, including that associated with growth and development, while also considering economic and equity issues associated with the design of communities. For example, businesses consider sustainability in their practices of environmental impact analysis, life-cycle assessment and industrial ecology methodologies, brownfield remediation techniques, green product design, and natural resource accounting. At the same time, there is some overlap between smart growth and urban sustainability. Tools that preserve open space (such as conservation easements and the clustered development and higher densities advocated by the new urbanists), growth controls (such as conversion taxes and concurrency), and tools that target growth (such as urban growth boundaries and urban service areas) all limit natural resource use. Thus smart growth appears to incorporate sustainability features implicitly into visions of desirable development, but these are limited to the land-use arena.

Of the three concepts, urban sustainability enjoys the least amount of public support. Like new regionalism, urban sustainability implicitly calls for redistribution. To some, it seems to call for reducing the standard of living of the affluent. In order to live in a sustainable manner, many persons need to live with less than they currently do, whether by their own directive or under the influence of public policies that make it easier for them to consume fewer resources, such as recycling, convenient public transit, and alternative energy programs. Smart growth makes no such demands.

Conceptualizing and Critiquing Smart Growth

Smart growth tools vary along three critical dimensions: primary goals, implementation mechanisms, and the government level at which each tool is deployed. The more than ninety examples of smart growth inventoried for this chapter may be clustered into eight primary goals: directing growth, preserving land, reducing auto dependence, controlling rate/amount of growth, redesigning communities, altering perception of the environment, encouraging regional cooperation, and altering the housing market.

The implementation mechanisms for smart growth tools are incentive based, market based, or regulatory in nature. (Note that these designations differ from traditional economic definitions.) *Incentive-based* tools are implemented through the use of government-sponsored incentives or other voluntary programs. For example, targeted development facilitates area development through incentives such as expedited permitting processes or reduced fees. Incentive-based tools include those that rely on goodwill (altruism as an incentive), such as supporting political leaders who advocate improved perceptions of the environment. *Market-based* tools operate within the market or modify the market and create demand for tools that in turn foster smart growth. For example, the use of taxpayer money to purchase land and preserve it as open space reflects the market value of the land. Also, transfers of development rights (TDRs) are created by local ordinance to allow development rights to be separated from land and sold to property owners in other areas. *Regulatory* tools require the compliance of all affected or participating parties. Some smart growth tools are implemented by multiple mechanisms.

Smart growth tools may be deployed at four identified geographic and/or administrative levels: local, regional, state, and/or federal.

Table 10.1 provides a brief descriptive listing of the smart growth tools identified in the course of this research, showing their implementation mechanisms and the levels of government at which they are deployed. Most tools are either incentive based (twenty-three) or regulatory (nineteen); relatively few are market based (eight). About half of all tools identified may be classified under the purpose of either directing growth (nine) or preserving land (eleven). On the other hand, there are relatively few tools for the purpose of altering the housing market (two) or for reducing auto dependence, redesigning communities, and increasing livability (four each). Finally, although some tools are implemented at more than one level of government (twelve), most are implemented at a single level. Most tools are implemented locally (twenty-four), followed by state (eighteen), regional (twelve), and federal (seven) implementation. Tables 10.2, 10.3, and 10.4 highlight the relationships among the purposes of smart growth tools, their implementation mechanisms, and their levels of deployment.

As Table 10.2 shows, incentive-based tools are usually used to direct growth and to redesign communities, whereas regulatory tools are used to encourage regional cooperation. Preserving land and controlling growth rate, the historical focus for managing growth, are addressed evenly by incentive-based, market-based, and regulatory

Table 10.1. Smart growth tools overview

Purpose	Tool	Implementation mechanism			Level of deployment			
		I	M	R	L	R	S	F
Direct growth	Urban service areas	X			X			
	Targeted development areas	X			X			
	Infill development (infill)	X			X			
	Rezoning	X			X			
	High-density/transit-oriented development	X		X	X			
	Expedited permitting	X			X			
	Transfer of development rights		X		X			
	Urban growth boundaries			X	X	X	X	
	Financial assistance for reuse	X					X	X
Preserve land	Voter control of land development			X	X	X		
	Sensitive land overlay restrictions			X	X	X		
	Conversion taxes	X					X	
	Exactions, fees, land dedications (exactions)			X	X			
	Density bonus for land conservation	X			X			
	Clustered development	X		X	X			
	Performance zoning	X			X			
	Transfer/sale conservation easements		X				X	
	Open-space land acquisition		X		X	X	X	
	Agricultural land conservation incentives	X					X	
	Purchase of farmland easements		X					X
Reduce auto dependence	Work-at-home provisions			X	X	X	X	
	Transit options	X				X	X	
	Provision of housing near work	X					X	
	Transportation funding policies			X				X
Control rate, amount of growth	Commercial development caps			X	X			
	New residential development caps			X	X			
	Concurrency	X		X			X	
	Litigation	X			X			
	Fiscal impact analysis		X				X	
Redesign communities	City/nature integration programs	X			X			
	Creation of "sustainable" communities	X		X	X			
	Fund site, building reuse	X					X	X
	City center plans	X		X	X			
Increase livability	Community/urban gardens	X			X			
	Strong political leadership	X					X	X
	Economic benefits of environmental resources (environmental cba)		X				X	
	Plan implementation strategies			X			X	
Encourage regional cooperation	Regional tax-base sharing			X	X			
	Regional growth management/ infrastructure allocation			X	X			
	Regional coalitions	X			X		X	
	Standards to guide growth			X	X	X	X	
	Regional impact analysis			X			X	
	Funds for regional planning			X				X
Alter housing market	Location-efficient mortgages		X		X			X
	Energy-efficient mortgages		X		X			

Note: For implementation mechanisms, I = incentive based, M = market based, R = regulatory; for level of deployment, L = local government, R = regional, S = state, F = federal. For more information on each tool, see the appendix to this chapter.

Table 10.2. Smart growth tools: implementaton mechanism by primary purpose

Purpose	Implementation mechanism		
	Incentive based	Market based	Regulatory
Direct growth	Urban service areas, targeted development areas, infill, rezoning, transit-oriented/high-density development, expedited permitting, reuse funds	Transfer of development rights	Transit-oriented / high-density development, urban growth boundaries
Preserve land	Conversion taxes, density bonuses, clustered development, agricultural land conservation, performance zoning	Conservation easements, land acquisition, farmland easements	Voter controls, overlay restrictions, exactions, clustered development
Reduce auto dependence	Transit options, jobs-housing balance incentives		Work-at-home provisions, transportation funding policies
Control rate, amount of growth	Concurrency, litigation	Fiscal impact analysis	Commercial caps, residential caps, concurrency
Redesign communities	City-nature integration, sustainable communities, reuse funds, city-center plans		Sustainable communities, city-center plans
Increase livability	Community gardens, political leadership	Cost-benefit analysis	Plan implementation strategies
Encourage regional cooperation	Regional coalitions		Tax-base sharing, regional growth management, growth standards, regional impact analysis, regional plan funds
Alter housing market		Location-efficient mortgages, energy-efficient mortgages	

tools. A newer focus, increasing livability, is also represented evenly by all three kinds of mechanisms, perhaps because of the broad interest in and relatively large scope of ways to address this purpose. Other new foci, altering the housing market and redesigning communities, are addressed through the use of fewer tools and in more fragmented fashion. Table 10.2 also illustrates two interesting omissions: there are no market-based tools, such as parking pricing, to reduce automobile dependence; and tools to encourage regional cooperation are primarily regulatory only, possibly reflecting the need for mandates to overcome interjurisdictional competition.

Table 10.3 shows that most tools are implemented at the local government level, highlighting the differences between smart growth and regionalism. Whereas locally implemented tools are used to address all eight tool purposes, regionally based tools address only five purposes. This seems logical given the general propensity of local governments to focus resources and programs locally, even when the issues addressed are regional. Policies and programs from decentralized levels of government may be less attuned to the requirements for success in a particular jurisdiction. Although federally implemented tools address seven of the eight goals, there is typically only one tool for each, possibly reflecting the limits to mobilization of political support. It is interesting to note that efforts to encourage regional cooperation are implemented at every government level, indicating widespread understanding of the need for inter-jurisdictional cooperation. Finally, housing market tools reflect a change in historical policy and explicitly incorporate local-federal collaboration.

As Table 10.4 illustrates, local governments tend to use a mix of incentive-based and regulatory tools to achieve smart growth. This reflects local governments' strength—localities are better at providing incentives or passing ordinances than they are at modifying regional land markets. State and federal governments, which have broader geographic ranges of control, appear to use a balanced mix of all three kinds of tools. The low number of regionally implemented tools as well as the emphasis on regulatory implementation is not surprising given the general weakness of regional governments in the United States. Although federally implemented tools are limited in number, they address a wide range of purposes and consistently use money, either directly or indirectly via funding policy, to provide incentives, affect the market, or facilitate regulatory compliance. Although two federally implemented tools represent departures from historical national policy—changing transportation funding poli-cies and altering the housing market—both are undertaken with limited scope and pass much of their authority down to the local level, potentially limiting any positive results.

Smart Growth Appropriations

The smart growth tools classified in Tables 10.1–10.4 and enumerated in the appen-dix to this chapter demonstrate the enormous range of purposes as well as the methods to direct growth that smart growth has appropriated from other planning traditions. Steven Masura (2000), a redevelopment project analyst, defines smart growth very broadly:

Table 10.3. Smart growth tools: government implementation scale by primary purpose

Purpose	Implementation scale			
	Local	Regional	State	Federal
Direct growth	Urban service areas, infill, rezoning, targeted development areas, uban growth boundaries, transit-oriented/high-density development, expedited permitting, transfer of development rights	Urban growth boundaries	Urban growth boundaries, reuse funds	Reuse funds
Preserve land	Voter controls, overlay restrictions, clustered development, performance zoning, land acquisition	Voter controls, overlay restrictions, exactions, density bonuses, land acquisition	Conversion taxes, conservation easements, agricultural land conservation, land acquisition	Farmland easements
Reduce auto dependence	Work-at-home provisions	Work-at-home provisions, transit options	Work-at-home provisions, transit options, jobs-housing balance incentives	Transportation funding policies
Control growth	Residential caps, litigation	Commercial caps	Concurrency, fiscal impact analysis	Reuse funds
Redesign communities	City/nature integration, sustainable cities, city-center plans			
Increase livability	Community gardens		Environmental cost-benefit analysis, plan implementation strategies, political leadership	Political leadership
Encourage regional cooperation	Regional coalitions, growth standards	Tax-base sharing, regional infrastructure allocation, growth standards	Regional coalitions, growth standards, regional impact analysis	Regional plan funds
Alter housing market	Location-efficient mortgages, energy-efficient mortgages			Location-efficient mortgages

Table 10.4. Smart growth tools: implementation mechanism by government implementation scale

Implementation scale	Implementation mechanism		
	Incentive Based	Market Based	Regulatory
Local	Urban service areas, targeted development areas, infill, rezoning, transit-oriented/high-density development, expedited permitting, clustered development, performance zoning, city-nature integration, sustainable communities, reuse funds, city-center plans, litigation, community gardens, regional coalitions	Transfer of development rights, land acquisition, location-efficient mortgages, energy-efficient mortgages	Transit-oriented / high-density development, urban growth boundaries, overlay restrictions, voter controls, clustered development, work-at-home provisions, residential caps, sustainable communities, city-center plans, growth standards
Regional	Density bonuses, transit options	Land acquisition	Urban growth boundaries, overlay restrictions, voter controls, exactions, work-at-home provisions, commercial development caps, tax-base sharing, regional growth management, growth standards
State	Conversion taxes, agricultural land conservation easements, transit options, jobs-housing balance, concurrency, reuse funds, political leadership	Conservation easements, land acquisition, fiscal impact analysis, environmental cost-benefit analysis	Urban growth boundaries, work-at-home provisions, concurrency, plan implementation strategies, regional coalitions, growth standards, regional impact analysis
Federal	Political leadership, reuse funds	Farmland easements, location-efficient mortgages	Transportation funding policies, regional plan funds

"Growth" includes how we plan, implement plans, and build for physical, social, and economic needs, both in developed and undeveloped areas; and "smart" means we can do a better job of addressing growth that reduces regional environmental impacts and results in sustainable quality of life for everyone, i.e., planning and development that is more efficient, effective, equitable, balanced, less environmentally degrading, conserving of resources and open space, creative, adaptive to old and news areas, productive, fiscally sound, and provides more diversity of choice for living, learning, working, playing, and traveling. (5)

Consider the following examples. Urban gardens provide nutritious food to low-income households and enhance their food security, preserve urban green space, and expand carbon dioxide assimilation capacity. Urban growth boundaries define developable land as well as conserve open space and allocate limited resources more efficiently. Do these planning options constitute "smart growth"? Although smart growth tools are being credited as innovations for directing growth in desirable new ways, the reality is that many of the tools identified are not new at all—they have been in the urban planning or related tool kits for decades. In 1991, the Greater Pittsburgh Community Food Bank established the Sustainable Food System, teaching the principles and techniques of gardening and providing food to low-income households. Portland, Oregon, has had an urban growth boundary since 1979.

Smart growth's appropriated continuum of programs and policies (see Figure 10.2) embraces the range of choices available to address future growth and development

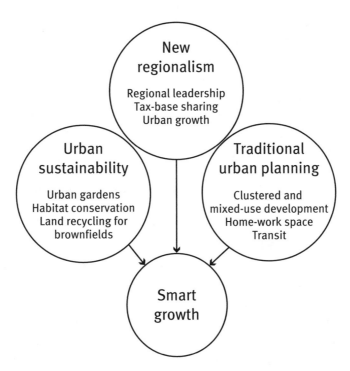

Figure 10.2. Examples of smart growth appropriations.

challenges (Urban Land Institute 2000). The tools are not new; only the rhetoric and unifying antisprawl impetus are new. This appropriation poses some serious limits to efficacy. The wide-ranging smart growth tools borrowed from urban sustainability and new regionalism are decoupled from those movements' demands for changed consumption and behavior, or equity, economic, or environmental underpinnings. Instead, they emphasize land use. The land-use focus of smart growth could work at cross-purposes with urban sustainability and regionalism and perpetuate inequalities associated with profits derived from land market transactions, as landowners and developers in favored areas continue to reap ever greater benefits stemming from their locational advantage alone. At the same time, although smart growth alone cannot be expected to achieve sustainability or regionalism, both of which incorporate greater considerations than simple land use, individual smart growth tools, acting as incremental steps toward change, may be more palatable than the calls for changes in consumer behavior and redistribution that characterize these other movements.

In sum, smart growth is a broadly defined, politically convenient concept, not a unifying movement. Today, individuals who invoke the term *smart growth* assume that it refers to their own normative ideologies or interpretations. Yet, as Downs (2001) notes, "smart growth should not mean the same thing everywhere" (25). The current dialogue on smart growth does not go far enough to uncover the inconsistencies among individual ideologies; smart growth encompasses developers who want to minimize risk in the development process as well as environmentalists who want to constrain development and preserve open space. As a movement, then, smart growth is currently stymied, because it covers a broad spectrum of conflicting viewpoints.

In order to transcend the limitations noted above and become a movement, smart growth advocates need to recognize what they share—desire for growth by design, not uncontrolled growth or a moratorium on all growth—and balance competing land-use interests across multiple situations and jurisdictions. Those who traditionally eschew compromise in the land-use arena—who believe the market is the sole arbiter of value, who feel the property owner alone is the best judge of how to develop his or her land, or who believe the natural environment should not be developed under any circumstances—will not support such a movement. Rather, it will attract pragmatists who are more concerned with finding mutually agreeable solutions than with fighting environmental protection requirements at all costs or holding out for no development at all.

Smart Growth in Southern California

Southern California seems both very appropriate and inappropriate for a smart growth movement. The region's increasing development and conservation pressures, and the spectrum of interested parties, are offset by political fragmentation, varying demographic and economic composition of regional communities, and the tendency of individual jurisdictions to compete to maximize their own advantages. Currently, smart growth in Southern California is more of a locally implemented response to sprawl concerns and development pressures than a unified regional movement.

Why would this region embrace smart growth but not the broader principles of urban sustainability and/or new regionalism? Several key constraints rooted in the area's politics and history make smart growth the easier option (Fulton 1997). First, since Proposition 13 was enacted in 1979, growth has been driven more by fiscal considerations than by the coordinated or proactive planning that forms the basis for a sustainable or regional community, and local jurisdictions compete for revenue-rich land uses and discourage construction and services that take a toll on the public coffers. In addition, rapid widespread growth of the Los Angeles region in the 1970s resulted in the establishment of numerous public agencies rather than a single strong regional planning body to satisfy water, transportation, waste management, and other service demands, and these agencies, as well as Southern California municipalities, cherish their independence and resist regional oversight.

Moreover, the vast metropolitan Los Angeles area is characterized by geographic and municipal dispersion of wealth and power, with undesirable land uses sited in less affluent communities in part because of a lack of organized opposition and in part because of these areas' critical need for any revenue source. Regional policy and planning work in Southern California in the past decade has focused primarily on economic efficiency rather than on a balance that includes environmental protection and improved social and economic equity (Pastor et al. 2000). Continued fiscally driven planning by numerous competitive agencies and jurisdictions is, without strong regional oversight, unlikely to change this trend.

Faced with these barriers to more fundamental reforms, Southern California jurisdictions, policy bodies, and politicians have hopped on the smart growth bandwagon. Not surprisingly, different proponents articulate different interpretations of smart growth. For example, environmental advocates borrow from urban sustainability and traditional urban planning, including new urbanism, to promote smart growth. The 2000 legislative platform of the California chapter of the American Planning Association (CAL-APA) recommends the use of general plan updates to accommodate smart growth, which CAL-APA describes as including everything from narrower streets and mixed use to habitat preserves and parks, to revitalized downtowns and reused brownfields.[10] The Sierra Club (2000) praises the Village Green housing development in Sylmar for its solar-powered, gas-fired heating and cooling system and its rail link. Citizen groups also use the concept of smart growth as a normative guide, as in the case of residents near the proposed site of Newhall Ranch, who formed the organization Santa Clarita Smart Growth "to slow the rapid pace of growth and encourage development and maintenance of a well-balanced, attractive and healthy place for all residents."[11] The California Public Employees Retirement System, which provides health services and retirement benefits to more than a million members in public agencies and school districts, has pledged to spend $100 million on smart growth projects, which it describes as "redirecting development and infrastructure investment in the existing [urban] core" in Southern California.[12] The Orange County Council of Governments has published two reports that advocate smart growth, interpreted as revitalizing downtowns, creating transit centers, preserving open space, and creating a sense of place as a way to balance the need for improved quality of life while accommodating demands for growth (see Bishop 2000, n.d.).

At the same time, the Los Angeles Department of Water and Power (LADWP) and the Southern California Building Industry Association (BIA) urge growth promotion to meet growing demands for single-family housing under a smart growth rubric. These advocates also borrow from planning and related fields, but even more explicitly use smart growth as a growth machine tool. The BIA Web site directs interested parties to the National Association of Home Builders Web site for that organization's "Statement of Policy on Smart Growth":

> In its broadest sense, Smart Growth means meeting the underlying demand for
> housing created by an ever-increasing population and prosperous economy by
> building a political consensus and employing market-sensitive and innovative land
> use planning concepts. . . . At the same time, Smart Growth means meeting that
> housing demand in "smarter ways" by planning for and building to higher densities,
> preserving meaningful open space and protecting environmentally-sensitive areas.[13]

NAHB's policy statement explicitly emphasizes the benefits of housing growth and an expanded tax base and criticizes those who use smart growth advocacy to slow or control growth.

The LADWP supports the Playa Vista development as a "sustainable, smart growth community" for its use of reclaimed water and solar-powered recharging station for electric buses, despite the fact that this massive new construction site is situated on and around the last remaining large coastal wetlands in Southern California.[14] As this example shows, some observers believe that growth is the ultimate solution to development pressures. Newhall Land and Farming Company, a major developer, promotes its planned Newhall Ranch—a proposed development of 12,000 acres of open space for 22,000 homes, an eighteen-hole golf course, and a fifteen-acre man-made lake in a floodplain in an area already plagued by poor traffic and air quality—as smart growth. Similarly, Newhall Land executives characterize Valencia, the company's new town on the urban fringe, as smart growth because of its transit service, clustered development, and neighborhood shopping opportunities.

The range of smart growth tools and their varied range of application in Southern California, as well as the underlying ideological positions of the advocates, indicate that there is no real unified smart growth movement in the region. Instead, smart growth is used to further local market preferences. At the same time, some advocates have situated themselves in the middle of the spectrum, relaxing more hard-line stances. Does this mean smart growth may be an answer for Southern California? It depends on who asks the question.

If one is primarily concerned with whether land-use tools can better direct growth, then smart growth as it stands now can improve land-use conditions in some parts of Southern California. Local examples of smart growth implementation indicate that the concept's strategic broad appeal has been exploited. Precisely because it is not a movement but rather a fragmented approach to growth, smart growth is well suited to this region's "increased opportunities through dispersion" (Hise, Dear, and Schockman 1996). Opposing parties characterize specific developments as either smart growth or not-smart growth to solidify support or opposition, and whereas the development industry uses smart growth to marshal support for increased single-family housing, others use it to illustrate a new paradigm in community design. Although smart growth has not created a single unified vision for development in Southern California, it has been used to unite sentiment at small, localized levels.

If one wants to know whether smart growth can provide a solution to the economic, environmental, and equity issues of Southern California, however, the answer is a qualified maybe. Recent successes of broad regional approaches to improving the quality of life in Southern California—from the Los Angeles Alliance for a New Economy's work to promote a citywide living wage to the Labor/Community Strategies Center's efforts to organize interested parties to sue the Metropolitan Transportation Authority for improved services—bode well for other widely supported regional efforts (Pastor et al. 2000). Smart growth has taken one of the steps identified as necessary to establish an equitable, efficient, environmentally sound regionwide agenda: it has amassed a broad advocacy base. Planners, developers, residents, business leaders, environmentalists, social advocates, and others who stand behind smart growth represent both suburbanites and city dwellers, transcending the geographic boundaries that typically divide local efforts (Rusk 1999).

What remains to be seen is whether the members of this informal coalition can unite and uncover mutually compatible aims that underlie their respective interests, such as assured property value and preserved wildlife habitat, both achieved via environmental preservation, or the strengthened workforce and greater work opportunities associated with greater social equity. Movement toward regional land-use decisions can increase fiscal equity by reducing wasteful competition between jurisdictions and improve cooperation, which may in turn yield broader social impacts (Orfield 2000). In this way, Southern California might exploit the superficial land-use orientation of smart growth to approximate an approach more aligned with new regionalism and urban sustainability.

Conclusion

This chapter has presented an analysis of smart growth through a typology of self-identified smart growth tools and comparisons with other planning trends. Although smart growth is indeed something that many support, its all-encompassing character weakens it as a movement to direct growth and change. Moreover, its widespread borrowing from other trends in planning limits its efficacy to land-use changes. Yet it is specifically the current fervor for smart growth that underscores this concept's potential to change the urban landscape, both nationally and perhaps especially in Southern California.

In our current information age, residents are more aware than they were in the past of the links between quality of life, including air and water quality and access to nature, and the effects of mass exurbanization. Moreover, in times of rapid economic

growth and consequent willingness to invest in growth-promoting urban infrastructure, residents observe firsthand the changes wrought—traffic congestion, air pollution,
and loss of open space. The planning lexicon and the positive connotations of the term
smart growth provide a way to classify any planning or land-use tool in a favorable
light and garner support for it. The majority of self-identified smart growth tools are
not new at all: what has changed is not the tools, but the rhetoric.

Furthermore, today many more regulations and regulatory agencies are involved
with land use and development than was the case in the past. Just as postwar models
of growth made metropolitan boosters anxious about opportunities for continued
expansion fifty years ago (Jonas and Wilson 1999), current zoning, permitting, and
environmental controls work against a purely decentralized land market while smart
growth tools both limit and generate growth by making more explicit the terms under
which a locality will allow development, reducing developer uncertainty.

These reflections are particularly appropriate in Southern California, where development and population pressures exacerbate the visible and varied effects of growth:
increased traffic, pollution problems, and battles over land development versus habitat and species preservation. Smart growth terminology has been appropriated for a
wide range of purposes and by a wide range of people and organizations in Southern
California, including national and state organizations, local politicians, local resident
groups, and planning departments and agencies. There is no escaping smart growth—
everyone knows about it and it seems to "work" for everyone. Masquerading as
something it is not, smart growth could provide a way for local organizations, which
have resisted regional coordination, to transcend the "tyranny of easy development
decisions"—easy because developers can readily transcend numerous competing local
government restrictions and develop at the urban fringe, where risk is predictable
and manageable (Lucy and Phillips 2000)—and expand the area's narrow land-use
and growth promotion focus to incorporate either the improved social equity and
environmental protection of the new regionalism or the limited resource consumption of urban sustainability.

Appendix: Smart Growth Tool Kit

Although smart growth seems to be everywhere, in that the types and impacts of
smart growth tools vary from one location to another, for purposes of this chapter I
sought out specific examples of smart growth tools implemented by government—
local, regional, state, and national—from published articles, professional documents,
Internet resources, and a limited number of planning practitioners.[15] Queries included
the term *smart growth* and therefore yielded tools that were so labeled. Examples of
implementation throughout the United States highlight smart growth's geographic
diversity. Although I did not include the new urbanism, per se, as a tool, as it is really
a movement in planning, several new urbanist tools (such as creating and maintaining city centers and providing housing near work) double as smart growth tools and
thus are included here. Although not exhaustive, this review is representative of the
current state of thinking about smart growth.

In this appendix, smart growth tools are categorized by their overall goals or purposes, such as to direct growth or encourage regional cooperation. I selected purpose as the salient classification characteristic as it transcends the specific opportunities or limitations of jurisdictions to design and implement tools and instead focuses on what implementing governments share—desired outcomes. The implementing level of government is noted for each tool (L = local, R = regional, S = state, F = federal), and a brief description is provided.

In addition to classifying the wide range of smart growth efforts, this typology underscores the import of smart growth tools. Although occasionally some smart growth tools, such as urban growth boundaries, yield long-term regional benefits, most smart growth tools are small-scale, locally implemented efforts. Most smart growth tools represent pragmatic solutions to localized land-use dilemmas; they have minimal impact on larger concerns of development because they fail to tackle the underlying problems that create sprawl, economic segregation, environmental injustice, skewed housing markets, and congestion.

A. *Tools to direct growth*
   1. Urban service areas (L, S): Fifteen cities in Silicon Valley, California, have identified land where they believe they can provide public services and therefore accommodate new development in those areas.
   2. Targeted development areas (L): Austin, Texas, uses a desired development zone and expedited permitting to target areas where development will be supported. The state of Maryland restricts state funds for roads, business, and economic and housing development to designated development areas. San Diego environmentalists, developers, and local government facilitate both desired development and desired land protection by identifying land available for land preservation or "as-of-right" development.[16]
   3. Infill development (L): California's Community Development Act of 1993 prohibits local redevelopment agencies from providing any direct assistance to retail projects that are located on five or more acres of land that have not previously been developed for urban purposes. Lancaster, California, encourages downtown investment through reduced fees.
   4. Rezoning (L): Contra Costa County in the San Francisco Bay Area rezoned an entire impoverished census tract to facilitate desired mixed-use development.
   5. Increased development density/transit-oriented development (L): Bay Area Rapid Transit stations in Contra Costa and Alameda Counties in the San Francisco Bay Area feature high-density housing, including affordable housing, and amenities such as coffee shops, restaurants, and health clubs.
   6. Expedited permitting (L): Jurisdictions offer simplified or shortened permitting and processing timelines to developers of projects in areas where such development is desired.
   7. Transfers of development rights (L): New Jersey and New York have created regional TDR programs for farmland protection to preserve New Jersey's Pinelands and Long Island Pine Barrens.[17]

8. Urban growth boundaries (L, R, S): Portland, Oregon, has used an urban growth boundary (UGB) since 1979 to target land for development. All land within the UGB is zoned for development, is assured links to public infrastructure, and enjoys expedited permit approval (and an appeals process, if necessary). In 1998, in the San Francisco Bay Area, residents of Cotati and Petaluma (Marin County), Milpitas (Santa Clara County), and Sonoma County approved UGBs and/or boundary ballot measures. In 1998, Ventura County voters passed a measure that provides the county with a two-pronged effort to manage growth, including implementation of UGBs.

9. Financial assistance to encourage reuse (S, F): Since 1995, the U.S. Environmental Protection Agency has provided more than $42 million to more than 227 communities for revitalization of abandoned or unused contaminated properties. The state of Maryland has several policies to spur redevelopment in specific areas, including limited liability paired with direct financial assistance to companies to clean up sites contaminated by others, a job creation tax credit for companies that create twenty-five or more jobs in targeted smart growth areas, "heritage" tax credits for redevelopment and reuse of historic structures, and low-interest (4 percent) mortgages for first-time home buyers who purchase homes in targeted smart growth areas. Minnesota's Metropolitan Livable Communities Act established a several-million-dollar program for the cleanup and redevelopment of contaminated urban sites.

B. *Tools to preserve land*

1. Voter control of land development (L, R): In 1998, Ventura County voters passed a measure that requires voter consent for development of unincorporated open space and farmland. Voters in four Ventura County cities supported similar measures that require voter approval to change city boundaries.

2. Sensitive lands overlay restrictions (L, R): Park City, Utah, and Summit County, Colorado, have imposed overlay regulations, or special development restrictions, in wetlands, wildlife habitats, ridgelands, and view corridors in excess of traditional development requirements.

3. Conversion taxes (S): To discourage land speculation, Vermont taxes at a rate of 80 percent the capital gains derived from land sales where the land has been held for less than four months and the gains exceed 200 percent of the initial value.

4. Exactions, land dedications, and impact fees (R): In Colorado, Adams County requires 20–25 percent land dedication for residential development, and El Paso County requires land dedication or cash-in-lieu for schools and parks.

5. Density bonuses for land conservation (R): Charlevoix County, Michigan, provides a density bonus to developers based on the amount of shoreline, ridgeland, or public road frontage that clustered development protects. Clallam County, Washington, on the Olympic Peninsula, permits landowners to develop at densities of one to five units per acre for clustered units or a minimum parcel size of thirty acres per unit if not clustered.

6. Clustered development (L): Southampton, New York, on Long Island, preserves scenic views and agricultural land by restricting new developments to 25 percent of the developable land per parcel.

7. Performance zoning (L): Fort Collins, Colorado, grants flexibility to developers and evaluates proposals based on quality of development as well as insulation of adjoining land uses from adverse impacts of development.

8. Transfer, sale, or donation of conservation easements (S): The state of California is considering legislation to expand the types of agencies that may be granted agricultural easements, including resource conservation, park, or open-space districts (AB1229), and to authorize credit against taxes assessed for land donations to government or nonprofit organizations for the purpose of protecting wildlife habitat, open space, or agricultural lands (SB680).

9. Open-space land acquisition (through taxes or bond authority) (L, R, S): Boulder, Colorado, voters approved sales taxes of 1.33 cents per dollar for the acquisition and maintenance of open space. Voters in Monroe County, Pennsylvania, approved a bond issue that will provide $25 million over ten years for the purchase of undeveloped land. Residents of Austin, Texas, supported increases in their water rates to fund the preservation of thousands of acres of environmentally sensitive land throughout the city. San Mateo and Santa Clara County residents voted in 1998 to expand the Mid-peninsula Regional Open Space District all the way to the coast, and Santa Cruz voters approved a $7 million bond that included an allocation of $1.7 million to pay for the purchase of greenbelt parkland. In 1990, the state of Florida enacted Preservation 2000 to provide $3 billion over ten years for the acquisition of conservation and recreation lands.

10. Agricultural land conservation incentives (S): Every state except Michigan uses a differential assessment program to assess farmland at its agricultural use value rather than fair market value, reducing local property tax bills and farmers' incentives to develop farmland. Michigan, New York, and Wisconsin permit farmers to take income tax credits against property taxes as a respite from taxes that exceed specified percentages of their income. Iowa provides a credit against school taxes for agricultural land. In all states, right-to-farm laws protect farmers from lawsuits by neighbors who move nearby after the agricultural operations are established and can prohibit local governments from placing unreasonable restrictions on agricultural land.

11. Provision of funds to preserve open space (F): The federal government has allocated funds for state and local governments to acquire title to or purchase easements to preserve farmland, open space, and wetlands.

C. *Tools to reduce auto dependence*

1. At-home work provisions (L, R, S): The Bucks County, Pennsylvania, Planning Commission created a home-based business ordinance for six of the fifty-four communities it serves. Escalon, California, facilitates home-based businesses with a simple two-page permit form.

2. Transit options (R, S): Portland, Oregon's, Metropolitan Area Express serves as a successful model of a thriving public transit system with high ridership and connections to bus and shuttle service. A regionally elected board sets transportation policies for the Portland area and guides new development.

3. Facilitating the provision of housing near work sources (S): The state of California allows landowners who are subject to agricultural preservation requirements to transfer up to five acres of land to a nonprofit or municipal corporation for the development and maintenance of farmworker housing, thereby providing much-needed housing on site (AB1505).

4. Changing transportation funding policies (F): The Transportation Equity Act for the Twenty-first Century expands federal transportation funding policies by broadening eligible uses and granting greater flexibility to local and metropolitan-area governments regarding fund use. The "Better America Bonds" program provides $700 million in federal tax credits allocated by the Environmental Protection Agency and is expected to generate $9.5 billion in state and local bonds for collaborative regional proposals to expand transit options.

D. *Tools to control rate/level of growth*

1. Commercial development size constraints (R): Calvert County, Maryland, limits the size of any single retail store to 30,000 square feet.

2. New residential development caps (L): In 1999 more than 240 jurisdictions nationwide considered antisprawl initiatives, including some that require voter approval before development permits may be issued for new subdivisions. Hudson, Ohio, planners and officials, citing water shortages, limit the number of new dwelling units to no more than 100 per year. Petaluma, California, limits the number of new residential unit approvals by the city council to no more than 1,500 in any consecutive three-year period, or an average of 500 per year (exempting senior and affordable housing and proposals for 30 or fewer units on five or fewer acres). Westminster, Colorado, limits annual water and sewer taps for residential development based on project design criteria.

3. Concurrency (S): The states of Florida and Washington require local governments to demonstrate that public facilities can adequately serve proposed development before they issue development permits. Montgomery County, Maryland, permits only those developers who can demonstrate their ability to pay the entire cost of new road construction to break ground.

4. Litigation (L): Towns neighboring Shelbourne, Vermont, sued Shelbourne, arguing that they would suffer the costs of a twenty-six-unit subdivision the city had approved.[18]

5. Fiscal impact analysis (S): The state of Colorado has produced a brochure and software program, "Small Town Guide to the Assessment of Growth and Development Activities," designed to help localities analyze the fiscal impacts of development projects through multiple methodologies.[19]

E. Tools to redesign communities

1. City/nature integration programs (L): Chattanooga, Tennessee, reclaimed the Tennessee River, which runs through downtown, and redeveloped the surrounding urban center as part of a community-led vision for a sustainable, desirable city. The rooftop of the Glynn Park Mall in Brunswick, Georgia, was modified to provide a habitat for nesting bird colonies in the southeast United States in response to the problem of dwindling wildlife habitats.

2. Creating/maintaining "sustainable communities" (L): The Civano-Tucson Solar Village, located on land owned by the Arizona State Land Department, will use solar energy, conserve water, and reduce waste. In California, the Santa Monica Sustainable City Program encourages use of nonhazardous materials and energy retrofit of city facilities.

3. Fund site/building reuse (S, F): The state of California has considered legislation to require the Department of Toxic Substances Control to prepare a report that identifies financial barriers to the restoration and reuse of contaminated property (SB324) and legislation that will provide tax relief and other financial incentives to parties that adapt and use existing buildings in designated urban areas (AB601).

4. Creating/maintaining town centers (including in edge cities) (L): City officials in Tyson's Corner, Virginia, have approved an approximately eighteen-acre grouping of small office and commercial uses and restaurants designed to replicate a traditional town center.[20]

F. Tools to increase livability

1. Creating community/urban gardens (L): The Greater Pittsburgh Community Food Bank developed the Green Harvest Sustainable Food System project in 1991 in order to teach gardening skills, provide low-income households with nutritious food, and involve youth in agricultural and environmental issues.[21]

2. Providing strong political leadership (S, F): Colorado Governor Roy Romer advertised smart growth as a primary direction for his state in an interview with *Europe* magazine just prior to the G7 Summit. Vice President Gore voiced smart growth themes in a September 2, 1998, speech: "In the future, livable communities will be the basis for our competitiveness and economic strength. Our efforts to make communities more livable today must emphasize the right kind of growth—sustainable growth." The principles of the California Futures Network, a statewide coalition of business, government, social, environmental, and agricultural leaders, promote a new development and conservation paradigm.[22]

3. Demonstrating economic benefits of the environment (S): The state of California has considered legislation to require the secretary of the state's Resources Agency to make findings regarding the environmental and economic benefits associated with watershed management as well as to implement a watershed management and restoration plan (AB730).

4. Attaching implementation strategies to plans (S): The state of California has considered requiring five-year capital outlay and infrastructure strategy reports and financing plans with the state's ten-year projections of capital and infrastructure needs as a way to connect identified need more closely to limited resources (SB915) as well as submission of a capital expenditure plan concurrent with the annual budget (SCA9).

G. *Tools to encourage regional cooperation*

1. Regional tax-based sharing (R, S): In Minneapolis–St. Paul, 40 percent of the increase in commercial or industrial property valuation in all 188 municipalities in the metro area is collected and redistributed based on population and per capita market value of property relative to the metro-area average. In New Jersey, tax-base sharing compensates jurisdictions for any negative financial impacts of land-use decisions made by a regional commission, such as land preserved for park purposes. The state of California prohibits the use of local public funds to subsidize relocation of big-box retailers or automobile dealerships within the same market area (AB178).

2. Regional growth management and infrastructure allocation (R): The San Diego Association of Governments serves as a lead agency to direct regional land-use planning in the San Diego area, as required by Proposition C and the creation of the Regional Growth Management Strategy, to which city and county plans must conform. Cape Cod, Massachusetts, uses a regional plan and commission to certify local plans for consistency with regional goals, to guide development, and to provide technical assistance, including sharing methodology for calculating carrying capacities.

3. Regional coalitions (L, S): Cleveland, Ohio, has developed a regional consortium in its older suburbs of city, civic, and business leaders to lobby state officials to focus resources in existing developed areas and roadways rather than construct new ones. The state of Georgia enacted a service delivery strategy in 1997 that requires every county to identify strategies for providing local government services and to resolve multijurisdictional land-use disputes.

4. Regional guidance/standards (L, R, S): Vermont's Environmental Commission reviews large-scale projects for conformance with state criteria. Florida requires state and regional approval of developments with regional impact, and local governments must demonstrate the adequacy of public facilities for proposed new development prior to approval and issuance of permits.[23] The action plan for the Treasure Valley area of Boise, Idaho, guides regional growth and development, links land use with transportation, reinforces the community's identity and sense of place, and protects and enhances open space and recreational options. The Utah Legislature Quality Growth Commission recommends areas for development based on the adequacy of infrastructure and administers the state's land conservation fund, including $32 million in legislature appropriations to acquire conservation easement. California prohibits cities and counties

from issuing permits for large subdivisions without local water conservation agency verification of adequacy of water to serve the proposed growth for at least twenty years (SB221).

5. Regional impact analysis (S): Florida, Vermont, Delaware, and Georgia have all implemented comprehensive review processes for projects expected to have regional impacts.

6. Funding for regional planning (F): The U.S. Department of Housing and Urban Development provides $50 million to match local funds spent to develop and implement smart growth strategies that involve two or more jurisdictions.

H. Tools to alter the housing market

1. Location-efficient mortgages (joint L/F): In a pilot program operating in Los Angeles and Chicago, the Federal National Mortgage Association (Fannie Mae) is allowing households that use mass transit to qualify for larger mortgages premised on smaller amounts of household income paid for transportation costs.

2. Energy-efficient mortgages (L): Baltimore Gas and Electric encourages construction of energy-efficient homes by offering marketing advantages to developers. Owners of energy-efficient homes pay proportionately less for utility costs than do owners of similar non-energy-efficient homes.

I. Non-government-sponsored examples of smart growth

This chapter focuses on government-sponsored and -implemented smart growth tools, but many private and nonprofit organizations, as well as individuals, have created and implemented such tools as well. For example, Sienna Architecture in Portland redesigns existing buildings to add floors to the tops of structures, modify basements to accommodate parking, and turn warehouses into needed residential space. The Nursing and Biomedical Science Building at the University of Texas at Houston provides 250,000 square feet in the form of an adaptable design, including clear-span structure, modular partitioning, and accessible floor plenums. The California Center for Land Recycling provides technical assistance and competitive grants of up to $25,000 to organizations that are redeveloping brownfields and other urban areas throughout California. In Chicago, the independent nonprofit Metropolitan Planning Council and Campaign for Sensible Development has published a guidebook of best development practices.[24]

Notes

1. The term *growth machine* refers to the collective efforts of place entrepreneurs, local government, businesspersons, political leaders, landowners, and others to create conditions that will attract development and promote local growth.

2. Albert Einstein, quoted at Stop Legacy Highway, http://www.stoplegacyhighway.org.

3. Energy-efficient mortgages assume that residents of units with energy-saving devices spend lower proportions of their income or revenue on utility costs. Scribcor, a real estate investment and management firm, increased the value of a suburban Chicago office building by

$1.3 million by improving its energy efficiency at a capital cost of $300,000 and with annual utility savings of $130,000. Green Clips.121.06.02.99, http://www.greendesign.net (accessed July 10, 1999).

4. See AB730 at California Senate Web site, http://www.sen.ca.gov (accessed June 22, 1999).

5. Interview of Parris Glendening by William Fulton.

6. Although the principles of the Charter for New Urbanism, as well as many of its proponents, call for a comprehensive approach to planning, the term *new urbanism* is often popularly used to refer to the design characteristics of a community.

7. At the same time, others assert that smart growth increases affordability, mainly through increased density and greater diversity of housing types in a given urban area.

8. See http://www.ahmansonland.com (accessed July 13, 2002) and http://www.ahmanson. org (accessed July 13, 2002).

9. Interviews with project opponents at the Playa Vista site, January 2002.

10. See CAL-APA's legislative platform, http://www.calapa.org/legislation/legrfc.htm.

11. See "About SC Smart Growth," http://www.scsmartgrowth.org/About.html. Village Green's design and amenities are estimated to reduce utility bills by 50–70 percent through the use of energy-efficient clothes washers and dryers as well as walls and windows with extra insulation; see http://www.biasc.org/SCBuilder/99magazines.

12. See the California Public Employees Retirement System Web site, http://www.CalPers. org/whatsnew/press/1999.

13. See the NAHB Web site, http://www.nahb.com/mainfeatures/smartpolicy.htm. This site's links to state and local associations include one to the Southern California BIA at http://www. biasc.org.

14. See LADWP, "Playa Vista/DWP Pact Advances Water Conservation and Alternative Energy," press release, May 16, 2000, http://www.ladwp.com/whatnew/dwpnews/051600.htm; and "Current Information: Dreamworks Pulls Out of the Proposed Playa Vista Development!" at http://ballona.org.News.html.

15. I discuss a handful of tools implemented by nonprofit organizations at the end of this appendix. The research reported here was conducted during the period June–August 1999.

16. Note that this vital process—the Natural Community Conservation Planning/multi-species planning process—has its roots in the Endangered Species Act, not in smart growth, although the Urban Land Institute has identified it as an example of smart growth.

17. TDRs are created by local ordinance to allow development rights to be separated from the land and sold to property owners in areas considered more desirable for growth.

18. Although this example of litigation was given as an example of smart growth, the legal system has always provided a way for dissatisfied citizens to fight questionable development practices, and hence it does not have its genesis in smart growth.

19. Colorado's guide advises localities to ensure that the revenue from new development, including tax revenue, is sufficient to meet or exceed the costs of infrastructure development, maintenance, and service that the proposed development will incur. Note that this can work against equity in the case of services and affordable housing.

20. Price Waterhouse has identified features required for "24-hour central cities," including mixed use for a diversified tax base, secure environment, access to mass transit, attractive and affordable housing, retail and entertainment services, high-quality office space, civic and cultural uses, hotels, parking, and a convention center (Petersen in Urban Land Institute 1998, 51).

21. Community gardens are another tool that local implementing governments identify as smart growth although they have a much earlier genesis than this movement.

22. The Rouse Enterprise Foundation has identified three components that are vital for successful investment in an urban area: good, committed leadership; honest government; and a willingness of the public and private sectors to work together (Petersen in Urban Land Institute 1998, 47). Political leadership, like litigation, is a tool with a long history and broad use that is currently being co-opted by the smart growth movement.

23. One unpredictable consequence of this requirement was that new development was propelled to rural areas. Hence the state has revised the adequacy requirement to reflect a review of the level of service available and required with the proposed development.

24. Sources for information on the tools described in this appendix are as follows: Urban Land Institute (1998) (A1, A2, B9, B10, D3, G2, G3, G4, G5, H1, I); O'Malley (1998) (A2, A6, D1, D2, D3); Lacayo (1999) (A2, A8, B1, D2, D4, E4); Froehlich (1998) (A2, A3, G3); Moe (1996) (A3, A8, D1); "Farmland Protection Toolbox," http://www.farm.fic.niu.edu (accessed July 10, 1999) (A6, B10); "Langdon," www.builderonline.com (accessed June 8, 1999) (A8, I); "Reinventing Environmental Protection," http://epa.gov (accessed July 11, 1999) (A9); "ECOS/AASHTO Conference on Smart Growth Proceedings," http://www.smartgrowth.org (accessed June 8, 1999) (A9); "Best Practices," http://www.rri.org (accessed July 9, 1999) (A9, E1); "White Paper on Smart Growth," http://www.state.co.us/smartgrowth/whalltls.htm (accessed July 9, 1999) (B2–B7, D2, D5); California State Senate Web site, http://www.sen.ca.gov (accessed June 1999 and October 2001) (B8, C3, E3, F3, F4, G1, G4); League of Women Voters Web site, http://bcn.boulder.co.us/lwv (accessed July 10, 1999) (B9); Bennett (1999) (C1); "Sprawl Solutions: Smart Growth," http://www.sierraclub.org (accessed July 10, 1999) (B9); Browner in "Partners for Smart Growth Conference," http://www.smartgrowth.org/library/gore_bonds.html (accessed October 8, 1999) (B11, C1); Peirce (1999) (C2); Peter Fimrite at *San Francisco Chronicle* Web site, http://www.sfchronicle.com (accessed September 14, 1998) (C2); Brauer (1999) (H1); U.S. House of Representatives Web site, http://www.house.gov/transportation/bestea/tea21sum.htm (accessed October 8, 1999) (C4); Peirce (1998) (C4); City of Petaluma (1991) (D2); Youth (1999) (E1); President's Council on Sustainable Development, http://www.whitehouse.gov/PCSD (accessed July 10, 1999) (E2, F1); Sprawl Watch Clearinghouse Web site, http://www.sprawlwatch.org (accessed July 10, 1999) (G1); American Planning Association (1998) (G1); "State Incentive Based Growth Management Laws," http://www.ncsl.org (accessed July 10, 1999) (G4); "Clinton-Gore Livability Agenda," http://www.smartgrowth.org/library/gore_pr11199.html (accessed July 1999) (G6); Green Clips.121.06.02.99 (H2), 111.01.13.99 (H2, I), at http://www.greendesign.net (accessed July 10, 1999); "CFN Email Update #2" (F2), "CFN Email Update #5" (F2), "CFN Email Update #10" (A8, B1, B9), "Land Use Lines" (I), http://www.cfn@nextgeneration.org (accessed various dates, 1998–99).

Works Cited

Abbott, Carl. 1997. "The Portland Region: Where City and Suburbs Talk to Each Other and Often Agree." *Housing Policy Debate* 8(1):11–53.

American Planning Association. 1998. *Growing Smart Legislative Guidebook: Model Statutes for Planning and the Management of Change.* Phases I and II interim ed. Chicago: American Planning Association.

Bennett, Julie. 1999. "Homebodies: Zoning Rushes to Catch Up with Home-Based Businesses." *Planning*, May, 10–15.

Bishop, Richard. 2000. "Here Comes the Neighborhood: Orange County, California." Prepared by RBB Policy Research and Planning, Santa Ana, CA, for presentation to the Orange County Council of Governments, June.

———. n.d. "Smart Growth Strategies to Accommodate Orange County's Future." Prepared by RBB Policy Research and Planning, Santa Ana, CA, for presentation to the Orange County Council of Governments.

Brauer, David. 1999. "Wheel Estate: New Mortgages Reward the No-Car Family." *Utne Reader*, July–August, 20–21.

Burchell, Robert W., David Listokin, and Catherine Galley. 2000. "Smart Growth: More than a Ghost of Urban Policy Past, Less than a Bold New Horizon." *Housing Policy Debate* 11(4):821–79.

City of Petaluma. 1991. "Residential Growth Management System User's Guide." September.

DiLorenzo, Thomas J. 2000. "The Myth of Urban Sprawl." *USA Today* 128 (2660):54–56.

Downs, Anthony. 2001. "What Does Smart Growth Really Mean?" *Planning*, April, 20–25.

Downs, Anthony, Arthur C. Nelson, and William A. Fischel. 2002. "Have Housing Prices Risen Faster in Portland than Elsewhere?" *Housing Policy Debate* 13(1):7–31.

Easterbrook, Gregg. 1999. Comments on "Retracting Suburbia: Smart Growth and the Future of Housing." *Housing Policy Debate* 10(3):513–40.

Froehlich, Maryann. 1998. "Smart Growth: Why Local Governments Are Taking a New Approach to Managing Growth in Their Communities." *Public Management* 80(5):5–9.

Fulton, William. 1997. *The Reluctant Metropolis: The Politics of Urban Growth in Los Angeles.* Point Arena, CA: Solano.

Growth/No Growth Alert. 1999. "How to Stop Sprawl in New Orleans." Vol. 2(11):3.

Harrison, Bennett. 1998. "It Takes a Region (or Does It?): The Material Basis for Metropolitanism and Metropolitics." Paper prepared for the conference Urban-Suburban Interdependence: New Directions for Research and Policy, cosponsored by the Great Cities Institute of the University of Illinois–Chicago, the Lincoln Institute of Land Policy, and the Center on Urban and Metropolitan Policy at the Brookings Institution, September.

Hise, Greg, Michael J. Dear, and H. Eric Schockman. 1996. "Rethinking Los Angeles." In *Rethinking Los Angeles*, ed. Michael J. Dear, H. Eric Schockman, and Greg Hise. Thousand Oaks, CA: Sage.

Hollis, Linda E. 1998. "Smart Growth and Regional Cooperation." In *ULI on the Future: Smart Growth: Economy, Community, Environment*, 36–45. Washington, DC: Urban Land Institute.

Jonas, Andrew E. G., and David Wilson. 1999. "The City as Growth Machine: Critical Reflections Two Decades Later." In *The Urban Growth Machine: Critical Perspectives Two Decades Later*, ed. Andrew E. G. Jonas and David Wilson. Albany: State University of New York Press.

Lacayo, Richard. 1999. "The Brawl over Sprawl." *Time*, March 22, 44–48.

Logan, John R., and Harvey L. Molotch. 1987. *Urban Fortunes: The Political Economy of Place.* Berkeley: University of California Press.

Lucy, William H., and David L. Phillips. 2000. *Confronting Suburban Decline: Strategic Planning for Metropolitan Renewal.* Washington, DC: Island.

Masura, Steven M. 2000. "Smart Growth: Missing Links and Next Steps." *American Planning Association California Planner*, March/April.

Moe, Richard. 1996. "Growing Smarter: Fighting Sprawl and Restoring Community in America." Address presented at San Joaquin Valley Town Hall, Fresno, CA, November 20.

O'Malley, Sharon. 1998. "Sprawl: Smart Growth." *Builder* 21(9):90, 96, 98.

Orfield, Myron. 2000. *Los Angeles Metropatterns: Social Separation and Sprawl in the Los Angeles Region.* Minneapolis, MN: Metropolitan Area Research Council.

Pastor, Manuel, Jr., Peter Dreier, J. Eugene Grigsby III, and Marta López-Garza. 2000. *Regions That Work: How Cities and Suburbs Can Grow Together.* Minneapolis: University of Minnesota Press.

Peirce, Neal. 1998. "Gore Rx: Fight Sprawl with Billions + Coalitions." In "The Washington Post Writers Group," npeirce@citistates.com, January 17.

———. 1999. "Rapid Rail for Intercity Corridors: Way beyond Choo-Choo Nostalgia." In "The Washington Post Writers Group," npeirce@citistates.com, May 16.

Porter, Douglas R. 1998. "The States: Growing Smarter?" In *ULI on the Future: Smart Growth: Economy, Community, Environment,* 28–35. Washington, DC: Urban Land Institute.

Rusk, David. 1999. *Inside Game, Outside Game.* Washington, DC: Brookings Institution.

Sierra Club. 2000. *Smart Choices or Sprawling Growth: A 50-State Survey of Development.* San Francisco: Sierra Club Foundation.

Soja, Edward W., and Allen J. Scott. 1996. "Introduction to Los Angeles: City and Region." In *The City: Los Angeles and the End of the Twentieth Century,* ed. Allen J. Scott and Edward W. Soja, 5–12. Berkeley: University of California Press.

Stroup, Richard. 2000. "Planning versus Market Solutions." In *A Guide to Smart Growth,* ed. Jane S. Shaw and Ronald D. Utt, 17–27. Washington, DC: Heritage Foundation.

Summers, Anita A. 1998. "Regionalization Efforts between Big Cities and Their Suburbs: Rhetoric and Reality." Paper prepared for the Conference of Central Cities and Suburbs: Current Knowledge and New Research Directions, September.

Urban Land Institute. 1998. *ULI on the Future: Smart Growth: Economy, Community, Environment.* Washington, DC: Urban Land Institute.

———. 2000. *Smart Growth Myth and Fact.* Washington, DC: Urban Land Institute.

Wackernagel, Mathis, and William E. Rees. 1996. *Our Ecological Footprint: Reducing Human Impact on the Earth.* Gabriola Island, BC: New Society.

Wheeler, Stephen. 2002. "The New Regionalism: Characteristics of an Emerging Movement." *Journal of the American Planning Association* 68(3):267–78.

Youth, Howard. 1999. "Unusual Habitats." *National Wildlife* 37(4):18–19.

11 | Living on the Edge: Growth Policy Choices for Ventura County

Christine M. Ryan, John P. Wilson, and William Fulton

The economic development and land-use policies pursued in Southern California throughout most of the twentieth century encouraged rapid population growth and urbanization of land. The five counties of Southern California—Los Angeles, Orange, Riverside, San Bernardino, and Ventura—currently support sixteen million people, a sevenfold increase since 1900. This growth shows no signs of waning, with the five counties adding two million people during the 1990s.

As a consequence, the conversion of pristine habitat and agricultural land to urban development has been rapid. This land conversion pattern is "spatially organized around the assumptions of the suburban era: that it serves a middle-class suburban population engaged in a middle-class suburban economy; that the supply of buildable land is practically unlimited"—that "Los Angeles has grown by moving on to 'the next valley'" (Southern California Studies Center 2001, 1, 2). However, this pattern has exerted considerable pressure on the region's resources, including its land resources. Most of Southern California's considerable agricultural land resources have been lost to urban development in the past fifty years. Much new "greenfield" development now occurs on natural land that was never converted to agriculture and, therefore, still contains significant natural resources, such as wetlands and wildlife. In particular, because of the region's varied topography and microclimates, Southern California is home to more endangered species (including many birds) and ecosystems than any other part of the country, and most of these resources are at risk because of urban development pressure.

As a result, policy makers and planners have been forced to reassess traditional development scenarios as they address future urban growth inside their borders. Increased awareness of the environmental consequences of growth has promoted future scenarios that incorporate the concepts of "urban sustainability," "regionalism," and "smart growth" in numerous jurisdictions. In chapter 10 of this volume, Gearin reviews the potential for these overlapping yet distinct concepts to improve our understanding and management of urban systems.

Local governments in Southern California have been at the forefront of attempts to manage urban growth for more than twenty years, using a variety of techniques, including overall restrictions on numbers of houses, downzoning, and—more recently—urban growth boundaries, which seek to use planning and regulatory mechanisms to direct urban growth to specific areas. However, these are local policy regimes that have responded mostly to local concerns rather than to large-scale landscape concerns (Glickfeld et al. 1999). At the other end of the spectrum, the federal and state Endangered Species Acts have forced the creation of large-scale conservation plans (known as habitat conservation plans and/or Natural Community Conservation Plans) designed to protect endangered species and habitats with little concern for the impact on human settlement patterns (see Pincetl, chapter 8, this volume).

Thus, even as Southern California has begun to use a variety of tools and techniques to manage urbanization, these tools and techniques have not been adopted or implemented in the context of a policy analysis framework that truly examines their impact. We undertook the study presented in this chapter to provide a "starting point" for such analysis.

We examined the likely impacts of different future land development scenarios on land-cover and land-use types in Ventura County, the county that has the smallest population, the strongest agricultural sector, and the most aggressive growth management regulations in Southern California. It was our hope that by modeling future urban growth in one county under different policy scenarios, we could assist policy makers in the region in examining and discussing the impacts that growth management policies are having—or could have—on urbanization in Southern California.

To examine this impact, we adapted Landis et al.'s (1998) California Urban and Biodiversity Analysis (CURBA) model, which was originally developed for Northern California. The research aimed to answer two empirical questions:

1. How is the spatial pattern of growth likely to vary under different local policy constraints if the population increases by 25 percent during the next fifteen to thirty years?
2. How would different policy scenarios affect the amounts of agricultural and environmentally sensitive land that would be consumed for new urbanization?

In modeling and analyzing six different growth policy scenarios for the future of Ventura County, we found the following:

- Different policy scenarios would have dramatic effects on the distribution of the county's future growth, both between farmland and habitat land and among the different geographic areas within the county.

- The current system of urban growth boundaries may permit the county to accommodate future growth without increasing densities, but it does not guarantee the protection of all important farmland and habitat land.
- Loss of farmland and habitat land could be minimized within the context of the current urban growth boundaries, but only if future urbanization occurs at ten persons per urbanized acre rather than the current seven.
- Any policy changes to alter the future growth pattern will require difficult trade-offs involving farmland, critical habitat areas, urban density, and the timing of future growth.

Urbanization Pressure and Growth Management in Ventura County

Ventura County is located northwest of Los Angeles County and south of Santa Barbara County. Its landscapes include coastal lowlands, wide river valleys, mountain ranges, and a dry inland desert. Elevations extend from sea level to approximately four thousand feet. Agriculture is confined to the river valleys and coastal lowlands. Substantial parts of these landscapes and the nearby gently rolling hills have been developed over the past century. Woodlands are now confined to riparian areas and chaparral to the steeper, dry areas that are often associated with publicly owned lands and protected open space.

The human occupation of Ventura County is typical of early California. Spanish explorers replaced Indian settlements with missions and ranchos, and these institutions were broken up when Americans turned to agriculture (Nunis 1993). The northern two-thirds of the county was placed in Los Padres National Forest. The remaining one-third (approximately 550,000 acres) was originally devoted mostly to agriculture, oil exploration, and towns designed to support both activities. The county spawned a series of vibrant towns such as Ventura, Oxnard, and Santa Paula, each with its own unique characteristics and without the hustle of neighboring Los Angeles County. The Oxnard Plain became an important agricultural area, producing sugar beets, lima beans, lemons, walnuts, avocados, strawberries, and vegetables. Oil was also discovered in the late 1800s, and its production, which peaked in the early 1900s, brought additional prosperity. Military bases were established at Point Mugu and Port Hueneme (Nunis 1993).

Further changes occurred when the Ventura Freeway (U.S. Highway 101) was extended into the Conejo Valley and across the coastal plain in the 1960s. Cities in the eastern part of the county, such as Thousand Oaks and Simi Valley, developed quickly beginning in the 1960s, when they emerged as commuter suburbs for the adjacent San Fernando Valley. More recently, they have experienced increased job and income growth due to an influx of high-technology businesses (Southern California Studies Center 2001).

Ventura County is also unique in Southern California in terms of its approach to growth. Beginning in the early 1970s, the county and its cities took strong steps to channel urban growth into cities and protect agricultural land in unincorporated areas. By agreeing on the so-called Guidelines for Orderly Development (GOD) and a series of greenbelts between cities, the county and its cities traditionally sought to contain urban development within cities' sphere of influence (SOI) boundaries but permitted those boundaries to expand as new urban development was required.[1] Agricultural zoning was retained in most unincorporated areas, and most agricultural landowners also participated in California's Williamson Act program, which provides lower property taxes in exchange for long-term commitments to retain undeveloped land in agriculture.

No other county in Southern California has used such consistent and wide-ranging growth management techniques for such a long period of time. Between 1970 and 1990, Ventura County accommodated a 50 percent increase in population growth (from 449,000 to 669,000 persons) while maintaining a significant agricultural base of more than 100,000 cultivated acres, mostly in row crops such as lettuce and strawberries and tree crops such as lemons and avocados. These agricultural areas are located mostly in the western part of the county, on the Oxnard Plain and in the Santa Clara River Valley.

In the eastern part of the county, growth management techniques—as well as open-space acquisition efforts—have also played an important role in shaping urban growth and protecting undeveloped areas. Much of the eastern part of the county is rangeland rather than cultivated agriculture, but the agriculture and open-space zoning controls have been applied there as well. Most of the remainder is environmentally sensitive wildland in the Santa Monica Mountains and related areas such as the Simi Hills, which have considerable habitat value.

Much of this land has been acquired by public agencies such as the National Park Service, which has placed some 150,000 acres into permanent open-space protection as part of the Santa Monica Mountains National Recreation Area since that entity was formed in 1978. (The Recreation Area straddles the Los Angeles and Ventura County lines, and most of the land acquired has been in Los Angeles County.) However, large areas of the Santa Monica Mountains remain in private hands, and their development in the future may threaten the viability of the protected areas. Local open-space districts also protect land in the eastern part of the county.

The result of all these efforts is a county that is both urban and rural, with a distinctive spatial structure. As of 2000, the county's population was approximately 753,000 persons. Ventura County has no dominant central city. Four cities (Oxnard, Simi Valley, Thousand Oaks, and Ventura) have populations of at least 100,000 persons, but no city is larger than 160,000 (Oxnard) (Table 11.1).

Of the 556,080 acres of land not included in Los Padres National Forest, in 2000 approximately 105,750 acres (19 percent) were developed, 46,380 acres (8.3 percent) were permanently protected open space, 112,580 acres (20.2 percent) were cultivated agriculture, 178,290 acres (32.1 percent) were undeveloped land with a slope of 25 percent or more, 23,350 acres (4.2 percent) were floodplain or wetlands, and the remaining 89,730 acres (16.1 percent) consisted of other private undeveloped land, mostly rangeland (Table 11.2).

Recent trends—that is, trends in the county from 1986 through 2000—suggest that the county's growth patterns are fairly stable, therefore providing a useful basis for a trend-based model such as CURBA.[2] The county grew from a population of 604,000 to 756,000 during this period, an increase of about 150,000 persons, or 25 percent.[3] The largest percentage population increase came in Moorpark, where population almost doubled during this period (Table 11.1). However, the amount of urbanized land or land designated for urbanization increased by 31.5 percent countywide during this period, increasing from about 80,000 to 105,000 acres (Figure 11.1). Of this amount, approximately 97,000 acres had actually been fully converted to urban use by the year 2000, and approximately 8,000 additional acres had been designated for urban use or were in the process of being converted at that time. Again, Moorpark led the county with about a 100 percent increase in urban land between 1986 and 2000 (Table 11.3).[4]

At the beginning of the study period (1986), the urban density for the county as a whole was 7.52 persons per urbanized acre (604,000 people living on 80,000 urbanized acres). During this period, the county's population grew by 150,000 persons and the urbanized land acreage grew by approximately 25,000, for a "marginal" urban density of 6 persons per acre. Thus by the end of the study period (2000), overall urban density had declined to 7.15 persons per urbanized acre (Table 11.1).

This urbanized land acreage figure does include some land that was designated for urbanization but had not been completely converted to urban use by 2000, such as the controversial Ahmanson Ranch property, which was approved for development in 1992 but had not started construction as of 2002, and considerable acreage in the northern part of Simi Valley. If these lands are removed (as Ahmanson Ranch was in 2003), the density figures change: marginal density is about 9 persons per urbanized acre rather than 6, and overall density increases slightly (from 7.52 to 7.80 persons per urbanized acre), rather than declines.

For purposes of this chapter, we have chosen to use the figure of 105,000 acres of land that is either urbanized or designated for urbanization. We checked the 300 additional parcels in the field and believe this to be the most accurate figure available

Table 11.1. Ventura County population totals and densities by political unit, 1986–2000

Political unit	1986 Population	2000 Population	Population change (%)	1986 density (persons per acre)	2000 density (persons per acre)	% Change in density, 1986–2000
Camarillo	46,100	63,300	37.3	7.06	7.12	0.8
Fillmore	11,000	13,250	20.5	12.03	11.63	−3.3
Moorpark	15,250	29,750	95.1	5.89	5.52	−6.3
Ojai	7,475	8,250	10.4	3.45	3.79	10.0
Oxnard	129,200	160,300	24.1	12.41	12.36	−0.4
Port Hueneme	19,750	23,500	19.0	7.33	8.58	17.1
Santa Paula	23,750	27,250	14.7	11.16	11.90	6.6
Simi Valley	88,500	113,000	27.7	7.47	8.49	13.7
Thousand Oaks	96,100	120,700	25.6	6.98	6.87	−1.5
Ventura	86,700	103,500	19.4	8.47	9.38	10.7
Unincorporated	80,500	93,600	16.3	4.71	3.31	−29.6
Totals	604,325	756,400	25.2	7.52	7.15	−4.8

Table 11.2. Landownership, land use, and environmental characteristics in nonurban areas of Ventura County by political unit, 2000

Political unit	2000 Nonurban land (acres)	Public land		Farmland		Slope < 25%		Floodplain		Wetland		Remainder	
		acres	%	acres	%	acres	%	acres	%	acres	%	acres	%
Camarillo	2,891	0	0.0	2,086	72.1	250	8.6	96	3.3	2	0.1	457	15.8
Fillmore	635	0	0.0	237	37.4	96	15.2	183	28.8	0	0.0	119	18.7
Moorpark	2,600	0	0.0	84	3.2	25	1.0	195	7.5	17	0.7	2,278	87.6
Ojai	425	0	0.0	109	25.6	0	0.0	59	14.0	0	0.0	257	60.5
Oxnard	4,174	0	0.0	2,790	66.8	0	0.0	445	10.7	91	2.2	848	20.3
Port Hueneme	54	0	0.0	0	0.0	0	0.0	47	86.4	0	0.0	7	13.6
Santa Paula	662	0	0.0	193	29.1	17	2.6	366	55.2	0	0.0	86	13.1
Simi Valley	8,009	566	7.1	32	0.4	3,022	37.7	287	3.6	12	0.2	4,090	51.1
Thousand Oaks	14,204	8,738	61.5	30	0.2	1,203	8.5	64	0.5	7	0.1	4,161	29.3
Ventura	1,967	205	10.4	534	27.1	558	28.4	306	15.6	12	0.6	351	17.8
County	414,719	36,868	8.9	106,490	25.7	173,122	41.7	18,264	4.4	2,896	0.7	77,080	18.6
Total	450,340	46,377	10.3	112,584	25.0	178,294	39.6	20,312	4.5	3,039	0.7	89,734	19.9

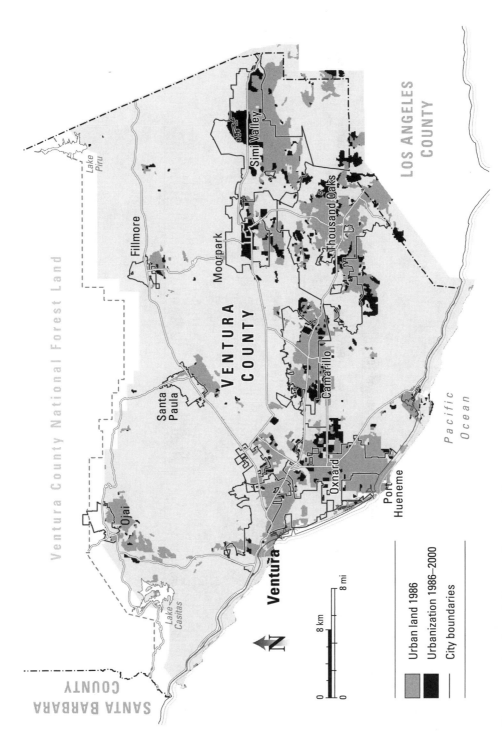

Figure 11.1. Land use in Ventura County, 1986–2000.

Table 11.3. Distribution of urban land in Ventura County by political unit, 1986 and 2000

Political unit	1986 Total land area (acres)	1986 Urban land area (acres)	Percentage urban 1986	Increase in urban land area 1986–2000 (acres)	Percentage increase in urban land area, 1986–2000
Camarillo	11,782	6,529	55.4	2,362	36.2
Fillmore	1,774	914	51.5	225	24.6
Moorpark	7,989	2,587	32.4	2,802	108.3
Ojai	2,600	2,167	83.4	7	0.3
Oxnard	17,142	10,413	60.7	2,555	24.5
Port Hueneme	2,792	2,693	96.5	44	1.7
Santa Paula	2,953	2,128	72.1	163	7.7
Simi Valley	21,318	11,854	55.6	1,455	12.3
Thousand Oaks	31,768	13,776	43.4	3,788	27.5
Ventura	13,000	10,233	78.7	801	7.8
Subtotal for Cities	113,117	63,294	56.0	14,204	22.4
Unincorporated	441,370	17,107	3.9	11,144	65.1
Totals	554,487	80,401	14.5	25,348	31.5

for urban land as of 2000, at least so far as modeling future growth patterns is concerned. It would be inaccurate to regard this land as not urbanized in our modeling, as the land is already "spoken for" in terms of urbanization. In addition, there is always a time lag between urbanization of land and the actual arrival of new urban population on that land.

The highest densities in 2000 were found in the county's three predominantly Latino cities (Fillmore, Oxnard, and Santa Paula), all of which had densities in excess of 11 persons per urbanized acre (Table 11.1).[5] The lowest densities were in Ojai and the unincorporated area. Using a somewhat different methodology, a study by Solimar Research Group and the Brookings Institution found that the national urban density in 1997 was 3.55 persons per urbanized acre, while the figure for the five-county Los Angeles area (including Ventura County) was 8.31 persons per urbanized acre (Fulton et al. 2001). Thus Ventura County appears to be developed at a slightly lower density than the remainder of Southern California.

Examining the use of land inside cities, we found that 56 percent of land inside city limits was urbanized in 1986 (compared with 3.9 percent in the unincorporated area). The highest percentage urbanized occurred in Port Hueneme, which is completely surrounded by Oxnard. The lowest percentage urbanized occurred in Moorpark, but this figure more than doubled between 1985 and 2000 (Table 11.3).

The vast majority of nonurban land is located in unincorporated county territory. However, Camarillo and Oxnard each had more than 2,000 acres of farmland inside their city limits in 2000. Simi Valley had more than 3,000 acres of steeply sloped land, and Thousand Oaks had approximately 8,700 acres of land in permanent open space—more than 60 percent of the nonurban land in the city (Table 11.2).

These were the patterns and trends that emerged from the growth management and open-space protection system that was in place in Ventura County from the early 1970s until the late 1990s. Beginning in 1995, however, citizen activists throughout the county began to promote a new growth management technique that seeks to create more formal urban growth boundaries that cannot be changed without the approval of voters. The Save Open Space and Agricultural Resources, or SOAR, movement began in Ventura in 1995 as the "Save Our Agricultural Resources" campaign. In a series of elections between 1995 and 2000, voters approved urban growth initiatives in eight of the county's ten cities.[6]

The SOAR movement came about for a variety of reasons. In part it emerged because local residents in various parts of the county opposed new development and did not trust their elected officials to make decisions they agreed with. On a broader scale, however, it emerged from the efforts of a widespread group of environmental and planning activists around the county who believed that it would be much more difficult in the future to protect undeveloped land using the traditional techniques that had been in place since the 1970s. Some of these activists were especially concerned that the county government would not have the political will to continue to resist suburban-style development in unincorporated areas. Indeed, two of SOAR's key organizers, Steve Bennett of Ventura and Linda Parks of Thousand Oaks, were eventually elected to the Ventura County Board of Supervisors, principally based on their support of limited growth.

Although the techniques have taken different forms in different parts of the county, most SOAR measures use the same approach. An urban growth boundary (technically known as a community urban restriction boundary, or CURB) is established for each city. Any alterations to the CURB require the approval of voters within that city. For land in unincorporated areas outside the CURB lines, any change in zoning away from agriculture and open space that would permit urbanization requires a county-wide vote. The sunset dates for the SOAR measures range from 2020 to 2030, depending on the city. Ventura County is the only county in the United States where voter approval is required to bring new land on line for urbanization throughout the entire county and its cities.

In general, the SOAR system was not shaped as the result of any analysis of current conditions and current constraints. No analysis was ever done to determine the demand for and supply of land for urbanization or the impact of SOAR on agricultural lands or wildlife habitats. This is not typical even of other West Coast areas that use urban growth boundaries and/or voter requirements. Metropolitan Portland is required by Oregon state law to have a twenty-year supply of land for urbanization inside its growth boundaries and to reassess that supply every five years. Even in the San Francisco Bay Area, where citizen groups such as Greenbelt Alliance have orchestrated voter passage of city-level urban growth boundaries, those boundaries contain estimates of how much urban land will be required over the next twenty years.

Instead of conducting such analyses, SOAR's citizen leaders drew the CURBs based mostly on current plans along with some negotiations they needed to conduct with cities in order to place the SOAR measures on the ballot.[7] As a result, some prime farmland is located inside CURBs, especially in Oxnard and Camarillo, and some extremely steep farmland is also located inside the boundaries, especially in Ventura and Santa Paula. By the same token, some flat and seemingly developable land with little habitat or agricultural value is located outside the boundaries, especially in the eastern part of the county.[8]

Modeling Different Growth Scenarios in Ventura County

Given this background, we applied the CURBA model to Ventura County in hopes of providing new insight into the probable future growth pattern of the county and, especially, the question of whether the county's current growth management system will preserve certain sensitive lands from urban development. The CURBA model is essentially a trend model that uses past development patterns to simulate future spatial patterns of population growth. In applying this model to the nine counties in the San Francisco Bay Area, Landis et al. (1998) concluded that the CURBA scenarios can reveal much about how alternative policies might affect conversion of farmland and environmentally sensitive land to urban use.

The CURBA model has two components: the urban growth submodel and the policy simulation and evaluation submodel. We provide a short description of each below and a more comprehensive explanation of each, along with its application to the Ventura County situation, in the appendix to this chapter. In addition, Figure 11.2 lists the tasks performed in each submodel.

The urban growth submodel compares observed changes in urbanized land during a specific time period with a variety of spatial and nonspatial factors, such as site variables (e.g., land cover, political status, slope) and neighborhood characteristics (e.g., distance to nearest major highway, percentage of neighboring cells that are urbanized) (Landis and Zhang 1998). Stepwise logit regression models are then developed and used to explain past patterns of growth. The preferred model seeks to use the fewest independent variables while still explaining the largest percentage of the overall change.

The geographic area being analyzed is divided into a series of square grid cells measuring one hundred meters on a side. Future population growth and density estimates are used to determine the quantity of land needed to accommodate the future growth. The model predicts the probability that each cell will be urbanized, and cells are then urbanized in their order of probability until the predicted amount of additional urban land has been consumed.

The policy simulation and evaluation submodel uses a series of spatial analytic techniques to examine a series of scenarios that include different policy constraints to predict land conversion magnitudes and patterns. In essence, this submodel removes certain cells from urbanization (e.g., cells containing agricultural land or cells outside the urban growth boundary) if the policy scenario being examined calls for that particular land-use cover to be protected from urbanization. In this way, the model

Urban growth submodel	Policy simulation and evaluation submodel
1. Prepare GIS layers used to depict past growth and a series of independent variables that may be invoked to explain the growth patterns.	1. Import future urbanization probabilities into ArcView GIS.
2. Use logit regression to estimate county-based urbanization equations In an appropriate statistical program.	2. Determine communitywide population growth increments and densities.
3. Use these equations to calculate future urbanization probabilities for undeveloped sites	3. Construct policy scenarios based on local development constraints—wetlands, floodplains, stream corridors, site slope, farmland, urban boundaries, and so on.
	4. Identify and change probabilities to zero for "nondevelopable" sites in each policy scenario.
	5. Predict urban growth patterns and habitat change/fragmentation under different policy scenarios.
	6. Summarize land-use change and compute before-and-after measures of land cover and species habitat fragmentation.
	7. Run additional scenarios (if necessary).

Figure 11.2. Tasks performed in urban growth and policy simulation and evaluation components of the California Urban and Biodiversity Analysis model (after Landis et al. 1998).

can be used to predict how spatial patterns of urbanization will vary under different policy scenarios.

Using the urban growth submodel described in more detail in the appendix to this chapter, we concluded that 95 percent of the spatial pattern of urban growth in Ventura County between 1986 and 2000 could be explained by a model containing eight variables weighted according to the equation shown in the appendix. Essentially, the model reveals that development probabilities are highest in areas (or cells) with the following characteristics:

1. At least half the cell is already located inside SOI boundaries.
2. Slopes are gentle.
3. The average distance of cells from major highways is large.
4. The average distance to cells already urbanized in 1986 is small.
5. At least half of the cell is classified as prime, unique, or state-important farmland by the state's Farmland Mapping and Monitoring Program (FMMP).
6. At least half the cell is located inside the city limits of Camarillo.
7. At least half the cell is located inside the city limits of Moorpark.
8. At least half the cell is located in a floodplain.

To summarize, nonfarmland cells close to existing urban areas but far from highways on floodplains and other gently sloping sites were the most likely to be urbanized. The likelihood that cells with these characteristics in Camarillo and Moorpark were urbanized was especially high, which is to be expected given their recent history of rapid urbanization. The positive sign for the variable we called HDIST (which indicates that the probability of a cell's being urbanized increased with increasing distance from freeways) was not expected, but it might be explained by the choice of major highways for this study. We reproduce the final equation that was generated using these variables in the appendix.

Using the policy simulation and evaluation submodel, we developed six policy scenarios for Ventura County that could be used as the basis for different CURBA model runs. We created the six scenarios to determine (1) how sensitive actual growth patterns might be to changes in the growth management regime and (2) how different growth patterns might affect the likelihood of converting certain sensitive land, especially farmland and wildlife habitat land, to urban use. For example, we were interested in knowing whether the likely overall growth patterns would be altered if the system of urban growth boundaries imposed by the voters were removed. We were also interested in knowing whether the system of urban growth boundaries would actually protect farmland and other sensitive land better than alternative policies.

For the purposes of the scenarios and the model runs, we specified the county's urban growth boundaries as being the CURBs and voter requirement areas that were in place prior to the 2000 election (for example, CURBs in Oxnard, Camarillo, Thousand Oaks, Simi Valley, and Moorpark and agricultural land in Ventura's SOI) and the spheres of influence for cities unaffected by SOAR at that time (for example, in

Fillmore, Ojai, Santa Paula, and the hillside areas of Ventura). Thus the scenarios and model runs did not take into account the passage of SOAR in Santa Paula and Fillmore and the vote requirement now in place for the Ventura hillsides.

Based on all these considerations, the six scenarios we chose (summarized in Figure 11.3) were as follows:

1. The "no constraints" scenario, which permitted future growth anywhere in the county except for public land and protected open space. This scenario assumed that the county's system of urban growth boundaries was not in place.
2. The "environmental and farmland protection" scenario, which prohibited growth on environmentally sensitive lands (steeply sloped lands, wetlands, and floodplains) and farmland in addition to publicly owned land and designated open space. This scenario also assumed that the urban growth boundaries were not in place.
3. The "compact growth" scenario, which prohibited growth outside the urban growth boundaries.
4. The "compact growth and farmland protection" scenario, which used Scenario 3 as a baseline but also prohibited development on farmland even if located inside the boundaries (although allowing it on environmentally sensitive land if it was inside the boundaries).
5. The "compact growth and environmental protection" scenario, which was the reverse of Scenario 4. This scenario used Scenario 3 as a baseline but prohibited development on environmentally sensitive land even if located inside the boundaries (although allowing it on farmland if it was inside the boundaries)
6. The "all constraints" scenario, which prohibited development of environmentally sensitive land, farmland, publicly owned land, designated open space, and areas located outside the SOI/SOAR boundaries.

In running the model with these policy scenarios, we attempted to predict how a 25 percent population increase (approximately 190,000 persons) would be distributed geographically within the county. In each scenario, we attempted to accommodate this additional growth at approximately 7.3 persons per urbanized acre, which we found to be representative of both the average density of the county as a whole and the urbanization density from 1986 through 2000. We applied this density across the county, although (as we have explained above) existing densities vary from city to city.

The Impact of Alternative Growth Scenarios for Ventura County's Future

In general, we found that the six scenarios fell into three distinct patterns, and for this reason we confined some of our analyses to only three scenarios. The analysis we did for all six scenarios is summarized in Table 11.4. The urban growth probability grid reproduced in Figure 11.4 shows which cells would have been urbanized had the policies and trends that characterized the period 1986–2000 been sustained indefinitely.

Figures 11.5, 11.6, and 11.7 depict the predicted spatial impacts of the three distinct scenarios chosen for further analysis (Scenarios 1, 3, and 6).

First, we found that Scenario 1 and Scenario 2 produced very similar results. Both scenarios would require approximately 25,000 acres to accommodate 190,000 additional persons. The vast majority of that newly urbanized land (more than 23,000 acres) would be located in unincorporated county territory. Loss of farmland and environmentally sensitive land would be significant but not irreparable.

Scenario 1, the no constraints scenario, was predisposed to favor nonfarmland in low-lying areas, close to existing urban land, and the map reproduced in Figure 11.5 shows that most development was predicted in or near Oxnard, south of Camarillo and Thousand Oaks, between Moorpark and Thousand Oaks, and immediately north of Moorpark and Simi Valley. The relatively large undeveloped areas inside the Simi Valley and Thousand Oaks city limits were not targeted for growth under this scenario, due in part to the large areas of public and/or steeply sloping lands in these cities. As Table 11.4 indicates, Scenario 2, the environmental and farmland protection scenario, produced similar results, although considerably more land would be urbanized in Moorpark and considerably less in Oxnard.

In short, the similarities in results for Scenarios 1 and 2 suggest that a policy designed explicitly to protect farmland and environmentally sensitive land (but one that does not have urban growth boundaries) would not produce a significantly different outcome than a market-based approach without any protections at all.

Scenario	Description
1. No constraints	Allows development anywhere in the study area except on public land and designated open space
2. Environmental and farmland protection	Prohibits development on farmland, wetland, floodplain, slopes greater than 25 percent, public land, and designated open space
3. Compact growth	Prohibits development outside SOI/SOAR boundaries and on public land and designated open space inside boundaries
4. Compact growth and farmland protection	Prohibits development outside SOI/SOAR boundaries and on farmland, public land, and designated open space inside boundaries
5. Compact growth and environmental protection	Prohibits development outside SOI/SOAR boundaries and on wetland, floodplain, slopes greater than 25 percent, public land, and designated open space inside boundaries
6. All constraints (compact growth with environmental and farmland protection)	Prohibits development outside SOI/SOAR boundaries and on farmland, wetland, floodplain, slopes greater than 25 percent, public land, and designated open space inside boundaries

Figure 11.3. Future policy scenarios used for runs of the California Urban and Biodiversity Analysis model. SOI = sphere of influence; SOAR = Save Open Space and Agricultural Resources initiatives.

Second, we found that Scenarios 3, 4, and 5 produced results that were different from the first two scenarios but similar to each other. Like Scenarios 1 and 2, Scenarios 3, 4, and 5 required approximately 25,000 acres of newly urbanized land to accommodate a population increase of 190,000 persons. However, in each of these three scenarios approximately two-thirds of the newly urbanized land was located inside cities. This outcome is simply the result of the fact that, because these scenarios prohibited urban growth outside the urban growth boundaries, growth was pushed from unincorporated areas back inside cities.

However, these three scenarios distributed growth differently among the cities, depending on whether they focused purely on the urban growth boundaries or sought to protect farmland and/or environmental land as well. By following the current (i.e., mid-2000) system of urban growth boundaries, Scenario 3, the compact growth scenario, distributed growth fairly evenly among the cities. As Figure 11.6 shows, most new urbanization was predicted to occur in Camarillo, Moorpark, Oxnard, Simi Valley, and Thousand Oaks, all of which have substantial undeveloped land inside their city limits. One-third of all urbanization still occured outside the city limits, especially near Simi Valley, Thousand Oaks, Ojai, and Oxnard.

As Table 11.4 indicates, Scenarios 4 and 5 (the compact growth/farmland protection scenario and the compact growth/environmental protection scenario) produced similar results but distributed the growth differently. The biggest difference is that in Scenario 4 far more growth was directed into Simi Valley and Thousand Oaks and far less into Oxnard and Camarillo. This is because there is a large amount of farmland located inside the city limits and urban growth boundaries of both Oxnard and Camarillo.

In short, the model runs for Scenarios 3 through 5 suggest that containing urban growth under the current system of urban growth boundaries would drive development into the cities, but it would not protect farmland as well as a policy that explicitly seeks to do so.

Scenario 6 was the only scenario that required the county to develop at higher densities to accommodate 190,000 additional persons. This scenario would prohibit growth outside the growth boundaries while protecting both farmland and environmentally sensitive land. Under these constraints, the county could not accommodate the additional population at 7.3 persons per urbanized acre; therefore, the density for future growth in this scenario had to be increased to 10.1 persons per acre. This is slightly less than the current density of Santa Paula.

Although it consumed less land and accommodated population at higher density, Scenario 6 distributed growth geographically in a fashion similar to Scenario 4, the compact growth and farmland protection scenario. Most new growth would be channeled into Thousand Oaks, Simi Valley, and Moorpark, and Camarillo and Oxnard would not receive as much urbanization because of the farmland protection provision (Figure 11.7).

In analyzing the potential impacts of different growth scenarios on the future of Ventura County, we also examined how these scenarios would affect existing supplies

Table 11.4. Magnitude of urban growth predicted for Ventura County with each policy scenario by political unit

Political unit	2000 Nonurban land (acres)	Scenario 1		Scenario 2		Scenario 3		Scenario 4		Scenario 5		Scenario 6	
		Acres	%	Acres	%	Acres	%	Acres	%	Acres	%	Acres	%
Camarillo	2,891	242	8.4	193	6.7	2,567	88.8	699	24.2	2,063	71.4	420	14.5
Fillmore	635	20	3.1	20	3.1	222	35.0	185	29.2	235	37.0	124	19.5
Moorpark	2,600	699	26.9	1,732	66.6	2,407	92.6	2,328	89.5	2,177	83.7	2,095	80.6
Ojai	425	15	3.5	0	0.0	269	63.4	297	69.8	321	75.6	240	56.4
Oxnard	4,174	793	19.0	292	7.0	2,454	58.8	566	13.6	2,387	57.2	494	11.8
Port Hueneme	54	7	13.6	7	13.6	54	100.0	54	100.0	7	13.6	7	13.6
Santa Paula	662	10	1.5	2	0.4	309	46.6	410	61.9	171	25.7	62	9.3
Simi Valley	8,009	5	0.1	131	1.6	4,453	55.6	6,385	79.7	4,196	52.4	4,144	51.7
Thousand Oaks	14,204	62	0.4	213	1.5	3,966	27.9	5,515	38.8	4,695	33.1	4,695	33.1
Ventura	1,967	91	4.6	10	0.5	736	37.4	788	40.1	549	27.9	269	13.7
County	414,719	23,275	5.6	23,381	5.6	8,246	2.0	8,659	2.1	9,227	2.2	6,353	1.5
Total	450,340	25,220	5.6	25,981	5.8	25,684	5.7	25,887	5.7	26,028	5.8	18,904	4.2

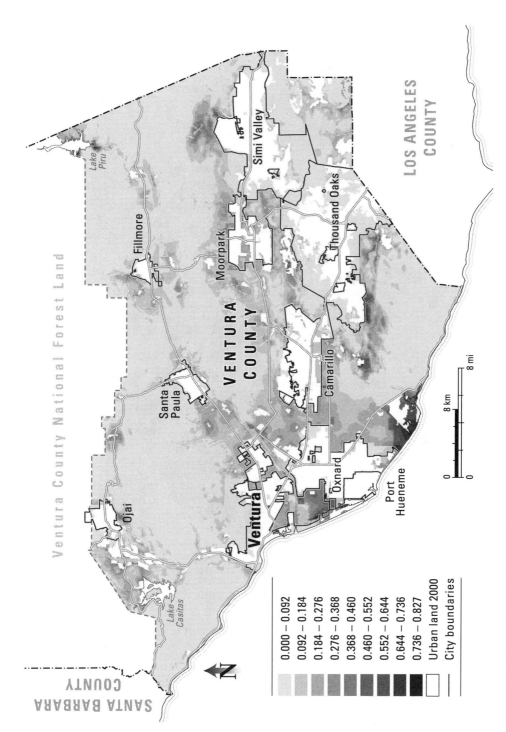

Figure 11.4. Probabilities for Ventura County.

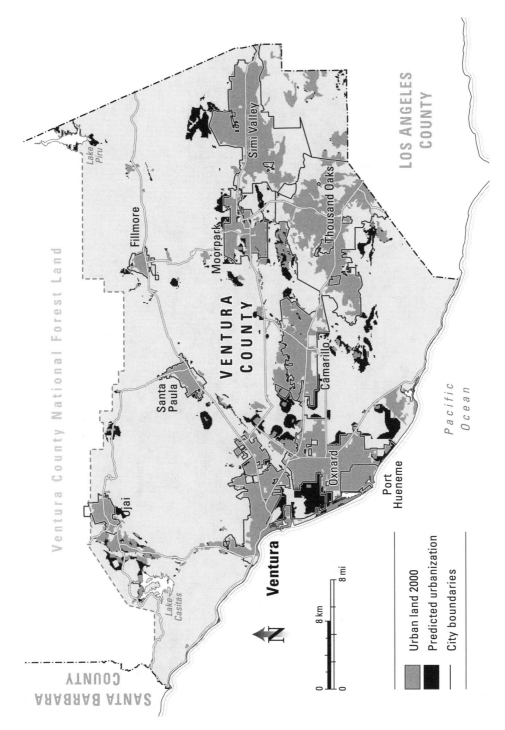

Figure 11.5. Impact on land use in Ventura County predicted by Scenario 1.

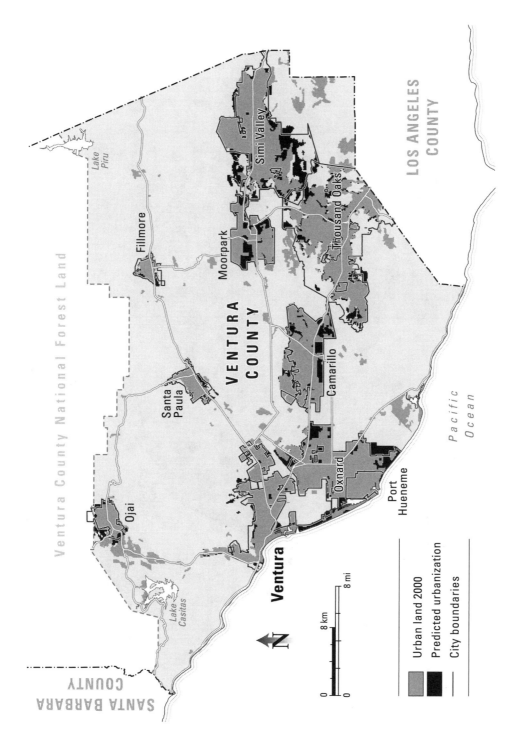

Figure 11.6. Impact on land use in Ventura County predicted by Scenario 3.

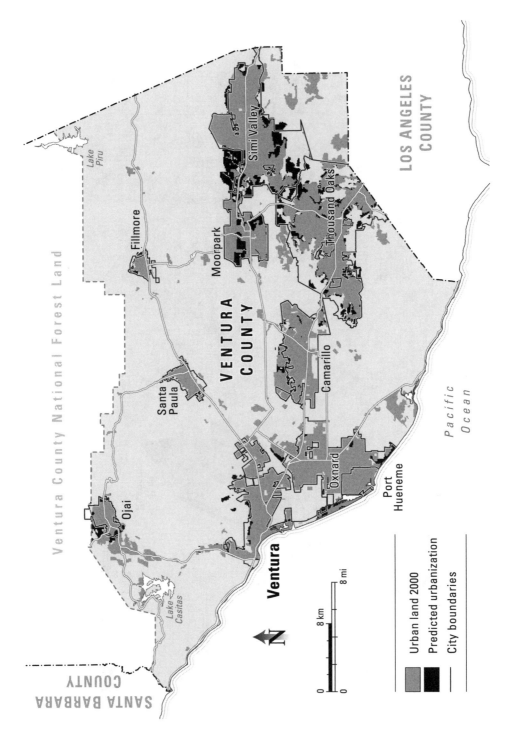

Figure 11.7. Impact on land use in Ventura County predicted by Scenario 6.

of natural land cover, partially as a "window" into their impacts on plant and animal species. As we stated at the outset, the protection of threatened wildlife has become a major land-use policy driver in some parts of Southern California, where the federal and state governments have designated "critical habitat" for those species. This has driven the creation of large-scale conservation plans, especially in Orange, Riverside, and San Diego Counties.

By contrast, Ventura County has not been heavily affected by the endangered species issue. Although the county is home to many ecosystems similar to those found elsewhere in Southern California, environmental scientists have less often found actual specimens of rare species in the county, and thus state and federal laws have been triggered less often. This is especially true in the farmland and rangeland areas of the county. In and around the Santa Monica Mountains, however, endangered species issues have arisen. Most recently, updated environmental analysis of the high-profile and controversial Ahmanson Ranch project found one federally listed species (the California red-legged frog) and one species previously thought to be extinct, which has now been listed by the state (the San Fernando Valley spineflower). These two environmental findings have formed the basis for renewed debate over whether or not the Ahmanson Ranch project, which was originally approved by Ventura County in 1992, should go forward.

To analyze the potential impacts of different scenarios, we examined the model results on twenty-five different classifications of land cover identified under the Holland (1986) land-cover classification system. We focused our analysis on Scenarios 1, 3, and 6.

As the land-cover classes shown in Table 11.5 reveal, Ventura County is dominated by Venturan coastal sage scrub (187,800 acres, or 42 percent of the nonurban area in 2000), six chaparral species (47,300 acres, or 10 percent), and nonnative grasses (approximately 31,900, or 7 percent). Agriculture remains an important economic activity, utilizing 25–26 percent of the study area (depending on the data source used). (The Holland system actually includes one classification for row crops called "agricultural" and two more for tree crops, called "orchard or vineyards" and "evergreen orchard.") The remainder of the study area is covered with various coastal and riparian forest and woodland cover types.[9]

Of the natural land covers, the Venturan coastal sage scrub is most important, both because it is so widespread and because it provides potential habitat to a wide range of threatened and endangered species. The Venturan variety is one of several types of sage scrub found in Southern California, and "the majority of plant species found within sage scrub communities are low-growing, summer deciduous or succulent plants such as California sagebrush, various sages, California buckwheat, and cacti" (U.S. Fish and Wildlife Service n.d.). Sage scrub serves as a key habitat for several endangered or threatened birds in Southern California, including the coastal California gnatcatcher, least Bell's vireo, and the cactus wren.

All of these scenarios would reduce the amount of acreage devoted to agricultural and natural land coverage in some way. But, as Table 11.5 shows, the scenarios involve a trade-off between agricultural land and natural land cover, especially Venturan coastal sage scrub and agriculture. So, for example, even though Scenario 6 (the all constraints scenario) would actually urbanize less land than the other two scenarios, it would cause the loss of more coastal sage scrub. This is largely because this scenario would shift growth from agricultural land on the Oxnard Plain to natural sage scrubland in the eastern part of the county, around Thousand Oaks and Simi Valley.

Similarly, Scenario 1, the no constraints scenario, would cause the most loss to agriculture (more than 12,000 acres in row crops alone) but far less loss to coastal sage scrub (4,100 acres, only half the loss in Scenario 6). Again, this is because making choices about which land to urbanize in Ventura County essentially requires making a choice between cultivated agricultural and natural land, which is most often covered by coastal sage scrub.

The habitat losses recorded in Table 11.5, however, tell only part of the story. Ryan (2001) used the policy simulation and evaluation submodel to calculate separate habitat fragmentation statistics for two Holland land-cover classes (Venturan coastal sage scrub and chamise chaparral) and three threatened or endangered species (the California red-legged frog, Savannah sparrow, and least Bell's vireo) that are thought to be present in the study area. Due to their differential habitat fragmentation effects, the six scenarios would impose varying impacts on these species and would also need to be considered in future land use policy.

Table 11.5 Habitat losses predicted for Ventura County under three local policy scenarios

Land-cover classes	2000 total	Scenario 1 Acres	%	Scenario 3 Acres	%	Scenario 6 Acres	%
Urban or built up	23,124	2,689	11.6	7,495	32.4	5,224	22.6
Agricultural	83,213	12,699	15.3	5,548	6.7	684	0.8
Orchard or vineyards	25,259	1,542	6.1	1,223	4.8	838	3.3
Evergreen orchard	7,144	230	3.2	0	0.0	0	0.0
Permanently flooded lacustrine habitat	3,637	556	15.3	52	1.4	42	1.2
Bays and estuaries	1,087	0	0.0	0	0.0	0	0.0
Sandy areas not beaches	6,390	324	5.1	138	2.2	42	0.7
Southern coastal bluff scrub	6,464	86	1.3	166	2.6	91	1.4
Venturan coastal sage scrub	187,780	4,122	2.2	7,218	3.8	8,211	4.4
Diegan coastal sage scrub	979	54	5.6	0	0.0	0	0.0
Upper sonoran sub-shrub scrub	1,446	0	0.0	0	0.0	2	0.2
Mule fat scrub	2,392	54	2.3	378	15.8	2	0.1
Southern alluvial fan scrub	237	0	0.0	0	0.0	0	0.0
Southern cottonwood-willow riparian forest	563	0	0.0	0	0.0	0	0.0
Southern willow scrub	5,291	156	2.9	348	6.6	74	1.4
Chamise chaparral (chamisal)	11,691	30	0.3	1,161	9.9	1,396	11.9
Redshank chaparral	1,693	25	1.5	10	0.6	42	2.5
Buck brush chaparral	3,857	52	1.3	0	0.0	0	0.0
Hoary-leafed chaparral	13,979	143	1.0	89	0.6	334	2.4
Big pod chaparral	16,079	126	0.8	398	2.5	497	3.1
Interior live oak chaparral	27	0	0.0	0	0.0	0	0.0
Coastal sage-chaparral scrub	4,856	25	0.5	37	0.8	17	0.4
Nonnative grassland	31,896	2,155	6.8	1,423	4.5	1,406	4.4
California walnut woodland	5,320	40	0.7	0	0.0	0	0.0
Coast live oak forest	7,715	109	1.4	0	0.0	0	0.0
Total	452,119	25,215	5.6	25,684	5.7	18,904	4.2

Policy Growth Choices in Ventura County

Managing growth to achieve multiple objectives is always a matter of making choices. In the case of Ventura County, an urban containment system—created in the 1970s and extended with the passage of the SOAR initiatives—has been focused primarily on channeling growth into cities, on maintaining physical separation between those urbanized cities, and, to some extent, on protecting farmland. It has not been focused on protecting or enhancing wildlife habitat, although some protection has probably occurred as a by-product of the system.

Yet we have already seen difficult policy choices forced throughout the region by the listing of endangered species, a lack of land supply, and a continuing suburban pattern. Despite its history of unusually strong growth management, Ventura County will certainly have to face a much more difficult set of choices in the future. Containing urban growth, protecting farmland, and preserving important wildlife habitat are not always consistent goals—in some cases, they may even be conflicting goals. Sometimes accommodating or protecting one involves sacrificing another, at least to a certain extent. To deal with any significant increment of additional population growth—such as the 25 percent increase analyzed in this chapter—the county has four distinct policy choices:

1. Accommodate urban growth and preserve existing habitat by converting existing farmland to urban use.
2. Accommodate urban growth and protect existing farmland by converting existing habitat to urban use.
3. Accommodate urban growth and protect both habitat and farmland by developing communities at higher densities.
4. Protect habitat and farmland without increasing densities by constraining the overall rate of growth.

These choices are not hypothetical. The county will almost certainly face them in the next few years.

Most of the county's 112,000 acres of farmland lie outside the county's growth boundaries and therefore will be protected if the existing growth boundaries remain in place. However, some significant amounts of farmland still lie inside the growth boundaries of Oxnard and Camarillo as a result of the negotiated agreement between SOAR initiative advocates and the two cities' city councils in 1998. Many of SOAR's political advocates have signaled that they may seek another ballot measure to alter the growth boundaries in both of these cities in order to protect that farmland. Our modeling suggests that this would almost certainly shift more urban growth to the grazing and rangeland of the eastern part of the county, around Simi Valley and Thousand Oaks, in order to accommodate the same amount of new urban growth.

Most habitat land—including the 187,000 acres of Venturan coastal sage scrub—also lies outside the county's growth boundaries and therefore would be protected if the existing growth boundaries remain in place. But, as our modeling reveals,

protecting this land in a comprehensive way would almost certainly require sacrificing farmland (especially the farmland inside Oxnard and Camarillo) if a significant
increment of new urban growth is to be accommodated. So far, Ventura County and
its cities have chosen to sacrifice habitat land in order accommodate urban growth
and preserve farmland.

But there is no guarantee that the county will have the luxury of making this
same choice in the future. Other communities throughout Southern California have
already been forced by the listing of endangered species to place protection of habitat at the "top of the list," above farmland and urbanization. Ventura County has
faced few endangered species issues up to now, but this may change. Already, newly
discovered endangered species altered the debate about Ahmanson Ranch; the project
was ultimately stopped. If endangered species become more of an issue in Ventura
County, then policy makers in the county may have no choice but to join their colleagues in Orange, San Diego, and Riverside Counties in making habitat preservation
the most important land priority.

Even if county policy makers made a choice to focus on protecting farmland
and/or preserving habitat land, there is no guarantee that the voters would alter or
abandon the existing system of urban growth boundaries to achieve those goals. It
is hard to predict whether voters will "hold the line" on these boundaries in future
elections. On the one hand, in the first three "SOAR override" elections in 1999 and
2000 (two in Ventura and one in unincorporated county territory near Ojai), voters
approved converting agricultural land to development. On the other hand, all three
projects involved community and institutional uses—a church, a park/sports complex,
and the expansion of a convalescent home—and none of the three projects was more
than one hundred acres in size.

A sterner test came in 2002, when ballot initiatives appeared in both Santa Paula
and Simi Valley to alter the CURB lines (expanding the line in Santa Paula, shrinking
it in Simi Valley). Both were stimulated by the prospect of more housing developments, but, as it turned out, both measures were defeated—and so the lines held as
they had previously been drawn. Furthermore, SOAR proponents have indicated their
desire to propose new ballot measures removing farmland from inside the CURB
lines in both Camarillo and Oxnard. Given the fact that the original SOAR measures
passed overwhelmingly, it is not clear that voters would "green-light" large private
development projects, especially those proposing a considerable amount of housing
or commercial construction. Nor is it clear, given events since 1998, that the CURB
lines will be permanent simply because voter approval is required to move them.

It is theoretically possible to protect farmland and environmentally sensitive land
and still maintain the county's system of urban growth boundaries—but only if future
development in the county occurs at higher densities inside the boundaries than has
been the case in recent years. Our results for Scenario 6 showed that a 25 percent
growth increment could be accommodated along with protection of all other resources
only with a density of 10 persons per newly urbanized acre, rather than the 7 persons
per acre assumed in the other scenarios.

Based on recent experience, it is not clear whether higher densities are either likely or politically feasible. Recent trends show little change given that Ventura County accommodated 7.52 persons for each acre of urbanized land in 1986 and the growth from 1986 through 2000 occurred at roughly the same density. Furthermore, a great deal of rhetoric since the passage of the SOAR initiatives in 1998 has suggested that many voters would prefer to protect land by constraining future population growth rather than by accommodating it at higher densities.

The choices about density and urban growth boundaries will not likely affect all cities equally. Some will feel more pressure than others. For example, under Scenario 3 (the urban growth boundary scenario without farmland and environmental land protection), 60 percent of the potentially available land would be consumed in six cities: Camarillo, Moorpark, Ojai, Port Hueneme, Simi Valley, and Thousand Oaks. Thousand Oaks faces particular pressure because, as of 2000, 62 percent of its nonurban area already consisted of publicly owned land and designated open space and was therefore unavailable for development.

The final policy choice—one that is often articulated by many SOAR supporters—is simply to use growth policy to attempt to reduce the rate of growth. Many cities in the county (and in California generally) have attempted to do this by restricting the number of residential units that may be permitted or built each year.[10]

However politically appealing such a policy is, it may be difficult to sustain in the face of urbanization pressure and political forces at the state and regional levels. California state housing policy requires that local governments plan for a specific increment of housing that is established through a formula based on population projections. Furthermore, there is considerable evidence that suppressing growth in one part of a metropolitan region simply shifts it to another location rather than eliminating it altogether (Glickfeld and Levine 1992). Even if local residents and policy makers care little about the regional impact of suppressing growth locally, other jurisdictions elsewhere, the state government, and housing advocates can sue to challenge the practice if they believe they are not benefiting from it.

Even if it is possible to limit the number of houses constructed, however, this does not mean that the pressure for urbanization will be reduced commensurately, for two reasons. First, demographic and economic change in California means that it is more difficult than it used to be to control the size of a local population by controlling the housing stock. With a greater percentage of population increase attributable to "natural increase," more residents live in each existing unit. With housing prices on the rise in expensive places like Ventura County, residents of modest means increasingly live in motels, garages, and other buildings not originally built with long-term residence in mind. Whether or not the number of homes is restricted, these additional residents increase the pressure for land urbanization by increasing the demand for employment, retail stores, social services, and other urban activities that consume land.

Second, a strategy of reducing the growth rate simply postpones, rather than eliminates, the need to make difficult policy choices. The 25 percent growth increment analyzed in this chapter's models represents the amount of increase that Ventura County received in a fifteen-year period, from 1986 through 2000. The next 25 percent increase may occur over a somewhat shorter or longer period, depending on economic conditions, growth policies, and other factors. But sooner or later, Ventura County's population will grow by 25 percent or more, and the county will be confronted with the difficult policy choices outlined in this chapter.

Conclusion

After more than a century of rapid urbanization, Southern California is running out of developable land, and the region has not yet devised a comprehensive—or coherent—strategy for accommodating additional growth in this new context of limited land supply. In the interim, the region has adopted a series of ad hoc policies and tools—many at the local level—designed to protect certain types of undeveloped land, contain urban expansion, and accommodate urban growth in this land-constrained context.

Yet different policies and tools may promote different values in different places. For example, large-scale plans such as those in Orange and San Diego Counties have promoted the protection of wildlife habitats with no consideration for human settlement patterns. As time goes on, it may be more difficult to manage multiple growth and land protection goals using policies and tools that have a single focus or are not well integrated into a larger growth strategy.

Ventura County's system of urban containment is one such policy that has emerged in response to regional growth pressure. It was first developed in the 1970s and has evolved over time, most recently with the passage of the SOAR initiatives. The Ventura County system was originally focused on channeling urban growth into cities, with the hope of protecting agricultural land. With the addition of voter-imposed urban growth boundaries, the goal appears to be to contain urban growth inside specific and rather small areas of the county unless voters specify otherwise.

By examining the likely impacts of different future land development scenarios in Ventura County in this chapter, we have highlighted the fact that the Ventura County system does not resolve all of the county's problems in attempting to cope with ongoing regional pressure for urbanization. As they are currently drawn, the county's urban growth boundaries accomplish a specific set of goals. They confine urban growth to specific areas. In the process, they protect most agricultural land, and—at least for the 25 percent increment of population growth examined here—they can accomplish these goals without increasing urban densities beyond the current figure of approximately seven persons per urbanized acre. However, the urban growth boundary system accomplishes these goals by creating clear trade-offs between different types of nonurban land and different geographic areas, and it does not address any possible secondary impacts of the resulting growth pattern, such as the jobs-housing balance.

According to the model results, the urban growth boundary system will achieve the goal of accommodating growth and protecting most farmland without increasing densities, but only by consuming almost six thousand acres of row crops (mostly near

Oxnard and Camarillo) and more than seven thousand acres of Venturan coastal sage scrub habitat (mostly near Thousand Oaks and Simi Valley) (see statistics for Scenario 3 in Table 11.5 for additional details).

Any attempt to alter this system will require a different set of trade-offs. It is possible to protect more habitat in the eastern part of the county by developing more farmland in the western part, or vice versa. It is possible to protect both, but only if densities are increased. It may be possible to reduce the rate of population growth, but this simply postpones the day when these difficult choices must be made. It does not eliminate the need to make the choices.

Furthermore, any such choices in the future will have significant impacts on the geographic relationships among jobs, housing, shopping, and other activities, and hence on the county's transportation system. Ventura County's urban growth boundary system does not address the question of how to deal with these concerns, or what types of trade-offs might be better or worse from this point of view.

California is unique in its widespread use of initiative and referendum power to affect land-use decisions. Ventura County is unique in having used that power to establish a countywide voter-created system of urban growth boundaries. This unique political history—and the growth patterns it has been creating and is likely to continue creating—represents part of Southern California's continuing struggle to deal with growth in a land-constrained context.

Like the large-scale conservation plans of Orange and San Diego Counties, the Ventura County system is one in which growth policy is driven by a specific set of policy concerns rather than by a comprehensive attempt to manage growth. In the case of Orange and San Diego Counties, the policy driver is the protection of endangered species. In the case of Ventura County, the policy driver is the maintenance of a suburban residential lifestyle using agricultural land as an open-space buffer. In both cases, other concerns—such as the jobs-housing balance and transportation—have not been taken into account.

Unfortunately, the Ventura County policy-making process has not been informed by careful analysis about the policy choices being made. This has come about partly because the current system was created by voter initiative. Because initiatives are often driven by citizen groups rather than government agencies—and because they are exempt from normal environmental review processes—voters often make choices without much information. All these difficulties stand in contrast to the Riverside County Integrated Project, in which the county has attempted to integrate land use, transportation, and open-space concerns through a process that has generated a great deal of information about the choices.

Even so, the Ventura County situation may well be the bellwether for the future. Residents throughout Southern California—especially in outlying counties—have given every indication that they favor retaining their suburban lifestyle, protecting as much open space as possible, and using the ballot box to make major land-use decisions. It is clear that future policy choices in Ventura County and elsewhere will have to be crafted within the context that we see in Ventura County today.

Appendix: CURBA Model Implementation

Urban Growth Submodel

The urban growth submodel of the CURBA model compares observed changes in urbanized land during some user-specified time period with a variety of spatial and nonspatial factors using logit regression equations of the following form:

$$\text{Prob}(Y) = f\{X1, X2, X3 \ldots Xn\}, \tag{1}$$

where Y = probability that an undeveloped grid cell is urbanized and $X1$, $X2$, $X3$ ... Xn are a series of site variables (e.g., land cover, political status, slope) and neighborhood characteristics (e.g., distance to nearest major highway, percentage of neighboring cells that are urbanized) that can be used to explain past growth patterns (Landis and Zhang 1998).

The dependent variable (Y) in equation (1) was calculated from FMMP land-use maps published by the Division of Land Resource Protection of the California Department of Conservation. The FMMP uses field mapping, air photo interpretation, computer analysis, and public reviews to map, monitor, and report on land use throughout California (California Department of Conservation 1994). FMMP data for 1986 and 1996 were downloaded directly from the Division of Land Resource Protection Web site in Intergraph formatted data files, converted to Arc/Info coverages, and used to identify existing urban areas in 1986 and those areas that were urbanized between 1986 and 1996. Urban land is defined as land occupied by structures with a building density of at least six structures per ten-acre parcel on these maps. There were no data for the northern two-thirds of the county owned by the U.S. Forest Service. These maps were shared with planners and policy makers in Ventura County in the third quarter of 2000 and their input was utilized to identify areas that had been urbanized between 1996 and 2000. This variable was assigned a value of one (if that grid cell was urbanized between 1986 and 2000), zero (if that grid cell was undeveloped in 1986 and not urbanized during the period 1986–2000), or –9999 (if that grid cell was already urbanized in 1986 or classified as a water feature).

A series of Arc/Info GIS map layers describing the environmental, land-use, zoning, density, and accessibility characteristics was compiled and used as explanatory variables in equation (1). These variables fell into four groups based on the type of GIS analysis required to generate maps depicting each of the variables (Ryan 2001). The first group of polygon features on maps was recoded and converted to raster layers with one-hectare cells. Polygon features were classified and converted into grids (as with the first group of variables), and one or more sets of Euclidean distances were calculated in Arc/Info GRID to generate the grid cell values for the second group of variables. The single variable included in the next group was computed with the buffer tools in Arc/Info 7.2.1 and used to distinguish those areas within 100 meters of major highways from the remainder of the study area. The fourth and final group of independent variables was computed with a series of operations performed on user-specified local neighborhoods. One variable recorded the percentage of neighboring cells that were classified as "urban" in 1986, and the others were computed from 30-meter USGS Digital Elevation Models. The maximum slope in three sets of user-specified windows was calculated using the SLOPE function in Arc/Info GRID and converted to 100-meter grids using an inverse distance weighted interpolation. The final three variables provided measures of landscape position by ranking the elevation of the center cell relative to all the cells in some user-specified window (Gallant and Wilson 2000). These percentile values were calculated in TAPES-G (Gallant and Wilson 1996), imported into Arc/Info 7.2.1, and converted to 100-meter grids with the same IDW function used for the slope variables. The full list of independent variables is summarized in Figure 11.8, and complete details of the data sources and GIS analysis tasks can be found in Ryan (2001).

A. Variables generated by converting polygon features to grid cell values
   1. GRO: annual population growth rates between 1986 and 2000 for specific cities and unincorporated areas
   2. FRM: cells with ≥ 50% of area classified as prime, unique, or state-important farmland
   3. FLO: cells with ≥ 50% of area classified as inside 100-year flood zone
   4. WET1: cells with ≥ 50% of area classified as wetland
   5. WET2: cells containing one or more wetland sites
   6. SPH86: cells with ≥ 50% of area classified inside sphere-of-influence boundaries
   7. CYCDP: cells with ≥ 50% of area classified inside city or census-designated place (CDP) boundaries
   8. CYIN: cells with ≥ 50% of area classified inside city boundaries
   9. CDPIN: cells with ≥ 50% of area classified inside CDP boundaries
   10–19. CAMO . . . VENO: cells with ≥ 50% of area classified inside specific city limits (i.e., Camarillo, Fillmore, Moorpark, Ojai, Oxnard, Port Hueneme, Santa Paula, Simi Valley, Thousand Oaks, and Ventura)
   20–26. CACO . . . OKVO: cells with ≥ 50% of area classified inside specific census-designated place boundaries (i.e., Casa Conejo, Channel Islands Beach, El Rio, Meiners Oak, Mira Oak, Oak Park, and Oakview)

B. Variables generated by converting polygon features to grid cells and calculating distances from each cell to previously selected cells
   27. UDIST: average distance from each cell to edge of nearest urbanized cell in 1986
   28. HDIST: average distance from each cell to edge of nearest cell crossed by a major highway
   29. CYCDPDIS: average distance form each cell to edge of nearest cell located inside city or CDP boundaries
   30. VCITYAL: average distance from each cell to edge of nearest cell located inside city boundaries
   31. VCDPAL: average distance from each cell to the edge of nearest cell located inside CDP boundaries
   32–41. CAMD . . . VEND: average distance from each cell to the edge of nearest cell located inside one of ten incorporated cities
   42–48. CACD . . . OKVD: average distance from each cell to the edge of nearest cell located inside one of seven census designated places

C. Variables generated by buffering line features
   49. HWYBUF: cells with ≥ 50% of area within 100 meters of a major highway

D. Variables generated with grids and local neighborhood operators
   50–52. SLP3 . . . SLP49: mean slope in 3-by-3, 15-by-15, or 49-by-49 30-meter cell windows averaged to 1-hectare cells
   53–55. PCT3 . . . PCT49: mean proportion of cells lower than center cell in 3-by-3, 15-by-15, or 49-by-49 cell windows averaged to 1-hectare cells
   56. NEIGH: percentage of neighboring grid cells in a 3-by-3 window classified as urban

---

Figure 11.8. Independent variables used in logit regression analysis.

These variables were then transferred to the Stata 6 statistical package used to perform the stepwise logistic regression analysis. Models with fewer and fewer independent variables were then constructed as follows: the most significant independent variables were identified from previous model runs, these variables were checked for multicollinearity (because numerous pairs of independent variables were highly correlated with one another), and the stepwise logit regression procedure was run again.

The final model, which incorporated eight variables and explained a substantial portion of the variability in the dependent variable (i.e., whether or not an undeveloped cell in 1986 was urbanized during the period 1986–2000), took the following form:

$$Y = -4.271 + 1.837\text{SPH86} - .0000761\text{SLP15} + .000322\text{HDIST} - .000687\text{UDIST}$$
$$+ 1.596\text{MINO} + .0907\text{FRM} + 1.282\text{CINO} + 1.306\text{FLO} \qquad (2)$$

where Y indicates whether or not a one-hectare cell was urbanized between 1986 and 2000 and the variables on the right side are as defined in Figure 11.8. This particular model has several desirable characteristics. First, it correctly predicted the fate of 95 percent of the nonurbanized cells during the period 1986–2000. Second, the model statistics ($R^2 = 0.3381$; log likelihood = –26489.06; chi-square = 27064.65) indicate a robust and highly significant model. Finally, the coefficient signs matched the expected results in seven of eight instances. Nonfarmland cells close to existing urban areas but far from highways on floodplains and other gently sloping sites were the most likely to be urbanized. The likelihood that cells with these characteristics in Camarillo and Moorpark were urbanized was especially high, which is to be expected given these cities' recent history of rapid urbanization. The positive sign for HDIST (which indicates that the probability of a cell being urbanized increased with increasing distance from freeways) was not expected but might be explained by the choice of major highways for this study (see Figure 11.1 for details). The SPH86, HDIST, UDIST, MINO, FRM, and CINO variables were then updated to show conditions in 2000 and used with the coefficients in equation (2) to calculate the urban growth probability grid reproduced in Figure 11.4.

Several of the variables were then updated (e.g., 2000 city limits were substituted for 1986 city limits) and used with the final regression model to calculate future urbanization probabilities for undeveloped grid cells in 2000. These probabilities were then imported into ArcView and turned into a probability grid for use in the CURBA policy simulation and evaluation submodel.

Policy Simulation and Evaluation Submodel

The six policy scenarios summarized in Figure 11.3 were implemented with a population growth increment of 25 percent and density of eighteen residents per hectare. The 25 percent population growth increment matched the number of people likely to be added during the next twenty years, and the density figure resulted from the division of the 2000 population by the 2000 urban area. The density actually changed very little from 1986 to 2000 (see Table 11.1 for details). This information enabled identification of the preferred number of cells with the highest probability scores.

The resulting growth predictions were then compared with the vegetative land-use cover classifications and cross-listed habitat designations found in the California GAP Analysis database (Davis et al. 1998) to quantify the impacts of growth on habitat extent and quality. The California GAP Analysis database incorporates both Jepson ecoregions and Holland vegetation classes. Species habitats were found by using the California Wildlife Habitat Relationships information system to assign vertebrate species to vegetation habitat types identified by the Holland vegetative land-use classes (Landis et al. 1998). The effects of urban growth on the following were quantified: (1) loss of vegetative land cover by type; (2) loss of mammal, reptile, and bird habitat for specific species; (3) loss of lands associated with various ecological values; and (4) changes in the level of vegetative land-cover fragmentation for specific species. The land-cover statistics generated in CURBA mimic those produced in the widely used FRAGSTATS program (McGarigal and Marks 1995).

Notes

1. Annexation and boundary decisions in California are made by each county's Local Agency Formation Commission, or LAFCo, a board made up of elected local officials. For each city, the LAFCo must identify a "sphere of influence," which is defined as the probable ultimate city boundary. Once this sphere area is identified, annexation becomes a routine matter.

2. We examined urban growth patterns from 1986 through 2000, partly to provide historical context but also to provide a baseline for developing the predictive CURBA model, which we describe below. We obtained data and map layers both for this descriptive analysis and for the modeling from a variety of sources. We obtained layers for urbanized land and various categories of farmland from the California Department of Conservation's Farmland Mapping and Monitoring Program and other layers from a variety of sources, as we describe in the appendix to this chapter.

3. The population figures we use in this chapter represent estimates from the California Department of Finance prior to the 2000 U.S. Census. We use these figures because the modeling we describe later was done prior to the release of the 2000 census data. The U.S. Census population for the county was virtually identical to the state estimate, although there were some variations among the individual cities.

4. The California Department of Conservation's FMMP estimated urban land in 2000 at approximately 97,000 acres. Our modeling was done prior to the release of these figures. Therefore, our estimate of 105,000 acres comes from the 1998 figure of approximately 92,500 acres as amended based on extensive conversations with planning staff throughout the county. This figure includes approximately 300 parcels of land that city and county planning staff have identified as urbanized for which permits had been granted as of 2000. Some of these projects were not completed as of 2000, hence the figure of 105,000 acres may be a slight overestimate.

5. This pattern is typical of the emerging pattern throughout California during this period, when many Latino families lived together at higher domestic densities than other racial and ethnic groups because of high fertility rates and relatively low incomes. Thus this phenomenon is the result of *human* density, not *building* density.

6. A ninth city, Ojai, had extremely stringent growth management policies in place and experienced little growth. The tenth city, Port Hueneme, is completely surrounded by Oxnard.

7. The SOAR movement needed city council support in some cities because SOAR's leaders made a technical error on their own petitions that caused a judge to disqualify the petitions. Thus, instead of being placed on the ballot via citizen petitions, many citywide SOAR measures were placed on the ballot by city councils.

8. The growth boundaries used in this analysis were the voter-imposed SOAR boundaries for those cities that had adopted SOAR initiatives by mid-2000 (Camarillo, Fillmore, Moorpark, Oxnard, Simi Valley, Thousand Oaks, and Ventura) and the SOI boundaries for the remaining three cities (Ojai, Port Hueneme, and Santa Paula). Subsequently, Santa Paula adopted a SOAR boundary that removed some hillside land that had been previously included in the SOI boundary. In addition, Ventura subsequently adopted a vote requirement on hillside land located inside the SOAR boundary.

9. Table 11.5 shows the Holland land-cover classes identified in the California GAP Analysis database and the habitat losses that are likely to occur under Scenarios 1, 3, and 6 for the nonurban areas identified with the 2000 FMMP land-cover/land-use database (see Table 11.2 for details). It should be noted that the land-cover classifications that identify potential wildlife habitat land are different from the nonurban land classifications used elsewhere in this analysis (steep slopes, floodplains, and wetlands), which are based on the nature of the land rather than the vegetative cover. (Agricultural land is also calculated separately, but the overall figure is very similar from both sources.) The results in Table 11.5 must be interpreted carefully—for example, the California GAP Analysis database identified 23,120 acres of urban and 4,740 acres of agricultural land (i.e., the agricultural, orchard and vineyards, and evergreen orchard categories in Table 11.5) that were not identified in the 2000 FMMP database. These additional "urban" and "agricultural" areas constitute 6.2 percent of the potentially developable land in the study area, and their presence in Table 11.5 points to a series of data quality problems. Geospatial data sets compiled from different sources and using different measurements, data structures, and automation techniques often show these types of variations, and it is impossible to tell which one or how much of each of these explanations is correct in this instance. However, the scenarios included in Table 11.5 do show that these problems were reduced over time, because additional losses of urban land ranging from 12 percent to 30 percent were predicted with the three local policy scenarios. This analysis means that the natural habitat area losses predicted with the three scenarios represent underestimates ranging from 4.6 percent (Scenario 3) to 5.6 percent (Scenario 1) on average. The key observation is that these discrepancies are small enough so as not to undermine the analysis and synthesis offered in the remainder of this chapter.

10. In Ventura County, this policy is in place in Ventura, Camarillo, Thousand Oaks, and Simi Valley, all of which also have SOAR initiatives in place. In California generally, about 10 percent of cities (sixty cities) have such policies.

Works Cited

California Department of Conservation. 1994. "A Guide to the Farmland Mapping and Monitoring Program." http://www.consrv.ca.gov/dlrp/fmmp/pubs/ guide.htm.

Davis, Frank W., David M. Stoms, A. D. Hollander, K. A.Thomas, P. A. Stine, D. Odion, M. I. Borchert, J. H. Thorne, V. Gray, R. E. Walker, K. Warner, and J. Graae. 1998. "The California GAP Analysis Database Project." http://www.ucsb.edu.

Fulton, William, Rolf Pendall, Mai Nguyen, and Alicia Harrison. 2001. *Who Sprawls Most? How Growth Patterns Differ across the U.S.* Washington, DC: Brookings Institution Center on Urban and Metropolitan Policy.

Gallant, John C., and John P. Wilson. 1996. "TAPES-G: A Grid-Based Terrain Analysis Program for the Environmental Sciences." *Computers and Geosciences* 22:713–22.

———. 2000. "Primary Topographic Attributes." In *Terrain Analysis: Principles and Applications*, ed. John P. Wilson and John C. Gallant, 51–86. New York: John Wiley.

Glickfeld, Madelyn, William Fulton, Grant McMurran, and Ned Levine. 1999. *Growth Governance in Southern California.* Claremont, CA: Claremont Graduate University Research Institute.

Glickfeld, Madelyn, and Ned Levine. 1992. *Regional Growth—Local Reaction: The Enactment and Effects of Local Growth Control and Management Measures in California.* Cambridge, MA: Lincoln Institute of Land Policy.

Holland, Robert F. 1986. *Preliminary Descriptions of the Terrestrial Natural Communities of California.* Sacramento: California Department of Fish and Game.

Landis, John D., Juan Pablo Monzon, Michael Reilly, and Chris Cogan. 1998. *Development and Pilot Application of the California Urban and Biodiversity Analysis (CURBA) Model.* Berkeley: University of California, Institute of Urban and Regional Development.

Landis, John D., and Ming Zhang. 1998. "The Second Generation of the California Urban Futures Model: Part 1, Model Logic and Theory." *Environment and Planning A* 30:657–66.

McGarigal, Kevin, and B. Marks. 1995. *FRAGSTATS: Spatial Pattern Analysis Program for Quantifying Landscape Structure.* Forest Service General Technical Report PNW-GTR-351. Portland, OR: U.S. Department of Agriculture.

Nunis, Doyce B., Jr., ed. 1993. *Southern California Local History: A Gathering of the Writings of W. W. Robinson.* Los Angeles: Historical Society of Southern California.

Ryan, Christine M. 2001. "Spatial Patterns of Population Growth and Habitat Change in Ventura County under Different Local Policy Scenarios." Master's thesis, University of Huddersfield (Queensgate, England), Department of Geography.

Southern California Studies Center. 2001. *Sprawl Hits the Wall: Confronting the Realities of Metropolitan Los Angeles.* Los Angeles: University of Southern California, Southern California Studies Center/Brookings Institution Center on Urban and Metropolitan Policy.

U.S. Fish and Wildlife Service, Pacific Region. n.d. "Frequently Asked Questions about Critical Habitat and the Coastal California Gnatcatcher." http://pacific.fws.gov/news/gnatcatcher/faqtext.htm.

12 | The Experimental Metropolis: Political Impediments and Opportunities for Innovation

Mara A. Marks, Elizabeth Gearin, and Carol S. Armstrong

Smart Growth, Sustainability, and Regionalism

The policy approaches described elsewhere in this volume represent promising responses to challenges posed by urbanization in Southern California and other growing regions:

- *Smart growth* that directs population growth away from undeveloped areas and into existing urban areas while maintaining or improving the quality of the existing urban fabric
- *Sustainable development* that promotes a competitive and vibrant economy, an equitable and civically engaged community, and a livable natural and built environment
- *Regional cooperation* on pressing economic, environmental, social, and governance problems that defy solution by independent local jurisdictions acting alone

Although not entirely new ideas, smart growth, sustainability, and regionalism have acquired particular cachet in current academic, policy making, and civic discussions. They are increasingly touted as enlightened policy approaches to combat negative effects of population growth and urbanization—including urban sprawl, degradation of the natural environment, traffic congestion, residential segregation, and social fragmentation. Champions of smart growth, sustainability, and regionalism, however, would do well to consider carefully the difficult terrain on which they operate. Clear-eyed understanding, not blind optimism, is required. As a noted scholar of urban development politics has observed, "The common good is something that doesn't just happen. It is something that must be brought into being, albeit imperfectly, by a set of political actors" (Stone 1987, 10).

That enterprise is particularly difficult in Southern California, noted for a political environment so fragmented that "many things are not done because it is impossible to secure the collaboration of all those whose collaboration is needed" (Banfield and Wilson 1963, 11). Unfortunately, many well-intentioned advocates of smart growth, sustainability, and regionalism gloss over the challenges of building coalitions and managing conflict in diverse, fragmented local regions. For example, an official with the Los Angeles chapter of the Urban Land Institute has blithely editorialized that an effective response to the challenge of Southern California's growth begins "with a change in attitude" and can be accomplished through a straightforward process. "The first step," he declares matter-of-factly, "is to agree on a common vision for the region." Once civic-minded leaders discern the best interests of the regional community, "the next logical steps are to create regional dialogues, build consensus, agree on goals and implement action plans to realize the vision" (McCormick 1999).

Implicit in this advice is the simplistic notion that there exists an objective conception of the public interest. In fact, it is terribly misleading to treat the region—or, for that matter, a city or even a neighborhood—as a corporate entity with a unitary interest. It is more appropriate to consider the factors that bestow advantages on some interests over others, the pervasiveness of conflict, and how that conflict is interwoven with opportunities for coalition building and conflict management (Bachrach and Baratz 1962).

In this chapter we analyze seven initiatives under way in Southern California that have been lauded as examples of smart growth, sustainability, and regionalism. The cases illustrate the challenges that bedevil these policy approaches as well as the political conditions that facilitate progress. The following section highlights these challenges and favorable conditions.

The Role of Politics in
Regional Growth and Development

The lack of a unitary interest in policies associated with urban growth, development, and change alluded to above warrants further elaboration, because it stands as the chief impediment to smart growth, sustainability, and regionalism. Henry Cisneros, former secretary of U.S. Department of Housing and Urban Development, has spoken eloquently of the "interwoven destinies" of people in urban regions (in Hiss n.d.). Without a doubt, people who live, work, and invest in local areas share a basic interest in a strong regional economy, a healthy natural environment, livable urban communities, outlets for constructive civic engagement, and widespread opportunities for social and economic advancement. However, beneath general agreement on net, long-term interests are clear and urgently felt concerns about who benefits and who bears the costs of various policy alternatives. Because the costs and benefits are not uniformly distributed, every policy alternative has the potential to spark factional struggle, as is routinely the case in efforts to find sites for desperately needed new schools, housing, and open space. To take another example, short-term interests often compel local jurisdictions to compete with one another although long-term interests suggest the need for collaboration toward a regional vision. In addition, the likelihood of "consensus" fades as the policy making process advances from the formulation of objectives to means of implementation. As programs are made concrete in the process of implementation, they are fashioned by value trade-offs and tactical concessions to unfolding conditions (Stone 1987). As difficult as it is to reach consensus on goals, it is more difficult to reach consensus on means.

Even when it is possible to articulate something approaching a collective interest, there is no guarantee that the necessary actors will exert themselves on behalf of that collective interest. This dilemma, which social scientists term the "free-rider problem," poses a second impediment to smart growth, sustainability, and regionalism (Olson 1971). For example, community residents all prefer clean parks to dirty ones, but, because all will benefit from a cleanup campaign, the incentives for an individual to participate are low. Selective benefits or side payments are often required to ensure that needed actions are performed.

A third impediment stems from a number of institutional, fiscal, regulatory, and other structural arrangements that discourage cooperation on many smart growth, sustainability, and regional initiatives. California's system of state and local government finance, for example, gives city officials incentives to encourage land uses that can promote retail sales tax or development fees. By contrast, officials have no fiscal incentives to approve land uses that most advocates of smart growth, sustainability, and regionalism say are desperately needed, including affordable housing, industrial capacity, and open space. Some of California's regulatory structures also frustrate smart growth, sustainability, and regional objectives. For example, the absence of clear and consistent remediation standards for the redevelopment of urban brownfields contributes to urban sprawl. Lacking regulatory certainty concerning "how clean is clean enough," developers have incentives to develop virgin real estate in outlying areas rather than incur liability on urban sites that may someday be deemed contaminated. Perhaps the most important structural impediment to cooperation and coordination on progressive policy objectives is the fragmentation of power among federal, state, and local authorities. This fragmentation provides multiple points of access for addressing smart growth, sustainability, and regionalism, but it also magnifies the difficulty of building and sustaining coalitions.

Initiatives for smart growth, sustainability, and regionalism must overcome hurdles posed by clashing interests, the free-rider problem, and structural disincentives to cooperation. "Coalition building on behalf of a program is therefore not a simple task of rallying support from among the indifferent," as Stone (1987) cautions; instead, "it is a complicated task of bringing together the people whose particular interests are served, allaying the concerns or isolating those whose particular interests are threatened, and presenting one's actions as being consistent with the good of at least a majority" (8). A number of political conditions help in this strategic task, chief among which are the following:

- Formal authority, the capacity to induce coordinated action
- The ability and willingness to offer selective benefits or side payments to see that needed actions are performed
- Promotion, the ability of leaders to frame issues to appeal to constituencies whose support is required

Laws, legal rulings, regulatory decisions, and other systems of authority improve advocates' capacity to induce coordinated action. Whereas spontaneous and uncoordinated actions of individuals and groups rarely advance smart growth, sustainability, or regional objectives, formal authority can go a long way toward supporting particular initiatives. Formal authority, however, does not guarantee initiatives' success. It is often possible to abide by the letter and not the spirit of a law, administrative ruling, or court decision. The ability and the willingness to provide selective benefits or side payments in exchange for support and cooperation can determine whether needed actions are performed. Among such benefits are financial incentives, political influence, special rights or privileges, and public recognition. In general, the more concrete and particular the benefits traded, the easier it is to secure cooperation. Regulatory exemptions, tax credits, development rights, direct grants, and other selective inducements can transform opponents into allies and free riders into collaborative partners.

Finally, the ability to influence how policy issues and alternatives are perceived can make it easier to mobilize support on behalf of smart growth, sustainability, and regional initiatives. This is not to deny that people have real interests. Rather, the way issues are framed can activate latent interests and create new alignments. As Rein and Schon (1993) have observed, "Framing is a way of selecting, organizing, interpreting, and making sense of a complex reality to provide guideposts for knowing, analyzing, persuading, and acting" (146). Promoting one frame over others is a crucial part of leadership where authority is fragmented among federal, state, regional, county, and local bodies as well among public and private actors. For example, defining problems of traffic congestion, loss of open space, and urban disinvestment as problems of "sprawl" has facilitated coalition building among public officials representing urban, suburban, and rural constituencies as well as corporate and civic interests, community-based organizations, farmers, and conservationists. Framing issues in ways that blur the line between local economic well-being and other aspects of the urban condition can also catalyze new coalitions. Skillful promotion might emphasize the interconnections between a community's quality of life and the attractiveness of an area as an investment site. Many high-wage, high-growth industries choose to locate in regions offering an educated labor force, an efficient transportation system, affordable housing, a healthful natural environment, and cultural amenities. In other words, social equity, urban livability, and environmental protection are good for business. Explicitly identifying common ground between policy concerns enhances prospects for forging coalitions—among business interests, environmentalists, antipoverty advocates, and others. Quantifying the costs or benefits of various policy alternatives is also a way of framing or crystallizing an issue. For example, some of Southern

California's municipal electorates voted to combine their fire and paramedic services after city leaders were able to demonstrate the savings that would result for local taxpayers (Stone 1987; California State Treasurer's Office 1999).[1]

To illustrate further the conditions that facilitate coalition building and conflict management, in the remainder of this chapter we examine seven initiatives to enhance economic, social, and environmental well-being in Southern California. Without a single regional governing authority to guide or restrict creativity and experimentation, a wide variety of policies are being adopted and implemented across the region. Although their objectives vary, coalitions working to advance the initiatives have benefited from favorable conditions that enabled them to overcome impediments. The policies highlighted here are nascent efforts, but they nevertheless offer valuable lessons for advocates of smart growth, sustainability, and regionalism in Southern California and beyond.

Because sustainability encompasses such a broad policy agenda, all the initiatives we discuss below are consistent with at least some objectives of sustainable development. Many of the initiatives are also consistent with smart growth and regional goals. Many reflect years of work to challenge existing arrangements and underscore widespread and varied efforts to develop and maintain an "insurgent regionalism" (Boudreau and Keil 2001). In southeast Los Angeles County, the Gateway Cities Partnership spearheads an effort to enhance the area's economic competitiveness by encouraging investment in human and physical assets. Following decades of antagonism and deadlock, developers and conservationists have adopted a less adversarial and more collaborative approach, planning natural conservation corridors that offer both habitat protection and development certainty in Orange County. Public officials are using the Riverside County Integrated Project to engage the public in strategic planning for Southern California's fastest-growing county. In the Los Angeles Unified School District, campuses participating in the Cool Schools initiative are replacing asphalt with landscaping to keep school buildings cooler and to reduce storm-water runoff. The Village Green residential development features energy-efficient technology projected to reduce energy costs by 30 to 50 percent as well as affordable homes that have easy accessibility to public transportation, child-care facilities, and park space. The Labor/Community Strategy Center leveraged years of grassroots organizing to form the Bus Riders Union, a coalition of the working poor mobilized to press for equity in public services. The city of Santa Monica built on a quarter of a century of a progressive regime of "middle-class radicals"—environmental progressives and renters (Boudreau and Keil 2001)—in its Sustainable City Program. These initiatives vary greatly in terms of policy objectives, geographic focus, and even the degree to which they have been implemented. Taken together, they illustrate a range of coalitional strategies that advocates of smart growth, sustainability, and regionalism may fruitfully employ.

Gateway Cities Partnership

In the absence of regional government, the Gateway Cities Partnership is attempting to provide sorely needed regional leadership to revitalize the economy of southeast

Los Angeles County, expand occupational opportunities for residents, and improve quality of life in the area. Founded in 1997 as a nonprofit collaborative of business, labor, education, and the public sector, the partnership has launched ambitious initiatives to develop a skilled workforce, promote the remediation and reuse of contaminated industrial land, and create a world-class logistics system in the Ports of Los Angeles and Long Beach.

The twenty-seven cities and unincorporated areas in southeast Los Angeles County, known collectively as the gateway cities, have long been Southern California's broad shoulders. Ford built cars in Pico Rivera. Firestone made tires in South Gate. The region's aerospace industry began in Downey, where companies such as Emsco and Consolidated Vultee manufactured the first airplanes on the West Coast and where the Apollo space capsules and space shuttles were built. With the Ports of Los Angeles and Long Beach to the south and cargo railheads and Los Angeles International Airport to the north, Southern California's original manufacturing belt now provides a crucial global gateway for the region (Flanigan 1999; Gateway Cities Partnership 1999b).

The gateway cities, however, have fallen on hard times. During the recession of the early 1990s, catastrophic job losses in the auto, aerospace, and defense industries reverberated throughout the Southern California economy. The number of jobs in the gateway cities decreased by 16.5 percent during the period from 1990 through 1994, contributing to the 10 percent decline in Los Angeles County's employment rate. The gateway cities have not shared in Southern California's stellar economic recovery, and the area remains a point of vulnerability for the region's long-term economic vitality (Gateway Cities Partnership 1999a).

The gateway cities still have the highest urban unemployment rate in California. Ten of the twenty-seven cities, including Compton, Lynwood, and Maywood, have unemployment rates that are two to three times the national average. The high-paying aerospace and defense jobs that vanished from the region during the late 1980s and early 1990s have not reappeared, and many of the new jobs in the gateway cities are relatively low-skill, low-value-added jobs that pay low wages. From 1992 through 1997, the gateway cities lost 24,000 jobs—more than a fifth of the area's job base— in high-wage industries such as aerospace, metals, trade, and transportation. During the same period, the number of jobs in low-wage industries, such as business services, apparel, and textiles, grew by 12 percent. If low-skill, low-wage jobs continue to replace high-skill, high-wage jobs, the area's skill base and spending power will decline. Low educational attainment, high unemployment, and expansion in the proportion of low-skill, low-wage jobs in the gateway cities are reflected in the area's rising poverty rate, which is at least 3 percent higher than the statewide average (Pastor et al. 2000).

Demographic transformations have accompanied economic restructuring in the gateway cities. In 1970, Anglos constituted 68 percent of the population of Los Angeles County. By 1990, they were 41 percent of the population. Many of the county's most dramatic demographic shifts occurred in the gateway cities during the decade of the 1980s. Compton's population shifted from 75 percent African American and

20 percent Latino in 1980 to 53 percent African American and 44 percent Latino in 1990. Several cities, including Bell, Bell Gardens, and Huntington Park, had slim Latino majorities in 1980 but 80 to 90 percent Latino majorities by 1990. Job losses in high-wage industrial sectors affected all residents but hit non-Anglo populations the hardest, in part because they were often the last hired in the growth of manufacturing prior to 1989. In areas of Los Angeles County most affected by the recession of the early 1990s, Latinos were 42 percent of the population and African Americans were 15 percent of the population, whereas in areas least affected by the recession, Latinos were 33 percent of the population and African Americans were 5 percent of the population. At the same time, the expansion of low-wage nondurable manufacturing and service industries relied on an expanding pool of unskilled Latino immigrants (Pastor 2001).

To retain their historic position as a center for high-paying manufacturing jobs, the gateway cities must channel investments into both human and physical assets. The area's precision machining, freight transportation and logistics, and information technology industries all face severe shortages of skilled workers. Unfortunately, 43 percent of all adult residents in the gateway cities have not completed a high school education, let alone specialized training. In terms of physical capital, much of the area's industrial space is in desperate need of modernization: 52 percent of the industrial buildings throughout Los Angeles County are more than thirty years old, and more than 70 percent are over twenty years old. Although many of the gateway cities' industrial facilities are outmoded, overwhelming demand for industrial space has squeezed the industrial vacancy rate to a mere 3 percent. The tight supply of modern industrial facilities undermines the area's ability to attract new high-value-added industries and to retain manufacturers looking to expand their operations. Unless the gateway cities can satisfy demand for both skilled workers and modern industrial facilities, high-wage industries will look to outlying areas of the region or will invest in areas outside of Southern California. The Gateway Cities Partnership's workforce development and land recycling initiatives work in tandem to tackle the human and physical capital needs of the area.

The partnership's ambitious initiatives to restore economic and social vitality to this area must overcome significant structural impediments, including California's inadequate brownfield cleanup policies, upside-down system of state and local government finance, and strong tradition of municipal independence. Most potential real estate sites in the gateway cities have some level of environmental contamination due to previous industrial uses. Despite more than twenty years of scientific studies and experience with toxic cleanup, California has no clear standard of "how clean is clean enough." Lack of certainty that future state and federal regulators will find particular toxic cleanups sufficient increases the liability for developers, the risks for private investors, and the financing costs for development projects.

Moreover, California's system of local government finance discourages cities from allocating municipal resources to assemble, clear, and remediate sites for industrial facilities, install improvements, and mitigate community concerns. Instead, as Lee

Harrington (1999), executive director of the Los Angeles Economic Development Corporation, has observed, "Most cities have battled tooth and nail for the next big box retailer or auto mall, consuming massive amounts of land which generates few livable wage jobs." In the gateway cities, developers have proposed converting major industrial acreage at the Boeing and NASA sites to large blocks of retail. Such land-use decisions would mean that where an aerospace firm once paid workers annual salaries of $60,000, a big-box retailer would pay workers $30,000 to $40,000 less.

The gateway cities' strong tradition of independence presents another impediment to the initiatives of the Gateway Cities Partnership. Beginning with the city of Lakewood's municipal incorporation in 1954, many of the gateway cities incorporated specifically to avoid annexation by one of the two largest cities in Los Angeles County—Los Angeles and Long Beach—and to insulate themselves from those cities' higher tax rates, government spending on social welfare and community services, and perceived urban problems. As Richard Hollingsworth, executive director of the Gateway Cities Partnership, has explained, "Many of our cities have been independent for fifty or sixty years, and they have a hard time envisioning themselves as part of a region" (quoted in *Planning Report* 1999; see also Miller 1981).

Promotion by the organization's leadership has played a key role in the partnership's efforts to knit together civic networks capable of overcoming structural barriers to workforce development and industrial land reuse. To overcome the fragmentation of authority among the area's cities, the partnership has concentrated on fostering a shared sense of geographic identity and a common civic agenda among the area's public officials and leading citizens. As Hollingsworth has put it, pursuing regional objectives has required "a marketing job within the region to remind them of what we are and what our potential is" (quoted in *Planning Report* 1999). To inspire a regional identity among city officials, business owners, and community groups, Hollingsworth has emphasized the area's historic strengths as a center for skilled manufacturing, as a leader in national and international freight transportation and logistics, and as a hub for information technology. To help spread the message among key constituencies, enlist support, and gain legitimacy, Hollingsworth assembled a twenty-nine-member board of directors for the Gateway Cities Partnership that includes representatives from the area's colleges, local governments, leading businesses, and labor unions (Lee 1999; James Irvine Foundation 1999).

Hollingsworth's sales pitch consists of a simple and compelling message that the area has a window of opportunity to shore up its historic strength as a center for skilled manufacturing. Hollingsworth initially identified the precision machining industry as the area's "economic backbone" and quantified the industry's need for skilled workers. Despite challenging times, the gateway cities remain home to about 25,000 precision machinists, the highest concentration in the United States. The area boasts another 3,700 tool and die makers. These skilled workers are employed by thousands of small and medium-sized manufacturers who provide precision-machined tools, parts, and finished products for a variety of industries. A failure to meet local demand for skilled workers would have a devastating impact on the area. The partnership's workforce development initiative aims to train some 15,000 new workers for skilled jobs that pay decent wages. "If we aren't successful," Hollingsworth has warned, "the region will lose about $1.4 billion annually in earnings from the precision machining industry alone" (quoted in *Planning Report* 1999).

Hollingsworth has taken great care in targeting this initiative to unemployed people, workers in transition, single mothers, and at-risk youth. Less than 30 percent of the young people who complete high school in the gateway cities go on to four-year colleges. Among the area's large Latino population, many adults have limited English proficiency and are hourly paid workers without experience with skilled career paths. Many African American families in the area are plagued by multigenerational unemployment and, like many Latinos, lack connections through family or friends to high-wage employment. Hollingsworth and the Gateway Cities Partnership board have called on high school counselors, welfare-to-work coordinators, and community organizations to spread the word that high school graduates with a desire to work and learn can earn "family wages" as skilled workers, with annual salaries in the range of $55,000 to $70,000 (James Irvine Foundation 1999; *Planning Report* 1999, 7).

Through promotion—articulating the workforce needs of a specific industry and focusing attention on the area's untapped human resource potential—the Gateway Cities Partnership has begun to galvanize employers, public and private organizations, educational institutions, and the broader community in support of workforce development efforts. Historically, for example, the area's community colleges and other training centers have turned out fewer than 200 precision machinists per year, compared with the 1,500 the partnership contends are needed to keep pace with the demand for skilled workers over the next decade. Hollingsworth has persuaded four community colleges to place greater emphasis on training for the precision machining industry and to develop new, fast-track curricula (Gateway Cities Partnership 1999a, 1999b). Building on this initial victory, Hollingsworth is exploring prospects for developing a regional high-tech training center that could offer fast-track training programs in the area's key growth industries—precision machining, national and international freight transportation/logistics, and information technology.[2]

In the meantime, the partnership—with the help of six community colleges and universities, area U.S. Congress members, and others—has secured a $2.8 million high-tech training grant from the U.S. Department of Labor to develop an interactive computer-based program to train precision machinists. According to Richard Proudfit, chair of the partnership, the grant "is a great example of harnessing the power of the region to do something really innovative and cutting edge." The grant also enables the partnership to offer selective benefits to move members of the public, private, and educational sectors across the gateway cities to expedite workforce training initiatives.[3]

In addition to increasing the pool of skilled workers for the area's aerospace, information technology, and international trade logistics industries, the Gateway Cities Partnership is promoting the reuse of industrial land in order to attract and retain high-value-added manufacturers. The partnership's land recycling initiative aims to eventually convert some five hundred acres of brownfields, oddly shaped parcels, and other dysfunctional real estate into new, high-quality, aesthetically pleasing industrial space that will "accommodate the companies of the new economy and improve neighborhoods."[4]

Nothing could sell Hollingsworth's land recycling program as well as a successful model. To demonstrate a strategy for redeveloping industrial sites in the gateway cities, Hollingsworth forged relationships with developers, bankers, local governments, and nonprofit organizations such as the California Center for Land Recycling. Under Hollingsworth's leadership, the partnership in 1999 inventoried underutilized and brownfield industrial sites within twenty-six of the gateway cites. Within five months, the partnership analyzed parcel data and met with city planning directors, real estate brokers, and developers to identify approximately 1,300 acres of underutilized or brownfield land on 381 parcels. After compiling poverty, education, and unemployment data for areas surrounding the sites, the partnership worked with city planning directors, private sector experts, and community-based organizations to prioritize the sites for development. This effort paid off for ten cities awarded federal Environmental Protection Agency grants to assess twenty sites for environmental cleanup and redevelopment as industrial sites. The partnership will apply for additional EPA funding for two of these sites.[5]

Hollingsworth's skill in promoting regional initiatives has been critical to the success the partnership has enjoyed so far. The organization has enlisted partners by methodically defining a civic identity for southern Los Angeles County and articulating a strategic vision for the area. Despite the lack of state regulatory standards for toxic cleanup, fiscal disincentives to industrial development, and a tradition of municipal independence, the partnership's ability to quantify the workforce needs of key industries, frame the area's unskilled and underemployed workforce as an untapped resource, and identify sites for industrial reuse has motivated public and private groups to work together to achieve areawide revitalization.

Natural Community Conservation Planning

Regulatory and financial barriers to infill development in urbanized areas such as the gateway cities exacerbate development pressures on "greenfield" sites. High land values in Southern California also create financial incentives to develop land inhabited by nearly two hundred threatened and endangered species. Enacting development moratoriums through the federal Endangered Species Act has been environmentalists' weapon of choice to prevent the destruction of species and habitat by encroaching development. However, the Endangered Species Act provides piecemeal protection for individual species, leaving their habitats at risk. Moreover, as seen in the battle over the spotted owl in the Pacific Northwest, the threat of development moratoriums has polarized conservationists and landowners, discouraging efforts toward negotiation or compromise.

Over the past decade, an alternative tool to protect threatened habitat has come into use in Southern California, relying initially on the formal authority of the U.S.

Department of the Interior and making use of selective benefits to induce cooperation. In an area of six thousand square miles spanning sections of Orange, San Diego,
Riverside, Los Angeles, and San Bernardino Counties, local governments, private landowners, and environmental and wildlife authorities are employing Natural Community
Conservation Planning (NCCP) to reconcile competing objectives of environmental
protection and economic development.[6] The California Natural Community Conservation Planning Act authorized the NCCP pilot program in 1991, giving conservationists and wildlife agencies long-term and ecosystemwide protection, giving
developers assurance against future environmental mitigation measures, and giving
local governments greater latitude to balance demands for growth and demands for
preservation.[7]

Common ground among all these interests seemed impossible during the late
1980s, when a political firestorm swirled around the California gnatcatcher, a tiny
songbird that makes its home in the coastal sage scrub. The Natural Resources Defense
Council petitioned the U.S. Department of the Interior to list the gnatcatcher on the
federal endangered species list, and the California Fish and Game Commission considered placing the gnatcatcher on the state endangered list. The California Building
Industry Association slowed both proceedings by filing for additional information
under the federal and state Endangered Species Acts. In the midst of California's severe
economic recession, politicians weighed in on the controversy, as when Orange County
Representative William Dannemeyer made a none-too subtle jab at conservationists
by introducing a bill in the U.S. Congress that would have declared the American
worker an endangered species.

Creation of the NCCP process appeared to offer a more politically expedient and
environmentally sound alternative to listing the gnatcatcher as an endangered species.
Initial response to the program was, however, underwhelming. Local governments
wanted to avoid enforcing an untested program, and protection of the gnatcatcher
and its habitat varied across local jurisdictions. Although some landowners and governments voluntarily protected coastal sage scrub from development, six months after
creation of the NCCP program, more than two thousand acres of the gnatcatcher
habitat had been destroyed (Fulton 1997).[8]

It took the formal authority of the federal government to make the NCCP process
viable. When U.S. Secretary of the Interior Bruce Babbitt declared the gnatcatcher
threatened—rather than endangered—he made use of an Endangered Species Act
provision permitting special regulations for real estate and economic development.
With the sweep of a pen, Babbitt issued special regulations *requiring* that those interested in developing the gnatcatcher's habitat participate in California's NCCP negotiation process. During the interim period when NCCPs are being negotiated, both the
California Department of Fish and Game and the U.S. Fish and Wildlife Service will
issue permits allowing development of up to 5 percent of low- and medium-quality
gnatcatcher habitat—coastal sage scrub—in each of the eleven pilot subregions. Individual landowners who wish to develop a greater portion are required to demonstrate
that their property is not gnatcatcher habitat.

If politics makes strange bedfellows, so too does regulation. By promoting the NCCP negotiation process, Babbitt's regulations encouraged competing interests to find common ground, providing an alternative to time-consuming and expensive legal battles in connection with Endangered Species Act listings. The provision of selective benefits plays a central role in the NCCP pilot program. The NCCP process gives conservationists something to offer local jurisdictions and landowners in exchange for their cooperation with habitat protection. Jurisdictions that elect not to participate in NCCP negotiations risk a development moratorium under Endangered Species Act litigation, whereas landowners in participating jurisdictions can negotiate agreements that give them development certainty. To help grease the wheels, the California Department of Fish and Game has shared the land acquisition costs in the NCCP pilot program with local jurisdictions.[9]

The NCCP process is not a panacea. Participation by local jurisdictions is voluntary, and some local governments with plan agreements are in no hurry to complete them. In southern Orange County, the primary landowner and key participant in the NCCP process is the Santa Margarita Company. The company's holdings include the San Mateo Creek watershed, the only intact, undammed coastal watershed in California south of Ventura. Santa Margarita has already received approval to build 8,000 homes on 2,400 acres of the site (Pincetl, in this volume). The company, however, does not appear to be in a great hurry to begin development, perhaps because if southern Orange County development exceeds the 5 percent allotment during the interim planning phase, the California Department of Fish and Game and the U.S. Fish and Wildlife Service will block any additional projects in the subregion.

Two of the eleven NCCP subregional plans are now complete, including the coastal/central Orange County subregional plan. Two additional subregional plans are under way in south and north Orange County. The coastal/central plan, approved in July 1996, includes areas previously protected through traditional land-use practices such as exactions, dedications, and purchases, as well as areas with at-risk habitat or species. The resulting preserve encompasses 37,380 acres containing twelve major habitats and thirty-nine threatened or endangered plant and animal species. Conservationists did not get everything they wanted. The U.S. Fish and Wildlife Service exempted the Orange County Transportation Authority from the NCCP, and the authority proceeded with its plans to build the San Joaquin toll road through part of the preserve. Still, the arrangement protects a massive swath of open space in some of the most valuable real estate in the country.[10]

It took intervention at the federal level to make the NCCP process attractive to developers. Today, the NCCP process offers a more flexible, collaborative mechanism for habitat protection than the blunt instrument of the Endangered Species Act. Under the NCCP process, the carrot of development certainty combines with the stick of threatened development moratorium to provide incentives for local jurisdictions and landowners to participate in negotiations, creating opportunities to mediate the conflicting interests of landowners and conservationists.

Riverside County Integrated Project

Southern Californians' sense of stake in their communities is critical to the region's ability to meet the challenges of population growth, yet many Southern Californians feel more connected to people in other parts of the world than to their own neighbors. Fortunately, a number of planning efforts under way throughout Southern California are shoring up civic capacity, deliberately engaging the public in planning processes. In the city of Los Angeles, the Los Angeles Neighborhood Initiative is helping to mobilize neighborhoods behind specific revitalization efforts. The New Schools/ Better Neighborhoods initiative is engaging residents in the Los Angeles Unified School District in the process of siting and designing schools that can serve as anchors for communities. The neighborhood improvement process in the city of Anaheim has engaged residents, landlords, school officials, businesspeople, police officers, and city officials in designing programs to stabilize neighborhoods and squelch drug and gang problems. Long Beach and other Southern California cities are using community workshops, focus groups, and public opinion surveys in their efforts to gauge public preferences and to mobilize communities behind strategic visions. Community consensus building is under way on a countywide scale in Riverside County.

Demographers expect Riverside County's population to reach three million by 2020. Government agencies, builders, and conservationists are struggling to determine where the county will house those people, where to put new roads to accommodate their commutes, where new industrial and commercial centers ought to be built, and how to avoid squeezing out rare plants and animals. County residents, employers, and community organizations have undertaken a bold effort to formulate a strategic vision for how Riverside ought to accommodate this growth. The Riverside County Integrated Project (RCIP) constitutes an ambitious effort that differs procedurally and substantively from traditional planning.[11] In an attempt to approximate a common, countywide interest, the integrated planning process engages Riverside County residents and other stakeholders through community meetings, focus groups, public opinion surveys, and public hearings. The scope of the project also differs considerably from traditional land-use plans, incorporating a state-required update of the county's general plan, a plan for four new transportation corridors, and a Natural Community Conservation Plan to preserve space for about 160 species of plants and wildlife (Haupt 2000).

Structural arrangements and competing interests pose impediments to integrated planning. First, fragmentation of governmental authority means that land-use decisions are typically made and funded on a city-by-city or project-by-project basis. Second, property owners, conservationists, commuters, and others with intensely held opinions about local land-use alternatives are seldom receptive to negotiation and compromise. Third, Riverside County has spent $24 million on the integrated planning process, but acquiring the land to build transportation corridors and preserve open space could cost billions of dollars. Without the confidence that they will be compensated for their property, landowners are reluctant to support the designation of habitat reserves (Downey 2000).

Backers of the integrated planning process have made headway in overcoming these challenges using the art of political promotion to augment the county's formal authority to fund elements of the planning effort. Although the state and federal governments have yet to commit the billions of dollars that will be necessary to implement the integrated plan, the county's success in securing $16 million in state and federal funds for land conservation has increased the credibility of the planning process in the eyes of private interests. Riverside County Supervisor Tom Mullen was key in championing the effort, and he framed the preliminary planning funds in the best possible light. "Securing these," Mullen insisted, "demonstrates our ability to meet this challenge and our commitment to private landowners as we keep this project moving forward." Indeed, area developers recently offered to pay a fee of $452 per unit on newly constructed homes to help the county reach its land acquisition goals. The state and federal funding, according to Borre Winckel, executive director of the Building Industry Association's Riverside County chapter, sends "a strong signal that we don't have to rely on all the money coming from the local level."[12] Furthermore, by fostering civic interest and involvement, integrated plan staff hope to create the impression that a popular mandate exists for coordinated governmental action and thus increase the pressure on local, state, and federal policy makers. Finally, by framing planning issues in a novel way—making explicit the interconnections among land use, jobs, housing, circulation, and conservation—planning staff seek to mediate diverse interests in how the county accommodates growth.

In meetings, focus groups, and polls, residents were challenged to contemplate what aspects of the county are worth preserving and what requires change, whether they wanted housing to enable their own children to reside in the area when they grow up, how Riverside's natural environment affects residents' quality of life, which transportation corridors should be further developed to accommodate population growth and economic activity, and how transportation resources should be allocated between highways and other modes of travel in specific corridors.[13] Through this process, the residents of Riverside County identified specific challenges that face the area over the next twenty years, including managing population growth, easing traffic congestion, maintaining the unique identities of Riverside's communities and neighborhoods, increasing the supply of housing, protecting the areas' natural habitat and air quality, promoting job growth and the local economy, safeguarding agricultural land, providing educational facilities, coping with fiscal limitations, and improving intergovernmental cooperation.[14]

RCIP staff held meetings almost weekly throughout the county to provide information about plan progress and to obtain public input. Staffers made working papers on the integrated plan available in advance of these meetings, enabling members of the public to reflect on alternatives under consideration. In addition to an advisory group comprising representatives from transit, environmental, farmer, builder, and property owner interests in the public and private sectors at the local, state, and federal levels, the public meeting process drew four thousand participants, mostly adults from rural areas and retirees.[15]

By soliciting the public's advice concerning how the county should accommodate the population growth projected, RCIP staff created an environment in which smart growth, sustainability, and regional goals are perceived as socially desirable and politically legitimate. For example, participants advised that niche farming would facilitate a more efficient use of farmland and water resources. Participants suggested that mixed-use opportunities for schools could promote more efficient land use, provide library and recreational facilities for residents, and promote vocational opportunities and superior education for students. Participants recommended that policy makers provide incentives for economic development near housing in order to reduce commute distances. To develop a skilled workforce, participants urged the establishment of education and training programs that concentrate on Riverside's strongest economic sectors. In addition, participants recommended greater intergovernmental coordination on issues such as transit and open-space corridors. Although only a small portion of Riverside's residents participated in the planning meetings, that the process was seen as open increased the odds that county leaders and the general public would regard some of the more novel recommendations as legitimate.

Political promotion is also evident in RCIP staff's efforts to advance the notion that the public reached consensus on a set of long-term goals for the county. In reality, the public-generated "vision plan" reflects a number of values that will need to be reconciled: economic development *and* environmental protection; a government that is both efficient *and* responsive; and protection of private property rights *as well as* preservation of habitat and open space.

Although Riverside's vision plan serves as an incomplete guide for policy makers, and although state and federal funding to implement the integrated plan remains in question, the process of civic engagement in planning issues seems to have fostered a new perspective on growth issues. To the extent that any communitywide vision has been expressed, it seems to be about balance: balance between the continued availability of open space for agriculture, recreation, and conservation and land for economic development and transportation corridors; balance between job growth and housing production and smooth traffic circulation; and balance between coordinated governmental planning and mechanisms for meaningful public participation in planning and governance. Most broadly, the Riverside County Integrated Project has made significant headway in overcoming the county's decentralization of authority as well as the competing visions of those with a stake in the area's future. By engaging the public, this integrated planning effort has already strengthened the county's civic capacity to meet the challenges that lie ahead as its population doubles over the next twenty years.

Bus Riders Union

Civic engagement of the sort under way in Riverside is essential to contend with the challenges of regional growth and change. However, a divide based on class and ethnicity breeds distrust and social separation, eroding a shared sense of stake in Southern

California's future. Repairing the fraying social fabric looms as one of the region's greatest challenges. A number of multiethnic organizing efforts focusing on regional issues of concern to the working poor have taken root in Southern California over the past decade. Action for Grassroots Empowerment and Neighborhood Development Alternatives (AGENDA) seeks to engage ordinary residents in local development policy. The Los Angeles Alliance for a New Economy has pushed for living wage ordinances and worker rights. The Bus Riders Union, a project of the Labor/Community Strategy Center, overcame collective action problems by framing inequities in the provision of public services in a way that has aided in "community" organizing at a regional level (Pastor 2001).

The Labor/Community Strategy Center's initial challenge to corporate polluters and regional regulators failed to spark community outrage beyond the directly affected local neighborhoods. Other residents, though sympathetic to the cause of environmental justice, chose not to invest time and energy in the issue. Hoping to inspire a regionwide progressive social movement, the center in 1992 began efforts to raise consciousness among a geographically diverse, multiethnic, working-class constituency about transportation inequity in Los Angeles County. It was that year that the Los Angeles County Transportation Commission and the Rapid Transit District merged to form the Metropolitan Transportation Authority (MTA). An important charge of the fledgling agency was expanding transit systems in Los Angeles County, and most of the MTA's twenty-year, $70 billion spending program was to be allocated to construction of a new light rail and subway system. Organizers from the Labor/Community Strategy Center contended that the rail lines, which tend to run from the suburbs to the central city, benefit suburban middle-class commuters and ignore the needs of the region's transit-dependent working poor.

Transit afforded the center a bread-and-butter issue to mobilize Los Angeles's working-class residents across geographic and ethnic lines (Pastor 2001). Most of those who ride MTA buses live in areas not served by rail, cannot afford private transportation, and depend on the bus system for access to jobs, schools, health care facilities, and other services throughout the region. Some 60 percent of MTA bus riders have annual household incomes below $15,000. Only 10 percent have annual household incomes above $30,000. These riders depend on the MTA bus system, characterized by MTA critics as underfunded, overcrowded, and insufficient (Lopez 1998). Especially during peak travel times, there are not enough seats for riders, and overfull buses often speed past bus stops with waiting commuters. Bus air conditioning is usually nonfunctioning, and buses are littered with trash. By contrast, suburban rail passengers travel in comfortable seats with pullout desks on clean trains. In recent years, the MTA has made huge capital investments to build rail lines. To service that debt and keep fares low to attract riders, the MTA subsidizes each commuter rail ticket to the tune of $2.92 to $21.00, depending on the rail line. In contrast, the average subsidy for a bus passenger is $1.17.[16]

Eric Mann, director of the Labor/Community Strategy Center, framed transit system inequities as evidence of "transit racism" when efforts got under way to organize the MTA's passengers as the Bus Riders Union. Initially, members of the Bus Riders Union attended MTA meetings to lobby for alternative policies. In 1994, when MTA decision makers met the union's demands for improved service with proposals for bus fare hikes, the tactics of the Bus Riders Union expanded from grassroots organizing to legal action. Promoting MTA's policies as racist helped the Bus Riders Union enlist key organizations as the locus of conflict shifted from hearing rooms to courtrooms. The NAACP Legal Defense Fund helped the Bus Riders Union bring a class-action lawsuit against the MTA. The Southern Christian Leadership Conference, the Korean Immigrant Workers' Advocates, and 350,000 mostly poor and minority bus riders joined in the suit. The plaintiffs charged that MTA policies violated U.S. civil rights laws, arguing that the MTA was subsidizing its commuter rail system on the backs of poor, mostly minority bus riders who would have to struggle to pay even the smallest fare increase.

The plaintiffs insisted that the court should require the MTA to bring its bus system to a respectable level of operations, including providing new buses and expanding service. In a 1996 consent decree, the MTA agreed to ensure that transit patrons—regardless of race, color, creed, or national origin—have equal access to an integrated transit system. As elements of the settlement, the MTA agreed to reduce the price of a monthly bus pass, lower the off-peak fare, and add more than 150 buses to its fleet within two years. The settlement also required the MTA to increase the number of transit police on buses, to provide new bus service to educational and job training centers and to county hospitals, and to spend $45 billion to upgrade bus shelters (Wachs 1997; Pastor 2001).[17]

The MTA has honored its agreement to hold bus fares steady. The success of the Bus Riders Union in diverting funding from middle-class-oriented rail projects to the bus system represents a significant victory. However, the MTA has flouted its commitment to add new buses and to increase bus service. Court monitors ordered the MTA to purchase 350 new buses, but under pressure from environmentalists to replace its diesel fleet with lower-emission vehicles and from its unionized drivers and mechanics not to reduce their overtime pay, the MTA has appealed this latest court action.[18]

Despite these mixed policy outcomes, the Bus Riders Union stands as an example of grassroots coalition building across geographic and ethnic lines. Whereas the Labor/Community Strategy Center had previously failed to mobilize a coalition for collective action, the transit issue struck a chord. By framing its organizing efforts in terms of immediate concern for the region's working poor, the Bus Riders Union managed to piece together a multiethnic progressive coalition that may be enlisted in future regional causes (Pastor 2001; Bell 1995; Environmental Defense 1999).

Cool Schools

Visitors to Los Angeles are sometimes taken aback by the sight of school playgrounds covered in asphalt, devoid of even a blade of grass. In the Los Angeles Unified School District, the nation's second largest, students play and practice on enough concrete to pave four hundred miles of four-lane highway (Los Angeles Department of Water and

Power n.d.). A number of local community organizations have been involved in urban greening and beautification programs in particular neighborhoods, but they have had to scramble for volunteers and have sometimes had to compete with each other for funding. Schools often rely on students, parents, and neighbors for help in pulling weeds and picking up trash on playgrounds, but they usually lack the resources to sustain cooperative efforts for larger-scale and longer-term projects. Under the leadership of Andy Lipkis, a local nonprofit environmental group called TreePeople initially overcame barriers to collective action by framing tree planting and asphalt removal as an issue of energy efficiency. Subsequently, the greening program won the financial and institutional support of the Los Angeles Department of Water and Power (DWP) and Los Angeles Unified School District.

With the help of scientists at the U.S. Department of Energy and Lawrence Livermore Laboratory, TreePeople quantified the benefits of planting trees to shade and cool school buildings. The scientists determined that properly placed, appropriate types of trees can reduce energy expenditures by 12–18 percent. TreePeople argued that these cost savings would more than offset the costs of installing and maintaining new landscaping. Armed with these figures, Lipkis and his organization were able to promote asphalt replacement and tree planting not as a mere campus beautification program, but rather as a cost-saving measure for school facilities—one with attractive environmental side benefits. By quantifying the cost savings that Los Angeles Unified School District would realize in exchange, TreePeople convinced the school board to allow schools to allocate part of their share of a recent $2.3 billion facilities bond to replace more than 30 percent of the asphalt on each campus with trees and greenery. The effort aligned nicely with conservation initiatives of the Los Angeles DWP, which got into the act by providing $6 million for the acquisition and planting of 8,200 trees and the development of an environmental curriculum emphasizing biology, botany, and horticulture.[19]

Generous public funding, along with institutional support from DWP and L.A. Unified, enabled TreePeople to build and maintain a coalition to implement the Cool Schools program. In addition to TreePeople, four other nonprofit community groups are helping to implement the Cool Schools program: North East Trees, the Hollywood Beautification Team, the Los Angeles Conservation Corps, and the Watts Labor Community Action Coalition. Although these organizations usually serve particular geographic areas, each has agreed to work with any school in the district on the Cool Schools project. Moreover, instead of having to compete for funding and other resources, these nonprofits are working together amicably. This level of cooperation is paying off at individual school sites where harried teachers, school administrators, parents, and community members know that their time, attention, and physical labor will be matched by public funding to make visible improvements. In short, TreePeople initially used promotional tactics, framing its tree-planting program as a cost-saving measure. The approach paid off, enabling the Cool Schools program to marshal the formal authority of the school board and to secure funding from the school district and from the DWP.

Cool Schools participants follow a three-step process. First, a given campus is analyzed for both its existing and potential trees and green space. Landscape professionals from a tree-planting organization walk the site and hold "Green Team" meetings with school administrators, teachers, students, parents, and other community members to identify tree-planting needs. Second, the tree-planting organization designs a landscape proposal that reflects the particular needs and unique character of the school. Once the school approves this plan, L.A. Unified officials check it for possible interference with underground utilities or vehicular access. Finally, L.A. Unified removes asphalt from the selected areas, and the tree-planting organization oversees a school and community-based team of volunteers in planting. As part of the Cool Schools learning curriculum, students give each tree a name and care for it over the first two years after planting. In 1999, the first year of the program, an average of 88 trees were planted at each of 42 schools. In the second phase of the program, Cool Schools provided an average of 105 trees per campus at another 40 schools.

With 708 square miles of campuses across the school district, the Cool Schools initiative could have a positive impact on the region's ecosystem. In Los Angeles, the large amount of school grounds covered over by asphalt creates a "heat island." Buildings and pavement absorb the sun's radiation as heat throughout the day, radiate the stored heat in the evening, and create convection patterns that exacerbate the effects of photochemical smog (Hough 1995). Replacing asphalt with vegetation decreases absorbed heat and promotes evening cooling. By trapping and absorbing up to 50 gallons of water each, the trees will also reduce the storm-water runoff that causes flooding and pollution during the rainy season and reduce schools' need to pump water for irrigation. Equally important, as the trees mature and shade the campus, they will make the schools cooler, more pleasant, and more attractive places for students.

The Cool Schools initiative has yielded other side benefits as well. Community participation in design and planting has promoted civic pride and a shared sense of stake in the schools' well-being. Working together on this shared project has also built trust and relationships that extend to other types of collaborative action. TreePeople's ability to quantify the energy and cost savings of the program and the willingness of the DWP and L.A. Unified to provide funding and institutional backing have encouraged collective action to flourish—along with trees.

Village Green

Widely shared aspirations for home ownership fueled a pro-housing civic agenda for most of Southern California's postwar history. Voters regularly approved by 70 to 80 percent majorities huge general-obligation bonds to build the infrastructure of streets, utilities, and schools required by suburban residential development. Federal government mortgage subsidies, state and local infrastructure subsidies, and postwar prosperity placed the dream of home ownership within reach of an expanded middle class. Developers covered the flatlands of greater Los Angeles with ranch homes as well as with modest "dingbat" apartments. As the plains filled up, developers transformed Southern California's hillsides into vast residential tracts (Brackman, Guerra, and Marks 2001).

Nothing approaching a pro-housing consensus exists today in Southern California. Residential construction in the region has lagged as population has increased. A recent report published by the California Department of Housing and Community Development and the University of California, Berkeley, Institute of Urban and Regional Development (2000) estimates that if current trends continue, the net housing deficit for the region will be 48,000 housing units by 2010. Clashes between developers and environmentalists are becoming more common, and growth opponents frequently raise environmental concerns to block regulatory approval for proposed housing and other development projects. Choosing their battles, most for-profit developers have consigned the low- and moderate-income housing market to nonprofit organizations that specialize in inner-city development.

The ability of environmentalists and other interests opposed to new development to block the construction of new housing has meant that the supply of housing has stagnated while the demand for housing has escalated. This imbalance in the region's housing market has had the predictable effect on housing prices. In Los Angeles County, for example, only about one in three households can afford to purchase the median-priced home, and more than half of all renters must work more than forty hours per week or spend more than 30 percent of their income on housing in order to afford a typical apartment (National Low-Income Housing Coalition 2000).

Some local residential developments manage to navigate the contentious construction approval process by co-opting or preempting potential opponents. Skillful promotion and the ability to offer selective benefits—in the form of cutting-edge construction techniques and creative financing—enabled locally based developers Lee Homes and Braemar Urban Ventures to build an ecologically sound and economically affordable community embodying smart growth principles.

Village Green, the largest transit-oriented affordable-housing community in Los Angeles County, comprises 186 new single-family detached homes within a short walk of the Sylmar/San Fernando Metrolink station. Village Green includes a child-care center, a 27,000-square-foot neighborhood park, and a "tot lot" playground.[20] Development density is about twelve units per acre, with average lot size approximately 3,000 square feet and each unit covering between 1,400 and 1,700 square feet. Home prices, considered affordable for low- and moderate-income buyers in the Los Angeles housing market, range from $150,000 to the mid-$190,000s for three- to four-bedroom family units (*Southern California Builder* 1999). Strong consumer demand sparked an early sellout for the first two phases of the project as first-time buyers snapped up 45 houses in a four-month period in 1999.[21]

A regional leader in urban infill development, the Lee Group seized several opportunities to make the project profitable for itself and affordable to buyers. Century Housing, a private financier, provided a reduced-interest construction loan as well as grants to reduce home buyers' closing costs and down payments. The Los Angeles Housing Department provided silent second mortgages to low- and moderate-income buyers.[22] In addition, the U.S. Department of Housing and Urban Development designated Village Green as the first pilot site for a national public-private program—

Partnership for Advancing Technology in Housing (PATH)—that enabled the developers to make the homes energy efficient as well as affordable. Under the HUD-administered PATH program, the homes were constructed according to the U.S. Department of Energy's Building America standards—designed to produce high-quality homes that require half the energy of typical homes but cost no more to build.[23] The U.S. Department of Energy, the Southern California Gas Company, BP Solar, the Los Angeles DWP, and Fannie Mae provided the technical assistance and cooperation that made these innovations possible. Village Green is the largest photovoltaic housing community in Southern California, with solar electric roof panels that generate a significant portion of electrical energy necessary to run lighting and appliances. The homes also feature upgraded superinsulation, window glazing designed to block 87 percent of the sun's ultraviolet rays, energy-efficient gas water- and space-heating systems, gas air conditioning, and mechanical ventilation. In addition, the homes showcase new structural steel and engineered wood products designed to reduce the amount of lumber needed and increase the efficiency of heating and cooling. These energy-saving technologies reduce home owners' energy bills by 30 to 50 percent and assist buyers in qualifying for mortgages.[24] Over time, the developers intend to achieve a 50 percent reduction in environmental impact, energy use, and maintenance costs and to reduce home owners' monthly maintenance costs by at least 20 percent.[25]

The Lee Group's success in framing this project as socially and ecologically responsible undercut potential opponents' ability to mobilize effectively against it. A well-orchestrated groundbreaking ceremony was typical of the sophistication of Village Green's promotional efforts. Then-President Clinton was among the dignitaries who attended the event. The developers have also publicized the praise Village Green has received from other elected officials, industry groups, and environmental organizations. For example, then-Vice President Gore called Village Green "a model for the U.S. construction industry . . . [demonstrating] the power of partnership between private industry and government to improve our homes and environment."[26] California State Treasurer Philip Angelides declared Village Green a model for smart growth. Los Angeles City Council member Ruth Galanter called the development "living proof that the building industry can combine new environmental technologies with affordable housing right here in one of the largest housing markets in the nation." The National Association of Home Builders named the project a Gold Energy Value Home, and Major Achievements in Marketing Excellence gave the project the 1999 Energy Efficient Home of the Year award. The environmental organization Global Green has proclaimed that Village Green gets "to the core of how we design, build, and maintain our homes and communities." These accolades are included in the developer's pitch at public hearings, on the project's Web site, and in other documentation promoting the project.

Although Southern California faces a severe housing deficit, opponents to new development have been highly successful in thwarting the construction of new homes. With financing and technical assistance from Century Housing, HUD, the U.S. Department of Energy, and others, Village Green's developers were able to promote the development as socially responsible and to make an innovative and much-needed project a reality (Petersen 1998; California State Treasurer's Office 1999).[27]

Santa Monica Sustainable City Program

Champions of sustainable development point to Austin, Chattanooga, San Francisco, and Seattle. In each of these cities, civic, business, and community leaders are crafting policy solutions to interrelated challenges of urbanization and tracking progress toward policy goals.[28] One of the most respected of these benchmarking programs is under way in Southern California. Through its Sustainable City Program, the city of Santa Monica has established targets for resource conservation, transportation, pollution prevention, public health protection, and community and economic development.

Most benchmarking programs confront two obstacles. First, as with any policy goal, the choice of benchmarks can be highly contentious as various groups struggle to safeguard their interests. Typically this difficulty is overcome through the removal of threats of penalties if the benchmarks are not met. This approach raises a second set of obstacles, however, in that facilitating collective action becomes more difficult. Santa Monica sidestepped these obstacles by directing the benchmarking program at the practices of city government itself, making policy formulation less controversial and making compliance easier to secure. Two political conditions—promotion by advocates of the program and the backing of formal political authority—facilitated Santa Monica's Sustainable City Program.

With renters and environmentalists ensconced for many years in Santa Monica's governing coalition, the city has a long tradition of progressive politics. In that context, the Sustainable City Program took root in 1991 when city officials created the Task Force on the Environment, composed of citizen volunteers with diverse environmental expertise to work with city staff in the existing Environmental and Public Works Management and Environmental Programs Divisions. To guide and coordinate the city's environmental policies and programs, the task force proposed framing its agenda under the rubric of sustainability. For more than a year, the task force promoted its sustainability agenda, engaging the community through questionnaires, presentations, community meetings, and a widely circulated draft Sustainable City Plan. Advocates of the program within city government were then in the position to promote the notion that a popular mandate exists for benchmarks, ranging from targets for water and energy conservation to pollution reduction to solid waste reduction. When in 1994 the city council held hearings on whether to adopt the program, advocates were able to claim that "resident stakeholders" recommended the benchmarks and indicators. Once the city council voted to adopt the sustainability indicators and benchmarks, the formal authority of city government was brought to bear on the Sustainable City Program. Going forward, the council's political self-interest in claiming credit for progress toward the sustainability indicators helps "compel them to act . . . to effect change," according to Dean Kubani, coordinator for the Sustainable City Program. As Kubani has observed, "If these indicators were developed by a group outside of the city government without the buy-in by the council, . . . I doubt that any of the positive changes that have been made would have occurred."[29]

Today, the benchmarks inform the policies, programs, and operations of Santa Monica city government. Rather than requiring businesses and residents to participate, the Sustainable City Program avoided battles over competing values that could have derailed the project. Instead, the effort brings formal governmental authority to bear on matters over which city officials have direct authority, such as city purchasing and contracting. Where the city of Santa Monica does in fact have formal authority, the city council can effect substantive changes. For example, a plan to reduce the use of toxic chemicals such as pesticides in all city operations has made Santa Monica a national model. In areas where the city lacks formal authority, progress toward sustainability has been more symbolic than substantive. In 1996, for example, the city council passed a resolution asking the GTE and Pacific Bell telephone companies to prevent the overproduction of telephone directories. The resolution drew praise from environmentalists opposed to the clear-cutting of rain forests for paper pulp but resulted in no concrete action by the phone companies.

Still, the city has wide latitude to make progress toward resource conservation and other goals on the strength of its own authority. In 1999, for example, Santa Monica became the first city in the nation to obtain all of its electrical power from renewable sources.[30] The result has been measurable progress toward a number of goals. Water usage in the city declined by 13.3 percent between 1990 and 1998. The number of city fleet vehicles operating on reduced emission fuels increased from 10 percent in 1993 to 65 percent in 1999. The amount of untreated dry-weather urban runoff entering the Santa Monica Bay from the city has declined by 92 percent since 1990, and construction of a new runoff treatment facility will lead to further reductions. Public open space in the city increased by 10 percent between 1990 and 1998.

The Santa Monica Sustainable City Program has garnered national attention. President Clinton's Council on Sustainable Development (1997) recognized Santa Monica as a "sustainable community," and the U.S. Department of Energy (n.d.) named Santa Monica a "clean city success story." The U.S. Environmental Protection Agency (1998) has lauded the city's "green purchasing program" and encourages other cities to emulate Santa Monica's purchasing practices. All of this has heightened awareness of sustainable practices among city staff and has set a positive example for Santa Monica's residents and businesses as well as for other municipalities (City of Santa Monica 1999). With the aura of a popular mandate and the weight of formal authority, the Santa Monica Sustainable City Program has aligned city policy with sustainability goals and has made Santa Monica an example to the region and beyond.

Conclusion

Southern California has long stood as a symbol of the possible, and today, many cities across the nation look to the region as a harbinger of their own urban destinies. In addition to the seven cases highlighted in this chapter, other initiatives throughout

Southern California provide reason for optimism. Location-efficient mortgages soon
to be offered in a new housing development in the city of Fillmore will lower housing costs for families that use mass transit.[31] The Metropolitan Water District, which
serves most of Southern California, has enlisted community-based organizations to
distribute free low-flush toilets in low-income communities. The old toilets are crushed
and used as roadbed material, water consumption is reduced, and the community
organizations receive operating support.[32] The Santa Monica Mountains Conservancy,
created in 1979 by the California State Legislature, manages thirty thousand acres
of parks and wildlife habitat. The conservancy recently joined forces with the cities
of Whittier, Diamond Bar, Brea, and La Habra Heights to connect green space and
to protect the Puente Hills ecosystem shared by those cities (California State Polytechnic University 1997). Other cities in densely populated southeast Los Angeles
County are rehabilitating abandoned industrial facilities along the Los Angeles River
with parks and bikeways.[33] The New Schools/Better Neighborhoods initiative engages
local communities to select sites and design desperately needed new schools in the
Los Angeles Unified School District. In neighborhoods that have little available land
but surging school-age populations, the initiative runs workshops that have generated creative ideas for school facilities planning, including joint-use arrangements
with libraries, parks, museums, and senior centers (Binger 1999). These and other
initiatives promoting smart growth, sustainability, and regionalism provide promising policy approaches to the complex challenges posed by growth, development, and
change.

The experiences of the people involved in these initiatives also offer warnings for
those pursuing similar agendas. First, competing conceptions of the public interest
remain regardless of how often the "common good" is invoked to advance particular
initiatives. For example, the civic engagement component of the Riverside County
Integrated Project has fostered a collaborative planning environment, but planners
will eventually have to reconcile the competing values of economic development and
environmental protection, government efficiency and responsiveness, and protection
of private property rights and environmental conservation. In the case of the Village
Green project, the developers effectively defused potential opposition, but Southern
California's landscape is dotted with failed attempts to build responsible projects
because opponents to growth of any kind have proven more powerful.

Second, even when key stakeholders do reach consensus, their cooperation is by
no means guaranteed. Funding provided by the DWP and L.A. Unified School District has created incentives for five separate nonprofit organizations to work together
and for school communities to participate in the Cool Schools program. By contrast,
although the gateway cities confront common challenges, including the need to improve residents' skill base and the need to attract and retain high-wage jobs, economic
restructuring, fiscal pressures, demographic shifts, and a tradition of municipal independence conspire against collective action.

Third, institutional, regulatory, and other structural arrangements make mobilization on behalf of some projects easier than mobilization on behalf of others. Once the

city of Santa Monica adopted its sustainability benchmarking program, city departments were compelled to cooperate: any foot-dragging could have negative impacts on future budget, staff, or programmatic requests that go before the city council. In Orange County, regulations issued by the U.S. secretary of the interior forced developers to participate in the NCCP negotiation process if they nurtured any hope of being awarded permits on gnatcatcher habitat. By contrast, achievement of the key goals of the Riverside County Integrated Project will require substantial state and federal funding commitments. Similarly, the Bus Riders Union lacks the authority to compel the MTA to abide by court orders to provide more buses, expand bus service, and improve transit conditions.

Many obstacles to smart growth, sustainability, and regionalism can be alleviated or even removed once barriers are identified, analyzed, and understood. The initiatives profiled in this chapter and scores of others under way throughout Southern California offer inspiration and strategic lessons to those who seek to make older urban areas more livable and more economically competitive, to safeguard natural areas and fragile ecosystems, and to shore up civic engagement and reduce social stratification. Operating in arenas of competing interests, beset by collective action problems, and bedeviled by political fragmentation and other structural impediments, efforts such as those highlighted here can be advanced through some combination of skillful promotion by policy champions who can compellingly frame and crystallize issues, formal authority to compel action and provide a stable institutional base, and participants' ability and willingness to exchange selective benefits for cooperation. In the absence of a central authority capable of inducing action, coalitions seeking smart growth, regionalism, and sustainability objectives must be pieced together on an issue-by-issue basis and nurtured at least until the policy initiatives can bear fruit. These coalitions can be fragile, short-lived, and narrowly focused. However, they provide great opportunity for local innovation.

Notes

1. Focus group with local elected officials, Loyola Marymount University, Los Angeles, January 8, 2001.

2. California Center for Regional Leadership (CCRL) Web site, http://www.calregions.org/civic/partners/south-gcp.html.

3. Gateway Cities Partnership, "Gateway Cities Region Receives $2.8 Million for High Tech Training," press release, http://www.gateway-partnership.org/document4.htm.

4. Gateway Cities Partnership Web site, http://www.gateway-partnership.org/initiatives.htm. See also the description of similar "high-road" economic strategies in Luria and Rogers (1999).

5. CCRL Web site, http://www.calregions.org/civic/partners/south-gcp.html. See also Cline and Garcia (2000). The city of Long Beach, the largest gateway city, has its own land recycling program.

6. *New York Times* editorial, March 24, 1997, cited on California Department of Fish and Game Web site, http://www.dfg.ca.gov/news/97023.html.

7. Codified as chapter 10 of division 3 of the California Fish and Game Code (2800 et seq.) per "Introduction to NCCP General Process Guidelines," http://ceres.ca.gov/CRA/NCCP.

8. Interview with Dr. Daniel Silver, Endangered Habitats League, May 18, 2000; interview with Gail Presley, California Department of Fish and Wildlife, May 18, 2000; California State Department of Fish and Game Web site, http://www.dfg.ca.gov/news.

9. For example, the California Department of Fish and Game and the U.S. Fish and Wildlife Service have agreed to shoulder 50 percent of the land acquisition costs for the San Diego NCCP, estimated at more than $200 million for 27,000 acres. Interview with Gail Presley.

10. Ibid.

11. Information regarding the basis for the plan, including population projections, comes from the RCIP Web site, http://www.rcip.org/stakeholdertext.htm; see also Verdin (2000).

12. Mullen and Winckel are both quoted in "Riverside County Integrated Project to Receive $10 Million," RCIP press release, February 1, 2001.

13. RCIP Web site, http://www.rcip.org.

14. Twelve community meetings were held to develop a general sense of issues throughout the county between June 17 and July 16, 1999. Our information sources include an interview with Beth Kuch, public relations manager for the RCIP consultant, May 18, 2001; an RCIP question-and-answer brochure; "RCIP: A Summary of the First Round of Community Workshops June/July 1999," prepared by Moore, Iacofano, Goltsman, Inc.; and "Riverside County Public Opinion Survey Report," January 14, 2000.

15. Interview with Beth Kuch.

16. Figures on subsidies and security expenses come from Environmental Defense (1999).

17. A summary of the consent decree is available on the Legal Defense Fund's Web site, http://www.ldfla.org/sumcd.html.

18. Information regarding the status of compliance with the consent decree was provided by Martin Hernandez, organizer, Los Angeles Labor/Community Strategy Center, in an interview on August 18, 2000.

19. Sources for the information in this paragraph are as follows: interview with Chuck Arnold, project coordinator, North East Trees, July 14 and August 4, 2000; Binger (1999); New Schools/Better Neighborhoods Web site, http://www.nsbn.org/community/building.html; Los Angeles Department of Water and Power (n.d.).

20. HFS Master Builders: The Braemar Group Web site, http://www.homesforsale-socal.com/mhb/mhb3.htm; Lee Group Web site, http://www.leehomes.net/about/about.html.

21. "ToolBase: PATH E-News," vol. 5, 1999, on National Association of Home Builders Research Center Web site, http://www.nahbrc.org/toolbase/rrr/pvol0599.htm.

22. Interview with Jay Stark, city liaison for the Lee Group, August 29, 2001; Lee Group Web site, http://www.leehomes.net/about/about.html.

23. Information about Building America is available on the U.S. Department of Energy Web site, http://www.eren.doe.gov/buildings/building_america/los_angeles.shtml.

24. Lee Group Web site, http://www.leehomes.net/about/about.html.

25. Ibid.; "National Pilot: Village Green," http://www.pathnet.org/inaction/sanfernando.html; U.S. Department of Housing and Urban Development (2000).

26. Quoted in "Village Green Unveils Energy-Efficient, Affordable Homes," May 17, 1999, http://www.pathnet.org/news/990517.html.

27. See also ibid.

28. City of Austin, Texas, Web site, http://www.ci.austin.tx.us/sustainable; Seattle Community Network Web site, http://www.scn.org/sustainable.

29. Remarks made during a presentation at the University of Southern California, Los Angeles, September 13, 1999.

30. Dean Kubani, in discussion of the importance of indicators on the Redefining Progress Community Indicators electronic Listserv, July 2000.

31. Natural Resource Defense Council Web site, http://www.nrdc.org/nrdc/nrdcpro/reports/lemrpt.html; National Housing Institute Web site, http://www.nhi.org/online/issues/103/lem.html.

32. MWD Web site, http://www.mwd.dst.ca.us.

33. Trust for Public Land Web site, http://www.tpl.org/onsite/entry-search.html; Friends of the Los Angeles River Web site, http://www.folar.org.

Works Cited

Bachrach, Peter, and Morton S. Baratz. 1962. "Two Faces of Power." *American Political Science Review* 56:947–92.

Banfield, Edward C., and James Q. Wilson. 1963. *City Politics.* New York: Vintage.

Bell, Tina Jenkins. 1995. "To Live and Ride in LA." *The Neighborhood Works*, June/July, 18.

Binger, Steven. 1999. *What If: New Schools, Better Neighborhoods, More Livable Communities.* San Francisco: James Irvine Foundation.

Boudreau, Julie-Anne, and Roger Keil. 2001. "Seceding from Responsibility? Secession Movements in Los Angeles." *Urban Studies* 38(10):1701–31.

Brackman, Harold, Fernando Guerra, and Mara Marks. 2001. "Rebuilding the Dream: A New Housing Agenda for Los Angeles." Unpublished report, Loyola Marymount University, Center for the Study of Los Angeles.

California Department of Housing and Community Development and University of California, Berkeley, Institute of Urban and Regional Development. 2000. *Raising the Roof.* Sacramento: California Department of Housing and Community Development.

California State Polytechnic University, Pomona. 1997. "Puente Hills Corridor: Greenspace Connectivity for Wildlife and People." Unpublished report.

California State Treasurer's Office. 1999. *Smart Investments: A Special Update of the California Debt Affordability Report.* Sacramento: California State Treasurer's Office.

City of Santa Monica, Task Force on the Environment. 1999. "Sustainable City Progress Report Update."

Cline, Susan, and Brianna Garcia. 2000. "Brownfield Redevelopment in the Los Angeles Basin." *DISP* 140:23–27.

Downey, Dave. 2000. "Regional Habitat Conservation Plan Taking Place Shape." *The Californian*, November 5.

Environmental Defense. 1999. "Fighting for Equality in Public Transit: Labor Community Strategy Center v. MTA." http://www.environmentaldefense.org/article.cfm?contentid=2826.

Flanigan, James. 1999. "Downey Takes Lead to Revive Gateway Cities." *Los Angeles Times*, June 16, C1, C4.

Fulton, William. 1997. *The Reluctant Metropolis: The Politics of Urban Growth in Los Angeles.* Point Arena, CA: Solano.

Gateway Cities Partnership. 1999a. "Gateway Cities Regional High Tech Training Center for the Region: Training for Family Wage Jobs and Careers." Unpublished report, Paramount, CA.

————. 1999b. "A Review of Social, Environmental, and Economic Performance Indicators for the Gateway Cities." Unpublished report, Paramount, CA.

Harrington, Lee. 1999. "Los Angeles' Economic Vitality Is at Risk Because We Disincentivize Industrial Land Uses." *Planning Report*, April 20.

Haupt, Wyatt, Jr. 2000. "Federal, State Officials Vow to Back County." *Californian*, September 26.

Hiss, Tony. n.d. "Outlining the New Metropolitan Initiative." http://www.cnt.org/mi/outline.htm.

Hough, Michael. 1995. *Cities and Natural Process*. London: Routledge.

James Irvine Foundation. 1999. "Workforce Development Case Studies." http://www. civicnavigator.com/workforce.pdf.

Lee, Don. 1999. "L.A. County Jobs Surge since '93, but Not Wages." *Los Angeles Times*, July 26.

Lopez, Steve. 1998. "The Few, the Proud, the Bus Riders." *Time*, August 31. http://www.time. come/time/magazine/1998/dom/980831/file.the_few_the_proud_t20.html.

Los Angeles Department of Water and Power. n.d. "Cool Schools Benefits." http://www.ladwp. com/coolschools/pages/benefits.html.

Luria, Daniel D., and Joel Rogers. 1999. *Metro Futures: Economic Solutions for Cities and Their Suburbs*. Boston: Beacon.

McCormick, James Watt. 1999. "Regional Approach Needed to Solve Land-Use Problems." *Real Estate Southern California*, November/December, 24.

Miller, Gary J. 1981. *Cities by Contract: The Politics of Municipal Incorporation*. Cambridge: MIT Press.

National Low-Income Housing Coalition. 2000. "Out of Reach: The Growing Gap between Housing Costs and Income of Poor People in the United States." http://www.nlihc.org/ cgi-bin/oor2000.pl?state=ca.

Olson, Mancur. 1971. *The Logic of Collective Action*. Cambridge, MA: Harvard University Press.

Pastor, Manuel, Jr. 2001. "Common Ground at Ground Zero? The New Economy and the New Organizing in Los Angeles." *Antipode* 22–23:265–66.

Pastor, Manuel, Jr., Peter Dreier, J. Eugene Grigsby III, and Marta López-Garza. 2000. *Regions That Work: How Cities and Suburbs Can Grow Together*. Minneapolis: University of Minnesota Press.

Petersen, Matthew. 1998. "Greening Our Homes: Protecting the Environment and Lowering Energy Bills." *Global Green Newsletter* 4:2.

Planning Report. 1999. "A New Region Emerges in Southern California: The Gateway Cities." May.

President's Council on Sustainable Development. 1997. "Sustainable Communities Task Force Report." http://www.whitehouse.gov/PCSD/Publications/suscomm/suscoc-am.html.

Rein, Martin, and Donald Schon. 1993. "Reframing Policy Discourse." In *The Argumentative Turn in Policy Analysis and Planning*, ed. Frank Fischer and John Forester. Durham, NC: Duke University Press.

Southern California Builder. 1999. "Smart Growth Begins with a Smart Housing Policy." August, 10.

Stone, Clarence N. 1987. "The Study of the Politics of Urban Development." In *The Politics of Urban Development*, ed. Clarence N. Stone and Heywood T. Sanders. Lawrence: University Press of Kansas.

U.S. Department of Energy. n.d. "A Department of Energy Clean Cities Success Story: Santa Monica, CA." http://www.ccities.doe.gov/success/santa_monica.shtml.

U.S. Department of Housing and Urban Development. 2000. *PATHways: Technology Making a Difference Where Americans Live.* Vol. 2(1).

U.S. Environmental Protection Agency, Office of Pollution Prevention and Toxics, Environmentally Preferable Purchasing. 1998. "The City of Santa Monica's Environmental Purchasing: A Case Study." http://www.epa.gov/opptintr/epp/santa.pdf.

Verdin, Tom. 2000. "New Plan Aims to Control Sprawl." *San Bernardino Sun*, September 26.

Wachs, Martin. 1997. "Public Transit and Social Equity." Lecture delivered at the University of Washington, May 29. http://www.ce.washington.edu/Transcp.html.

Contributors

Carolyn B. Aldana is associate professor of economics at California State University, San Bernardino. She has published papers on inequality, economic performance and well-being, minority bank performance, and health care for nonstandard labor. Her current research focuses on wealth accumulation issues for people of color.

Carol S. Armstrong is a Ph.D. candidate in urban planning at the University of Southern California, where she conducts research on environmental planning in the context of international development.

Michael Dear is professor of geography and founding director of the Southern California Studies Center at the University of Southern California. He is the author or editor of eleven books, including *The Postmodern Urban Condition* and the edited collections *Urban Latino Cultures: La vida latina en L.A.* and *The Postborder City: Cultural Spaces in Bajalta California.*

Peter Dreier is the Dr. E. P. Clapp Distinguished Professor of Politics and director of the Urban and Environmental Policy Program at Occidental College in Los Angeles, where he teaches courses on urban politics and policy, community organizing and leadership, and movements for social justice. He has served as senior policy adviser to the mayor of Boston and as that city's director of housing. His books include *Place Matters: Metropolitics for the Twenty-first Century* (coauthored with John Mollenkopf and Todd Swanstrom), which won the Michael Harrington Book Award from the American Political Science Association; *Regions That Work: How Cities and Suburbs Can Grow Together* (Minnesota, 2000; coauthored with Manuel Pastor Jr., J. Eugene Grigsby III, and Marta López-Garza), and the forthcoming *The Next L.A.: The Struggle for a Livable City* (with Robert Gottlieb, Regina Freer, and Mark Vallianatos).

Gary A. Dymski is director of the University of California Center, Sacramento, and professor of economics at the University of California, Riverside. He is also a research associate of the Economic Policy Institute and a member of the editorial boards of *Geoforum*, the *International Review of Applied Economics*, and the *Journal of Economic*

Issues. His publications include *The Bank Merger Wave*; three coedited volumes, including *Seeking Shelter on the Pacific Rim*; and articles and book chapters on banking, financial fragility, urban development, credit-market discrimination, the Latin American and Asian financial crises, exploitation, and housing finance.

Steven P. Erie is professor of political science and director of the urban studies and planning program at the University of California, San Diego. His book *Rainbow's End* won best urban book awards from the American Political Science Association and the American Sociological Association. His book *Globalizing L.A.* is a study of trade, infrastructure, and regional development in Southern California, and he is currently conducting research for his next project, *Beyond "Chinatown": MWD and Water, Development, and Environment in Southern California.* He is actively involved in public policy debates in the state and region, and served as a member of the Governor's Commission on Building for the Twenty-first Century.

Gregory Freeman is director of policy consulting for the Los Angeles County Economic Development Corporation (LAEDC), where his research focuses on trade, transportation infrastructure, brownfields, industrial redevelopment, and the fiscalization of land use. He conducts economic impact analysis work for LAEDC's consulting group, the California Economic Research Center.

William Fulton is a senior research fellow at the Southern California Studies Center at the University of Southern California and president of Solimar Research Group, a public policy research firm dealing with metropolitan growth, urban planning, and economic development. He is founding editor of *California Planning and Development Report* and the author of four books, including *The Reluctant Metropolis: The Politics of Urban Growth in Los Angeles* and (with Peter Calthorpe) *The Regional City.*

Elizabeth Gearin is a doctoral candidate in the School of Policy, Planning, and Development at the University of Southern California and a member of the American Institute of Certified Planners. Her research interests focus on sustainable development and the role of children's perspectives in our understanding of the built environment. Prior to her academic work, she spent seven years as a practicing planner in the San Francisco Bay Area, working principally in the areas of affordable housing and community development.

Genevieve Giuliano is professor in the School of Policy, Planning, and Development and director of the METRANS Transportation Center of the University of Southern California/California State University, Long Beach. Her research interests include relationships between transportation and land use, transportation policy evaluation, and impacts of information technology on transportation, land use, and travel behavior. She is a member and past chair of the Transportation Research Board Executive Committee and a national associate of the National Academies, serves on the editorial boards of *Urban Studies* and *Journal of Transportation and Statistics*, and participates on advisory boards for transportation programs at the University of Minnesota and the University of California, Davis.

Pascale Joassart-Marcelli is assistant professor of economics at the University of Massachusetts, Boston. Her research focuses on urban poverty, intrametropolitan fiscal disparities, and locally segmented labor markets. She has taught courses in urban geography, public finance, and development economics.

Enrico A. Marcelli is assistant professor of economics and public policy at the University of Massachusetts, Boston, and research fellow at Harvard University's Department of Society, Human Development, and Health. His research investigates the economic impact and integration of undocumented Mexican and other Latino immigrants residing in the United States and the contributions of and benefits to urban neighborhoods from metropolitan or regional economic development efforts. He teaches courses on labor, health and urban economics, and demography and U.S. immigration.

Mara A. Marks is associate director of the Center for the Study of Los Angeles at Loyola Marymount University. She studies the patterns and trends shaping Los Angeles as a way to understand urban America, focusing on ethnic relations, local leadership, and land-use politics. She has served as a consultant to several public and private organizations, including Los Angeles World Airports, the Southern California Association of Governments, the California Assembly Commission on State and Local Finance, and the City of Los Angeles Human Relations Commission.

Juliet Musso is associate professor of public policy in the School of Policy, Planning, and Development, University of Southern California. Her expertise is in urban policy, with specific research interests in community governance and sustainability, intergovernmental fiscal policy, and local institutional reform. She has written widely on the political economy of municipal incorporation and is now studying the development of neighborhood councils in the city of Los Angeles. Her other research topics include local government use of advanced telecommunications technologies to improve participation and service delivery, and intergovernmental fiscal relations in California.

Manuel Pastor Jr. is professor of Latin American and Latino studies and director of the Center for Justice, Tolerance, and Community at the University of California, Santa Cruz. His research on U.S. urban issues focuses on labor market and social conditions of low-income urban communities, with a recent emphasis on environmental justice. His most recent book, coauthored with Angela Glover Blackwell and Stewart Kwoh, is *Searching for the Uncommon Common Ground: New Dimensions on Race in America*; he also coauthored (with Peter Dreier, J. Eugene Grigsby III, and Marta López-Garza) *Regions That Work: How Cities and Suburbs Can Grow Together* (Minnesota,

2000), which has become a reference for those seeking to better link community and regional development.

Stephanie Pincetl is visiting professor at the Institute of the Environment at the University of California, Los Angeles, where she is developing the Urban Center for People and the Environment. She is the author of *Transforming California: A Political History of Land Use and Development* as well as articles and book chapters that explore the evolution of land use.

Laura Pulido is associate professor of geography and a member of the Program in American Studies and Ethnicity faculty at the University of Southern California. She is the author of *Environmentalism and Economic Justice: Two Chicano Struggles in the Southwest* and the forthcoming *Black, Brown, Yellow, and Left: Radical Activism in Los Angeles, 1968–78.*

Christine M. Ryan is a GIS consultant. During the past fifteen years, she has worked extensively with the ESRI family of GIS software products on numerous environmental and urban analysis and modeling projects in California and Montana.

John P. Wilson is professor of geography and director of the GIS Research Laboratory at the University of Southern California. He teaches courses on geographic information science, spatial analysis, and environmental modeling. He is the founding editor of *Transactions in GIS*, one of the series editors for Wiley's Mastering GIS book series, and an active participant in the UNIGIS International Network, a worldwide consortium of more than twenty institutions that collaborate on the development and delivery of geographic information science learning materials. He coedited *Terrain Analysis: Principles and Applications* and has authored or coauthored many book chapters and journal articles about GPS data capture, terrain analysis methods, and the spatial modeling and analysis of urban and environmental systems.

Jennifer Wolch is professor of geography and director of the Center for Sustainable Cities at the University of Southern California, where she teaches courses on Los Angeles, urban social problems, and sustainable cities. Her books include *Landscapes of Despair: From Deinstitutionalization to Homelessness* and *Malign Neglect: Homelessness in an American City* (with Michael Dear); *The Shadow State: Government and Voluntary Sector in Transition*; and *Animal Geographies: Place, Politics, and Identity in the Nature-Culture Borderlands* (edited with Jody Emel).

Index